Applying

Principles

Also by Jerry Kirkpatrick

*In Defense of Advertising:
Arguments from Reason, Ethical Egoism,
and Laissez-Faire Capitalism*

*Montessori, Dewey, and Capitalism:
Educational Theory for a
Free Market in Education*

*Independent Judgment and Introspection:
Fundamental Requirements
of the Free Society*

Applying Principles

Short Essays

Based on the

Philosophy of Ayn Rand, Economics of Ludwig von Mises, and Psychology of Edith Packer

Jerry Kirkpatrick

Kirkpatrick Books
Upland, California

Publisher's Cataloging-in-Publication Data

Names: Kirkpatrick, Jerry, author.
Title: Applying principles : short essays based on the philosophy of Ayn
   Rand , economics of Ludwig von Mises , and psychology of Edith
   Packer / Jerry Kirkpatrick.
Description: Includes bibliographical references and index. | Upland, CA:
   Kirkpatrick Books, 2021.
Identifiers: LCCN: 2021908577 | ISBN: 978-0-9787803-8-8 (hardcover) |
   978-0-9787803-9-5 (paperback) | 978-1-7371387-0-9 (ebook)
Subjects: LCSH Capitalism—Essays. | Economics—Essays. |
   Psychology—Essays. | Rand, Ayn—Criticism and interpretation.
   | Von Mises, Ludwig, 1881-1973—Criticism and interpretation. |
   Packer, Edith—Criticism and interpretation. | BISAC POLITICAL
   SCIENCE / Political Ideologies / Capitalism | EDUCATION /
   Essays | PSYCHOLOGY / Applied Psychology | PHILOSOPHY /
   Epistemology
Classification: LCC HB501 .K57 2021 | DDC 330.12/2—dc23

Copyright © 2021 by Jerry Kirkpatrick

All rights reserved. No portion of this book may be reproduced, by any
   process or technique, without the express written consent of the
   publisher.

Library of Congress Catalog Card Number: 2021908577

Kirkpatrick Books (formerly TLJ Books), Upland, CA 91784
https://books.jkirkpatrick.net, jkirkpa380@gmail.com

Printed in the United States of America

Contents

Preface	11
1. Capitalism and Politics	
Does Subliminal Advertising Exist?	19
Healthy and Unhealthy Competition	21
Why Does Capitalism Need To Be Defended?	23
The Market Gives Privilege to No One	25
The Market Function of Piracy	27
"It's Just Being Turned into a Business"	31
Postmodernism and the Next Failure of Socialism	33
The Two Liberalisms	36
Coerced Altruism, Involuntary Servitude, and Contempt for the Less Well Off	39
Why the World Is Not Going to Hell in a Basket	41
The Importance of Philosophy to a Successful Business Career	44
Ideas Kill	47
Choice Theory and Capitalism versus Dictatorship	49
Working in Business as Opposed to Being a Student	52
The Blender Principle	54

Altruistic Twaddle and the Harm It Causes … 56

The Triumph of Ethics over Practicality: A Tale of Two Cities … 59

Politics Is a Bore (Retitled: Who Are We Going to Coerce Today?) … 62

The Comparative Society … 65

The Sovietization of Federal Law … 68

Return of the Blackshirts? … 71

How the Government Kills Industries … 74

The Whistleblowers: An Indictment of the Mixed Economy and Bureaucracy … 77

The Elites and the Underground: No Law vs. Rule of Law vs. Excessive Law … 81

The PhD Cop … 84

The Not-So-Visible Gun: Government Is Not Our Friend … 86

Ayn Rand, of Course, Was Right … 88

The Galilean Personality vs. Wall-to-Wall Marxism and Human Sexual Identity … 90

Further Comment on *Galileo's Middle Finger* … 94

Americanized Maoism, the "Narrative" of Political Correctness, and Racist Minimum Wage Legislation … 98

The Communist Era and Capitalism vs. Democracy … 101

On Involuntary Servitude: "You'll Do Something, Mr. Cook. . . . If You Don't, We'll Make You." … 105

The Fascist Early Progressives … 110

Who Are We Going to Coerce Today?—Also Known As: Politics Is a Bore 2016 Version … 113

The Reductio of Bureaucracy: Totalitarian Dictatorship … 117

2. Academia

Drop Errors and the Trouble with Peer Review … 123

Privilege, Peer Review, and Piracy: Q & A … 127

The Ethics and Epistemology of Peer Review … 130

Because the Stakes are So Small	133
The Ethics of Accreditation	135
Ignorance versus Dishonesty	138
The Flawed Environment of Academic Research	140
Challenging the New McCarthyism	143
Trigger Warnings	146
Crybullies, Non-Negotiable Demands, Micro-Totalitarianisms, Academic Fascism . . . and *Cabaret*	149

3. EDUCATION

Go Fish!	153
On Judging the Quality of Today's Students	155
Peddlers of Ideas	159
The Child As Small Adult	161
Interest and the Core Curriculum	163
The Primacy of Method	166
Education and the Rent Control Model of Monopoly	168
Education in One Lesson	170
"You Can Get It in the Book"	174
The Factory Model of Education, Technocracy, and the Free School Movement	176
Teaching versus Learning versus Doing	178
Rankism and the Well-Earned Disrespect of Some Teachers	180
Control and Choice in Education	182
Group Projects: The Bell Has Tolled	185
Educational Innovation from Outside the Establishment	187
Look It Up, Look It Up: The Open-Book Test	190
On Killing Creativity	192
Plagiarism—Beyond a Reasonable Doubt	194
Filling the Swiss Cheese Holes	197

4. Psychology

Describe, Don't Evaluate	201
Curiosity for Subtle Detail	204
Sound or Independent Judgment?	206
Rules vs. Principles	208
Ensuring That Disposition Trumps Situation	210
Faking Your Way Through Life	213
The Von Domarus Principle and the Nature of the Subconscious Mind	215
The Courage to be Patient	217
Questions about Independent Judgment	219
Standing Down from External Control	221
Theory of the Big Mouth	224
The Primacy of Psychology	227
On Hitting... Dogs and Children	229
Should Spanking Be a Felony?	232
Look at Your Premises. Look. Look. Look!	234
"Children Don't Have Disorders; They Live in a Disordered World"	237
Statements of Independence	239
Introversion, Quiet Persistence, and the Tortoise	242
The Barbarity of Modern Psychiatry	244
Kindness versus "Hard Science"	248
The Science Isn't There	251
"Men of Hard Science" and the Denial of Animal Emotions	256
The Root of Dictatorship	258
In Praise of Quitters and Failures	262
Parents: Be Your Children's Friend—Give Them the Easy Life	264
Thoughts, Not Environmental Conditions, Cause Criminal Behavior	267

The Role of Honor in Moral Revolutions	269
A Neoconservative's Defense of Pseudo-Honor	271
Fixed vs. Growth Mindsets	274
"They'll Be Fine"—Two Takes on Indifference to Psychology	277
The Bureaucratic Personality: Similarities to the Criminal Mind?	280
On Hitting Dogs and Children . . . and Prisoners of War	284
Defending Hate Speech and Satire against the Criminal Mind	284
From the Stick Motivation Department: Chores	285
From the Stick Motivation Department, Part Two: Class Participation	288

5. Epistemology

The Dangerous Admiration of BS	293
Dewey in Context	295
The Epistemology of Ethics, Salesmanship, and Basket Weaving	299
Nutrition and The Argument from Uncertainty	301
Virulent Absolutism in an Age of Relativism	304
Facts Don't Matter, Or: The Art of BS	307
Polylogism, the Right to Lie, and Serial Embellishers	309
Why Don't Facts Matter?	311
Genes vs. Environment: Anyone for Free Will?	315
Is Intelligence Inborn?	318
Statistical Projection vs. Scientific Generalization	322

6. Youth Sports

Caterpillars into Butterflies	325
On Extrinsic Motivation, Bureaucracy, and the Stage-Mother Syndrome	327
Yes, There Is Crying in Softball	329
Tiger Mom or Stage Mom?	332

There Are More Important Things in Life Than Softball … 334

"Miniature Adults," the Marketing Concept, and a Montessori Approach to Organized Youth Sports … 337

Life Lessons from Sports: What about the Sixty Years after College? … 340

The Obsession with Scholarships … 343

Not-So-Good Life Lessons from Sports … 345

More, More, More Does Not Mean Better … 349

And Now, the Concussion Issue … 352

Overuse Injuries—What the Experts Are Saying … 354

Year-Round Single Sport Specialization: Not Good for Kids or Skill Development, Experts Say … 357

7. THE ARTS

Life in Three-Quarter Time … 363

Evita: Why We Love That Musical about a Dictator … 365

INDEX … 369

Preface

Applying Principles is a collection of short essays published between January 2007 and December 2016, my first ten years of blogging at jerry-kirkpatrick.blogspot.com. In the blog's masthead, I write the following:

> This blog comments on business, education, philosophy, psychology, and economics, among other topics, based on my understanding of Ayn Rand's philosophy, Ludwig von Mises' economics, and Edith Packer's psychology. Epistemology and psychology are my special interests. Note that I assume ethical egoism and laissez-faire capitalism are morally and economically unassailable. My interest is in applying, not defending, them.

Although I spent thirty-six years in college classrooms teaching undergraduate and graduate students business marketing, my bachelor's degree was in philosophy. That subject influenced and underscored my entire career. As a result, I never let the day job of teaching students how to sell soap (as I would often describe my academic duties) become disconnected from its foundations in psychology, economics, or philosophy.

Indeed, I recognized early in graduate school that marketing, as well as the other business disciplines, are properly described as applied sciences that rest on those more fundamental fields. "Art" is sometimes used to describe applied science, but the usage is correct only if it is meant as a synonym. Often the word is meant to disparage applied fields because they are allegedly less precise or rigorous than "real" science, which means the physical or quantitative sciences. A student many years ago complimented me when she realized that advertising was as disciplined (her word) as finance, her major. There may not be universal equations in the applied human sciences, but the principles are universal in their appropriate context and the fields are "disciplined."

Business as applied science is analogous to medicine and engineering. Medicine rests on biology for its more fundamental foundation and engineering on physics and chemistry. All fundamental and derivative special sciences, again in turn, rest on philosophy. All such fields are related and should be integrated, rather than isolated as they so often are in today's academic world.

Thus, what I did when researching, writing, and teaching was to apply principles from the other, more fundamental fields, which explains my interest in epistemology and psychology, as well as the principles unique to marketing and advertising.

To illustrate further, the civil engineer whose goal is to build a bridge must know not just the fundamentals of physics and chemistry, but also the nature and composition of materials (used to build the bridge), and also the nature and behavior of rivers, which includes the history of the particular river over which the bridge will span and the nature and behavior of the river's soil and water.

Applied science gathers all relevant concrete facts of the specific case it is working on, then uses, that is, applies, the universal concepts and principles of the fundamental sciences on which it rests, plus the narrower concepts and principles of its discipline.

Application is one of the two fundamental methods of cognition and is deductive. Generalization is the other and is inductive. We all use both every day in our lives. The two methods, as I say in my 2018 blog post, "are not the monopoly of scientists, philosophers, or academics in general."[1] Generalization gives us concepts and principles to guide our lives, while it also gives us theory and theoretical science. Application,

---

[1] Jerry Kirkpatrick, "On the Correct Roles of Induction and Deduction in Human Life: Two Sentences from Ayn Rand's Theory of Concepts," December 11, 2018, jerrykirkpatrick.blogspot.com.

which requires the previously acquired knowledge that generalization gives us, is what our medical doctors do, what Sherlock Holmes did, and what we do on a daily basis.

Application means we identify "a this as an instance of a that." We present a cough and runny nose to our doctor and he or she quickly concludes, based on accumulated knowledge and patient history, that we have a cold. Similarly, Holmes saw that Watson was tanned and showed signs of having been wounded in a war; thus he concluded Watson recently came back from Afghanistan. And a child applies the previously learned concept of balance by shifting weight when learning to ride a bicycle. All three examples are processes of deduction, and illustrate how deduction is the predominant method of applied sciences, as well as everyday life.*

Deduction, therefore, is essentially what I have been doing when writing my blog posts. I am not in any intended way coming up with new concepts or principles, nor am I repeating the proofs of the great writers listed in my masthead, or others I may cite in a post as a reference. I take their ideas and apply them to specific issues.

The following essays are not journalistic as a newspaper column might be. I gave myself the assignment always to come up with something more fundamental than the news of the day, whether theoretical or historical, which last includes relevant citation of research.

I also gave myself the assignment initially to write essays of between 800 and 1200 words. In later years, the length increased and a couple of essays are long enough to have been split into two parts as might have occurred in the days of printed four-page newsletters. I saw no reason to split them in today's electronic age.

My goal was to write one post a month, though in 2007 there are two months with two posts each. I settled quickly on publishing the one post at some point during the month, with no particular deadline confronting me. When I was still teaching in the earlier years, that posting date was sometimes rather late. Now I try to post within the first one or two weeks.

There are 125 posts in this collection. In the calendar year 2015 I added a note saying that I was not going write one post a month, or even standard-length posts, as I needed time to work on my book *Independent Judgment and Introspection*. Not a lot of visible progress, however, was made on the book, so by October I was back to one standard-length post per month. I realized that I enjoy the stimulation of writing something on a more or less regular schedule.

The posts are organized into seven chapters, listed chronologically within chapter. Because of the way I write—"interdisciplinary" to use the academic jargon—one may quibble over some classifications. Chapter 6 on "Youth Sports" began as individual posts on the main blog, but for about a year, 2013–14, I posted those first essays, along with some new ones, in a sports blog that is still online at youthsportsgoodforkids.blogspot.com. (Our daughter was playing softball, which gave us a front row seat in the culture of youth sports.) For some posts I found that a book recently read provided opportunity for comment, though I do not call these book reviews. And some posts are either excerpted from one of my books or were drafts of what finally appeared.

I do have favorites. It was difficult to choose one per chapter, but here they are, in chapter order:

- "The Reductio of Bureaucracy: Totalitarian Dictatorship"
- "Because the Stakes Are So Small"
- "Go Fish!"
- "Look at Your Premises. Look. Look. Look!"
- "Why Don't Facts Matter?"
- "Yes, There Is Crying in Softball"
- "Life in Three-Quarter Time"

All links in the present collection have been checked, though not as many degraded as I would have thought. New-found locations or good substitutes in almost all cases were found with some substitutes from a later year than the date of original posting. Light edits and comments not included in the original are bracketed. Date of publication of each post is at the end of its posting in parentheses. Editorial footnotes, indicated by one, two, or three asterisks, are also positioned at the end of their respective posts.

My idea for publishing this collection comes from two books of columns: *All It Takes Is Guts* by economist Walter Williams and

Double Standards by radio show host Larry Elder. I did not read these books from beginning to end. I skimmed the table of contents and read whatever caught my attention. Readers of this work might want to do the same.

My primary acknowledgement is to my wife, philosopher Linda Reardan, my soulmate for forty years, philosophical consultant, and editor. I also owe a considerable gratitude to economist George Reisman, who was a student of Ludwig von Mises and could easily have been listed in the blog's masthead. Through his writing and teaching, Professor Reisman taught me how to be a scholar; his work permeates my understanding of a free society.

* It is in this sense that history is also an applied science. We, as well as professional historians, look at past events, natural or human, and try to explain them, that is, identify their causes, by reference to our accumulated theoretical knowledge. Historians in the human sciences rely in particular on political philosophy, economics, and psychology. See Ludwig von Mises, *Theory and History*, amazon.com.

Note to the print edition. The challenge of turning electronic posts, now available in Kindle and epub versions, into print was what do I do with the hyperlinks. In some posts there are over thirty links. My solution was to put them in footnotes with abbreviated, less formal citations. Article or book title and date and author, if available, are included, but the link itself is reduced to the domain name—such as amazon.com or wikipedia.org. The title, when searched, almost always appears in top results. If not, putting the title in quotation marks and including the author's name and domain will reveal the citation's location. (Most note numbers in the text are at the location of the Kindle and epub links.)

Applying

Principles

1
Capitalism and Politics

2007
Does Subliminal Advertising Exist?

STARTING A NEW BLOG—and especially since the paperback edition of my book defending advertising (*In Defense of Advertising: Arguments from Reason, Ethical Egoism, and Laissez-Faire Capitalism*[1]) has just been published—I suppose I should begin with a post about advertising. So let me deal with a question that frequently arises: "What about subliminal advertising?," to which I typically respond, "What about it? It doesn't exist!"

That's the short answer. Some elaboration is required.

The term "subliminal" means beneath the threshold of perception. Many things are subliminal, such as the circulation of our blood, which we normally do not feel, experience, or perceive moving throughout our bodies. And it is possible to have our skin touched in such a way that we do not notice the touch. Subliminal advertising, however, is supposedly the power to motivate action based on something that no one can perceive, such as a message flashed on a movie or television screen at 1/3000th of a second or the word "sex" unrecognizably embedded in ice cubes in a liquor print ad. James Vicary and Wilson

---

[1] Jerry Kirkpatrick, *In Defense of Advertising*, amazon.com. See also books.jkirkpatrick.net.

Bryan Key, respectively, are the two proponents of these claims. See this brief recap of their roles in the history of subliminal advertising.[2] Marketing professor Stuart Rogers argues that Vicary's movie theater "experiment" was a hoax.[3]

The notion of subliminal perception is a self-contradiction because it is not possible to perceive something that is beneath one's threshold of perception. Add to this the fact that advertisers exert great effort to make their messages blatantly explicit—innuendo, sexual or otherwise, is intended to be noticed—and you have no grounds for the subliminal advertising complaint. Critics are never satisfied, though, so they now talk about "semi-subliminal" advertising and "secondary imagery" that is often missed on an initial look. The latter is just a variation on the subliminal-embed theme of Wilson Key. The former is what Ayn Rand would call an "anti-concept." Either something is above the threshold of perception or it is not; it cannot be half-way between. There are, of course, levels of perception, once above the threshold, but the lower the level, the less likely we are to be influenced by the message.

Repetitiveness is then thrown into the mix with the argument that we are manipulated by a constant repetition of ads that makes us change our desires without being aware of the process. Hmm. There are quite a few influencers in our lives who use repetition to get us to change our minds (or to reinforce a value or view we already hold): parents in relation to their children, teachers in relation to their students, journalists in relation to their audiences, and, oh yes, politicians—who have been known to use many different communication techniques to win votes—in relation to their constituencies. As I say in my book, when it comes to ethics and taste in communication, advertisers can hold their own against any of these four groups of influencers. Advertising just happens to be a convenient fall guy.

Then there is the flap last winter [2006] over Kentucky Fried Chicken's alleged subliminal advertising. A code word was inserted in one frame of a thirty-second commercial. When taken to KFC's web site, the code word would produce a coupon for a Buffalo Snacker sandwich.

---

[2]David Mikkelson, "Popcorn Subliminal Advertising," May 3, 2011, snopes.com.
[3]Stuart Rogers, "How a Publicity Blitz Created the Myth of Subliminal Advertising," winter 1993, jkirkpatrick.net/Rogers.pdf.

ABC thought it was subliminal advertising and only ran the commercial minus the frame containing the code word—despite KFC's wide publicizing of the stunt and their obvious desire for everyone to go looking for the code word. That the commercial had to be recorded and played slowly enough to view each individual frame speaks volumes about the people who still want to believe in subliminal advertising. Their motivation, as I demonstrate in my book, runs deep and is rooted in hostility toward capitalism, egoism, and, ultimately, reason.

Failure to understand the nature and causes of one's emotions and, more generally, ignorance of the influence of the subconscious on one's conscious perceptions are the sources of belief in subliminal communication. A commercial showing a sizzling T-bone steak, for example, at 5PM may trigger salivation in some, perhaps many. Why? Because of the viewers' stored evaluations of steak as deliciously satisfying when hungry. A person who has just eaten, however, will not react that way. And a vegetarian may react with indifference or even indignation. The contents of our subconscious minds can indeed be triggered by conscious (not subliminal) perceptions, but the material in the subconscious is a conclusion that was drawn—an evaluation made—some time earlier.

Hmm. All this hostility toward advertising, capitalism, egoism, and reason must be triggered by "subliminal" communication from the parents, teachers, journalists, and politicians who repetitiously harp about those institutions' alleged flaws and evils!

(January 1, 2007)

Healthy and Unhealthy Competition

EDUCATION AND SOCIAL CRITIC Alfie Kohn is an exhaustive researcher and engaging writer.[4] I have not read all of his eleven original books, but I do highly recommend these two: *Punished by Rewards: The Trouble with Gold Stars, Incentive Plans, A's, Praise, and Other Bribes* and *Unconditional Parenting: Moving from Rewards and Punishments to Love and Reason*. The titles and subtitles make clear his premises about human motivation and behavior. In his first book,

---

[4] Alfie Kohn (website), alfiekohn.org.

however, *No Contest: The Case against Competition*,[5] Kohn writes (p. 9), "The more closely I have examined the topic, the more firmly I have become convinced that competition is an inherently undesirable arrangement, that the phrase *healthy competition* is actually a contradiction in terms." To this, I must take exception.

Kohn, a strong defender of intrinsic motivation, frames his critique of competition—an extrinsic motivator—by setting up an irreconcilable conflict between doing well and beating others, by focusing on competence and accomplishment vs. trying to do something better than someone else. But healthy competition, especially the economic type, requires strong focus on doing well; beating someone else in the process, if it is focused on at all, is consequence. Kohn's understanding of economic competition, unfortunately, is laced with Marxist mythology, Galbraith's dependence effect, and the doctrine of pure and perfect competition, so he sees competition as an unfair and arbitrary creator of desires. Even at the highest levels of athletic competition— think John Wooden—winning is consequence of doing well. Winning for its own sake is indeed not an attractive character trait.[6]

Other forms of competition, however, do tend to focus exclusively, or nearly so, on beating others. Competition in the animal kingdom is the extreme example where, because of the limited supply of food and territory, competition often becomes a fight-to-the-death encounter. Among humans living in a society of abundance, a different kind of fight-to-the-death desperation is sometimes seen—not physical desperation as animals might face, but psychological. Because of the anxiety that many people feel, "competitiveness," or a desperate need to defeat others, becomes a defensive motivator. Doing well takes a back seat. Occasionally, a highly talented and accomplished person exhibits defense-driven competitiveness, but this does not detract from the point that the source of the competitiveness is psychology and the source of the accomplishment is ability.

One form of competition that devalues doing well and encourages beating others is that caused by government intervention into

---

[5] Alfie Kohn, *No Contest*, amazon.com.
[6] "John Wooden," wikipedia.org, and John Wooden, Coach and Teacher (website), coachwooden.com.

the economy. Ludwig von Mises points out that totalitarian states encourage people to "court the favor of those in power," but this is true of any bureaucratic intrusion into the economy.[7] Licensed professionals, because of the privileges extended to them by the government, will focus less on doing their jobs well and more on making sure the bureaucrats keep the unlicensed out of their market. Because of the restriction in supply brought about by the licensing monopoly, the consumers of that profession must now scramble—not too differently from what animals must do in their kingdom—to compete with each other, that is, to try to *beat* others, to obtain that limited supply. The beaten ones, as in the medical market, go without.

Kohn's book is filled with examples of bureaucratic and defensive competition, two types that I would agree are unhealthy, but he does not always identify them as such. He, of course, confuses the two with healthy, economic competition. If read with an understanding of this confusion in mind, Kohn's book can provide a detailed analysis of the less savory forms of competition that exist in our society.

(January 21, 2007)

Why Does Capitalism Need To Be Defended?

I ADMIT THAT I HAVE NOT HEARD this question—why does capitalism need to be defended?—in precisely that form. After the hardcover edition of my book *In Defense of Advertising: Arguments from Reason, Ethical Egoism, and Laissez-Faire Capitalism* was published, I did hear the question this way: Why does advertising need to be defended? As advertising is the point man and product of capitalism, the two questions are intimately related.

The question about advertising initially surprised me. When the look on my face expressed a "Did you read the book?" reply, my questioners promptly continued, "Advertising in the U.S. is an $xxx billion [fill in the current number] a year business. It doesn't need to be defended!" Somehow, apparently, the amount of money spent by the industry was supposed to be its own justification. Similarly, I could imagine someone

---

[7]Ludwig von Mises, *Human Action*, mises.org. See also amazon.com.

thinking or saying, "The United States is an $xx trillion [use current number] a year economy. Capitalism doesn't need to be defended!"

I soon came to realize where my advertising questioners were coming from: their question is motivated by the premises of what I call the critics' world view. As I argue in my book, the social and economic criticisms of advertising—namely that advertising is coercive, offensive, and monopolistic—are based on false philosophic and economic ideas that at root are authoritarian.

The discussion with my questioners usually runs as follows. The questioners comment that advertising is a "big bucks" industry and, like any other big business, assume it eventually becomes immune to competition—and to criticism. "It's just words," they say, "like water falling off a duck's back. The criticisms have no effect on advertisers who, after all, are so big and powerful that they can easily ignore the complaints. Therefore, advertising does not need to be defended." QED. Subsequent discussion then brings out the premise that a little (or a lot) of legislation is needed to help cut these guys down to size. Why? Because advertising is so ... well, coercive, offensive, and monopolistic. At that point, we are off to the litany of criticisms that ranges from alleged sexual orgies subliminally embedded in a Howard Johnson's restaurant menu to the four-firm concentration ratio.

No doubt, anyone who has engaged the critics of capitalism has observed a similar pattern. It involves a move from surface appearances—advertising doesn't need to defended—to underlying causal principles that initially seem unconnected to the appearances—these big advertisers need to be brought down a few notches. It is a move from what is seen, to use Bastiat's phrase, to what is not seen.[8] Bastiat explained the seen and unseen in terms of economic events, but the more fundamental psychological issue here is that conscious perceptions (the seen) are shaped by the contents of one's subconscious (the unseen). Defenders of advertising and capitalism must probe to those deeper levels and make the critics aware of, and answer, all of the buried fallacies that motivate their surface comments.

---

[8]Frederic Bastiat, *That Which Is Seen, and That Which Is Not Seen*, in *The Bastiat Collection*, Mark Thornton, ed., amazon.com.

Contrary to what the critics of advertising—or capitalism—may think, their criticisms do have an effect. When left unanswered, the criticisms reinforce ignorance and misunderstandings about the nature of advertising and, by implication, capitalism. They reinforce and encourage hostility toward both. And they implicitly and explicitly provide a call for legislation to restrain what are perceived by the critics to be "abuses" of advertising and big business.

(February 15, 2007)

The Market Gives Privilege to No One

"BANKERS' HOURS" IS AN OLD PHRASE that actually reflects monopolistic privilege. The 10AM to 3PM that banks formerly were open to serve customers was made possible by government regulation and the consequent lack of competition to force bankers to be more available when customers needed them. With modest deregulation (and the electronic bookkeeping that deregulation encouraged) banks today are open a little longer than the former hours and some are even open on Saturdays.

Doctors, dentists, lawyers, and professors, however—a distinguished group that enjoy government-granted privileges in the form of licensing and other regulatory protections—still do not usually work weekends. Free-market service firms must be open and available when their customers need them. Why should medical or educational services only be available Monday through Friday, 8AM to 5PM? The significantly unregulated computer industry's "24/7" indicates the ultimate in service. The free market gives privilege to no one.

Privilege is a remnant of aristocratic life, special enjoyments granted due to birth or rank in society. Today, the rank stems directly from bureaucratic intrusions into the marketplace. Its key trait is that it is unearned, making the holder of the rank exempt from competition. Regulations restrict a portion of the market to the exclusive enjoyment of those protected at the expense of those who are not so protected. Sometimes, those enjoying this rank exhibit aristocratic arrogance, such as the professor who says to a student, during the professor's posted office hours: "I can't talk now. I have a meeting."

The meeting is with other professors and the message conveyed is that other professors are more important than paying customers.*

Robert Fuller, former president of Oberlin College, has coined a word that actually is broader than the monopolistic privileges I am talking about here. And Fuller, who is a social liberal, would certainly not agree with my application of his term.[9] Fuller recognizes that there is legitimate rank that can be earned, so he coined the term "rankism" to mean "the abuse of rank." Rankism, he says, describes a concept similar to, but broader than, racism, sexism, and bullying in general. "Rankism insults the dignity of subordinates by treating them as invisible, as nobodies. Nobody is another n-word and, like the original, it is used to justify denigration and inequity" (*Somebodies and Nobodies: Overcoming the Abuse of Rank*,[10] p. 5). Fuller argues that equality means "equal dignity" and everyone has a right to it; equality does not mean equal wealth or equal rank. As a social liberal, he thinks the government, as in the case of race and gender inequities, must step in. My interpretation is that the government was a cause or magnifier of these particular inequities.

Despite his social liberalism, Fuller's concept provides valuable insight into the psychological underpinnings of the abuse of rank by those in higher or privileged authority. Earned rank does exist naturally in society—parents hold rank over children, teachers over students, and employers over employees—and more *earned* rank would exist in a truly free-market economy because bureaucrats would have to get jobs in business and compete for their positions of authority. From the standpoint of psychology, though, as Fuller demonstrates, "lording it over" one's subordinates derives from defensive anxiety and the necessity of setting oneself up as special or superior to others. Sometimes this necessity is made manifest through regulatory privilege. Rankism, says Fuller, is the last "vestige of aristocratic class" that must be eliminated from the home, school, workplace, and social order before we can achieve a just society based on equal dignity. The first step, in contrast to what Fuller would say, involves removing the

---

[9] "Social Liberalism," wikipedia.org.
[10] Robert Fuller, *Somebodies and Nobodies*, amazon.com.

last semblance of regulatory privilege by getting government out of our lives and economy.

Fuller's website is called Breaking Ranks.[11]

* Oops! Did say students were paying customers? I realize that many professors—a privileged group I know well—object strenuously to this characterization. Yet students in a state-financed university, such as mine, often work thirty or more hours per week to pay for their education. This means they are paying substantial taxes to pay for their professors' meal tickets. And this doesn't count the taxes the students' parents have paid over the years. So, yes, I do believe it is correct to call my students paying customers.

(March 13, 2007)

The Market Function of Piracy

IN MARKETING THE MOST EFFECTIVE WAY to introduce new products is the free sample. In 1978 Lever Brothers spent $15 million ($63.57 million in today's 2021 currency) delivering a free sample of Signal Mouthwash to two-thirds of all US households [about 51 million in 1978]. The strategy was a success and the product remained on the market well into the 1990s.

The significance of the free sample is product trial; it gets the product into consumers' hands. If consumers use the sample and like it, they may go on to buy the product and buy it again and again, that is, become repeat purchasers; they may even spread the good word to others. When repeat purchasing and favorable word of mouth kick in, the product's sales will experience a shift from slow to rapid growth and management will consider the product a success.

Free sampling is the best method of introducing new products, but it is also the most expensive. Not surprisingly, then, *Forbes ASAP* magazine* reports this alternative way to practice free sampling:

> One security manager for a major manufacturer, who asked not to be identified, says she is sure some companies actu-

---

[11] Dignity Works (website), breakingranks.net.

ally view being counterfeited as a boon to their efforts to build brand awareness. After all, she says, if some companies give away merchandise to expand market share, what's not to like about having someone else take on the expense of manufacturing and distributing the goods, as long as they're high-quality copies?

Imitation is a universal trait of human behavior, ranging from the use of phrases and mannerisms of admired others to the reuse of hummable themes in music, recognizable images in paintings, and well-known plots in literature and Disney movies. Imitation is a normal part of the competitive process in growth markets. As the sales of an innovative new product takes off, competitors enter the market with their own, often cheaper, versions.

If the innovative product is patented, competitors make minor design or functional changes to secure their own patents. Knock-offs are unauthorized, usually cheaper copies. And, of course, the innovative marketer often produces its own cheap version, sometimes called a fighting brand, to fend off the competition. Over time real prices in the product category decline and quality improves.

Knock-offs are pirated products. Because they are usually cheaper than the original, knock-offs tend to appeal to a more price-conscious segment of the market; that is, the buyers of pirated products are probably not legitimate prospects for the innovative new product, either because they cannot afford, or do not want to pay, the higher price. Message to the innovative marketer? Either drop the price of the new product or produce a cheaper version—or be the first to exploit a new technology, something the movie and recording industries chose not to do.** Many, including these two industries, would rather sue than practice good marketing.

One study found that users of pirated software sufficiently influenced—by word-of-mouth communication—eighty percent of the software's prospects to buy the legal product and another described several scenarios in which piracy can help increase the sales of legal products.*** The pirated product functions as a free sample that the innovator does not have to fund.

So what about free copies? How do you compete with free, to state the battle cry of the new Luddites who fear digital technology? It's done all the time. One of the most dramatic recent instances of this was the strategy of science fiction writer Cory Doctorow[12] who, over the course of three years, gave away 700,000 electronic copies of *Down and Out in the Magic Kingdom*. Sales of the hard copy went through six printings and surpassed his publisher's expectations. Many of the downloaders, Doctorow said, did not buy the hard copy and probably would not have regardless, but the giveaway created considerable buzz and a significant minority did buy the hard copy. Compare the experience of the Mises Institute with *Omnipotent Government*.[13]

Free—no matter where it comes from—can help sell.

* "Faker's Paradise," April 5, 1999, p. 54.

** See Ray Beckerman's blog *Recording Industry vs. The People*[14] to read how the Recording Industry Association of America (RIAA) uses questionable legal tactics to sue teenagers and grandmothers instead of designing creative money-making uses of peer-to-peer (P2P) file sharing.

*** Moshe Givon, Vijay Mahajan, and Eitan Muller, "Software Piracy: Estimation of Lost Sales and the Impact on Software Diffusion," *Journal of Marketing*, 59:1 (January 1995), 29–37; Julio O. de Castro, David B. Balkin, and Dean A. Shepherd, "Knock-Off or Knockout?," *Business Strategy Review*, Spring 2007, 28–32. Thanks to Gil Guillory on the Mises Scholars List for alerting me to the former study.

(May 21, 2007, cross-posted at Mises.org[15])

Addendum. Comment made on the Mises.org posting (no longer available):

There are two issues underlying my post.

---

[12] Cory Doctorow, "Giving It Away," December 1, 2006, forbes.com.
[13] Jeffrey A. Tucker, "Books, Online and Off," March 22, 2004, mises.org.
[14] Ray Beckerman, Recording Industry vs The People (website), recordingindustryvspeople.blogspot.com.
[15] Jerry Kirkpatrick, "The Market Function of Piracy," May 21, 2007, mises.org.

The first is a practical one: what's a marketer to do when hit with a price attack? Use the legal system to defeat the competition (which in the past has included using antitrust laws and lobbying Congress to pass new laws) or creatively come up with new entrepreneurial ways of offering greater overall value to prospects than the competition? The RIAA could have been a leader in P2P file sharing technology; instead, they have become just another example of an industry using the legal system to maintain a leg up on innovative competitors.

In Mozart's day, to give a contrast from before the age of copyright law, it was common to arrange popular opera tunes for wind ensembles, which tunes then became the rock'n'roll hits of the day. Mozart wrote his father that he had to get busy arranging one of his operas before the copiers got to it. Mozart was interested in making money, so he did do his own arrangements.

One more example from the late nineteenth century. Sheet music publishers tried to silence, or demand royalties from, the phonograph and player piano industries. In fact both technologies increased the sale of sheet music. From a marketing perspective, the publishers should have paid the phonograph and piano industries a sales commission.

The other issue underlying my post is the question of ethics: is piracy unethical or are copyrights and patents instances of monopoly power and privilege? Piracy means making copies; the innovator still has the originals to sell. Is piracy theft? It depends on your theory of property.

I admit in this issue to being a long-time Objectivist who was weened on intellectual property as property. I'm not so sure it is anymore. Creative people are notoriously un-entrepreneurial. Could it be that they (feel that they) need government protection and monopoly prices because they do not know how, or do not want, to get down in the trenches of marketing and actually sell their products?? "God forbid," I can see many creatives saying, "that I should have to rub shoulders with those grubby sales people!"

Mark Twain and Jack Valenti (President of the Motion Picture Association of America, 1966–2004) both advocated copyright in perpetuity. That's essentially what we have today: lifetime plus seventy years.

That may kill creativity, so say Lawrence Lessig in *Free Culture*[16] and Siva Vaidhyanathan in *Copyrights and Copywrongs*.[17]

(May 21, 2007)

"It's Just Being Turned into a Business"

THIS LAMENT IS OFTEN HEARD TODAY about medicine and education, among other fields. Business, however, is the last thing medicine and education have been turned into. Bureaus of the government would be a more accurate description. Why the confusion between bureaucracy and business?

The simplest answer is that most people do not understand the difference between the two. A bureaucracy, as Ludwig von Mises[18] points out, is an organization dominated by methods of managing the affairs of government, whereas a business is dominated by the goal of making a profit through customer satisfaction.

Bureaucracy, or rather, bureaucratic management, is a set of rules and a budget handed down from a higher authority to guide the running of a government department, such as the police, the courts, or the military. A business may have guidelines, usually called policies, and each department within the organization may have a budget, but the ultimate yardstick by which business activity is evaluated is profit-making by producing need- and want-satisfying products. When market conditions change, meaning customer needs and wants have changed, policies and budgets must be adapted lest the company fail to keep up with the competition and go out of business. Bureaucracy has no such ultimate yardstick. That is why the rules and budgets of government offices often ossify leading to the familiar refrain of the bureaucrat: "Rules are rules, fella; I don't make 'em, I just enforce 'em."

When bureaucratic rules, in the form of laws and regulations of business, intrude on the marketplace, businesses that are regulated will take on the characteristics of bureaucracies. This is because the laws and regulations of our mixed economy deflect attention away from

---

[16] Lawrence Lessig, *Free Culture*, amazon.com.
[17] Siva Vaidhyanathan, *Copyrights and Copywrongs*, amazon.com.
[18] Ludwig von Mises, *Bureaucracy*, mises.org. See also amazon.com.

profit-making through customer satisfaction to compliance with the rules of the bureaucracy. And the rules almost never coincide with what is best for the market. Ossification sets in and a "rules are rules" mentality eventually takes over. To the extent that a business is regulated by the government, to that extent it will be bureaucratic. Small businesses, except for local zoning ordinances and licensing requirements, usually escape regulation, that is, until they grow in size to a certain number of employees or level of sales; more rules, then, kick in.

Bureaucracy does not mean a large, hierarchically structured organization, such as General Motors or the Department of Justice. This is the popular misconception given by the media and management professors. General Motors is a private business that is highly regulated by the government; bureaucratic intrusions into the profit-making, customer-satisfying operation of the company are what make GM today seem so bureaucratic, not its size or structure. The Department of Justice makes no pretense at being a private business; it was founded as a bureaucracy.

The postal service, on the other hand, does pretend to be a business by mimicking the operations of private enterprise, such as subtracting costs from revenues and conducting market research surveys. But the post office is so thoroughly regulated and controlled by the government—it is a quasi-governmental agency[19] under the executive branch—that it is a joke to consider it anything other than a bureaucracy. Public schools and state universities are government entities, making them bureaucracies by definition; private schools are highly regulated by the education czars and so are nearly as bureaucratic. Almost all operators of both types of school abhor the prospect of making a profit or of having to satisfy paying customers.

Yet occasionally the trustees of these institutions will demand that expenses be accounted for or that pay be tied to merit. This is when the screams of faculty are heard to say that education is just being turned into a business. More accurately, the demands are the bureaucracy trying to mimic business accountability by imposing additional rules on the system. The result is a stilted, heavy-handed decree of arbitrary edicts administered by a "rules are rules" mentality. (And pay tied to

---

[19] "United States Postal Service, Governance and Organization," wikipedia.org.

merit becomes a political popularity contest.) Add to this the fact that education today, which once was controlled at the local and state level, is rapidly becoming nationalized by the US Department of Education and you have education as a bureau of the national government.

The same attempts at mimicking business accountability can be seen in medicine with the cartel-imposed cost constraints of the insurance industry and Medicare. Medicine is hardly a free market today, nor was it prior to the current health-maintenance-organization/Medicare era. In the early twentieth century, the licensing monopoly of the American Medical Association drastically reduced the number of medical schools and hospitals and continues to keep that number low.[20] The mess that we have now is just one bureaucratic monstrosity piled on top of the previous model. Calls for cost containment and accountability are not the calls of free enterprise. They are the panicked cries of bureaucrats who have no clue what they are doing.

But they do have their rules and the rules must be enforced.

(November 26, 2007)

2008

Postmodernism and the Next Failure of Socialism

SOCIALISM, AND MORE BROADLY COLLECTIVISM, as Ayn Rand pointed out, died as a moral ideal in 1945. As a practical ideal, socialism died with the collapse of the Soviet Union in 1991. Yet socialism and the principle that government might is required to make right is still with us. How can that be?

Answer: epistemological errors of Enlightenment thinkers, specifically their failure to identify the true nature of consciousness and thereby describe reason's method of knowing reality, allowed irrationalism and collectivism to take root and grow into today's spectacle of a virulently absolutist and nihilistic postmodernism.

---

[20]Llewellyn H. Rockwell, Jr., "Medical Control, Medical Corruption," June 1994, lewrockwell.com; Dale Steinreich, "100 Years of Medical Robbery," June 10, 2004, Mises.org; Dale Steinreich, "Real Medical Freedom," August 27, 2004, mises.org.

Stephen Hicks' 2004 book *Explaining Postmodernism: Skepticism and Socialism from Rousseau to Foucault*[21] chronicles this process with brilliant simplicity. Beginning with an overview of the contrast between modernism and postmodernism, that is, the Enlightenment's pro-reason, pro-individualist, pro-capitalist philosophies and the postmodernists' rejection of those views, Hicks essentializes the ideas of the major players in this evolution.

Cashing in on the errors of the Enlightenment, Kant and Hegel were among the first (Rousseau preceded them in opposing fundamental Enlightenment values) to narrow the effectiveness of reason—in order to make room for faith and religion—and to devalue the autonomy of the individual. As the nineteenth century progressed, subsequent philosophers, including Kierkegaard, Schopenhauer, and Nietzsche, declared reality a subjective, contradictory creation known only through feeling or instinct and the individual's identity a function of group membership. Contempt for reason was their conclusion. Heidegger in the twentieth century elevated morbid, anxious feelings to the role of guides to knowledge and declared war against the entire Western tradition based on the law of non-contradiction. When logical positivism and linguistic analysis failed to correct the Enlightenment's errors, the path was cleared for the postmodernists—among them Foucault, Lyotard, Derrida, and Rorty—to take over.

When reason and reality are gone and feelings, especially those of anxiety, dread, and alienation, guide action, and when the group defines the individual, "group balkanization," as Hicks observes, "and conflict must necessarily result." A "nasty political correctness"—arising ironically in an age of relativism—became the tactic for accomplishing political goals (p. 82). And those goals are all of a socialist hue. The problem for the postmodernists, though, is that socialism has suffered a number of setbacks. The proletariat has not rebelled spontaneously, nor has capitalism collapsed. Indeed, Hicks cites six dramatic failures of socialism that have led to various reincarnations. The postmodern variety resulted most particularly from Khrushchev's[22] revelations of 1956. The postmodernists moved socialism away from its traditional

---

[21] Stephen Hicks, *Explaining Postmodernism*, amazon.com.
[22] "On the Cult of Personality and Its Consequences," wikipedia.org.

emphasis on need, wealth, and science and technology to the form we see today: egalitarianism, the notion that wealth is bad and environmentalism good (that is, the shift from "red" to "green"), and from universalism to multiculturalism.

Epistemological trends of the past 200 years, plus the failures of socialism, have culminated in the virulent absolutism of political correctness. Socialists have always advocated the coercion of government might to achieve their goals, but the postmodernists today are academics who realize that past revolutions have failed and capitalism has not collapsed. As a result, they are left with the only weapons they know how to use, namely words. Thus, they use words—not facts or overt force—as their means of swaying others and the words express hostility at Enlightenment values and despair about the present and future.

Cynical and envy-ridden, as Hicks points out in his grippingly eloquent conclusion, the postmodernists are the Iagos to the Enlightenment's Othellos.[23] The postmodernists' goal is no longer revolution; their goal, like Iago's, is to inject doubt into modernity's values and "let that doubt work like a slow poison" (p. 200).

I must emphasize that this brief post cannot do justice to the clarity and persuasive power with which Hicks' 200-page book exposes the insidious deviousness of postmodernism. Some reviewers have said the book is scary, but I find it inspiring and encouraging, if for no other reason than the fact that Hicks makes the reader want to go out on a limb to predict the next failure of socialism. The more significant reason for being encouraged is the negativity of postmodernism; negative programs never last.

But allow me to make that prediction. Ayn Rand said[24] that collectivism had to fail precisely at its height because its claims to intellectuality and idealism were both frauds. I think the same point must eventually be applied to the environmental movement—those "reds" who have become "greens"—especially the global warming crowd. And it seems like everyone is going green today. However, when a Harvard

---

[23] "Othello," wikipedia.org.
[24] *Ayn Rand Lexicon*, "Collectivism," aynrandlexicon.com.

psychologist writing in the *New York Times Magazine*[25] acknowledges that the numbers about curbing carbon emissions "don't add up" and science staffer John Tierney[26] on the same newspaper makes fun of the exaggerated predictions routinely made today in the name of environmental "science," establishment media would seem to be moving in the direction of more openness to facts and less blind acceptance of the red/green litany.

The antidote to postmodernism is better ideas and those ideas are making their way through our culture. Will I see postmodernism overthrown in my lifetime? Perhaps not, but my daughter might.

(February 21, 2008)

The Two Liberalisms

POLITICS BORES ME. That's why I have not written a blog on politics or on the upcoming election. Let this post suffice as my comment on today's politics.

The Democrats' loss in 2004 led to much soul-searching[27] to define what the Democratic brand of liberalism should be or represent. Advice given focused on the usual concretes—guns, abortion, gay rights—the kinds of issues that would excite no one except conservatives. My advice is this. Reexamine the meaning of liberalism. Note its fundamental principles, especially as they evolved out of the Enlightenment. Then, in a radical departure from "politics as usual," adopt those principles as vanguard for freedom worldwide.

The problem is that two liberalisms came out of the Enlightenment. The first was classical[28] or market[29] liberalism (today also called libertarianism[30]). The second, developing in the latter part of the nineteenth century in England and the United States, is social liberalism,

---

[25] Steven Pinker, "The Moral Instinct," January 13, 2008, nytimes.com.
[26] John Tierney, "In 2008, a 100 Percent Chance of Alarm," January 1, 2008, nytimes.com.
[27] Adam Nagourney, "Baffled in Loss, Democrats Seek Way Foward," November 7, 2007, nytimes.com.
[28] "Classical Liberalism," wikipedia.org.
[29] "Market Liberalism," wikipedia.org.
[30] "Libertarianism," wikipedia.org.

an amalgam of ideas ranging from mixed-economy features of part capitalism, part socialism, to Fabian[31] or democratic socialism.[32]

Market and social liberalism have the same genus, which means they share certain principles, and for advocates of market liberalism, this is an argument for possibly seeking common ground with some of their social counterparts. The common principles are these: emphasis on self-realization or self-actualization of the individual human mind as the essence of liberty, which translates to demands for the freedom of speech and press; strong value placed on reason, science, and technology as the source of modern material civilization; and the complete separation of church and state, with an emphasis on secular naturalism, including the naturalization of consciousness.

Where market and social liberalism differ is in their attitude toward business. Social liberalism holds that business, especially big business, is the new aristocracy that, through its positions of power and privilege, coerce the poor into remaining poor and generally disrupt the good taste of society. Hence, government might must be brought in to make right.

The history and theory of capitalism as understood by social liberals, of course, is patently false and has been demonstrated so by Ayn Rand and Ludwig von Mises, among many others. And social liberals are mistaken to think that reason, science, and technology by themselves created modern material civilization. Without capitalism, at the end of the eighteenth century, reason, science, and technology would have remained, respectively, little more than a mental exercise, a curiosity, and a hobby. Instead, capitalism unleashed their creative and productive powers.

It is these errors of social liberals that market liberals must articulate in conversations. Reality exists in a continuum; so do people. Social liberals range in thought from those who are merely mistaken to those who are explicitly and rabidly socialist and are out to destroy business. It is the former with whom one can make common cause, because such social and market liberals share many of the same values, namely freedom of the individual human mind, reason, science, technology,

---

[31] "Fabian Society," wikipedia.org.
[32] "Democratic Socialism," wikipedia.org.

separation of church and state, and naturalization of consciousness. It is a challenge to the market liberal, then, to convince the mistaken social liberal that true liberalism is the market or libertarian variety. If Democrats want to remain advocates of freedom, they should make their liberalism consistent and adopt market liberalism.

So what about religious conservatives and today's Republicans? People exist in a continuum, so some conservatives do still understand capitalism and promote it correctly, but most pretend to advocate capitalism, while rushing to outdo the Democrats, and usually succeeding at the job, in expanding the welfare-warfare state.

Lew Rockwell,[33] president of the Mises Institute, has this to say about conservatives:

> The problem with American conservatism is that it hates the left more than the state, loves the past more than liberty, feels a greater attachment to nationalism than to the idea of self-determination, believes brute force is the answer to all social problems, and thinks it is better to impose truth rather than risk losing one soul to heresy.

This is a good statement about conservatism, but one question remains: why does conservatism hate the left? The answer is the secular naturalism of liberalism; from its beginnings in the Enlightenment, liberalism has always seen religion and the church as enemies of individual rights and freedom. The phrase "pinko-commie atheists," with emphasis on the last word, summarizes the motivation of conservatism. It is intolerant of irreligion. That identifies conservatism as a movement that is pre-Enlightenment.

Conservatism is not a friend of capitalism, nor is it a philosophy of liberalism.

The fundamental problem with both social liberalism and religious conservatism is that both identify morality with altruism. Social liberals may force their children to give all proceeds from a lemonade-stand sale to charity, but the religious conservatives force their children to

---

[33] Llewellyn H. Rockwell, Jr., "The Great Conservative Hoax," May 4, 2006, lewrockwell.com.

give ten percent or more of their allowance to the church. Both advocate as gospel self-sacrifice in their personal, social, and political lives.

Eliminating the premise that government might makes right requires first that the premise of self-sacrifice be challenged and replaced by the right, whether child or adult, peaceably and cooperatively to pursue ones' own values.

(September 8, 2008)

Coerced Altruism, Involuntary Servitude, and Contempt for the Less Well Off

"MANY PEOPLE NEED TO BE COERCED to do things for their own good." This is a common refrain heard from social liberals and religious conservatives alike.

National service[34] was advocated by both presidential candidates in the recent election; young people are to be coerced to "do good for their own good." Advocates of the military draft have always argued that it is the duty of eighteen-year-olds to serve their country and to die for it; unless current ideological trends change, future drafts will extend involuntary servitude to young women, putting them next to the young men so they may also die for their country. And in the government-run, government-coerced education system "service learning"[35]—the notion of learning about the poor and downtrodden while at the same time receiving an altruistic jolt by serving them—is abuzz. Students are forced to clean bedpans in nursing homes and give food to the homeless.

Such notions are usually put forth by the more highly educated. The less educated just follow along in agreement. Two questions come to mind: Why do so many people think this way? And how do they come to think of children, young people, and others in general as their slaves? The first is readily answered as the two-and-a-half thousand years of

---

[34]"McCain, Obama Find Common Ground on National Service," September 12, 2008, cnn.com.
[35]"Service-Learning," wikipedia.org.

cultural tradition[36] that equates altruism and self-sacrifice to ethics. The second is more subtle and takes us into psychology.

Of course, most advocates of these ideas do not think of their victims as slaves. The word is harsh, but forcing someone to do something against his or her will does not make that person an autonomous individual. That it is the highly educated who espouse these notions indicates an air of superiority over those who are coerced. Historically, it has always been the upper-class aristocrats who have taken it upon themselves to make decisions that control the lives of their subjects, the lower, less educated classes. Today, we do not have an official aristocracy, but Plato's philosopher kings[37] have most certainly been replaced by our present-day PhD kings, the ones who hold authoritative (and authoritarian) positions in various government agencies.

Interestingly, this elite, when pressed for details about why they believe what they do, exhibits not just an air of condescension over the lower- and less-educated, but also an apprehension to let the uncultivated guide their own lives. There appears to be a fear, not unlike that of the old aristocracy, to the effect: "I know what's best for the uneducated, but I don't want to associate with them. We have nothing in common." Do I dare say that the attitude of this contemporary elite is "I don't want to associate with the 'great unwashed.'"[38] The elite fears a loss of status or rank, and therefore power, over its subordinates by hobnobbing with them; the dirt may rub off and cause contamination. The elite fears that they might lose their pseudo self-esteem.[39]

The essence of this attitude is a profound lack of respect for the less well off accompanied by the contemptuous sorrow known as pity that apparently gives rise to the need to lord it over them. The need to lord it over others, as I pointed out in a previous post,[40] derives from defensive anxiety. Having grown up in the ranks of the "less well off" and "less educated," I can attest to the lack of respect communicated by those who thought they knew what was best for me. Ironically, neither

---

[36] "Ayn Rand Mike Wallace 1959 Full Interview," youtube.com.
[37] "Philosopher King," wikipedia.org; Plato, *The Republic*, classics.mit.edu.
[38] "Hoi Polloi," wikipedia.org.
[39] "Self-Esteem," wikipedia.org.
[40] See above, "The Market Gives Privilege to No One," p. 25.

I nor most of my friends or relatives considered ourselves "less well off" or "disadvantaged." Our unquestioned assumption was that we would do better than our parents. Self-esteem, it seems, is precondition not just to raise oneself above one's original station in life, but also, and perhaps more importantly, to avoid turning around and looking down on those whence one came.

The conviction to impose altruism and involuntary servitude on others stems from unexamined premises embedded in our culture for thousands of years. The root of the premises, though, is the thousands-of-years old view of human nature that certain types of people are incapable of helping themselves or, especially, making sound decisions for themselves. And "types of people" here means anyone of a certain skin color, gender, religion, nationality, or level of income, education, and occupation, etc. The source of this theory of human nature, in turn, seems to be rationalization for the fears those in power feel toward those who are lower in status. This is a case of psychology influencing and determining perception.

Altruism is the main premise in our culture that needs to be examined. It does not mean kindness or gentleness. It means giving up a higher value for the sake of a lower or non-value. It means self-sacrifice. The first step to questioning altruism is to acknowledge the full meaning of the adage, "We were put on earth to serve others." The full meaning is implied in what one wag added to the familiar phrase: "but I don't know why the others were put here." The others were put here to collect our sacrifices and it is our duty to continue sacrificing to those others. That is the meaning of altruism. It is ancient ethics still reigning over us in the twenty-first century.

(November 26, 2008)

2009

Why the World Is Not Going to Hell in a Basket

ONE OF THE UNFORTUNATE DISEASES of older age is the tendency to pessimism or even cynicism. Nostalgia for the good old days is rampant, with complaints about how the young don't know what we knew at their age and how they are so ill-mannered and unworldly. When generalized to the political and cultural arenas, Armageddon is said to be imminent. For advocates of capitalism and admirers of Ayn Rand, it sometimes becomes a prediction of a new Dark Age.

I wish to take exception to these dire prophecies and venture an alternative scenario. One argument for the coming Dark Age is the analogy that is drawn between the twentieth and third centuries. The third century AD in the Roman Empire was a century of inflation[41]; so was the twentieth century in the modern world, including the United States. In the Roman Empire, it was a century of war, chaotic leadership by ineffective emperors, and collapse of cultural institutions. Similar statements are made about the twentieth century of wars, chaos, weak leadership, and cultural collapse. The third century AD paved the way for the barbarians and ultimate collapse of ancient civilization. Obviously, the cynics conclude, we are headed in the same direction.

The decline of ancient Rome is a fascinating topic. I see the beginning of its end occurring about 150 BC, when Greek slaves were brought to Rome to educate the children of aristocrats. These Greek slaves were influenced mostly by the philosophy of Stoicism,[42] the notion of turning away from the material world, and the Romans fell in love with the view. With Stoicism tapping into what apparently was an existing sense of life among Romans, the path was then prepared for Christianity and its view of turning-away. By the fourth century AD, Paulinus of Nola,[43] a Roman senator of great wealth and property, simply renounced the material world and retreated to an austere, monastic life. In symbolic, if not actual, form ancient civilization sought refuge in the monastery. Turning away from material civilization is not a characteristic of contemporary culture or philosophy.

In the title essay of her book *For the New Intellectual*, Ayn Rand said[44] that Descartes reintroduced the Witch Doctor into modern philosophy, thus setting up an opposition between the material and spiritual that

---

[41] "Roman Empire," wikipedia.org; Bruce Bartlett, "How Excessive Government Killed Ancient Rome," Fall 1994, cato.org; Joseph R. Peden, "Inflation and the Fall of the Roman Empire," transcript of lecture delivered October 17, 1984, mises.org.
[42] "Stoicism," wikipedia.org.
[43] "Paulinus of Nola," wikipedia.org.
[44] "Prior Certainty of Consciousness," aynrandlexicon.com.

exists to this day. This opposition gave rise to Kant's subjectivism and the resurgence of mysticism, which, Rand says, will lead to a new Dark Age.

I disagree with this interpretation. Based on conversations with my wife, philosopher Linda Reardan, I would say that Descartes made a valiant effort to bring consciousness down to earth—God being the metaphor of consciousness—and the entire modern and contemporary periods in philosophy have been an attempt to integrate consciousness into the material world and to naturalize it. There has not been a complete success, but this notion is at the root of my interpretation of John Dewey's epistemology and the comment in *Montessori, Dewey, and Capitalism*[45] (p. 70) that the rejection of intrinsicism in philosophy began "if only as a glimmer" in the late nineteenth century. Philosophy, I conclude, has been progressing, albeit not always in a straight line.

And viewing historical progress as requiring a straight line is surely a prescription for pessimism and cynicism. The Magna Carta[46] was signed in 1215, but it was another six centuries before the Age of Enlightenment and the American Bill of Rights came into existence. In between there was the Black Death that wiped out as much as half of Europe's population and the Hundred Years' War, among other atrocities, yet the spirit to live and better ideas survived throughout that period to give us the world we have today. My notion of optimism derives from taking a very long view of civilization—centuries long. I do not expect life to improve much, if at all, in the next four years of the current presidential administration. I do not expect the current (or previous) administration to be the indicator of the beginning of the end of civilization as we know it. I see the twentieth and maybe even the twenty-first centuries to be a blip in the progress of civilization. My optimism in no small part is also aided by a commitment to avoid condemning someone merely for espousing ideas with which I disagree.

Good—meaning rational—ideas win out in the long run. The ancient Greeks suffered a Dark Age[47] from about 1200 to 800 BC. When they obtained the Phoenician alphabet and learned to write,

---

[45] Jerry Kirkpatrick, *Montessori, Dewey, and Capitalism*, amazon.com. See also books.jkirkpatrick.net.
[46] "Magna Carta," wikipedia.org.
[47] "Greek Dark Ages," wikipedia.org.

they immediately recorded their entire oral tradition, paving the way for the golden age of Greco-Roman civilization. When moveable type was invented in the fifteenth century, every extant written work that could be found was, within a hundred years, published in permanent form, making education of the masses possible. The current century is proving to be the age of digitization, the aim of which is to make every written work in existence available in electronic form. The advantages of this cannot begin to be imagined.

The twentieth century produced two enormously destructive wars, but they did not silence either Ludwig von Mises or Ayn Rand. Their ideas now flourish—not on the front pages of leading newspapers or on nightly newscasts, but they are making their way through our culture. As I frequently tell my daughter, patience is a virtue. I may not in my lifetime see any significant intellectual change in our culture, and my daughter may not see much of a change either. But barring a meteor strike that wipes out ninety-five percent of all living species—and that assumes the destruction of all paper and electronic literature—the will to live will win out and civilization will continue.

(February 15, 2009)

The Importance of Philosophy to a Successful Business Career

Understanding the broad abstractions of ethics and epistemology can instill confidence in one's work life. Such understanding is especially helpful in a business career, not for the purpose of preaching to co-workers, employees, or customers, but to maintain clear thoughts about what is right and wrong in decision making and to correctly perceive facts in complicated situations.

Most ethical issues in business center on honesty. For example, a boss might say to a young worker, "Tell the customer it's on the truck," when in fact the order has not yet been processed. The assumption is that the company will scramble to get the order on the truck before a major delay occurs and customer dissatisfaction results. The problem with this stretching of the truth is that as days, weeks, months, and years go by it often gets stretched further and further from reality leading to "what the customers don't know won't hurt 'em." This can eventually culminate in an Enron[48] or Bernard Madoff[49] scenario. Such is the importance of honesty in a business career.

Telling the truth is the simplest solution to business problems even if it results in being yelled at or temporarily losing business. It is far better than living a life of fakery.[50] The tricky part about honesty is that lying and dishonesty are not the same. Honesty does not require truth telling under threat of force. A misdirection lie to deceive a potential thief of the whereabouts of your money is quite honest and moral. Everyone has a right to self-defense. Everyone also enjoys a right to privacy—no one, for example, has a right to your financial situation. A negotiator might ask, "Tell me the truth. What is your rock bottom price?" or "Is this [specific amount] your final price?" You may properly respond evasively or with an incorrect specific price. This is not game playing or bluffing[51]; it is sound, ethical decision-making.

Bribery is an omnipresent issue in the press and in discussions of business ethics. It also is an issue of honesty—because of the deception that occurs—but it is compounded by its similarity to a number of other concepts that it too often is not differentiated from. Epistemology, particularly the theory of definition, can help clarify this.

Most bribes involve a payment of money or offer of gift to influence others. But so does a perk, a grease payment, extortion, subornation, and a commission or broker's fee. And then there is the gift of candy to children, often called a bribe, to get them to clean their rooms. How are these to be distinguished from each other? The rules of definition say that our concepts must be classified in terms of genus and differentia, that is, concepts must be put into a broad category first, then differentiated from the other items that are similar to the one being defined. This is the situation we have with bribery.

---

[48] "Enron," wikipedia.org.
[49] "Bernie Madoff," wikipedia.org.
[50] See below, "Faking Your Way through Life," p. 213.
[51] Jerry Kirkpatrick, "A Critique of 'Is Business Bluffing Ethical?'" April 21, 2002, cpp.edu/faculty/jkirkpatrick.

The genus of all the concepts in the previous paragraph is a payment or gift to influence others. The differentia of each does the clarifying. A perk (or perquisite) is an above-board prize that accompanies one's job, such as a tip or company car. "Above-board" means it is not covert or secretive. A grease payment is a modest incentive to induce foot-dragging bureaucrats to perform their normal duties. Extortion is a demand for payment under threat of force, whereas subornation is a covert payment to persuade someone to ignore or violate the law, rules, or one's ethics. A commission or broker's fee is payment for a job well done, such as a closed sale. The candy given to children? It's just an incentive to action. To call it a bribe is metaphorical extension of the original concept.

So what is a bribe? Most similar to subornation, it is a covert payment designed to undermine a relation of trust. A sales rep, for example, offers an extra payment to a buyer, unbeknownst to the owner of the buyer's company, in exchange for a contract. The deceit and breach of trust occurs by cheating the owner of the buyer's company. Bribery is a precise concept that should not be slung around lightly and applied to all of these other actions. It is a specific type of unsavory behavior that, when not understood clearly, becomes applied to and confused with decent, respectable outcomes, such as perks, commissions, and parental management of children. Such is how philosophy, particularly epistemology, can parse complicated issues.

The resulting clarity inspires strength and conviction that paying a perk, commission, or maybe even making a grease payment are not unsavory behavior.

The most important place in which philosophy can instill confidence in one's work life in business is in the understanding of self-interest as moral and in the guiltless acceptance and promotion of the profit motive of capitalism. For a wealth of resources on these issues, I refer readers to the works of Ayn Rand[52] and Ludwig von Mises.[53]

(August 24, 2009)

---

[52] Ayn Rand, *The Virtue of Selfishness,* amazon.com.
[53] Ludwig von Mises, *Human Action,* amazon.com.

2010

Ideas Kill

IDEAS HAVE CONSEQUENCES and one consequence is that, when implemented, certain ideas can kill.

Two recent stints of sitting six-plus hours in the emergency room of a local hospital stimulated thoughts on the state of socialized medicine today. As a marketing professor, the first sarcastic comment that came to mind was just how little the hospital staff cared about their paying customers who were sitting agonizingly in those oh-so-comfortable chairs. Beyond this, I had to ask, "Where is the excess capacity—of doctors and examining rooms—to be called upon to meet high demand?" Supermarkets, after all, promptly open additional registers when more than three customers are waiting in line to check out. Of course, this last just as promptly usually generates from the medical profession the indignant response "We're not a business! How dare you!!"

The answer to my question is that, by design, there has been no excess capacity in medicine since at least the mid-nineteenth century. The goal of the licensing monopoly created by the American Medical Association[54] in 1847 was to restrict supply in order to increase the income of a certain type[55] of doctor. The 1910 *Flexner Report*[56] led to a further restriction of the supply of medical schools. Regulation and taxation of for-profit hospitals throughout the twentieth century drove most out of business, leaving such institutions to be taken over either by an arm of the government or by government-sanctioned and protected nonprofit organizations. That is to say, to be taken over by those idols of customer service, the bureaucrats.

Nonetheless, the system has not been as bad as it is today. In the 1950s, when I was a child, our family doctor made house calls and twice, once after a bang on my head and the second time after I suffered a baseball in the eye, the doctor met my father and me at the hospital

---

[54] "American Medical Association, Criticism," wikipedia.org; Llewellyn H. Rockwell, Jr., "The Trouble with Licensure," August 1, 1990, lewrockwell.com.
[55] Linda Johnston, MD, DHt, "Homeopathy, Economics, and Government," October 3, 2002, lewrockwell.com.
[56] "Flexner Report," wikipedia.org; Dale Steinreich, "100 Years of US Medical Fascism," April 17, 2010, lewrockwell.com.

where more resources were available than in the doctor's office. There was no wait when we got to the hospital and my father paid for all of this out of his pocket—we had no medical insurance. And, oh yes, my father was not wealthy. He worked as a clerk in the post office. The connection between seller and customer was direct and the market performed relatively smoothly.

What has happened in the years since is the solidification of medical bureaucratization that began at its point of inflection during the wage and price controls of World War II.* Health insurance that businesses could deduct from their taxes was the only way wages could be increased. This began the slippery slope of putting the government-regulated cartel of insurance companies between doctors and patients. Medicare in 1965 iced the government takeover of medicine with strict price controls. Skyrocketing costs, shortages, and the charade of billing as much as five times what is actually paid for medical procedures have become the norm.

What kills, in the form of long waits, is price-control-caused shortages and other regulations that restrict innovation and supply. People die waiting to get appointments with doctors, waiting for surgeries, for transplant organs, for drug approvals from the FDA. Think Canada and the UK. One doctor[57] estimates that 80,000 men over a three-year period died in the US awaiting the approval of a prostate cancer drug that was already in use in Europe.

Our adventure in the hospital that I began this post with ultimately had a happy ending, but in the intervening hours of waiting a parade of doctors looked at our daughter offering diagnoses ranging from tendonitis to viral infection to (the correct) bacterial infection, a possibly serious problem if not caught early. The range of diagnoses could only make me think of Jerome Groopman's[58] book on *How Doctors Think*,[59] where Groopman points out that 10–15% of diagnoses are wrong. The likely issue in my daughter's case is that the doctors are so frazzled by lack of time to listen to or take a full patient history that they cannot consider all alternative explanations of the symptoms.

---

[57] Mark Thornton, "The FDA vs. Bone Cancer Patients," May 7, 2010, wsj.com.
[58] See below, "Curiosity for Subtle Detail," p. 204.
[59] Jerome Groopman, *How Doctors Think*, amazon.com.

The doctors are caught in a bureaucratic web spun by the advocates of socialized medicine. The doctors, as a result, have become no better and no worse than college professors at a state-run university. That is to say, they have become bureaucrats just like me. Some are better than others. The challenge is to find the good ones.

Even before these two visits to the ER, the state of the system had become personal to me. Some twenty months ago I had a date with the cardiologist. My response, therefore, to those who want more government involvement in medicine is simple: "You would have me dead. With your ideas in place twenty months ago, with the increased shortages and waiting time those ideas cause, I might not be here today. Your ideas kill."

* The seeds of socialized medicine go back to Prussia's Bismarck. And, according to Melchior Palyi[60] (chap. 4), Bismarck just governmentalized ideas that were plentiful during the medieval guild era.

(May 20, 2010)

Choice Theory and Capitalism versus Dictatorship

IN MY BOOK *MONTESSORI, DEWEY, AND CAPITALISM*[61] (p. 118, note 8), I speculate that the root of dictatorship may be the parent/child relationship, stemming from the millenniums old theory of teaching and parenting based on authoritarianism. "If it is okay to coerce children," I write, "why should it not also be okay to coerce adults?"

I drew this conclusion not just from the work of Maria Montessori,[62] but also from Thomas Gordon,[63] Haim Ginott,[64] and Alfie Kohn.[65] All are

---

[60] Melchior Palyi, *Compulsory Medical Care and the Welfare State*, mises.org.
[61] Jerry Kirkpatrick, *Montessori, Dewey, and Capitalism*, amazon.com. See also books.jkirkpatrick.net.
[62] Maria Montessori, *The Montessori Method*, amazon.com.
[63] Thomas Gordon, *Parent Effectiveness Training*, amazon.com.
[64] Haim G. Ginott, *Between Parent and Child*, amazon.com.
[65] Alfie Kohn, *Punished by Rewards*, amazon.com.

advocates in varying degrees of so-called intrinsic motivation.[66] Some have even suggested a connection between external control psychology and dictatorship, but none have linked internal control with the need for laissez-faire capitalism. Psychiatrist William Glasser[67] goes furthest by commenting extensively on our "external control society" and the need for less of it. Glasser indeed provides an extremely simple and fundamental foundation of my statement in his discussions of choice theory versus external control.

Choice theory, according to Glasser, means that we choose most of our behavior, including the alleged mental illness of depression. Glasser prefers verbs to nouns, emphasizing what we choose to do rather than dwelling on what we think is done to us. So he says that we do not suffer depression. Rather, we depress, or choose to depress, when we experience a disappointment. The way out of depressing, he says, is to take internal control of our lives by making value judgments to choose other, happier behaviors and then acting on those judgments.

The broader implication is that we control only our own behaviors and not that of others. Even though we may try at length to change other people's behaviors, the result on our part is usually frustration, or worse, and on the part of the person we are trying to change resistance, rebellion, resignation, or withdrawal. The relationship—whether it is between parent and child, husband and wife, teacher and student, or manager and employee—ultimately ends in unhappiness, and sometimes complete separation. The solution, says Glasser, is to stop trying to change other people's behavior, acknowledging and acting on the fact that we can only control or change our own.

This means avoiding Glasser's seven deadly habits that destroy personal relationships: criticizing, blaming, complaining, nagging, threatening, punishing, and rewarding to control (bribing) (*Unhappy Teenagers*,[68] p. 13). These are all tools of external control psychology and their aim is to coerce behavioral change by bypassing the other person's consent or understanding. Criticizing and blaming, says Glasser, are the worst, though all of the habits erode closeness.

---

[66] "Motivation, Intrinsic and Extrinsic," wikipedia.org.
[67] William Glasser, *Choice Theory*, amazon.com.
[68] William Glasser, *Unhappy Teenagers*, amazon.com.

When the aim of coercive behavioral change is taken to the extreme, direct physical force may result, such as spanking, hitting, or the use of weapons. Caring, trusting, listening, supporting, negotiating, befriending, and encouraging are the connecting habits that Glasser recommends as replacements for the deadly ones (p. 14).

External control psychology is the belief that we know what is best for others and that we have the right to impose our will on those others. It is the use of rewards and punishments as motivation. When elevated to the relationship of politician and citizen (Glasser does not quite go this far), external control psychology becomes the right to impose—by legislation or fiat—laws, regulations, and edicts to force citizens to do or not do what the politicians think is best. External control psychology assumes and attempts to invoke dependence. It is the real root of dictatorship.

Internal control psychology, on the other hand, is the foundation of independent judgment. It assumes that each of us controls our own destiny by choosing our values and behaviors. Interaction with others is conducted through reason and logic, that is, persuasion, rather than Glasser's manipulative deadly habits. Motivating others requires appealing to the others' self-interest, communicating in such a way that the others see the benefit to themselves of the requested action. Internal control psychology treats others with dignity.[69] It derives from a high level of self-esteem and respect for others and acknowledges that the others have or are capable of a similar disposition.

At the political level, internal control psychology means each individual has the right to choose his or her own values and behaviors. To the politicians and government in general, it means: leave us alone. Internal control psychology is the root of capitalism.

(July 16, 2010)

---

[69] See below, "Rankism and the Well-Earned Disrespect of Some Teachers," p. 180.

Working in Business as Opposed to Being a Student

When I began working in business, shortly after receiving my bachelor's degree, I experienced a pleasant surprise: I immensely enjoyed what I was doing. Indeed, I felt that working in business was a lot more fun than being a student, so much so that it took nearly six-and-a-half years before I could summon the strength to go to graduate school. I have related this story to a number of people, but never had a good explanation or understanding why being an employee is so much more enjoyable than being a student.

The answer is not the money difference—being paid to do work as opposed to paying the school for an education. It is the feeling of importance. The work itself may not be top-level decision making, which in my case it was not, but every stroke of my pencil mattered. It made the difference in customer satisfaction and company earnings. Everyone in the company contributed to both. The sense of importance also came from the familial atmosphere I experienced with my co-workers and boss, an atmosphere I experienced in every business that I worked for but have not found in any of my academic jobs. Is there something fundamentally different about business and education?

Ask a group of students if they feel important in their school and you are likely to get a blank or incredulous "are you kidding?" stare (Glasser,[70] p. 45). Importance in school, they say, comes from their friends or their extracurricular activities (sports, music, theater, etc.). As a student they feel more like a number on a roster, not overly seen or respected as a person, but as just another piece of produce to be graded and sorted. This, of course, comes from the bureaucratic nature of government-run and -regulated education.[71] Grading and sorting are among the main functions of bureaucracy. Students do not feel important because they are not treated the way customers are in privately-run businesses.* Students are not customers, but they should be.

---

[70] William Glasser, *Choice Theory in the Classroom*, amazon.com.

[71] See above, "It's Just Being Turned into a Business," p. 31. see below, "The Factory Model of Education, Technocracy, and the Free School Movement," p. 176. see below, "On Extrinsic Motivation and the Stage-Mother Syndrome," p. 327.

How are customers treated in private businesses? The slogans "customers are number one" and "the customer is always right" give an indication of the importance of customers to businesses and the importance customers should feel when patronizing most well-run businesses. But what businesses can we compare to education to see what an education customer in a free market might feel? There are today several (relatively) free markets in education. Private lessons, whether piano, personal training, or tutoring, are one. The customer is given the instructor's full attention and is rarely graded or made to suffer rewards and punishments. Importance is built-in to this type of learning.

Team lessons, especially in sports, are another. While softball and basketball coaches do evaluate players for best position and first or second team, they usually do not employ rewards and punishments of the type that carry the weight of school grades. The players, as a result, have fun working as a team to beat the other teams. There are small private classes, sometimes held in an instructor's living room or in a rented hotel room. Customers feel relaxed and important to the instructor because they are there just to learn and have fun in the process. They are not there to be graded or tested, the source of anxiety and decreased feelings of importance. Finally, there are large private classes—lectures—sometimes given in hotel ballrooms. No grades, no tests. The customers are there to learn and take away from the lecture what they want. They are important to the lecturer for the revenue he or she earns. They may not have personal contact and receive personal attention from the lecturer, but the atmosphere nevertheless is pleasant—far more pleasant than the impersonal graduate-student run megasections many of us have endured in research universities.

Clearly, it is the critical, comparative grade-and-sort atmosphere of government-run education that eliminates almost any chance for the student (customer) to acquire a sense of importance. Throw in at the K-12 level the compulsory attendance laws and you have students, especially at the secondary level, who have the sense of being in jail.**

The bureaucratic nature of education also makes it difficult for faculty to enjoy the familial atmosphere I experienced in private businesses. As professors, we have to fill out the right forms (and get our hands slapped if we don't) and comply with the myriad rules. Customer satisfaction and earnings are irrelevant, so there is no benchmark of performance or importance. Conflict frequently erupts with the lack of a common goal. With guaranteed lifetime employment, the "family" sometimes becomes enmeshed in what seems like a marriage "without the possibility of divorce."[72] The stakes[73] in such a situation have become too small.

* I include private universities, including the for-profits, in the category of bureaucratic education, because they are regulated and therefore their culture is controlled and defined by the government.

** Craig Haney and Philip Zimbardo, "It's Tough to Tell a High School from a Prison," *Psychology Today*, June 1975. Also, see John Holt, *The Underachieving School*.[74]

(October 13, 2010)

The Blender Principle

MANY YEARS AGO WHEN I WAS A YOUNG MAN, I bought a kitchen blender for my then girlfriend as a birthday present. I proudly mentioned this gift to a friend and the friend's reaction was best described by the expression, "If looks could kill, ..." Lesson learned. Not quite the best romantic choice.

The blender principle refers to the art of gift giving and since this is the holiday season, I would like to comment on observations I've made in the years since that incident. Of course, *Scroogenomics*[75] has already chimed in with the economist's perspective on gift giving, namely that when others shop for us they are unlikely to do as well as

---

[72] Thomas H. Benton,"The 7 Deadly Sins of Professors," May 12, 2006, chronicle.com.
[73] See below, "Because the Stakes Are So Small," p. 133.
[74] John Holt, *The Underachieving School*, amazon.com.
[75] Joel Waldfogel, *Scroogenomics*, amazon.com.

we would when we shop for ourselves. And the *Wall Street Journal*[76] last year provided plenty of horror stories about ill-chosen gifts.

The blender principle states that the gift must match the desires of the recipient. Anything else is a disappointment. This means that it is not impossible for a blender to be appreciated by someone who loves to cook, has little money, and talks constantly about the dishes she could make if only she had a blender. For most, women in particular, a blender is just too utilitarian. As my friend put it, "You want to give something that is 'useless,' not practical, such as perfume or jewelry."

The adage "it's the thought that counts" is correct, and I would add "not the price tag." The art of gift giving is not easy. It requires knowing well the desires of the recipient, which cannot always be known in advance. No doubt this is why many people throw money at the gift, these days seemingly acting on the premise that the more money thrown, the better the gift—and, presumably for some, the more appreciation expected. Giving according to price, though, is an evasion of thought. It's as bad a giving a blender, or socks or underwear, or cash or gift card (except perhaps when grandparents do the latter).

One of the most enjoyable and challenging purchases I had to make in my younger years was a gift for a Christmas grab bag. The limit on the gifts was $10, which today would probably be about $25 or $30. Not a large amount of money and even less information about who was attending the party, except that the attendees were all admirers of capitalism. The challenge was to come up with a gift that was not too specific and not too generic but somewhere in between such that any one of fifteen to twenty people could appreciate it. I think I succeeded, though I no longer remember who got the gift (a book about the monopoly board game) or whether it was appreciated. At least one gift in the bag was non-G rated, indicating a decided misunderstanding of the concept.

A limited price tag on gifts is appealing. It forces the issue on thought. Like the wedding registry, however, most kids and even adults

---

[76] Elizabeth Bernstein, "The Gift That Needs Forgiving," December 15, 2009, wsj.com; Rachel Emma Silverman, "Oh, Honey, You Shouldn't Have: When Well-Intentioned Gifts Go Bad," December 17, 2009, wsj.com; Elizabeth Bernstein, "Gifts That Backfired," December 18, 2009, wsj.com.

today have resorted to providing givers long lists of preferred items. Add the faux surprise and hyperbolic gushing "how did you know—just what I wanted" upon opening the gift and I begin thinking of the h-word [hypocrisy] for the whole season. Yes, I am one who suffers holiday season stress.[77] As a result, I have often wished that my family were Jewish. Eight gifts for the children during Hanukkah and the family goes out to dinner at a nice restaurant on Christmas day. That's it. Instead, lists are beginning to accumulate around our house and the panic I feel on the first day of each month when I have to think of a new blog topic is beginning to set in for the current holiday season.

What I really wish for this holiday season is the elevation of thought and demotion of price in process of gift giving. Victorian England is apparently the origin of our modern tradition, and the Victorians were creative. For example, they had cobweb parties,[78] only vaguely reminiscent of spiders. Gifts are tied to yarn of different colors and the yarn is elaborately spun around the room. Guests are given or may choose a particular color of yarn and then follow it to their gift.

Sounds fun to me! The usual arsenal of gifts under a tree, though, will still probably be required this year.

(December 4, 2010)

2012

Altruistic Twaddle and the Harm It Causes

Twaddle, as the dictionary says, is "empty silly talk," that is, "empty" in the sense that nothing is really being said, "silly" in the sense of being ridiculous or trivial or frivolous, and "talk" . . . well, in the sense that someone is saying or writing it. "Drivel" and "nonsense" might be other descriptives of the word.

When I put "altruistic" in front of it, I am talking about the tiresome nonsense that today is praised and promoted as ethical behavior, such as cleaning bedpans in nursing homes to demonstrate one's unselfish

---

[77] Elizabeth Scott, "Managing the Seemingly Inevitable Holiday Season Stress," January 15, 2021, verywellmind.com.

[78] Jessica Bloustein Marshall, "Yankee Swap vs. White Elephant vs. Dirty Santa," December 22, 2014, mentalfloss.com.

public service and thereby become eligible to attend an Ivy League or other highly reputed college. Or the ads encouraging us to give five dollars to the Starbucks Foundation to help create jobs. (On job creation, see this.[79]) Or to help promote economic development and create world peace by digging ditches in a third-world country

Not that there is anything wrong, demeaning, or unethical about these behaviors. I have not cleaned bedpans, but I have donated to charity and for pay I have dug at least one ditch. It is the disconnect stemming from a screaming ignorance of economics that stands out among those who say we should work side by side old people, poor people, and people living in abject poverty on the other side of the world to achieve world peace and prosperity.

The reasoning seems to flow like this.[80] If we work side by side these people, we will acquire a mutual understanding of each other, gain respect, and become friends. This, somehow, will make war obsolete because peace must necessarily follow from our friendships. Then justice, and finally—the greatest leap of all—economic prosperity (presumably, by digging ditches and building schools), will follow.

Friendship certainly does develop over weeks or months when one works beside a total stranger. It's almost impossible not to become friendly on some level. But friendship does not guarantee peace. Blood relatives and neighbors have fought and killed each other in many a civil war.[81] Clearly, something more fundamental about human relationships than friendship must determine the causes of war and peace.[82]

There is good reason why culture has been likened to an iceberg,[83] with nine-tenths of its core values buried beneath surface appearances (and beneath surface friendships that may develop in the Peace Corps[84] and other missionary organizations). It is this depth of what defines a culture, or rather, the ignorance of it, that has led American

---

[79] George Reisman, "Consumers Don't 'Create Jobs': Reisman vs. Blodget," December 13, 2011, mises.org.
[80] Global Volunteers (website), globalvolunteers.org; "Make a Positive Impact," globalvolunteers.org.
[81] "Brother against Brother," en.wikipedia.org; "Rwandan Genocide," wikipedia.org.
[82] "War," aynrandlexicon.com.
[83] "Edward T. Hall's Cultural Iceberg Model," 1976, spps.org.
[84] The Peace Corps (website), peacecorps.gov.

presidents to naively assume boots on the ground can quickly turn a dictatorship into a free state.

The core value that made the United States great is its respect for individual rights, especially property rights. "Make trade, not war" is the slogan that should replace the familiar fluff from the 1960s.[85] Trading goods and services with, as opposed to shooting bullets at, each other is the only way to prevent war and alleviate poverty. It means, however, keeping the government out of both our bedrooms and board rooms, something advocates of altruism almost never agree with.

Other forms of altruistic twaddle include buying expensive hybrid or electric cars or installing expensive solar panels—and I say "expensive" to emphasize that low income people are unlikely to participate in these markets.* And the newly approved benefit corporation[86] that allows businesses to put social and environmental objectives ahead of profits. But about this last, Doug French[87] at the Mises Institute commented: "While a business owner may make grand pronouncements that the environment or some social issue is more important than profits, what he or she is really saying is that the company believes these issues are more important than customers." And: "The idea at the root of benefit corporations is that profit should be abolished."

This is the ultimate consequence of altruistic twaddle. The twaddle may strike some, as it does me, as tiresome nonsense, but it is not harmless. People who perform these behaviors may do them for the warm, fuzzy feeling of being moral, or even more moral than thou, according the altruistic ethics, but in truth their ideas and actions harm consumers, harm the poor, harm the old, and harm those living in abject poverty on the other side of the world.

Self-interest, the profit motive, and capitalism are what create. Altruism destroys.

* I never say never to entrepreneurs, because some entrepreneur, some day, somewhere may, even in today's government-hampered markets, figure out how to make these products cost effective and

---

[85] "Make Love, Not War," wikipedia.org.
[86] Angus Loten, "With New Law, Profits Take a Back Seat," January 19, 2012, wsj.com.
[87] Doug French, "Profits Are Socially Responsible," June 26, 2012, mises.org.

profitable when sold to low income buyers. Today, of course, aside from the inefficiencies of the technologies, these markets are shot through with government meddling and favoritism, ranging from tax credits to bailouts.

Postscript. I have never been a fan of the Peace Corps but the source of the reasoning in paragraph four above is the private nonprofit organization Global Volunteers.[88] A labor of love of its entrepreneurial founders, the organization is billed as leader in the volunteer vacation movement. As I read through the site, I found myself faintly attracted to its mission and I think it is because anyone who works or aspires to work in a helping profession naturally would like to test his or her skills at helping. I know too much about economics, however, to think that this kind of volunteer work will ever achieve world peace or alleviate poverty.

One more question remains. Who actually is helped by missionary work? The helper's self-esteem is surely boosted, but what about the unseen nine-tenths of the helpee? When rich Americans fly halfway around the world to spend their two-week vacations helping others who supposedly cannot help themselves, might there not be a touch of resentment lurking beneath the surface, not to mention feelings of inferiority?

For a different angle on this topic, see above, "Coerced Altruism, Involuntary Servitude, and Contempt for the Less Well Off," p. 39.

(February 13, 2012)

The Triumph of Ethics over Practicality: A Tale of Two Cities

MY TITLE THIS MONTH—the triumph of ethics over practicality—is sarcastic because I believe, as Ayn Rand taught, that the moral is the practical. My reference is to the continued unquestioned acceptance and dominance of altruism as the equivalent of ethics. And just as unquestioned, the premise that self-interest is bad.

---

[88] Global Volunteers (website), globalvolunteers.org.

The two cities[89] are Joplin, Missouri, and Tuscaloosa, Alabama. About a year ago, a month apart, both were hit with devastating tornadoes. A year later Joplin is thriving, largely revived and rebuilt. Tuscaloosa, on the other hand, still has undemolished ruins, vacant lots, and businesses awaiting permit approvals to rebuild.

This is an old story, of course: West vs. East Germany, South vs. North Korea, the US vs. the USSR. Why is the lesson never learned that capitalism works and socialism—central planning of any kind, including urban planning—does not? The answer once again is ethics, especially the primacy of altruism.

The pursuit of profit, the alleged reasoning goes, especially in an emergency situation such as the aftermath of a tornado, is unconscionably selfish and self-evidently harmful. This requires careful thought and planning by experts who know what is best for the public, those poor distraught victims. "It is our duty to serve," the urban planners and other do-gooding bureaucrats rush in to say, "and serve we will."

To be more explicit, the reasoning continues, egoism is evil and self-sacrifice is noble, the public servant being the most noble of all. All work and effort is expended for the sake of others, often at great personal sacrifice. This largesse is manifested, as Ayn Rand scathingly pointed out, in "the most wasteful, useless and meaningless activity of all: the building of public monuments" (*The Virtue of Selfishness*, p. 89[90]). Monument builders in return expect gratitude and prestige from their constituents, a form of "you scratch my back, I'll scratch yours."

The public monument of these two cities is Tuscaloosa, a "showpiece," as the city's recovery plan states, of "state-of-the-art urban planning," with "unique neighborhoods that are healthy, safe, accessible, connected, and sustainable," anchored by "village centers"—and unfinished, one year later. The Tuscaloosa plan, however, the *Wall Street Journal*[91] comments, "never mentions protecting property rights." It's the monument that counts, the "state-of-the-art" plan.

That is because a public monument, according to Rand, is always presented as "a munificent gift to the victims whose forced labor or

---

[89] "Tornado Recovery: How Joplin Is Beating Tuscaloosa," April 13, 2012, wsj.com.
[90] Ayn Rand, "The Monument Builders," in *The Virtue of Selfishness*, amazon.com.
[91] "Tornado Recovery: How Joplin Is Beating Tuscaloosa," April 13, 2012, wsj.com.

extorted money had paid for it." In the case of Tuscaloosa the "forced labor and extorted money" was taxation, construction moratoria, and restrictions and regulations that increased the cost of doing business by thousands, even hundreds of thousands of dollars. Rights were irrelevant.

Joplin, on the other hand, took the free market route by suspending licensing and zoning regulations and allowing home and business owners to make their own decisions as to when and how they were going to rebuild. No monuments were built in Joplin.

What underlies the monument building mentality, whether it was construction of the pyramids in ancient Egypt or a military arch in the local park, is a theory of human nature. Egoism assumes that human beings are capable, resilient, self-directing and self-controlling. Altruism assumes that we are weak, inept, and in need of leadership from the more knowing and competent others, a ruling elite. It is not surprising then that a self-responsibility theory of human nature underlies egoism and capitalism. A theory of dependence underlies altruism and socialism in all of its variants. It is what underlies the theory of external control psychology.[92]

The monument builder is the one who vocally preaches self-sacrifice and in the end collects the sacrifices. The monument builder is a public servant who thinks of him- or herself as doing very important work. Practicality is irrelevant. Ethics—the ethics of altruism—is paramount. Thus, monument building becomes self-congratulatory but it often lacks external praise, as from one's constituents who might not always see the builder's work as "very important" or appreciate the builder's "sacrifices" that have been made.

The need to build more monuments becomes significant. More "forced labor and extorted money"—in today's parlance, increased taxes, more regulations, and elaborate public works programs—become required.

The monument building mentality quite simply is that of a dictator.

(May 23, 2012)

---

[92] See above, "Choice Theory and Capitalism versus Dictatorship," p. 49.

Politics Is a Bore (Retitled: Who Are We Going to Coerce Today?)

The term "political junkie" is familiar to all of us today, but when I first heard it years ago used by a news reporter to describe herself, I was puzzled. Why, I thought, would anyone be so obsessed with politics to spend every waking minute following every conceivable tidbit of information coming out of the political arena?

Perhaps the reporter's interest in politics was strictly professional, to cover what was going on, but I suspect that many in her position, as well as others who follow political news closely, admire the entire system and consider it important to support. Many political junkies, I fear, are those who admire the coercive apparatus of the state and relish the thought of being in a position of political power to make political decisions.

To me, politics is a bore—precisely because it is all about coercion, the government-initiated type; it's seldom about reducing government involvement in our lives. And following politics closely, as many do, means their interest really comes down to: who is going to be coerced today? Let's see who's going to be told by the anointed authorities what they can and cannot do. Protecting individual rights has long since disappeared from our political landscape such that decisions in today's government-by-lobby mixed economy invariably constitute violations of innocent victims' rights for the sake of someone else's rent-seeking[93] benefit.

Just look at the disgraceful shakedown of Gibson Guitar,[94] carried out in the name of the environmental lobby. Flimsily suspected, but never charged, of illegally importing wood from Madagascar and India, the company was twice raided with Gestapo-like tactics by armed, bullet-proof clad SWAT teams. At a 2011 press conference,[95] Gibson CEO Henry Juszkiewicz courageously called the Justice Department on its flagrantly unjust laws and tyrannical procedures. Because of

---

[93]"Rent Seeking," wikipedia.org.
[94]Craig Havighurst, "Why Gibson Guitar Was Raided By The Justice Department," August 31, 2011, npr.org.
[95]"Gibson Guitar vs. The Obama Regime," September 4, 2011, wwwwakeupamericans-spree.blogspot.com.

the outcry that followed, the Department compromised by allowing Gibson off the hook with a settlement: $350 thousand in fines and censorship (a gag order) not ever to do again what Juszkiewicz did at his press conference, namely to contradict the alleged facts claimed by the government.[96] If this is not coercion in politics—the initiation of the use of physical force against innocent victims—what is?

Now I suppose one could say that some politicians are trying to do good things in Washington and the state capital. And I will grant that maybe one or two may be trying to roll back government intrusions into our bedrooms and board rooms. Ron Paul's two presidential runs have certainly given a hearing to new ideas and Paul Ryan has put Ayn Rand's name in the news.*

But, seriously, what have Democrats and Republicans done in the last hundred years to increase the protections of individual rights? Democrats make no pretense at rolling back government interventions; they are only too eager to pass more laws increasing the state's size and power. Republicans, on the other hand, are notorious for paying lip service to the free market and capitalism, but when in office they end up increasing the government's coercive powers more than the Democrats would have done. Look at the two previous Bush administrations.

"Passing a law" for over a century has almost always meant increasing coercion against an innocent party for the gain of a pressure group. The "squeakiest wheel," of course, gets the grease in a mixed economy; that's the fundamental theory of the system because there is no just way to determine who gets the favors, or should I say, rents. But the laws are democratically passed by vote, one might object? Democracy, as the Greeks taught, can be a form of dictatorship and Hong Kong[97] survived quite well for decades under the British common law *without general elections.***

That's not to say that I don't believe in voting, though not voting is just as valid a participation in the system as pulling a lever. In the current political season, I will vote against the many California tax

---

[96] Kris Maher, "Gibson Guitar to Pay Fine Over Wood Imports," August 7, 2012, wsj.com; Harvey Silverglate, "Gibson Is Off the Feds' Hook. Who's Next?," August 19, 2012, wsj.com.
[97] "History of Hong Kong," wikipedia.org.

propositions and probably vote for the lesser of two evils for president. I was going to write in Ron Paul's name, as I did four years ago, but I think a statement does need to be made in this election. I realize that my vote in this very blue state is virtually worthless and, after the election, politics will resume its usual games of playing "who are we going to coerce today"?

Yawn! Wake me up when something really good and important happens.

Altering a bit what I have said before,[98] "I do not expect life to improve much, if at all, in the next four years of the [next] presidential administration. I do not expect the [next] (or [current]) administration to be the indicator of the beginning of the end of civilization as we know it." Life goes on. Cultural and political systems change slowly. Political junkies can continue to obsess over every coercive decision that is made in positions of power. I will read and write about other topics.

* A recent informal search of *The NY Times* produced these mentions of Ayn Rand's name: 97 for all of 2011, 10 for the first quarter of 2012, 68 for the second quarter, and 147 for the third. Paul Ryan seems to be doing some good, though most comments about Ayn Rand in the Old Gray Lady[99] remain smarmy, snarky, ignorant, and hostile. Perhaps after I am dead, these Times writers will also be dead and younger ones will take their place, ones who have actually read Rand's works and are capable of separating her personality and followers from her ideas.

** I'm not convinced that the vote is fundamental to a genuine liberalism. The classical liberals saw it that way, but Hong Kong has shown us that a constitution and legal system that are adhered to do not require voting to keep the system going. When African Americans and women attained the right to vote, that did not guarantee them the protection of other, more important rights to liberty and property.

Postscript. I retitled this post just a few months after its initial appearance, because I realized what I was saying is that politics today

---

[98] See above, "Why the World Is Not Going to Hell in a Basket," p. 41.
[99] "Old Gray Lady," urbandictionary.com.

is all about using initiated coercion to say what we can and cannot do. I also, more fundamentally, became bored with politics because of the unfortunate lack of courage and integrity of many Republicans. After November 2016, politics ceased to be boring!

(November 12, 2012)

2013

The Comparative Society

HIGH SCHOOL ENGLISH TEACHER AND POET, John Wooden,[100] also known as the highly successful, 27-year coach of UCLA basketball from 1948 to 1975, learned from his father that the key to success was never to compare oneself to others.

Compete only with yourself, Wooden the son would tell his players, by striving to do better than you did yesterday, last month, or last hour. During halftime Wooden would often not even talk about the other team, only about how each of his own players could improve in the second half.

Focus on bettering oneself, says Wooden, is what builds confidence, poise, and integrity, not to mention winning ball teams.

A "competitive society" is what most think our pseudo-capitalistic economy today is and beating the other guy—the ultimate comparison—is what competition supposedly is all about. But economic competition, as I have written before,[101] is precisely the comparison-free bettering of oneself that Wooden describes.

Capitalism is a system of social cooperation where everyone wins by trading value for value. Entrepreneurs do not spend their days and nights thinking about how to beat the competition, but about how to improve their products and make them more affordable. Winning large market share is consequence of the focus on improvement, not the goal. Wooden would certainly concur with this description of economic competition.

In today's obsessively comparative society, beating others shows up everywhere, especially and unfortunately in areas that relate to children.

---

[100] John Wooden, "The Difference between Winning and Succeeding," February 2001, ted.com; John Wooden, *Wooden on Leadership*, amazon.com.
[101] See above, "Healthy and Unhealthy Competition," p. 21.

We have tiger moms[102] forcing their children to take the "right" courses, attend the "right" schools, and play the "right" musical instruments. Why? To keep up with the Joneses, or rather, more specifically, to do better than the Joneses.

Our entire educational system, through grades, exams, and degrees, is institutionalized comparison. The no-child-left-behind act[103] has merely ossified the system by making teaching to the test[104] virtually mandatory and pushing advanced topics to lower and lower levels, such as algebra in sixth grade and reading and writing in kindergarten. And, of course, requiring lots of officiously mind-numbing busywork, usually called homework.* Why? American test scores are lower than those of the Japanese. We must be better!

"Pushing to lower levels," meaning to younger ages, is not the prerogative of our education system. Organized youth sports continues its trend of putting younger and younger children through increasing hours of practice and game playing, week after week after week. Why? We have to be better than the other guy, we have to get our kids scholarships to get into college, and we have to prepare them properly, starting at the youngest age, or they won't be able to compete at the high school or college level.

Indeed, education and youth sports share a similarity: both are dominated and controlled by adults. Traditional education systems, as Ken Robinson[105] has amusingly pointed out, are created by college professors, which means their ultimate goal is not to meet the needs of students, but to turn out more college professors just like them.

Organized youth sports are organized and operated by adults for the sake of their own, adult needs. If the sports were organized for the children, fun and development would still be the primary goals. For many youth sports today, winning has become the only thing.

In education much can be accomplished by turning learning activities over to the kids. Hole-in-the-wall experiments conducted by 2013

---

[102] See below, "Tiger Mom or Stage Mom?," p. 332.
[103] "No Child Left Behind Act," wikipedia.org.
[104] "Teaching to the Test," wikipedia.org.
[105] Ken Robinson, "Do Schools Kill Creativity?," February 2006, ted.com.

TED Prize winner, Sugata Mitra,[106] have spectacularly demonstrated how children can eagerly and without adult supervision teach themselves.

In a New Delhi slum, Mitra literally put a computer in a building wall, then walked away. The slum children, who had never seen a computer before, not only learned how to use it, but also learned English and, in other experiments, learned all about DNA! Most of the teaching came from each other. Minimal facilitation by grannies, not Oxford- or Cambridge-trained instructors, are all that has been needed to increase the learning.

If "truth is what works," to borrow a much-reviled phrase from William James, then removal of the comparisons of grades, exams, and degrees in education seems to work. It works in Montessori schools. It works in hole-in-the-wall experiments.

Now if we can only implement the Wooden philosophy of removing comparison in sports. Regrettably, short of a return to the sandlot where kids are in charge, this does not seem likely.

When enormous amounts of money drive sports at the college and professional levels—twelve times as much money, for example, spent on athletes in one athletic conference[107] as on academic students—can anyone seriously expect parents to turn their backs and say, "Let's just do it because it's fun"?

Perhaps what we need is to encourage more English teachers and poets to become coaches!

* This is not to say that advanced math and reading and writing cannot be learned at early ages. Montessori schools, by adapting the topics carefully to stage of development, inspire early learning every day, and without homework. But our traditional public and private schools do not teach via the Montessori method. They use the carrot and stick—grades, exams, and degrees—as motivators. Independence is not their goal. Obedience to authority is.

(March 22, 2013)

---

[106]Sugata Mitra, "Build a School in the Cloud," February 2013, ted.com.
[107]"Some Schools Spend 10 Times More On Athletes Than Students: Report," huffpost.com.

The Sovietization of Federal Law

"SHOW ME THE MAN and I'll find you the crime."

That paean to nonobjective law is attributed to Lavrenti Beria[108] Joseph Stalin's chief of secret police. It is cited by Harvard Law School professor Alan Dershowitz in his foreword to *Three Felonies a Day: How the Feds Target the Innocent*,[109] by Harvey Silverglate (p. xxxvi).

Objective law consists of simple, clear, concrete statements of what citizens cannot do in a free society. Nonobjective law is pliable; it is excessively broad and vague such that both prosecutors and ordinary citizens can come up with contradictory interpretations. As a result, prosecutors can use those contradictions, "creatively" bending the law, to charge crimes against anyone they want to get. Hence, the Beria claim.

Nonobjective law is an essential tool of dictatorship.

The modern Berias are federal prosecutors who work for the United States Department of Justice (DOJ). As thoroughly argued and documented in Silverglate's book, thousands of federal criminal laws are so broad and vague that prosecutors can find something in them to charge any one of us with up to three felonies a day.*

Consider two high profile cases. Michael Milken, the so-called junk-bond king, pled guilty to six felony counts only after prosecutor Rudolph Giuliani threatened to send his younger brother to prison. Yet editorials in the Wall Street Journal and research by law school deans concluded that "the entire original indictment [against Milken] described perfectly lawful transactions that required a huge stretch to be even remotely considered criminal" (Silverglate, p. 102).

And the late Arthur Anderson LLP, one of the then Big Five accounting firms in the US, was indicted by Enron prosecutors for destroying documents that the prosecutors needed to go after Enron. Arthur Anderson at the time was following generally accepted accounting practices. That, of course, did not stop the prosecutors from indicting the firm for obstruction of justice. Clients began leaving the firm and Anderson soon went out of business. In 2005, the US Supreme

---

[108] "Lavrenti Beria," wikipedia.org.
[109] Harvey Silverglate, *Three Felonies a Day*, amazon.com.

Court unanimously exonerated the firm, which unfortunately for Anderson was a "Pyrrhic victory," as Silverglate puts it (p. 136).

In subsequent cases business firms have learned the Arthur Anderson lesson: instead of fighting the Justice Department and possibly going out of business, they now send sacrificial lambs (usually, individual executives) to the prosecutorial wolves.

The ruthlessness with which prosecutors pursue their targets is reminiscent of Javert, Victor Hugo's maniacal police inspector in *Les Miserables* who obsessively stalked the "vicious" bread thief Jean Valjean. Javert's mantra, however, was strict adherence and obedience to the law, which in the nineteenth century was simple and clear: don't steal bread. Javert's punishments were harsh, but his character still seems a little too nice when compared to the prosecutors in Silverglate's reports.

Playing especially to a gullible and supportive press, today's prosecutors hunt for victims who may not have done anything harmful or illegal at all or at most have taken an action considered legal at the time of the act, only to be indicted later. Most politicians are former prosecutors, so most prosecutors are wannabe governors and senators. They aim to win and will do anything to establish that victory, seemingly caring little about truth or justice.

To change the comparison, prosecutors are like gunslingers in the old west who are only too eager to add notches to their prosecutorial guns, such notches paraded later in political campaigns for public office.

The tactics of prosecutors, to say the least, are less than admirable. "Ladder climbing" is common. To get a high profile target, prosecutors threaten lower level employees with stiff fines and prison terms to get them to testify against the bigger fish. The prosecutors then "move up the ladder" until they have something on their target. However, as Dershowitz puts it, these "cooperating" witnesses often "are taught not only to sing, but also to compose" (quoted in Silverglate, p. xliv). Offering these witnesses something of value in exchange for testimony—witness bribery in Silverglate's words—is also not uncommon.

Merciless hounding, Javert-style, lasting ten or more years, is routine for prosecutors who refuse to stop even after appellate courts have overturned their verdicts. Piling on charges, sometimes in the hundreds, usually insures that the target will be found guilty of something. Midnight FBI interrogations to intimidate defense witnesses have occurred, as have the use of Gestapo-like (SWAT team) raids of medical offices, with assistants told at gunpoint to hang up the phone. Doctors who are partners have been charged with conspiracy, based on no more evidence than the fact that they were partners. And doctors who specialize in pain management are treated like street pushers.**

And, of course, there is more. Prosecutors freeze defendant assets, often making it nearly impossible for a victim to finance a legal defense. They impose gag orders, thereby preventing defendants, or their attorneys, from talking to the press about the case. When Martha Stewart defended her case via press release, the DOJ took this as evidence of securities fraud (p. 121). Prosecutors, of course, still retain the right to try their cases in public, relishing especially the nightly news "perp walk."[110]

Among themselves[111] prosecutors reportedly play a game to see how long it takes their junior colleagues to come up with crimes to charge famous personalities, such as Mother Theresa or John Lennon.

Sovietization is here. Beria would be proud of our system!

---

* The DOJ also prosecutes the notoriously nonobjective antitrust laws that can find businesses guilty of monopolization if they price their products above the market, guilty of predatory pricing if they set prices below the market, and guilty of collusion and conspiracy if they match the prices of competitors.

** "Sick culture" are the words Silverglate uses to describe the DOJ's current amoral mindset. See Silverglate's and two other writers' discussions of the disgraceful persecution of the late Aaron Swartz.[112]

(June 24, 2013)

---

[110] "Perp Walk," wikipedia.org.
[111] Tim Wu, "Jurisprudence: Introduction," October 14, 2007, slate.com.
[112] Harvey Silverglate, "The Swartz Suicide and the Sick Culture of the Justice Dept.," January 24, 2013, dankennedy.net; Lawrence Lessig, "Aaron's Law: Violating a Site's Terms of Service Should Not Land You in Jail," January 16, 2013, theatlantic.com; Tim Wu, "How the Legal System Failed Aaron Swartz—and Us," January 14, 2013, newyorker.com.

Return of the Blackshirts?

THE ATTIRE OF ARMED PARAMILITARY SQUADS in Mussolini's Italy were known as Blackshirts.[113] Their wardrobe and behavior were later adopted by other militant fascists, especially the German Schutzstaffel (SS).[114]

These groups of young men were known for gleefully shooting innocent victims first and asking questions later.

Radley Balko, in his book *Rise of the Warrior Cop: The Militarization of America's Police Forces*,[115] does not go so far as to say that the United States has become a fascist police state . . . yet. We're still free to travel, he says, we still have habeas corpus, and we don't have mass censorship.

> But perhaps we *have* entered a police state writ small. At the individual level, a police officer's power and authority over the people he interacts with day to day is near complete (p. 335, Balko's emphasis).

The cause is the tremendous growth over the last forty years of callously indifferent, brutal, and frequently botched SWAT raids conducted initially in the name of the drug war but now expanded to enforcing even minor regulations, for example, barbers operating without a license and guitar manufacturers[116] allegedly using contraband wood. SWAT teams have also been sent as follow-up on purse snatchings from cars. Routine police work, in other words, is now being handled by the men and women wearing black pants, black shirts, bulging bullet-proof protectors, and Darth Vader helmets.

The cause of the cause is judicial erosion of the castle doctrine and billions of dollars of federal money made available to police forces to buy military equipment, such as automatic assault weapons, flashbang grenades, helicopters, armored personnel carriers, and tanks.

---

[113] "Blackshirts," wikipedia.org; "Blackshirt: Italian History," britannica.com.
[114] "Schutzstaffel," wikipedia.org.
[115] Radley Balko, *Rise of the Warrior Cop*, amazon.com.
[116] See above, "Politics Is a Bore (Retitled: Who Are We Going to Coerce Today?)," p. 62.

Police in towns as small at 25,000 people have joined the militarization gravy train.

The castle doctrine in common law says your home is your castle and no one, including the police, may enter without knocking and being invited in by you. And the police may not search your premises without a warrant. In the name of the drug war—promoted self-righteously and fervently by both Republicans and Democrats—no-knock entrance has become standard, because knocking supposedly alerts drug dealers to destroy evidence (by flushing drugs down the toilet). Search warrants can be dispensed with if police fear for their safety. Drug dealers are always assumed to be armed and dangerous, which is often not the case.

Never mind that turning the water off or hiring a plumber to put a catch net on the drain would save flushed evidence. Or that one reason for the knock-and-announce castle doctrine is to prevent cops from being shot by citizens who naturally think their homes are being invaded by scummy crooks, perhaps even terrorists. Permits to carry concealed weapons have not helped such citizens. If a cop is killed in one of these raids, the citizen is arrested for murder.

The typical SWAT raid, using the latest military gear, begins with a flash-bang grenade, emitting a blinding burst of light and deafeningly explosive clap to paralyze the targets. (Never mind that heart attack deaths of innocent victims caused by this "shock and awe" have occurred or that target houses plus neighboring ones have burned to the ground from the fires started by the grenades.)

Next step is to bash down the door, throw anyone present, including grandparents and children, to the floor, zip-tie them, point guns at their heads, and scream expletives. Dogs are shot and the house is trashed while searching for drugs. Sometimes the teams have found only one or two joints of pot or two or three marijuana plants . . . or, quite frequently, nothing.

In Denver in 1999, according to Balko in an earlier paper[117] written for the Cato Institute, 149 no-knock raids produced only 49 charges of any kind with only two targets receiving prison time. The rest? Botched

---

[117] Radley Balko, "Overkill: The Rise of Paramilitary Police Raids in America," July 17, 2006, cato.org.

raids. Seventy-three wrong-address case histories are described by Balko in the same paper. An interactive map,[118] produced by Cato, shows several hundred botched raids since 1985.

Even when a SWAT team has the correct address, many innocent relatives and children are treated like criminals and sometimes killed. The perpetrators—the cops—are exonerated and even praised for not arresting the innocents. "Collateral damage" in a war is acceptable, according to SWAT leaders and police chiefs. Apologies are rare. If media noise is made, victims may win a civil judgment, paid, of course, by taxpayers.

The senseless, needless drug war is merely a much longer repeat of the alcohol prohibition fiasco that lasted from 1920 to 1933. Its major accomplishments were to give us Nascar and the Mafia. Today, we are moving precariously close to a blackshirted police state, because of unsound moral, economic, and political policy.

Any hope for reform? Cheye Calvo, mayor of Berwyn Heights, Maryland, succeeded in getting a modest bill passed in the state legislature requiring police departments to keep statistics on the use of SWAT teams—something that had never been done before or considered important. In the last six months of 2009 in Maryland, SWAT teams were deployed 4.5 times a day (804 times total). Ninety-four percent of their outings were to serve search or arrest warrants, half of them for misdemeanors or nonserious felonies.

How was Calvo able to get this much accomplished? In 2004 his front door was bashed down and his two black labs were immediately shot. Calvo and his mother-in-law were forced into the usual positions, screamed at, and interrogated for four hours. The house was trashed, with the dogs' blood tracked all over.*

It was a mistake.[119]

No apologies. No punishment of the perpetrators. County officials said they would do it all over again. The cops, after all, exercised "restraint and compassion" and did not arrest anyone.

---

[118] "Cato Institute Uses Google Maps to Show Botched SWAT Raids," fastcompany.com.
[119] "Cheye Calvo Details the SWAT Raid that Killed His Family Dogs" (video), October 5, 2008, cato.org.

Calvo, fortunately for the rest of us, took action. The ACLU[120] has joined in. Balko continues to wage intellectual war against these "special forces" mentalities by writing and speaking frequently.[121] And Cato Institute has founded the National Police Misconduct Reporting Project.[122]

Much more needs to be done.

* The cruel and unsympathetic killing of dogs requires comment. Mail carriers have been known to have run-ins with dogs. How has the postal service handled such "threats"? They adopted the novel idea of giving carriers training in how to distract dogs, make friends with them, or, if necessary, to use mace to keep them at bay. Dog attacks on mail carriers, according to Balko, "are almost nonexistent" (p. 292). In the Calvo raid, one detective, upon seeing the dead labs, was heard making a phone call to remind a family member to schedule a vet appointment for her own animal. Such callous, almost psychopathic indifference is reminiscent of the Abu Ghraib scandal.[123]

(October 14, 2013)

2014

How the Government Kills Industries

GROWING UP IN A SMALL MIDWESTERN TOWN in the 1950's, I had two fantasies: traveling the country someday as member of the saxophone section of a big band and traveling to far away places on sleek, swift passenger trains. At some point in my adolescence I came to the considerably disappointing realization that both industries were dying, if not already halfway in the ground. As a result, I felt compelled to switch interests to other areas.

The government played no small part in destroying both the big bands and railroads, especially the passenger trains.

---

[120] "War Comes Home: The Excessive Militarization of American Police," aclu.org.
[121] Radley Balko, "The Agitator," huffpost.com. See also theagitator.com.
[122] Bob Adelmann, "Cato Institute Starts National Police Misconduct Reporting Project," May 29, 2012, thenewamerican.com; "Unlawful Shield: A Cato Institute Website Dedicated to Abolishing Qualified Immunity," policemisconduct.net.
[123] See below, "Ensuring that Disposition Trumps Situation," p. 210.

As for the big bands, the conventional wisdom about why they declined is often reported in such gems of economic analysis as "cultural shift," "changing tastes," and "the kids needed their own music."

The real reason for their decline was a 30% cabaret tax on any venue that allowed dancing. Eric Felten, writing in the *Wall Street Journal*,[124] succinctly describes the effect of the 1944 tax: "By 1949, the hotel dine-and-dance-room trade was a third of what it had been three years earlier. The Swing Era was over." Venues exhibiting instrumental music for which there was no dancing were not taxed; this gave rise to the bebop era of small jazz combos. In 1960 the tax was reduced to 10% and in 1965 eliminated. Felten concludes, "By then, the Swing Era ballrooms and other 'terperies' were long gone, and public dancing was done in front of stages where young men wielded electric guitars."

Taxes have consequences. So do price controls.

The railroad industry, of course, is said to have succumbed to plain old capitalistic competition from other modes of transport. Nothing could be further from the truth.

From its beginning to the present, the American railroad industry has been promoted, manipulated, and shackled by government interference.

The "meetup"[125] at Promontory Point, Utah, between the Union Pacific and Central Pacific railroads in 1869, occurred only after each of the political entrepreneurs[126] involved had graded 250 miles of earth, parallel to each other, in some cases separated only by a hill, with no track ever laid. Why did this occur? Because they both were after the government subsidies. Almost immediately after the meetup, the shabbily laid track that was installed for the famous photograph was torn up and redone.

The worst interference in railroading prior to World War I was the price controls on freight rates, imposed by the Interstate Commerce Commission (ICC). The story is told in *Throttling the Railroads*[127] by Clarence B. Carson. As with most government regulatory lingo, the

---

[124] Eric Felten, "How the Taxman Cleared the Dance Floor," March 17, 2013, wsj.com.
[125] Mark A. Pribonic, "The Myth of the Great Railroad Meetup," mises.org.
[126] "Political Entrepreneur," wikipedia.org.
[127] Clarence B. Carson, *Throttling the Railroads*, amazon.com.

ICC said rates had to be "just and reasonable," which in practice meant that railroads could not charge different rates for the same distances traveled or the same rates for different distances. Thus, grapefruit, as Carson illustrates it (p. 58), can be shipped to Baltimore from Florida, Texas, or California. To be competitive, the economics of railroading required that the California railroad match the prices of the other two. This was not allowed.

This and many other instances of restrictive price controls leading up to the first world war produced earnings and service declines. As a result the economics of railroading—high fixed costs dictating long trains pulled over long distances with few stops (the western roads) and the pooling of resources to support shorter lines with more stops (the eastern roads)—an effective transcontinental railroad system was prevented from developing. From 1917 to 1920, the US government nationalized the railroads, insuring that they would not develop further. In fact, miles of track laid in the country peaked in 1920.

After 1920 regulation continued to hobble and eventually destroy railroading. Increasingly tightened regulation and rising competition from highways, waterways, airports, and airlines—all subsidized—continued to hurt the railroads, but the killer was featherbedding.[128] Firemen who stoked the fires on steam locomotives continued by law to work well into the 1980s on the efficient and safer diesel-powered engines. The railroads faced great difficulty in attempting to fire or lay off anyone.

The passenger lines in this environment could not survive. The once proud 20th Century Limited,[129] all-Pullman passenger train of the New York Central, used to make its non-stop run from New York to Chicago in sixteen hours. With a change of train station, one could then hop on the equally proud Super Chief[130] of the Santa Fe and be in Los Angeles thirty-seven hours later. In 1971 nearly all privately-owned passenger service in the United States came to an end.

The railroad goose was cooked by 1920. The feeding frenzy then took over. Today there is hardly a carcass left.

---

[128] "Featherbedding," wikipedia.org.
[129] "20th Century Limited," wikipedia.org.
[130] "Super Chief," wikipedia.org.

Granted that in the absence of government interference competition from other modes of transport, especially air, would have changed the landscape of travel. There is no reason, however, to think that there would not be sleek, profitable passenger trains operating on specialized routes, most likely high-speed lines in well-traveled corridors that government bureaucrats in the current political climate think should be run by them.

In Florida private entrepreneurs have a better idea. "We just ask that government get out of the way," so said a VP[131] of All Aboard Florida[132] [now called Brightline], soon to be launched three-hour passenger rail service between Miami and Orlando, with planned extensions to Tampa and Jacksonville.

Perhaps there is hope for the railroads.

The big bands of the swing era, unfortunately, along with their dine-and-dance-room trade sponsors, seem nearly completely gone.

(January 24, 2014)

The Whistleblowers: An Indictment of the Mixed Economy and Bureaucracy

SOCRATES WAS AN EARLY WHISTLEBLOWER. He exposed many leaders of ancient Athens as hot-air know-it-alls and was executed for his efforts.

Today, whistleblowers usually avoid execution, though the enemies[133] of Edward Snowden would like to bring the death penalty back for him. Most whistleblowers are harassed, labeled as troublemakers and, perhaps, as unstable; they are demoted, fired, prevented from collecting unemployment insurance, blacklisted from obtaining new employment in the same field, and sometimes sent to prison.

This is the reward they get for exposing the sleazy, dishonest practices of their superiors in the political-power-laden bureaucratic management of government.[134]

---

[131] Holman W. Jenkins, Jr. "A Private Railroad Is Born," January 14, 2014, wsj.com.
[132] "Brightline" (website), gobrightline.com.
[133] "Fox News' Ralph Peters: 'Bring Back The Death Penalty' For Edward Snowden" (video), June 10, 2013, huffpost.com.
[134] Ludwig von Mises, *Bureaucracy*, amazon.com.

78 • *Applying Principles*

The Whistleblowers[135] by Myron Peretz Glazer and Penina Migdal Glazer, published in 1989, reviews some sixty-four cases of informing on and exposing less than savory behavior of superiors. Contrary to the Glazers' intent, the book is an indictment of the mixed economy and government bureaucracy.

The Glazers' premises are standard Marxist social liberalism,[136] so they assume that the profit motive in capitalism is anathema to customer satisfaction, health, and well-being. They also assume that government waste and dangerous policies are the result of profit-seeking lobbying from private businesses.

If unethical behavior goes on entirely within the government, that is, with no private lobbyists or businesses as participants, they assume that a few bad apples in a normally white-hatted environment are the ones the whistleblowers are going after. Over two-thirds of the Glazers' cases took place exclusively within the government bureaucracy.

The cases focus mostly on the exposure of wrongdoing and its aftermath, usually retaliation from superiors who had demanded silence and team-playing loyalty. Facts of each case are minimal, or assumed to be unquestioned, and are often difficult to judge.

History, however, has proven a few whistleblower cases wrong involving private businesses. Ralph Nader's Corvair[137] was not a dangerous automobile, as was thought at the time, nor was Ford's Pinto.[138] Nor, for that matter, is nuclear power[139] dangerous when compared to other forms of energy.

Several cases in the book deal with nuclear power plant licensing and illustrate the disease called government intervention in the marketplace. Absent the free market yardstick of earning profit through customer satisfaction, bureaucrats regulate the licensing of nuclear power plants based on their own "expert" judgments.

Compliance to the regulations requires mountains of paper, diverting attention from operation of the business, namely the

---

[135] Myron Peretz Glazer and Penina Migdal Glazer, *The Whistleblowers*, amazon.com.
[136] "Social Liberalism," wikipedia.org.
[137] "Chevrolet Corvair," wikipedia.org.
[138] "Ford Pinto," wikipedia.org.
[139] Petr Beckmann, *The Health Hazards of NOT Going Nuclear*, amazon.com.

production of a service that meets the consumer's needs and wants. In the process of completing the mountains of paper, some employees may neglect the compliance regulations, inaccurately fill out the forms, or even falsify them.

This last produces the hailstorm of corruption complaints against private businesses and the subsequent whistleblowing. Remove the government from business affairs, leaving the issue of "satisfaction, health, and well-being" to the customers, and the corruption would most likely not occur.*

Similarly, the Frank Serpico[140] case, in which the New York City policeman blew the whistle on fellow cops for accepting bribes from drug dealers and gamblers, would become moot in a free market. Legalize gambling and drugs—what is left to blow the whistle on?

Make a legitimate product illegal and the incentive is to cheat! That's how black markets arise.[141]

Probably the worst of the Glazers' cases was the Census Bureau bureaucrat who had political ambitions. He told his employee she had to provide sex to politicians and provide other candidates for the same thing. After she blew the whistle, the woman's boss told her, among other retaliations, that he was making sure her ex-husband would get her children and that she would never see them again.

Another example, in the Department of Education, entailed theft and illegal withholding and destruction of documents in a case alleging misuse of federal money by the state of Illinois and city of Chicago.

The whistleblower was told a "very good" letter of recommendation, signed by the Secretary of Education, would be given to him if he would just get a new job and keep his mouth shut. When he didn't keep his mouth shut, he was fired—but that wasn't the end of it. He was eventually framed on a criminal charge, spent time in jail, then was finally exonerated after he had served his time.

Loyalty to superiors and not going over their heads is a big thing in bureaucracies. The purpose of retaliation against whistleblowers who do not remain silent and are not loyal is to destroy their credibility as witnesses against wrongdoing. This, whether coming from a frail ego

---

[140] "Frank Serpico," wikipedia.org.
[141] "Black Market," wikipedia.org.

that cannot tolerate criticism or from a criminal personality,[142] explains why dictators kill their critics.

Socrates would not remain silent, so he had to go.

Naive as I may be, I am frankly astounded that such unsavory behavior goes on within government bureaucracies. When I was a young man, working in a small (50–60 employee) private business in mid-town Manhattan, it never occurred to me not to question my boss or go over his head. And no one was offended if I was "disloyal" and went to the general manager or president of the company to ask how to resolve a problem. Everyone in the company understood that the reason for being in business was to satisfy customers.**

Whistleblowing and retaliation against whistleblowers continues today unabated within the bureaucracies. Shortly after 9/11, Jesselyn Radack,[143] who is now Edward Snowden's American lawyer, found herself on the receiving end of an extremely negative job evaluation and was strongly encouraged to resign from the Department of Justice. Later, she was put on indefinite leave from her private sector job, was stopped for extra screenings at airports, put on a no-fly list, and threatened with arrest.

Her crime? She gave the press copies of emails she had sent to the FBI advising them of correct ethics and legality in relation to John Walker Lindh,[144] the American Taliban. The emails had somehow disappeared from the FBI file and her recommendations against illegal interrogation of Lindh were flatly ignored. Radack was then alleged to have violated attorney-client privilege and obstructed justice. The Bars of Virginia, Maryland, and the District of Columbia were asked to sanction her. No charges were ever filed, but the harassment continued for several years.

Such is the way bureaucrats seem to operate when they have no rational, objective yardstick by which to measure their actions.

---

[142] See below, "Thoughts, Not Environmental Conditions, Cause Criminal Behavior," p. 267.
[143] Russell Brandom, "Edward Snowden's Lawyer Will Keep Your Secrets," June 24, 2014, theverge.com; "Jesslyn Radack," wikipedia.org; Jesslyn Radack, "Conscience Over Career: The Prosecution of the American Taliban," June 7, 2008, fff.org.
[144] "John Walker Lindh," wikipedia.org.

* This is not to say that there are not "bad apples" in private businesses. My point, contrary to the Glazers and most social liberals today, is that capitalistic incentives to satisfy customers in order to generate a profit require integrity and courage.

** No one in that profit-making business, or in any others that I have worked in, were sleazy or dishonest.

(August 25, 2014)

The Elites and the Underground: No Law vs. Rule of Law vs. Excessive Law

"Rule of law" is an unquestioned prerequisite today for any free society and growing economy. Unfortunately, there is too little rule of law for 80–95% of the world's population and too much for the rest.

The former population are what Hernando de Soto calls "extralegal" poor who want and need to be able to join the middle classes and thrive in those segments of the developed world that are now a decided minority.[145]

The latter are the political and economic elites who live in varying degrees, depending on country, officially under the rule of law but are facing, year after year, increasing erosion of that protection with the growth of dictatorship by excessive law.[146]

The extralegals, as de Soto's research has found at his Institute for Liberty and Democracy[147] in Lima, Peru, have no legal existence in most third-world countries. They have no titles to their property, no legal descriptions of its location and other public records, and therefore no way to accumulate and protect assets—also known as capital. Yet most of these productive and innovative black-market entrepreneurs want to join the rest of their societies and be just as prosperous as everyone else.

---

[145] "The Hidden Architecture of Capital," ild.org.pe; "Property Paradigm—ILD," ild.org.pe.
[146] See below, "On Extrinsic Motivation, Bureaucracy, and the Stage-Mother Syndrome," p. 327.
[147] Institute for Liberty and Democracy (website), ild.org.pe.

The problem is that most of the ruling elites don't want them to prosper. The solution is property rights and the rule of law.

Indeed, de Soto argues persuasively,[148] property rights for the extralegals would go a long way toward eliminating terrorism—as it did in his country of Peru. And the impetus for the "Arab Spring" of 2010–11, his research has shown, was not religious revolution, but the economic desire of small entrepreneurs to be recognized and respected.[149]

The problem with the phrase "rule of law" when mentioned to most members of the developed world is that they assume they live under firm and objective rule of law.

To the Founding Fathers of the United States sound criminal law meant law "so clear that it could be understood when read by a person 'while running'" (p. xxxviii, preface to Silverglate).[150] We certainly live under law, but what we have is too much of it, and most of that is vague, overly broad, and arbitrarily applied.

No less than 87,000 rules[151] have been implemented by the various federal administrative agencies in the US since 1993 [through 2013] and 4500 laws[152] [through 2013] have been enacted by Congress during the same period. This does not include state, county, and city laws that are approved every year, a number that has been estimated at 40,000.[153]

"Ignorance of the law is no defense," our citizenship education classes have taught us. Just how are we supposed to keep up with this litany of decrees?

We aren't, according to Harvey Silverglate in his book *Three Felonies a Day*[154] Federal prosecutors relish the prospect of being able to find a law on the books that can be, and is increasingly, used against anyone, innocent or not.

---

[148] Hernando de Soto, "The Capitalist Cure for Terrorism," October 10, 2014, wsj.com
[149] "Property Paradigm—ILD," ild.org.pe; "There's No Rule Book for Eradicating Corruption," ild.org.pe.
[150] Harvey Silverglate, *Three Felonies a Day*, amazon.com.
[151] Clyde Wayne Crews, "Red Tapeworm 2014: Cumulative Final Rules in the Federal Register," July 1, 2014, cei.org.
[152] "Statistics and Historical Comparison—GovTrack.us," govtrack.us.
[153] "New Laws Toughen Rules on Abortions, Immigrants, Voters," December 31, 2011, nbcnews.com.
[154] Harvey Silverglate, *Three Felonies a Day*, amazon.com.

The vague and overly broad edicts of college administrations and the US Department of Education, as well documented in Greg Lukianoff's book *Unlearning Liberty*,[155] have made free speech a rarity in the ivory tower. And judicial erosion has allowed no-knock searches, along with the militarization of our police forces.[156]

The worst confusion over rule of law is the nearly total ignorance of the origins of administrative or regulatory law. In addition to showing that it unconstitutionally puts legislative, executive, and judicial powers in one agency, Columbia University law professor, Philip Hamburger,[157] details the origin of administrative law as the prerogative of kings to issue binding proclamations. This, Hamburger points out, was the prerogative of absolute power, especially since judges were expected to defer to their kings.

That this was the origin of our modern administrative or regulatory "rules" was even acknowledged approvingly by a "leading Progressive theorist" in 1927. Since that time, the issue has been rarely, if ever, discussed. As for modern judicial deference to administrative power, Hamburger says, "our judges do [it] far more systematically than even the worst of 17th century English judges."

There you have it. The world today divided into the extremes of elites and poor.

Elites enjoying a good life while their countries ride on express trains toward dictatorship and poor living an underground life in shanties likely with no indoor plumbing or running water.

Genuinely objective rule of law, which means in particular clear and concise property rights, is urgently required to bail both groups out of their precarious situations.

Such a social system based on clear and concise property rights is capitalism.

(October 23, 2014)

---

[155] Greg Lukianoff, *Unlearning Liberty*, amazon.com.
[156] Radley Balko, *Rise of the Warrior Cop*, amazon.com; see above, "Return of the Blackshirts?," p. 71.
[157] Philip Hamburger, *The Administrative Threat*, amazon.com.

The PhD Cop

As I have written before,[158] I am not terribly impressed by credentials, especially those granted by universities. Nevertheless, when a policeman earns a PhD degree, and does so from Harvard, I have to take note.

The late Joseph McNamara[159] was a by-the-bootstraps scholar and cop. He earned his bachelor's degree attending night classes while walking a daytime beat in Harlem. He was granted a fellowship to Harvard in 1968 and wrote his dissertation[160] on law enforcement's handling of drug use before 1914. He became deputy inspector of crime analysis in New York, then served three years as Kansas City's police chief and fifteen as San Jose's. He concluded his career as research fellow at the Hoover Institution.

Somewhere in that career, he found time to write five crime novels and many op-ed essays criticizing today's police culture. He was called the father of community policing[161] and hailed as twenty years before his time.

Though politically conservative, he vehemently opposed the drug war and militarization of the police. He advocated the legalization of marijuana and the end of mandatory sentencing.

Community policing operates on the assumption that even in high-crime areas, the vast majority of citizens are law-abiding and want the police to be there to protect them from criminals. It's the "we're on the same side" notion that the policemen and the citizens, paraphrasing the song from *Oklahoma!*,[162] should be friends, not enemies.

McNamara learned this lesson on the streets of Harlem and, as a result, insisted on dialogue and cooperation between cops and citizens in his two cities as chief.

---

[158] See below, "Peddlers of Ideas," p. 159. See below, "Interest and the Core Curriculum," p. 163..
[159] Paul Vitello, "Joseph D. McNamara, Father of Community Policing, Dies at 79," September 26, 2014, nytimes.com.
[160] Radley Balko, "Joseph McNamara: An Appreciation," September 22, 2014, washingtonpost.com.
[161] "Community Policing," wikipedia.org.
[162] "*Oklahoma!*," wikipedia.org.

Statistics don't lie (usually)—crime decreased.

In 1991, after the videotaped beating of Rodney King, McNamara called for the resignation[163] of Los Angeles Police Chief Daryl Gates. His point? The viciousness of the beating could only mean that this was not an isolated incident and that the credibility of policing was called into question.

His last op-ed, written for Reuters[164] on August 19 after the Ferguson, Missouri, shooting, is titled "Never an Excuse for Shooting Unarmed Suspects . . ." The cops' primary goal, he maintained, is to protect human life and only shoot when confronted with imminent danger from a gun or knife.

In a 2006 *Wall Street Journal*[165] op-ed, referring to two shootings of unarmed victims in New York, McNamara stated that in the two cases neither he, his father, his older brother, nor other relatives—all of whom had worked a cumulative total of 150 years in the NYPD—would have fired a shot.

Though in the Ferguson situation[166] there may have been a justifiably perceived danger from an under-the-influence big man trying to take the officer's gun away from him, the message from McNamara is clear. Police need to remember they are the citizens' champions, not their intimidators or oppressors, garbed up in paramilitary, black-shirted[167] outfits with weapons and explosives designed for the battlefield.

The phrases "soldier's general," "player's coach," "student's teacher," and "worker's manager" describe someone in authority who worked his or her way up to that position but who also has not forgotten what it was like in the lower level.

Empathy and understanding, which is just another way of saying being nice, make respected and accomplished leaders. While there certainly are exceptions, many privileged generals, coaches, teachers,

---

[163] Tunku Varadarajan, "A Most Consequential Cop," October 10, 2014, wsj.com.
[164] Joseph D. McNamara, "Never An Excuse for Shooting Unarmed Suspects, Former Police Chief Says," August 19, 2014, reuters.com.
[165] Joseph D. McNamara, "50 Shots," wsj.com.
[166] Curtis Kalin, "10 Key Facts Ferguson Grand Jury Discovered," November 25, 2014, cnsnews.com.
[167] See above, "Return of the Blackshirts," p. 71.

and managers who either do not work their way up to the positions of authority or who arrogantly and deliberately forget their pasts only become fixed-mindset[168] bullies.

Dr. McNamara was the citizen's policeman and chief. We need far more like him.

(December 12, 2014)

2015

The Not-So-Visible Gun: Government Is Not Our Friend

A RELATIVE IN YEARS PAST would frequently tell his children, when coming upon a representative of law enforcement, "See that policeman? He is our friend!"

The militarization of police forces in recent years notwithstanding, and trigger happiness of some cops aside, the police by and large are our protectors against the bad guys. They use self-defensive force to protect us from those who initiate its use.

But government per se? The 22 million[169] or so elected and unelected members of federal, state, and local governments still hold the legal monopoly on the use of physical force. They can initiate coercion against the rest of us to do what they say, or what the law says we ought to do, supposedly for our own good or to protect us from presumed bad guys.

Some writers have contrasted Adam Smith's invisible hand of the marketplace with an alternative metaphor: the visible fist of government. While fists can do damage, the symbol of the fist usually indicates intimidation.

Governmental coercion is much more than intimidation.

"Who Are We Going to Coerce Today?"[170] is how I recently retitled a previous post, because coercion is the essence of governing in

---

[168] See below, "Fixed vs. Growth Mindsets, p. 274.
[169] Mike Patton, "The Growth of Government: 1980 to 2012," forbes.com.
[170] See above, "Politics Is a Bore (Retitled: Who Are We Going to Coerce Today?)," p. 62.

our mixed economy. A gun—initiated coercion—backs up every decision of the bureaucrats and law that they enforce.

The problem today is that not many citizens see or acknowledge the presence of the gun.

Special interest groups—and by that I mean not just "crony capitalists"[171] but most significantly leftist intellectual organizations and their leaders—lobby hard to pass laws in the name of the "public good." In fact, however, they are unabashed rent-seekers whose laws benefit the lobby at the expense of everyone else, often to the detriment of the very groups they claim to benefit.

There are too many examples to cite, but the supposed Robin Hood (redistributionist) principle[172] of taking from the rich to give to the poor usually enriches the better off at the expense of the less well off. Wage controls cause unemployment and enhance the incomes of those who manage to keep their jobs. Price controls of the ceiling type cause shortages and price floors cause surpluses; they benefit the first dwellers, such as existing renters and farmers.

"But we are the government and we can change it," the naïve might say. No, only the army of 22 million, mostly unelected bureaucrats,[173] constitute the government. And change? Maybe a tiny bit can be changed every two, four, or six years when we vote, but that often is for the worse.

Fight City Hall? Not easily, and with extremely rare success. Government prosecutors[174] are often powerful and unaccountable.

The attitude and battle cry of many bureaucrats, unfortunately, seems to be: "We have the power. You don't. So Get lost!"

That is the gun talking. And that is why government is not our friend.

(May 13, 2015)

---

[171] "Crony Capitalism," wikipedia.org.
[172] Gary Galles, "Extorting Low-Income Individuals to Help 'the Poor,'" May 11, 2015, mises.org.
[173] Jeffrey A. Tucker, "What about the Unelected?," November 7, 2014, fee.org.
[174] Michael N. Giuliano, "The Problem with Government Prosecutors," May 13, 2015, mises.org; see above, "The Sovietization of Federal Law," p. 68.

Ayn Rand, of Course, Was Right

"It turns out, of course, that Mises was right."

The quote is from that "worldly philosopher,"[175] socialist Robert Heilbroner, in a *New Yorker* article in 1989. (See Skousen.[176]) It acknowledges that Austrian economist Ludwig von Mises correctly predicted the decline and collapse of the worker's paradise known as the USSR.

Bureaucrats in planned economies, as Mises pointed out in 1920,[177] have no God's-eye view (that is, omniscience), capable of flawlessly determining who should produce what, in what quantities, at what price, and who should get what, in what quantities, at what price.

In other words, socialism is incapable of economic calculation.

Ayn Rand, unfortunately, has yet to find her Heilbroner. Someday, perhaps, a distinguished member of the philosophical profession will announce that "Ayn Rand, of course, was right . . . about many things, but especially altruism."

Even a cursory reading of Rand's writings makes it abundantly clear that she did not understand altruism to mean kindness and gentleness or, for that matter, that she did not think it altruistic—or wrong—to aid a deserving friend or relative or to help little old ladies across the street.

To Rand, altruism means self-sacrifice, the giving up a higher value for the sake of a lower- or non-value, the pursuit of a career to please one's parents instead of the career one truly loves and wants. It means marrying a person one does not love—again, to please those "significant others" who may disapprove of your choice's religion, social class, race, ethnicity, . . . or sexual orientation.

It means doing your job because it's your duty, not because you enjoy it. It means giving birth to a child you do not want and enslaving yourself to a mistake or accident that occurred when you were young.

"Moral purification through suffering" is how the ascetic life is sometimes described. It is the motto of altruism.

---

[175] Robert L. Heilbroner, *The Worldly Philosophers*, amazon.com.
[176] Mark Skousen, "They Were Right," September 1, 1999, fee.org.
[177] Ludwig von Mises, "Economic Calculation in the Socialist Commonwealth," 1920, mises.org.

Immanuel Kant did not not know the word "altruism," but he did give us the essence of it: always act from duty, not inclination.

It was Auguste Comte who coined the word, and he meant every bit of the notion of self-sacrifice. For Comte, the golden rule is too selfish, as is Jesus' prescription to love your neighbor as yourself. Suicide is selfish and so are rights.

Fortunately, George Smith[178] at libertarianism.org has read Comte's "tiresome writings" that explain his theory in "excruciating detail." In a five-part article, Smith demonstrates that Ayn Rand correctly understood the meaning of altruism.

Comte's ethics, as quoted by Smith:

> never admits anything but duties, of all to all. For its persistently social point of view cannot tolerate the notion of rights, constantly based on individualism. We are born loaded with obligations of every kind, to our predecessors, to our successors, and to our contemporaries.... All human rights then are as absurd as they are immoral.

The agnostic Comte developed a secular religion such that our duty, harkening back to the devout Kant, is to all of humanity. As Kant said, our duty is to humanity as an end in itself; humanity is never a means to our own ends. Comte put it this way: "To live for others affords the only means of freely developing the whole existence of man."

Rights, therefore, are out. The collective is in.

Does the individual even exist? No, says Comte. "Man . . . as an individual, cannot properly be said to exist, except in the too abstract brain of modern metaphysicians. Existence in the true sense can only be predicated of Humanity."

So sacrifice the individual to the collective. On this, too, of course, Ayn Rand was right: altruism and collectivism go hand in hand.

---

[178] George Smith, "Ayn Rand and Altruism, Part 1," October 23, 2012, libertarianism.org.

And she was right that the unprecedented devastation of the twentieth century—between 100 and 300 million war deaths,[179] depending on source—was caused by the two doctrines.

Kindness and gentleness are not what altruism is all about. Self-sacrifice is.

Postscript: The 1988 book *The Altruistic Personality*[180] by Oliner and Oliner is sometimes taken to be the epitome of altruistic behavior. The book consists of a myriad of reflections by rescuers of Jews in Nazi Europe. Fascinating reading, the book shows that there were many Anne Franks[181] throughout the occupied countries and several Schindlers.[182] The authors correctly identify Comte as coiner of the word "altruism," meaning duty, selflessness, and not acting on inclination, but then they redefine it for purposes of their study as "rescue behavior," which means anyone who has the courage to act in the face of considerable risk.

Ayn Rand said she would take a bullet for her husband. This did not make her an altruist, nor does the behavior of these heroic rescuers make them altruists!

(August 20, 2015)

The Galilean Personality vs. Wall-to-Wall Marxism and Human Sexual Identity

MEDICAL HISTORIAN AND BIOETHICIST ALICE DREGER, in her provocatively titled book *Galileo's Middle Finger*,[183] provides a variety of descriptions of what she calls the Galilean Personality:

> It consists of "men and women who are smart, egotistical, innovative, and know they're right" (p. 180), who "tend to believe that the truth will save them, and to insist on the truth even when giving up on it might reduce their suffer-

---

[179] "Necrometrics Estimated Totals for the Entire 20th Century," 2010, necrometrics.com.
[180] Samuel P. Oliner and Pearl M. Oliner, *The Altruistic Personality*, amazon.com.
[181] "Anne Frank," wikipedia.org.
[182] "Oskar Schindler," wikipedia.org.
[183] Alice Dreger, *Galileo's Middle Finger*, amazon.com.

ing" (181). Such personalities are "pugnacious, articulate, [and] politically incorrect." Like the namesake of their personalities, they believe they are "right in the fight but never infallible" (185).

Confidence, independence, integrity, and, above all, commitment to facts. These traits apply equally to Dreger, as to the several heroes she chronicles in her book.

The title, as some reviewers have noted, is a bit misleading, because the book is not a history of scientists from Galileo's day to the present who rebelled against dogmatic authorities. Nor is it particularly about Galileo's middle finger, though after observing the scientist's mummified digit in a Florence museum Dreger did get inspired by the thought of Galileo flipping off the Pope.*

Galileo's science that confirmed the Copernican revolution, as Dreger observes, asserts that human identity is not what we thought it was, because humans, as consequence of Galileo's work, can no longer be understood as occupying the center of the universe. The Pope took exception.

Similarly, scientists today who assert their research outcomes on human sexual identity find themselves engaged in battles with the dogmatic authorities of sexual identity politics. This theme became central to Dreger's book.

"Wall-to-wall Marxism"** refers to the activist intellectual context in which Dreger operated while researching and writing the book. Dreger would probably describe herself as a "moderate liberal," but it was her Galilean commitment to facts that got her into hot water with the radical Marxist left. They didn't like what she said and wrote, let alone what the scientists she wrote about had said and written.

In fact, in one depressed moment during her research—depressed because of the hostility and, at one point, threat, thrown at her—she captured the essence of her modern Marxist colleagues and reported her feeling in the book:

> We have to use our privilege to advance the rights of the marginalized. We can't let people [like two good guys] say what is true about the world. We have to give voice and power to the oppressed and let them say what is true. Science is as

biased as all human endeavors, and so we have to empower the disempowered, and speak always with them (p. 137).

These are Dreger's words describing the way her Marxist colleagues think. The two good guys are J. Michael Bailey and Craig Palmer.

Bailey's research reported that many men who have sex change operations do so for erotic reasons, not, as transgender political activists insist, because they are "born with the brain of one sex and the body of the other" (p. 9).

Palmer co-authored a book asserting that rape often includes a sexual component, meaning that rapists do not always rape solely for reasons of power and conquest, but also because they enjoy sex.

The activists fiercely attacked Bailey and Palmer, charging them, among other alleged crimes, with rights abuse of research subjects and falsifying data. One scientific journal, cited by Dreger, published an article saying Palmer and his co-author deserve to be hung (p. 116).

Dreger's role in this, as a historian of fact, was to pore over everything relevant to the controversies, ranging from the works of the scientists involved to all of the various criticisms offered, some of them found in forgotten transcripts and archives.

Bailey and Palmer fought valiantly to defend themselves, which is why Dreger gave them the accolade of Galilean personality. Dreger's work has cleared their names—at least, to anyone interested in reading the facts.

Bailey and Palmer are not the only ones profiled and defended in Dreger's book. Napoleon Chagnon spent many years studying the Yanomamö tribe in Venezuela, describing them as a fierce, male dominated tribe that fought violently over females, practiced domestic brutality, used drugs ritualistically, and couldn't care less about the environment.

This was not the right thing to say.

Chagnon's enemies unleashed a torrent of character assassinations, from the usual charges of cooked data to hints and not-so-subtle hints of beliefs in eugenics and intentional use of a bad vaccine that infected the whole tribe.

Dreger's indefatigable efforts to dig for facts also cleared this Galilean personality.

So what is Dreger's conclusion from these stories? Facts don't matter—to today's identity activists, as summed up in her depressed feeling quoted above.

In a somewhat understated way, she does acknowledge that the activists get their motivating ideology straight from Karl Marx, but I would add: Marxist polylogism[184] is emboldened by our current atmosphere of postmodern[185] epistemological relativism. Only the "oppressed classes" have changed.

The premise remains that opposition to dogma must be silenced. And Dreger's book makes it clear that relativism results in the same authoritarianism as does religion.

* The book's dust jacket shows half of an 1873 painting[186] with Galileo sitting in front of a globe, his right hand obscured. A student to whom Galileo is lecturing was cut out of the picture and it is Galileo's index—not middle—finger that is extended in the original painting.

** The phrase "wall-to-wall Marxism" is from the feisty and indefatigable Christopher Monckton,[187] Viscount of Brenchley. Monckton was referring to the National Socialist Workers' Party in Scotland and the Royal Society in England, but the words seem an appropriate description of our current cultural environment. Monckton is a prominent "climate change doubter," as the Associated Press's revised stylebook[188] now prefers to call "climate deniers."

(October 31, 2015)

---

[184] See below, "Polylogism, the Right Lie, and Serial Embellishers," p. 309.
[185] See above, "Postmodernism and the Next Failure of Socialism," p. 33.
[186] "Galileo Demonstrating the New Astronomical Theories at the University of Padua," artsandculture.google.com.
[187] "Christopher Monckton of Brenchley, "The Unspeakable BBC Parks Its Tanks On My Lawn," May 18, 2015, wattsupwiththat.com.
[188] Paul Colford, "An Addition to AP Stylebook Entry on Global Warming," September 22, 2015, ap.org.

Further Comment on *Galileo's Middle Finger*

MY PREVIOUS POST[189] DID NOT DO JUSTICE to the Alice Dreger book *Galileo's Middle Finger*.[190] Here are a few additional comments.

Intersex people. Intersex infants, children, and adults, formerly referred to by the pejorative "hermaphrodite," are born with ambiguous genitalia—for example, with external penis and vagina, usually of different sizes, or with an external vagina and internal testes but no uterus or ovaries.

Dreger's doctoral dissertation focused on late nineteenth and early twentieth century hermaphroditism. Because such sexual differences were seldom ever talked about, most intersex people in that period lived relatively normal lives, presumably because they assumed that everyone else was built the same way. As Dreger put it, perhaps a little surprise on the doctor's face when examining the patient was the only awareness anyone had of the medical issue!

Sometime during the twentieth century, doctors decided they should do something about the "shameful" condition. They decided, usually only telling the parents that some infant surgery was necessary, to play God and change intersex infants into boys or girls, based entirely on their judgment of which way the infant should go.

In recent times, it seems doctors have become more transparent by telling parents what they are doing . . . but rarely, even today, have doctors or parents told their patients and children what was done to them as infants.

"Shame, secrecy, and lies" is how Dreger describes the attitudes and behavior of doctors and parents. And it is this shame, secrecy, and lying that has incensed the human sexual identity activists. Intersex people are individuals with rights just like everyone else, but they have been denied honesty, have been discriminated against, and even denied choice—over which way they want to go, or whether to go at all.

Several early chapters of Dreger's book detail her own activism to get the medical profession to fess up and change its ways. The stone

---

[189] See above, "The Galilean Personality vs. Wall-to-Wall Marxism and Human Sexual Identity," p. 90.
[190] Alice Dreger, *Galileo's Middle Finger*, amazon.com.

wall she hit is part of the reason she felt the depression mentioned in my previous post.*

Congenital adrenal hyperplasia. Another stone wall was hit and described in the latter chapters of Dreger's book. A doctor in New York City has made a career of administering dexamethasone, a powerful steroid, to in utero fetuses to prevent the formation of ambiguous genitalia and other sexual anomalies that can result from this inherited disease.

Dreger tallied a number of problems with this medical practice and lobbied hard, but failed, to stop it. The off-label[191] drug—many drugs are so used—must be administered before there is any evidence the fetus is developing in an anomalous manner.

Dreger's math found that only one out of ten such treated fetuses stood to benefit from the drug. On the other hand, the risks? Only one study—and only one—has been conducted to discern long-term consequences. The findings of that study indicated a significant minority of the sample suffered retardation, memory difficulties, and growth disorders; as a result, the study was shut down.

The controversy centered around informed consent, much of which seems not to have been given, and bureaucratic approval to proceed with such a treatment.

At one point, charges of fraud for phantom research projects were brought up, but the whistleblower, like many operating in bureaucratic environments,[192] was attacked and threatened with psychiatric treatment. The Feds, responsible for protecting the public from risky medical practice, did little to stop a prestigious and well-established doctor.

Dreger lost the battle.

Social justice. Dr. Dreger views herself as an activist fighting for social justice. This has pushed me to clarify in my mind the difference between social and individual justice. "Social justice" has a long history, so it is not unique to Karl Marx, but today's advocates use it in a distinctively Marxian flavor.

---

[191] "Off-Label Use," wikipedia.org.
[192] See above, "The Whistleblowers: An Indictment of the Mixed Economy and Bureaucracy," p. 77.

Is Dreger an advocate of social justice? Not really, though I'm sure she would disagree with my interpretation of her work.

Social justice, as I define it using today's Marxian flavor, is the virtue of fairly and accurately judging oppressed classes as underprivileged and granting them restitution in the form of additional wealth, education, employment, along with other favors that they otherwise have not been able to attain. The underprivileged include anyone who is deemed unsuccessful, but especially African Americans, women, and LGBTs. This is a collectivist definition.

Individual justice is the virtue of fairly and accurately judging individuals—oneself and others—according to the standards of honesty, integrity, courage, independence, and especially productiveness. This is the individualist definition.

I think Dr. Dreger, because of her uncompromising commitment to facts, is closer to practicing the latter form of justice than the former. This, I would say, is why she could not accept her Marxist colleagues' epistemological relativism. Yes, African Americans, women, and LGBTs have been badly discriminated against, even enslaved, but each individual must be judged on his or her own merits. No "class," to use Marx's terminology, owes any other "class" anything, especially when restitution is made at the point of a gun.

To use a reductio argument against the Marxists one might say this: Ayn Rand wrote that the individual is the smallest minority on earth. Turning the thought around, can we not say that the group or "class" of individuals is the largest "class" on earth? And therefore the largest "class" on earth that has been discriminated against and oppressed??

Individuals of the world should unite! And fight off their oppressors!!

Marxists should be advocates of individualism if they are seriously concerned about justice for the oppressed.

Free speech at Northwestern. An unwavering defender of First Amendment rights, Dreger has, since the publication of her book, performed a little flipping off herself. She has resigned[193] from the Northwestern University Medical School over her dean's attempts

---

[193] Tyler Kingkade, "Noted Author Resigns from Northwestern in Censorship Protest," August 25, 2015, huffpost.com.

to censor the content of a faculty magazine she edited. The content? About sex, of course, but also possibly "offensive" content—to the hospital's *brand name*!

Sigh! As a marketing prof, I have to make one comment. Bureaucrats, whether in academia or government, have no clue what sound marketing, including branding, means. They think the usual BS that marketing is just that and that a brand image is something made up and pawned off on the helpless, unsuspecting public. This is just good Marxist thinking about business.

Sound branding—that is, product identification—of a first class hospital should run something like this:

> We use the latest, most advanced knowledge and techniques to treat and cure our patients. In the process we entertain and examine all ideas—the wilder and more offensive the better.
>
> The better because we will then know that we have left no stone unturned in order to come up with treatments and cures to do justice—there's that word again!—for our patients.

* To the sheltered, like yours truly, this was an eye-opening read. It also struck me as the perfect "borderline case" in the philosophical problem of universals.[194] The existence of intersex people (and animals) demonstrates that there is no intrinsic maleness or femaleness "out there, in the thing" as the intrinsic theory of essences claims. It also took my teenage daughter to explain the difference between gender, which is social (actually, psychological [i.e., not arbitrary]), and sex, which is biological. Now I understand! [See this 2018 blog post for the objective, non-arbitrary psychological basis of gender.[195]]

(November 2, 2015)

---

[194] "Problem of Universals," wikipedia.org.
[195] "Masculinity and Femininity: The Differences Are Not Arbitrary 'Social Constructs,'" August 8, 2018, jerrykirkpatrick.blogspot.com.

2016

Americanized Maoism, the "Narrative" of Political Correctness, and Racist Minimum Wage Legislation

DANIEL HENNINGER[196] IN THE *WALL STREET JOURNAL* has referred to our current political correctness madness as "a kind of Americanized Maoism." This is an interesting characterization.*

China did not have a proletariat of factory workers, so Mao chose peasants as the oppressed class we should worship and model our lives on and, of course, protect from the evil capitalists.

Today's American leftists certainly would not seem to mind having us all wear Mao tunics, nor would they mind reducing our standard of living to the level of Mao's peasants.

Note a few of the consumer products that have been banned by those who know what is best for us: phosphates in laundry and dish detergents, high-flow water valves, incandescent light bulbs, plastic shopping bags, and the vent hole in the lowly gasoline can.

Jeffrey Tucker[197] has examined a number of these civilization killers. On the light bulb ban, he writes, "It's the plot of [Ayn Rand's] *Anthem* lived in real time."

The gasoline can? Apparently, wealthy leftists have never had to mow their own lawns and don't care to remember their elementary physics. That second hole makes it easy and spillage-free to pour gas into the mower's tank. Tucker's conclusion: the bureaucrats in power want us to reduce our lives to the misery of pre-capitalist eras.

The Americanized part of "Americanized Maoism," however, is just another import from Europe. It is the postmodern rejection of Enlightenment values and establishment of what I referred to in a previous

---

[196] Daniel Henninger, "Revolt of the Politically Incorrect," January 6, 2016, wsj.com.
[197] Jeffrey A. Tucker, "Three More Attacks on Civilization," April 20, 2011, mises.org; "Why Everything Is Dirtier," May 5, 2011, mises.org; "How Government Wrecked the Gas Can," May 7, 2012, fee.org; "How We Destroyed Indoor Plumbing," March 31, 2015, fee.org; "Anthem and the Meaning of the Light Bulb Ban," April 20, 2015, fee.org.

post[198] as a virulent absolutism in an age of epistemological and moral relativism. (Some terms were borrowed from Stephen Hicks.[199])

This is what has given us the word "narrative." When challenging the left, the dismissive response will often be, "That's only your narrative." Which is another way of saying what's true for you is not necessarily true for me. And it's also Marx's polylogism[200] dressed up in new garb.

So why should we listen to the left? The unspoken and sometimes not so unspoken reply is, "We have the power. You don't. Our narrative is in charge."

One current "narrative" taken as a given is that opposition to minimum wage is racist. Fortunately, a recent column[201] by Professor Williams has taught us an important history lesson about who really is the racist.

The 1931 origin and design of minimum wage legislation was to prevent African Americans from getting work. Nearly every economist in the United States knows minimum wage laws prevent the least skilled—mostly African Americans at that time, and still today—from being hired. Similar motivation operated in South Africa's 1925 Apartheid legislation to prevent the hiring of "Natives."

The true racists are the advocates of minimum wage, and since capitalism is the cure for racism,[202] anyone who opposes free markets should be labelled haters of the minority disadvantaged and oppressed.

Trigger warning for the poor babies on college campuses:

> The left has it wrong.
>
> Capitalism—free markets and free speech—are what you should be studying and supporting. It's time to get your feelings hurt. You might learn something in the process.

* Henninger also argues that the popularity of certain "outsiders" in the 2016 Republican presidential circus is a revolt of the politically

---

[198] See below, "Virulent Absolutism in an Age of Relativism," p. 304.
[199] Stephen Hicks, *Explaining Postmodernism*, amazon.com; see above, "Postmodernism and the Next Failure of Socialism," p. 33.
[200] "Polylogism," wikipedia.org.
[201] Walter E. Williams, "Minimum Wage Dishonesty," January 13, 2016, creators.com.
[202] George Reisman, "Capitalism: the Cure for Racism," amazon.com.

incorrect, meaning that Americans, probably through their "you can't push me around" sense of life, are sick of being badgered by the left and told what to think, feel, and do.

A Note on Correctness. The term usually means free from error, accurate, or precise, but in the pejorative sense in which the word is used today, it means conformity to an orthodoxy with deviation calling for punishment.

Penalties for failure to conform range from expressions of disapproval, shock, contempt, and condemnation to the more serious excommunication, expulsion, or termination to the ultimate of imprisonment, and death.

Today's radical Marxist left—in the form of political correctness—is not unique in insisting on such conformity.

Just ask Socrates about Athenian correctness in the fifth century BC or Galileo about the Inquisition's Catholic correctness in 1633.

Throughout history, religious, ideological, and intellectual movements have produced their share of correctness zealots. Christian and Islamic correctness, as in "radical Christianity" and "radical Islam," are not inappropriate designations.

Nor is Freudian correctness. See Jeffrey Masson[203] on his expulsion from the Freud Archives and other psychoanalytic societies over his view of Freud's seduction theory.

The motivation for correctness zealotry is intolerance of difference, especially as manifested in language and behavior that deviates from the orthodoxy. The goal is control, initially censorship of language but in the end total control of thought and behavior.

(January 21, 2016)

---

[203] Jeffrey Moussaieff Masson, *The Assault on Truth*, amazon.com.

The Communist Era and Capitalism vs. Democracy

SIDNEY HOOK'S 600-PAGE AUTOBIOGRAPHY *OUT OF STEP*[204] provides a wealth of information about New York intellectual life in the twentieth century, especially the communist era from the 1930s to 1960s.

It also indicates that the main debate today is not, or should not be, capitalism vs. socialism, but capitalism vs. democracy.

As Marxist scholar, communist fellow traveler, anti-Stalinist, pro-Cold Warrior, anti-New Leftist, and adamant defender of democracy, Hook knew or was acquainted with nearly all of the players of the communist era.

The difference between Hook and his Communist Party colleagues is that, as a philosophy professor at New York University, he actually read and thoroughly understood Karl Marx, so if he had been a professor in a USSR university in the 1920s and '30s, he, like others before him, certainly would have been purged.

The names of many of these players should be familiar to anyone who has read about or lived through any portion of the communist era, for example, playwright Bertolt Brecht, who was worshipped by my 1960s New Left professors, and journalist Whittaker Chambers. Hook has stories about all of them.

Brecht, one day in Hook's apartment in 1935, made a casual remark about a Stalin-assigned assassination: "The more innocent they are, the more they deserve to be shot." Hook showed Brecht the door and never saw him again.

Chambers was a Stalinist spy in the 1930s who, when he came in from the cold, was immediately hired by *Time* magazine. Chambers later testified against Alger Hiss, accusing the high-level State Department official of also being a former spy. Hiss was subsequently convicted of perjury and went to his death denying it all. Hook concluded the evidence was against him.*

Never a card-carrying Party member, Hook became anti-communist after the Moscow Show Trial[205] revelations of 1936–38. He supported

---
[204] Sidney Hook, *Out of Step*, amazon.com.
[205] "Moscow Trials," wikipedia.org.

US entry into World War II against the Nazis while Party members, who took their orders from the Kremlin, opposed any support for the evil capitalist regime of the United States.

During the Cold War, when communist apologists were advocating unilateral disarmament on the part of the US and saying it was better to be red than dead, Hook supported a strong defense and pushed the slogan "better free than slave."

His chapter on the New Left's spring 1969 uprising at NYU, that is, its occupation and disruption of academic life, is detailed and alarming. His description of the corresponding spinelessness of the school's administration is equally detailed and alarming.

Not a friend of the New Left in the 1960s, Hook declared its campaigners "anti-intellectual" and "barbarians of virtue."

And to set the record straight on whether or not, in earlier years, Communist Party members had infiltrated US educational institutions—the New Left had rewritten history to say otherwise—Hook cites Communist Party instructions to its members to teach Marxist-Leninism in every class without being caught or exposed. This confirms what I once heard Ayn Rand[206] say, this time in Hook's words: the duty of card-carrying communists was "to deceive and to cheat."

The main political debate throughout Hook's life, especially as stated by him, was democracy vs. totalitarianism. Nazism, fascism, and Soviet communism represented the latter, but as a lifelong socialist—on moral, not economic, grounds—the former meant democratic socialism.

For Hook and his socialist colleagues, socialism is the ultimate end [goal] of Jeffersonian democracy and the Bill of Rights. This is sometimes called social democracy, though more often in the United States its close cousin is social or progressive—as opposed to classical—liberalism. Social liberalism is an alleged improvement on the classical type.

At the end of his life (and book), Hook acknowledged that collective ownership of the means of production—the socialist state as giant post office, to use Lenin's metaphor—does not work. Thus, he describes himself as "an unreconstructed believer in the welfare state and in a steeply progressive income tax." Interventionism, in other words, with a strong leftward bias.

---

[206] See above, "Ayn Rand, of Course, Was Right," p. 88.

Although he spent many of his last years at Stanford's Hoover Institution and was awarded the Medal of Freedom in 1985 by President Reagan, Hook was no conservative. He was a secular humanist (and naturalist), which means he was a lifelong atheist and ardent supporter of science and scientific method.**

Democracy for Hook, however, was primary. He and nearly everyone else in the world today, including the Marxists and communists, seem to advocate democracy. So what does Hook mean by it?

In the absence of genus and differentia, he gives descriptions, such as "free discussion," "freely given consent," "voluntary [consent], not subject to coercion," and, most importantly, the absence of economic obstructions to that consent and to the pursuit of education, jobs, and happiness.

Hook's moral basis for being a socialist was, of course, his unexamined assumption that capitalism exploits workers. Socialists are more moral because they are "nicer" (meaning more altruistic, though Hook does not use the term) than the capitalists who are mean and selfish. Therefore, a crucial prerequisite of modern democracy is that economic power must be put under political control.

I say the main debate today is, or should be, capitalism vs. democracy, rather than vs. socialism, because of the near-universal endorsement of democracy and equally near-universal failure to define it. Hook's somewhat muddled understanding is how most currently see it.

Socialism, to be sure, still needs to be refuted, though Ludwig von Mises[207] did it thoroughly in 1922. And telling a näive voter that the government often abuses its legal monopoly on the use of physical force is likely to produce a "but we are the government and we can change it" response.

What percentage influence does a voter have in a typical US presidential election? Less than a millionth of a percent!

As I suggested in an earlier post,[208] the vote is not unimportant in a free society, but it is neither primary nor fundamental. Hong Kong,

---

[207] Ludwig von Mises, *Socialism*, mises.org. See also amazon.com.
[208] See above, "Politics Is a Bore (Retitled: Who Are We Going to Coerce Today?)," p. 62.

after all, did quite well for decades with no general elections. What it did have was the English constitution and legal system.

This means that if democracy is a term to be endorsed at all, it must be defined as voting restrained by individual rights and those rights must be clearly distinguished from the collectivized[209] versions of the social liberals. Individual rights are freedoms to take action, not entitlements to things, that is, to food, shelter, clothing, education, jobs, and happiness.

I'm tempted to say that democracy should be tossed entirely in defenses of the free society. If capitalism is understood as a social system,[210] not just economic, it can be put where it belongs—in philosophy—and therefore cannot be dismissed as "just economic," which most opponents and the ignorant alike do when the term comes up.

Discussions of social systems come from the fourth branch of philosophy called social (or political) philosophy. Social philosophy defines the nature and proper function of government, which brings rights and ethics into the discussion of capitalism, which means egoism should also be brought in, as well as a theory of human nature, and a theory of consciousness and universals, among other fundamental issues of epistemology and metaphysics.

Sidney Hook was a philosopher who knew about discussions of this sort, at the fundamental level, and used fundamentals to defend Marx and socialism. He was an advocate of Enlightenment values: reason, science, technology, freedom, and, of course, rights and democracy, as most socialists of his era were.

Defenders of the free society cannot just say they are advocates of the Enlightenment values of reason, science, technology, freedom, rights, and democracy . . . and expect to win arguments.

What is required today for a proper defense is the elevation—that is, the boosting, heightening, raising up—of discussion from our current concrete-bound, trivial, and disconnected mess to universal and fundamental principles.

Socialism was a moral ideal in the 1920s, '30s, and, according to Ayn Rand, until the end of World War II. As a practical ideal it died with

---

[209] "Collective Rights," aynrandlexicon.com,
[210] "Capitalism," aynrandlexicon.com.

the USSR collapse in 1991, yet its flotsam lingers in 2016 to obstruct passage to a genuinely free society.

It lingers by default because of the lack of principled opposition.

Sidney Hook was a significant member of the generation that sought to promote a moral ideal. His book provides lessons for anyone in 2016 who wishes to do the same, this time, one would hope, promoting the ideal of laissez-faire capitalism and all that it rests on.

* Chambers became a neoconservative and wrote the infamously sleazy review of *Atlas Shrugged* in William Buckley's *National Review*.[211] "From almost any page," says Chambers, "a voice can be heard . . . commanding: 'To a gas chamber—go!'" Chambers was posthumously awarded the Medal of Freedom in 1984 by President Reagan.

** F. A. Hayek,[212] in "Why I Am Not a Conservative," points out that conservatives are not averse to using coercion to achieve their goals and he even suggests that coercion is the common denominator uniting "repentant socialists" (like Whittaker Chambers) and conservatism. True (classical) liberalism, says Hayek, supports liberty over equality or democracy.

(March 4, 2016)

On Involuntary Servitude: "You'll Do Something, Mr. Cook. . . . If You Don't, We'll Make You."

THE MARCH 28 *TIME* MAGAZINE cover story[213] about Apple Inc.'s legal battle against the FBI and the lengthy interview[214] with CEO

---

[211] Whittaker Chambers, "Big Sister Is Watching You," December 28, 1957, nationalreview.com.
[212] F. A. Hayek, "Why I Am Not a Conservative," cato.org.
[213] Lev Grossman, "Inside Apple CEO Tim Cook's Fight With the FBI," March 17, 2016, time.com.
[214] Nancy Gibbs and Lev Grossman, "Here's the Full Transcript of TIME's Interview with Apple CEO Tim Cook," March 17, 2016, time.com.

Tim Cook are well worth the read.* So also is the earlier February 25 column on this case by Judge Andrew Napolitano.[215]

There are several conclusions from the three pieces.

The FBI in February had ordered Apple to create new software to hack the encrypted iPhone of a dead terrorist. Apple contested the order, saying it would be a violation of civil liberties and that such software would put a master key in the hands of bad guys all over the world, including authoritarian governments. This, Cook says, is tantamount to banning encryption.

The case is now moot, because the FBI did what it should have done in the first place: it hired an independent firm to hack the phone, presumably achieved without creating new software. The order at the FBI's request has been vacated, but the issues, including the possible future coercing of Apple and other tech firms, remain.

Tim Cook in the *Time* article and interview says that banning encryption means only the bad guys—such as terrorists—will have it, because encryption software is widely available beyond the borders of the United States. I doubt that Cook intended this, but he is making the same argument as the defenders of the Second Amendment: ban guns and only the bad guys will have them!

Cook says the court order amounted to a violation of the civil liberties of Apple's customers, especially their right to privacy. Judge Andrew Napolitano made it an issue of due process, because Apple was not given proper notice, and, more significantly, a case of involuntary servitude.

Let's take involuntary servitude first. The phrase comes from the Thirteenth Amendment to the US Constitution that outlaws slavery. The Supreme Court, however, has issued a number of rationalizations[216] why a military draft and other forms of forced labor do not constitute servitude. The main excuse is that the amendment was passed specifically to apply to African slavery, not to other forms of forced labor. That is, all young, able-bodied men—and today, women—owe a duty,

---

[215] Judge Andrew P. Napolitano, "Apple's Involuntary Servitude," February 24, 2016, creators.com.
[216] "Selective Draft Law Cases," wikipedia.org.

when so ordered, to perform work for their government and, if "necessary," to go die for the old men (and women) in power in Washington.

The justices of the Supreme Court, not to mention legal experts and other intellectual leaders, both today and yesterday, have failed to understand that rights are absolute and universal. A freedom to take action, when not infringing anyone else's freedoms, is a freedom to take action.

And slavery is slavery, as Judge Napolitano argued. Slave labor is precisely what Apple was asked to perform.

Indeed, the FBI vs. Apple case was an *Atlas Shrugged* moment on at least two counts. Several Apple engineers[217] had stated that they would refuse to write such requested new software for the FBI, risking fines and imprisonment. Or quit. In effect, they were threatening to strike.

The working title of Ayn Rand's novel was *The Strike*.

The case most amazingly was a Hank Rearden moment. I'm referring to the passage in the novel where the steel titan is ordered by James Taggart and his cronies to produce at a loss and therefore make the irrational work. When Rearden asks how he is supposed to accomplish that, Taggart responds, "Oh, you'll do something."

A major theme of the novel is that creativity and innovation do not work at the point of a gun, but that was what the FBI was asking and expecting Apple to do.

What our country needs more of today are business CEO's with the integrity and courage of Mr. Cook—to stand up to their government.

In fact, this confrontation between the FBI and Apple would make an excellent business ethics case for future (or even current) executives to discuss.

The civil liberties issue that Cook talks about brings up the canard about privacy versus security. Cook wants to defend his customers' privacy. The FBI and Washington don't give a hoot.

When a crisis occurs, the politicians and bureaucrats scream security over privacy. Rights be damned. And the use of fear by the government usually succeeds in getting citizens to cough up their rights.

---

[217] Jordan Kahn, "Apple Engineers Say They Could Refuse or Quit If Ordered to Unlock iPhone by FBI," March 17, 2016, 9to5mac.com

Cook points out that the government wanted Apple to create a master key and give up the privacy—which really means security and safety—of millions of people around the world in order to go after a "sliver" of bad guys.

Somehow the lawyers in Washington seem to have forgotten the training that taught them a most important principle of the free society, namely that it is better for a guilty person to go free—that would be Cook's sliver of bad guys—than for an innocent one to be sent to jail.

Plus, as long as I am talking about involuntary servitude, this brings up the related Vietnam War era discussions of the prospects of an all-volunteer army. "There might not be enough volunteers," the supporters of the draft yelped incredulously. Two answers were given, aside from the prickly issue of rights versus slavery: one, perhaps the war was not just and we shouldn't be involved at all, or two, if the war is just and the country does not have enough volunteers, then the country deserves what is coming to it.

This last applies similarly to the FBI's attempt to force Apple into involuntary servitude, for unjust means to a just end can never be moral. Coercing Apple to hack a dead terrorist's phone to obtain information that might prevent the occurrence of a future event destroys the principle of justice and ethics.

If, however, in the name of justice the FBI refused to coerce Apple and, as consequence, failed to obtain such information, at the very least it could then stand tall and say that it upheld a cardinal principle of the free society.

The real—practical—issue here, though, is that the FBI (and government as a whole) needs to become proactive in creating better crossbows. In any weapons race, the bad guys will sooner or later obtain the latest crossbow, or encryption technology, which means the good guys must stay one step ahead of the bad. Apple has done, and is continuing to do, just that.

It is time for the government to do the same, instead of wasting money and resources trying the coerce Apple to correct the FBI's own mistakes.

The FBI's mistake was the order to reset the iPhone's passcode, which resulted accidentally in the Bureau's inability to access the phone's information.

In the few weeks of this FBI standoff, Apple fortunately was not raided by gangs of armed, bulletproof vested SWAT teams. Apple is a high profile, well-liked firm and escaped—for now—such inexcusable tyranny.

Tennessee based Gibson Guitar[218] a few years ago was not so fortunate.

After the SWAT teams left, Gibson CEO Henry Juszkiewicz, like Tim Cook, spoke up to defend his business. Never charged (for illegally importing wood from Madagascar and India), and, of course, no apologies given, Gibson was slapped with a fine and a gag order—to never again speak up to point out how unjust the US Justice Department is, which is to say: to never again attempt to defend itself.

* Dated March 17 in the digital versions.

Postscript. I cannot pretend to keep up with all the issues involved in this post's encryption battle, but WhatsApp,[219] the online messaging service, has just announced that it has encrypted all messages of its billion or so worldwide users. No one in the WhatsApp office can listen in to or hack what is being, or has been, said.

WhatsApp's analogy to defend encryption is that what is now being done electronically has been done for centuries without the electronics, because it is just conversation that formerly was done at the water cooler or under an old oak tree. If the FBI wants the information that is being discussed, it either needs to subpoena the participants or send spies to the coolers and trees.

Spooks on the ground to gather intelligence. What a novel idea! It used to be done but, as I recall, budget cuts going back to the Clinton administration led to the post-9/11 hysteria about weapons of mass

---

[218] See above, "Politics Is a Bore (Retitled: Who Are We Going to Coerce Today?)," p. 62.
[219] Cade Metz, "Forget Apple vs. the FBI: WhatsApp Just Switched on Encryption for a Billion People," April 5, 2016, wired.com.

destruction in Iraq. The Bush administration had to rely on satellite photographs to verify information that should have been obtained with real people seeing with their own eyes.

(April 6, 2016)

The Fascist Early Progressives

THIS POST TITLE MAY BE A BIT EXTREME, to call progressivism "fascist," but not by much.

After all, Ludwig von Mises referred to fascism as "socialism of the German pattern" to distinguish it from the Russian version. Instead of expropriation of private property to achieve socialist states, Nazi Germany and Fascist Spain and Italy imposed extensive government regulations to control private life, both business and personal.

The Progressive Era in the United States, from about 1890 to 1930, established the same pattern, but it was based on the leaders' learning of democratic socialism in Prussian universities.

The early progressives' specific policies, as comprehensively documented in Thomas C. Leonard's book *Illiberal Reformers: Race, Eugenics, and American Economics in the Progressive Era*,[220] would not be considered politically correct today, but their fundamental principles of using think-tank-guided "experts" and government guns to achieve socialist goals have been internalized by modern liberals and conservatives alike, and vastly extended to control nearly all aspects of private life.

Most of the early progressives were reared in old New England families, which made them evangelical white Anglo-Saxon Protestant males, and their program was largely independent of political affiliation: it was strongly supported, for example, by both the Republican Theodore Roosevelt and Democrat Woodrow Wilson.

Here's a first taste of the progressives' thinking, as stated in a review of Leonard's book: "In the early twentieth century, progressives displayed an open contempt for individual rights. In a 1915 unsigned

---

[220] Thomas C. Leonard, *Illiberal Reformers*, wsj.com.

editorial at this magazine [*The New Republic*[221]], the editors ridiculed the Bill of Rights as a joke."

The reviewer continues, "If Leonard didn't have the quotes from prominent progressives to back up his claims, this would read like right-wing paranoia . . . ." And the quotes are numerous.

This book is an important corrective to the history profession's biased glamorizing of early progressivism.

The liberal individualism of the Scottish Enlightenment was viewed by these early progressives as selfish and therefore un-Christian and immoral. Their evangelical focus shifted from saving souls to saving society, from the individual to the collective. The "public" or "common good" became the standard for policy.

Indeed, one of the motivations for founding the American Economic Association in 1885 was to counter and exclude the ideas of classical liberals Herbert Spencer and William Graham Sumner.* The promoters of progressivism were mostly economists and sociologists: Richard T. Ely, John R. Commons, Edward A. Ross, and Irving Fisher, plus many more.

Elitism and social engineering, not democracy, were their motivating aspirations.

Their form of elitism sought to exclude certain groups, believed to be inferior, from participating in much of society. For example, they eagerly sought to preserve race purity and maintain a living wage for workers of northern European extraction.

Among the groups targeted for exclusion were African Americans, women, and immigrants—especially the Chinese and those from southern and eastern Europe, which especially meant Jews. The disabled, feeble minded, and insane were also inferiors who were excluded to asylums and special farms away from the cities; in some cases they were sterilized.

The former three groups (the early progressives were not Marxists and did not use the term "classes") were less skilled than their white Anglo-Saxon Protestant male counterparts, so by their willingness to accept a lower wage, they threatened to reduce earnings of the "more deserving" male workers.

---

[221] Malcolm Harris, "The Dark History of Liberal Reform," January 21, 2016, newrepublic.com.

Minimum wage and immigration laws were the progressives' solution.

Maintaining racial purity was more of a challenge, but the "state-of-the-art science" of eugenics came to the rescue. "Well-born" is the meaning of the term, coined by Darwin's half-cousin, Francis Galton. The aim of eugenics was hereditary control of the race through compulsory sterilization and euthanasia.

Up to 60,000 sterilizations were performed in the United States, as late as 1972. Justification for the practice was given in a Supreme Court[222] decision in 1927, authored by the progressive justices William Howard Taft, Louis Brandeis, and Oliver Wendell Holmes. The legal argument said compulsory sterilization was no different from compulsory vaccination.

Cancelling compulsion in either case was not an option—to those who knew best.

American psychiatrists[223] promoted and supported the Nazi sterilization program that ran from 1934–39. A few supported compulsory euthanasia. The euphemistically labeled "mercy killings" began in Nazi Germany in 1938—in gas chambers disguised as showers.

Eugenics is not much talked about today, or taught in the schools—for the obvious reason that modern progressives do not want to be associated with Nazi Germany. The eugenic connection to progressivism is also seldom mentioned or taught, but it fit the progressives' program like a glove.

Fascist progressivism? Theodore Roosevelt saw race suicide as the greatest problem of civilization and, according to H. L. Mencken, whom Leonard quotes, "believed simply in government," not democracy.

The "quality" of the vote, not quantity, was what counted for progressives. Wealth and literacy tests were recommended to determine who should be allowed. Voter turnout in national elections fell thirty percent between 1896 and 1924, even more in the Jim Crow South.

Woodrow Wilson praised those "sturdy stocks... [from] the North of Europe" and denigrated immigrants from southern and eastern

---

[222] "Buck v. Bell," wikipedia.org.
[223] Peter R. Breggin, "Psychiatry's Role in the Holocaust," 1993, breggin.com

Europe. He also derided inalienable rights as "nonsense." The Wilson administration *re-segregated* the federal government.

Fascist progressivism? Much, much more can be found in Leonard's book.

* "Social Darwinism," Leonard points out in a journal article,[224] was a less-than-accurate construct of Richard Hofstadter[225] in 1944. It then became a favorite pejorative of modern historians, used to disparage the Progressive Era's capitalism and capitalism's advocates. The phrase was hardly used during the period, least of all by Spencer or Sumner.

(July 7, 2016)

Who Are We Going to Coerce Today?—Also Known As: Politics Is a Bore 2016 Version

IN NOVEMBER 2012,[226] I PUBLISHED A PAEAN to our national elections titled "Politics Is a Bore." Some months afterwards I changed the title to the more apt "Who Are We Going To Coerce Today?," because coercing innocent people is what contemporary politics is all about.

Below is a lightly edited and updated version of the 2012 tribute.

The term "political junkie" is familiar to all of us today, but when I first heard it years ago, used by a news reporter to describe herself, I was puzzled. Why, I thought, would anyone be so obsessed with politics to spend every waking minute following every conceivable tidbit of information coming out of the political arena?

Perhaps the reporter's interest in politics was strictly professional, to cover what was going on, but I suspect that many in her position, as well others who follow political news closely, admire the entire system and consider it important to support. Many political junkies, I fear,

---

[224] Thomas C. Leonard, "Origins of the Myth of Social Darwinism: The Ambiguous Legacy of Richard Hofstadter's Social Darwinism in American Thought," 2009, princeton.edu.
[225] Richard Hofstadter, *Social Darwinism in American Thought*," amazon.com.
[226] See above, "Politics Is a Bore (Retitled: Who Are We Going to Coerce Today?)," p. 62.

are those who admire the coercive apparatus of the state and relish the thought of being in a position of political power to make political decisions.

To me, politics is a bore—precisely because it is all about coercion, the government-initiated type; it's seldom about reducing government involvement in our lives. And following politics closely, as many do, means their interest really comes down to: who is going to be coerced today? Let's see who's going to be told by the anointed authorities what they can and cannot do. Protecting individual rights has long since disappeared from our political landscape such that decisions in today's government-by-lobby mixed economy invariably constitute violations of innocent victims' rights for the sake of someone else's rent-seeking[227] benefit.

Just look at the disgraceful shakedown of Gibson Guitar[228] [in 2011], carried out in the name of the environmental lobby. Flimsily suspected, but never charged, of illegally importing wood from Madagascar and India, the company was twice raided with Gestapo-like tactics by armed, bullet-proof clad SWAT teams. At a 2011 press conference,[229] Gibson CEO Henry Juszkiewicz courageously called the Justice Department on its flagrantly unjust laws and tyrannical procedures. Because of the outcry that followed, the Department compromised by allowing Gibson off the hook with a settlement: $350 thousand in fines and censorship (a gag order) not ever to do again what Juszkiewicz did at his press conference, namely to contradict the alleged facts claimed by the government.[230] If this is not coercion in politics—the initiation of the use of physical force against innocent victims—what is?

Now I suppose one could say that some politicians are trying to do good things in Washington and the state capital. And I will grant that maybe one or two may be trying to roll back government intrusions

---

[227] "Rent Seeking," wikipedia.org.
[228] Craig Havighurst, "Why Gibson Guitar Was Raided By The Justice Department," August 31, 2011, npr.org.
[229] "Gibson Guitar vs. The Obama Regime," September 4, 2011, wwwwakeupamericans-spree.blogspot.com.
[230] Kris Maher, "Gibson Guitar to Pay Fine Over Wood Imports," August 7, 2012, wsj.com; Harvey Silverglate, "Gibson Is Off the Feds' Hook. Who's Next?," August 19, 2012, wsj.com.

into our bedrooms and board rooms. Ron Paul's two presidential runs have certainly given a hearing to new ideas and Paul Ryan has put Ayn Rand's name in the news [in 2012, not 2016!].*

But, seriously, what have Democrats and Republicans done in the last hundred years to increase the protections of individual rights? Democrats make no pretense at rolling back government interventions; they are only too eager to pass more laws increasing the state's size and power. Republicans, on the other hand, are notorious for paying lip service to the free market and capitalism, but when in office they end up increasing the government's coercive powers more than the Democrats would have done. Look at the two previous Bush administrations.

"Passing a law" for over a century has almost always meant increasing coercion against an innocent party for the gain of a pressure group. The "squeakiest wheel," of course, gets the grease in a mixed economy; that's the fundamental theory of the system because there is no just way to determine who gets the favors, or should I say, rents. But the laws are democratically passed by vote, one might object? Democracy, as the Greeks taught, can be a form of dictatorship and Hong Kong[231] survived quite well for decades under the British common law *without general elections.***

That's not to say that I don't believe in voting, though not voting is just as valid a participation in the system as pulling a lever. In the current political season, I will vote against the many California tax propositions and probably vote for the lesser of two evils for president. [Not in 2016. I'm voting for Gary Johnson.] I was going to write in Ron Paul's name, as I did four years ago, but I think a statement does need to be made in this election. I realize that my vote in this very blue state is virtually worthless and, after the election, politics will resume its usual games of playing "who are we going to coerce today"?

Yawn! Wake me up when something really good and important happens.

Altering a bit what I have said before,[232] "I do not expect life to improve much, if at all, in the next four years of the [next] presidential administration. I do not expect the [next] (or [current]) administration

---

[231] "History of Hong Kong," wikipedia.org.
[232] See above, "Why the World Is Not Going to Hell in a Basket," p. 41.

to be the indicator of the beginning of the end of civilization as we know it." Life goes on. Cultural and political systems change slowly. Political junkies can continue to obsess over every coercive decision that is made in positions of power. I will read and write about other topics.

* A recent informal search of *The NY Times* produced these mentions of Ayn Rand's name: 97 for all of 2011, 10 for the first quarter of 2012, 68 for the second quarter, and 147 for the third. Paul Ryan seems to be doing some good, though most comments about Ayn Rand in the Old Gray Lady[233] remain smarmy, snarky, ignorant, and hostile. Perhaps after I am dead, these *Times* writers will also be dead and younger ones will take their place, ones who have actually read Rand's works and are capable of separating her personality and followers from her ideas.

[**Update**: 38 mentions for all of 2015, 6 for the first quarter of 2016, 8 for the second quarter, and 6 for the third. A few mentions in the past five years have seemed a little more neutral. Most recently, in a book-review-page author interview,[234] mystery writer Otto Penzler said he has "virtually all the books written by Ayn Rand, several read more than once" and his favorite fictional hero is Howard Roark. Are times (or *The Times*) changing?]

** I'm not convinced that the vote is fundamental to a genuine liberalism. The classical liberals saw it that way, but Hong Kong has shown us that a constitution and legal system that are adhered to do not require voting to keep the system going. When African Americans and women attained the right to vote, that did not guarantee them the protection of other, more important rights to liberty and property. See section 8, chapter 1, of Ludwig von Mises' *Liberalism*.[235] The primary purpose of democracy, he says, is to avoid civil war by ensuring a peaceful transition of leadership.

---

[233] "Old Gray Lady," urbandictionary.com.
[234] "Otto Penzler: By the Book," October 13, 2016, nytimes.com.
[235] Ludwig von Mises, *Liberalism*, mises.org.

Postscript, 2016. It seems I used the phrase "politics bores me" in my September 2008[236] hymn to our political system. I was talking about the two liberalisms, the left's version and the Misesian one. In September of this year, Jeffrey Tucker[237] wrote at fee.org urging us all to take back the Misesian word. Why? Because the left is tending not to use liberalism to describe their brand of politics, preferring to call themselves progressives. To those who know what is happening on college campuses, it is obvious why the left is abandoning the word: they no longer pretend to be advocates of freedom. In July[238] I used the f-word (fascist) to describe the early progressives; the shoe seems to fit. And Tucker, in this recent piece,[239] implies that the premise of a total state began with the early progressives.

Postscript, 2021. Politics stopped boring me on November 9, 2016, the day after the presidential election, when the putsch mentality crawled out of its holes. Since then, I have been terrified by the left's explicitly stated aims to do what they have always said they would do: set up a totalitarian dictatorship! I was admittedly far too naïve.

(November 1, 2016)

The Reductio of Bureaucracy: Totalitarian Dictatorship

THE CONTINUED EXPANSION OF BUREAUCRATIC MANAGEMENT leads ultimately to totalitarian dictatorship.

Viktor Frankl, a Holocaust survivor, describes this termination point:

> The emaciated bodies of the sick were thrown on two-wheeled carts which were drawn by prisoners for many miles, often through snowstorms, to the next camp. If one of the sick men had died before the cart left, he was thrown

---

[236] See above, "The Two Liberalisms," p. 36.
[237] Jeffrey A. Tucker, "If the Word Liberal Is Up for Grabs, Can We Have It Back?," September 25, 2016, fee.org.
[238] See above, "The Fascist Early Progressives," p. 110.
[239] Jeffrey A. Tucker, "Salon Journalist Panics Over 'Political Crisis,'" October 26, 2016, fee.org.

on anyway—the list had to be correct! The list was the only thing that mattered. A man counted only because he had a prison number. One literally became a number: dead or alive—that was unimportant; the life of a "number" was completely irrelevant.[240]

In several previous posts[241] I have used the following words to represent the generally acknowledged mindset of a bureaucrat: "Rules are rules, fella. I don't make 'em. I just enforce 'em."

Rules, lists, paperwork. This is bureaucracy.

As Ludwig von Mises[242] has taught us, bureaucracy is not a large, hierarchically structured organization, whether of big government or big business. It is the government's method of managing its affairs, which means it is the "peaceful" method of managing coercion. Laws of the land, a budget for each bureau, and regulatory rules dictate to citizens what they can and cannot do. Disobedience brings punishment. The method is top-down; the higher authority must be obeyed.*

Business management is bottom-up, deriving its legitimacy from customer satisfaction, the only means in a free market of earning profits. Policies, not rules, are guidelines informing everyone in the company, from president to stock clerk, how to function in order to achieve optimal customer satisfaction and therefore optimal profits.

If a large, hierarchically structured business today seems bureaucratic, in the sense of being inefficient and insensitive to customers, look for the government's demands for compliance to laws and rules. Compliance means obedience to a higher power, which consequently deflects attention from customer needs and wants. This is what makes businesses in a mixed economy take on the "rules are rules" mentality.

So why the bureaucratic indifference to people? Paperwork is the only yardstick bureaucracy has to measure its "success." Laws and rules are commands that compel citizens to obey, and citizens usually do

---

[240] Victor Frankl, *Man's Search for Meaning*, pp. 52–53, amazon.com. In this work, Frankl, an Austrian psychiatrist, describes his experiences in the concentration camps and his struggles to survive.

[241] See above, "It's Just Being Turned into a Business," p. 31. see above, "The Whistleblowers: An Indictment of the Mixed Economy and Bureaucracy," p. 77.

[242] Ludwig von Mises, *Bureaucracy*, mises.org. See also amazon.com.

obey to avoid punishment. Paperwork records the compliance—but it must be correct.

The objective yardstick of a business is its bottom line, profits, which means it is successfully meeting its customer's needs and wants.

A bureaucratic society is a rule-bound society. Freedom and creativity are not valued. (Creativity, after all, means breaking rules.) The more bureaucratic the society, the more rule-bound it will become. The socialist state, therefore, is a society dominated almost entirely by laws and rules. The more laws and rules, the more total the regulation of human affairs, the less value it places on its citizens' lives.

Total bureaucracy—the totalitarian socialist state—is dictatorship by excessive law. This describes Nazi Germany during World War II, as well as the USSR and many similar regimes in the twentieth century.

The list has to be correct because all paperwork has to be correct. William Shirer made this clear in *The Rise and Fall of the Third Reich*,[243] when he described gangs of German secretaries dutifully typing orders to send Jewish people to their deaths.

Even a few members of Kerensky's provisional Russian government, who were discovered by illiterate Bolshevik revolutionaries during the 1917 October Revolution,[244] were compelled to write their own arrest papers. The paperwork had to be correct!

In a bureaucratic society, thought is neither required nor appreciated, only compliance. Thus, paperwork has to be correct for the lower-ranked official to avoid punishment and for the higher to justify his or her actions, by reference to a law or rule.

Concern for the person behind a bureaucratic number is minimal or non-existent. Just ask students at state-run universities what it is like to be a number on a roster. (And the rosters do have to be correct!)

Message for advocates of a free society? The fewer laws and rules, the better. Indeed, a strong argument[245] has been made that we could easily do without legislature-made, statutory law by replacing it with common law.

---

[243] William L. Shirer, *The Rise and Fall of the Third Reich*, amazon.com.
[244] "October Revolution," wikipedia.org.
[245] N. Stephan Kinsella, "Legislation and Law in a Free Society," September 1, 1995, fee.org.

Central planning requires centralized law-making, that is, deliberative assemblies (legislatures) and regulatory agencies to write and pass thousands of pages of laws and rules, all of which are subject to ossification, officious manipulation, and arbitrary application. This gives us the nefarious rule by men under a pretext of rule by law.**

Common law is decentralized and requires conceptual thinking by each citizen and judge to resolve specific disputes with reference to principles. Justice evolves and improves on a case by case basis, as wealth and well-being do in the decentralized free market.

Conceptual thinking requires the discovery and understanding of universal principles that can be applied to many concrete instances. Common law, therefore, is general and guided by rights, such as the requirement to prove intent in criminal cases, but it is constrained by precedent and usually confined to specific parties. Change in common law occurs slowly and deliberately.

Legislature-made laws and rules, in contrast, aside from their flagrant violations of individual rights, are at the same time concrete and sweeping, such as a ban on smoking in all public places and within twenty feet of a building. And because legislature-made law is *made*, not discovered [recognized or identified], change occurs quickly and frequently, thus leading to a continual increase of laws and rules—and paperwork.

Thinking in principles and independent judgment are prerequisites for building and sustaining a free society. When our minds are driven to focus on lists and paperwork that must be accurate, conceptual thinking becomes difficult, though not impossible. For many, however, in bureaucratic situations, morality—honesty, integrity, courage, dignity ... and human decency—go out the window.

The list has to be correct.

For more on the relationship between bureaucracy, socialism, and dictatorship, see Mises' 1944 book *Bureaucracy*.[246] Here is his one-paragraph summary and conclusion (p. 125):

> The champions of socialism call themselves progressives, but they recommend a system which is characterized by

---

[246] Ludwig von Mises, *Bureaucracy*, mises.org.

rigid observance of routine and by a resistance to every kind of improvement. They call themselves liberals, but they are intent upon abolishing liberty. They call themselves democrats, but they yearn for dictatorship. They call themselves revolutionaries, but they want to make the government omnipotent. They promise the blessings of the Garden of Eden, but they plan to transform the world into a gigantic post office. Every man but one a subordinate clerk in a bureau, what an alluring utopia! What a noble cause to fight for!

Bureaucracy is not a benign institution.

* "Peaceful" is in scare quotes because any expansion of laws and rules beyond retaliatory force to protect individual rights, through administration of the police, military, and legal system, is a violation of rights and therefore becomes a declaration of war on citizens. The overt use of guns is not usually required in many bureaucratic systems, because of citizen compliance, but the guns nonetheless are there in the background.

** "Show me the man and I'll find you the crime," said Stalin's chief of secret police.[247] See this post[248] where I discuss similarities between criminal and bureaucratic personalities.

(December 6, 2016)

---

[247] See above, "The Sovietization of Federal Law," p. 68.
[248] See below, "The Bureaucratic Personality: Similarities to the Criminal Mind?," p. 280.

2

Academia

2007

Drop Errors and the Trouble with Peer Review

IN PRODUCT DEVELOPMENT there are two kinds of errors. A "go" error occurs when the green light is given to a product that eventually fails. The Edsel, a $250 million write-off by the Ford Motor Company in 1959, is one example. The "drop" error occurs when an idea that could have been highly profitable is eliminated from further consideration. How do we know that the idea could have been profitable? In a free market dropped ideas have the habit of being picked up by someone else. Chester Carlson's invention was dropped by such notables as General Electric, 3M, Kodak, RCA, and IBM, but picked up by the small Haloid Company. In 1961 Haloid changed its name to Xerox. Even go errors in a free market often get corrected; just a few years after the Edsel fiasco, Ford rolled out a better idea called the Mustang.

Peer review is the process by which millions of dollars of government money are handed out to researchers in medicine and the physical sciences; the process by which recognition, promotion, and tenure are determined for professors, especially those in the "softer" sciences who do not need or use grants for their research; and one of the criteria—numbers of peer-reviewed journal articles, for example—used to determine accreditation for universities.

Peer review, a "blind" process in which the names of author and evaluator are concealed from each other, requires two or three so-called peers to read a paper or proposal to judge the quality of actual or proposed research before acceptance. As such, peer review is a product development process that protects only against go errors. It is at best quality control that insures accuracy and reliability of research done. At worst it holds back innovation through drop errors. Since there is no free market in scholarly research—today's government-university-science complex is a severely hampered market—dropped ideas either never get a hearing or take many more years than they otherwise should to surface.

Medical researcher and long-time critic of peer review, David Horrobin, argued that the peer-review process, which developed in its current form largely as a screening device after World War II, has perhaps improved the accuracy and reliability of conventional research published in medicine, but it has done so at the price of innovation. Prior to World War II, unknown researchers could submit papers to journals only with the endorsement of a published author. The editor would then decide whether or not to publish. Peer review was ad hoc and not common. It was the growth of government involvement in education and, especially, the government's lavishing of money on research that called for the blind-review screening process.

In a paper titled "The Philosophical Basis of Peer Review and the Suppression of Innovation"* Horrobin urged that more unconventional and innovative research be encouraged by journal editors. When a reviewer questioned the need for such a statement, Horrobin produced eighteen incidences of medical innovations rejected by the peer-review process. In 1995 Horrobin's paper was cited by the US Supreme Court as support for the argument that some "well-grounded but innovative theories" may not be published in peer-reviewed outlets.**

Horrobin's solution to divvying up grant money was to give funds equally to all researchers and let each work on whatever his or her interests indicated. Prior to 1960, said Horrobin, this interest-as-guide process was essentially how funding was distributed in the UK and more innovation in medicine resulted in those years than in the years since 1960. Horrobin approved of government involvement in and funding of research, but the analogy to free markets in his solution—bottom-up, self-interested choice by researchers—versus central planning—top-down, "expert" direction by peer reviewers—cannot be escaped.

Never mind that Socrates and Galileo were badly treated by their peer reviewers or that frauds and hoaxes sometimes dodge the quality controllers or, further, that you may want to cite Ayn Rand and Ludwig von Mises but can't figure out how to get past your peer-review gatekeepers, the real problem of peer review is the severely hampered market in scholarly research. What would a truly free market in scholarly research be like?

First, publishers of journals and scholarly books would have to earn a profit from their buyers and not live off the donations of their authors or other benefactors. Some university presses, for example, are now publishing what are called "supported books," which means someone, usually the author's department, must contribute one or two thousand dollars to the publication of the author's book. And at least one commercial press requires authors to do their own copy edit and provide camera-ready typeset text; this can add up to two thousand dollars or more that authors must fund. Twenty-five dollars per page, charged to authors or their departments, has long been the going rate for published papers in some fields. (In some quarters today this method of getting into print would be called subsidy or vanity publishing.)

In addition, the so-called nonprofits, which finance a portion of today's research and journals, are in fact creatures of the tax system and must, despite their descriptive name, show an excess of donations over expenses lest their organization become some philanthropist's very expensive hobby. Under laissez-faire, in the absence of tax write-offs and the guilt that wealthy business people tend to exhibit, as well as, or especially because of, their ignorance of economics, there probably would be far fewer such organizations than exist today.

Second, there would be no government money to dangle in front of researchers and no government-owned or -regulated universities filled with bureaucratized product lines (curricula designed by committee), bureaucratized sales reps (the professors), or bureaucratized performance evaluations (those mounds of paper, which include lists of published research, that must be produced for promotion, tenure, and most every other consideration). All of this distorts the market and probably encourages the overabundance of pretentious minutia that fills today's overabundance of academic journals.

Under laissez-faire, only the market would decide who produces what and who gets what in scholarly output. Indeed, the market for this research might not differ much from the product development market in automobiles. Private, profit-making firms, both traditional businesses and universities, would finance the work and effectively and efficiently produce market-satisfying results. Portions of the results might be published in profit-making journals and books, much of it perhaps not.

Yes, there might be some Edsels created by this free-market development process and there might still be some delayed acceptances of Xeroxes, but there also might be a lot more Mustangs! Absent the government-encouraged gatekeepers and other hurdles that must be jumped in order to get into the market, researchers who cannot find an outlet will be free to start their own journals, publishing companies, businesses, or even universities. The hampered market today, which includes the "golden handcuffs" of tenure, makes this quite difficult.

* *JAMA, The Journal of the American Medical Association*, March 9, 1990, 263:1438–41. See abstract.[1]

** Daubert v. Merrell Dow Pharmaceuticals, 509 U.S. 579. [Albert Einstein[2] had his run-in with peer review in 1936. His theory of relativity and Watson and Crick's description[3] of the double helix would not likely make it through the current process!]

(April 11, 2007)

---

[1] David F. Horrobin, "The Philosophical Basis of Peer Review and the Suppression of Innovation," March 9, 1990, jammanetwork.com.
[2] Ariel Procaccia, "Einstein's Contempt for Peer Review Wasn't Misplaced, It Is Something of a Lottery," January 30, 2020, theprint.in.
[3] Andre Spicer and Thomas Roulet, "Hate the Peer-Review Process? Einstein Did Too," June 2, 2014, theconversation.com. [Also: Mark Humphries, "The Absurdity of Peer Review," June 3, 2021, medium.com.]

Privilege, Peer Review, and Piracy: Q & A

THREE RECENT POSTS produced several questions and comments.

Follow the Government Intervention. In "The Market Gives Privilege to No One"[4] I stated that certain groups of professionals do not usually work weekends and that the computer industry's "24/7" indicates the ultimate in free-market service. "But I work weekends," protested one doctor and one professor and shock was expressed that I was asking them to work around the clock!

Concerning the latter, no one person that I know of in the computer industry works twenty-four hours a day, seven days a week. The designation "24/7" means that customers can get service whenever they need it; the 24/7 company covers the entire week, around the clock, with service workers. Educational services on Saturdays and Sundays are scarce. Medical services are nonexistent, unless you are willing to subject yourself to waiting six hours or more in a socialized hospital emergency room. Government intervention, especially restriction of the supply of doctors and hospitals in the medical market, creates these service distortions and gives the professors and doctors a privileged life. On the medical market, see "100 Years of Medical Robbery"[5] and "Real Medical Freedom"[6] by Dale Steinreich.

One professor recited a common view that some academics hold: students are not customers, but products to be sold to businesses, that is, students are "work in progress" that become "finished goods" upon graduation. At best, this description of students is metaphor, at worst it is profound insult. The product of education is the knowledge the professor is supposed to be conveying to students and knowledge is what students are buying with their tuition payments. If professors view students as products in a production line, is it any wonder that students feel like numbers on a roster? Why do professors view them this way? Follow the government intervention: because that is precisely how the bureaucracy views students.

---

[4]See above, "The Market Gives Privilege to No One," p. 25.
[5]Dale Steinreich, "100 Years of Medical Robbery," June 10, 2004, mises.org.
[6]Dale Steinreich, "Real Medical Freedom," August 27, 2004, mises.org.

Playing the Game. In "Drop Errors and the Trouble with Peer Review"[7] I said that peer reviewers are gatekeepers that prevent or delay the acceptance of innovative ideas. One reader wrote that entrepreneurs are getting around the gatekeepers by establishing online journals.

True. Technological innovation, such as the internet, has made it easier for writers to get into print without having to jump through the usual hoops and there has been a proliferation of academic journals, many of them online. Much of the proliferation, however, is driven by the publish-or-perish atmosphere of academic life, which is expanding beyond research universities to what used to be called teaching schools. Accreditation requirements for "academic qualification," usually defined as a certain number of peer-reviewed journal articles—books don't count or, at most, count only as equivalent to one article—have created the need for more outlets to accommodate this increased "original research."

University administrators have become bean counters and professors plan strategies for getting around the peer-review gatekeepers. Hallway discussion among faculty is about how to play the game.

Is Unauthorized Copying Theft? In "The Market Function of Piracy"[8] I said that pirated goods may function as a free sample in accelerating the acceptance of new products. The question arises, am I defending theft? No, I'm trying to recast the intellectual property debate; I addressed the issue to some extent in a comment I made to my post on the Mises blog (available as an addendum to "The Market Function of Piracy.")

As Siva Vaidnyanathan said in *Copyrights and Copywrongs*,[9] "You cannot argue for theft" (p. 253). Neither Vaidnyanathan nor Lawrence Lessig in *Free Culture*[10] are against intellectual property but both are attempting to rein in the lunacy of recent trends, such as the war against peer-to-peer file sharing and the push for perpetuity in copyrights. Their focus is on reforming intellectual property law to foster

---

[7] See above, "Drop Errors and the Trouble with Peer Review," p. 123.
[8] See above, "The Market Function of Piracy," p. 27.
[9] Siva Vaidnyanathan, *Copyrights and Copywrongs*, amazon.com.
[10] Lawrence, Lessig, *Free Culture*, amazon.com.

creativity, not stifle it. Roll it back, perhaps, to fourteen or twenty-eight years for copyrights.

The problem I have with their discussions, and others, is that interest-group and collectivist terminology dominate. Beginning with the Constitution, the aim of patents and copyrights is "to promote the Progress of Science and Useful Arts." Why not promote business in general? The aim of intellectual property legislation, they say, is to balance the needs of society with the rights of creators and the public good should dictate when property should go into the public domain. And so on.

When some advocates of intellectual property rights, on the other hand, make a case for the perpetuity, they have the collectivist and utilitarian defenders in a bind. Rights do not expire, they say. Why should my patent or copyright expire? Time limits are arbitrary, justified only on grounds of the public good. It is the failure to answer this argument, I think, that today is causing the continued lengthening of copyright, and to a lesser extent, patent terms.

The fundamental question to be answered in intellectual property debates is, where does your property end and my rights begin? How is it that you can come into my house and tell me that I cannot copy something I already paid you for? Or, to put it in historical context, is intellectual property really property or is it an instance of monopoly power and privilege? Historically, until the mid-nineteenth century, patents and copyrights were considered monopolies granted by the government; that's why time limits were put on them. And many economists in the nineteenth century considered patents just another form of protectionism.

My knowledge of marketing theory adds an additional perspective to this debate. There are actions creators can take—mainly the relentless search for customers—to market their innovations without resort to patents and copyrights. Clothing designs, for example, are largely unprotected, but some designers, despite the rapid availability of knock-offs, do quite well. By initiating lawsuits, especially the kind that occur today, creators' actions begin to look like monopoly protectionism cloaked in the self-righteous guise of property rights. Add to this the mind/body dichotomy—namely that creators do not like, and some even despise, having to aggressively market their wares—and you have a case for concluding that patents and copyrights are more about monopoly and less about property.

Property or monopoly. That is the issue. I'm not 100% certain that patents and copyrights are monopolies, but I'm no longer convinced that intellectual property is property. More research on my part must be done. I will have more to say about this topic at some other time. [not yet written].

(June 26, 2007)

The Ethics and Epistemology of Peer Review

IN A previous post,[11] I argued that academic peer review is a gate-keeping process brought about by the post-World War II growth of government involvement in research and scholarship. Though it may control quality in a narrow, conventional sense, one significant consequence of this process is the suppression of innovation. The present post takes a look at the underlying ethics and epistemology of peer review.

Medical researcher David Horrobin,[12] whom I quoted in the previous post, says that critics of peer review "are almost always dismissed in pejorative terms such as 'maverick,' 'failure,' and 'driven by failure.'" Lest those epithets be ascribed to me, I hasten to say that I have had some success in the process and that I am not denigrating anyone who uses it to advance his or her career. The process nonetheless does have serious flaws.

Most significant of its flaws is the view that peer review must be blind in order to maintain objectivity, that is, to prevent bias from entering the process. However, as the *British Medical Journal*,[13] which has not used blind peer review since 1999, points out, "A court with an unidentified judge makes us think immediately of totalitarian states and the world of Franz Kafka." Objectivity is the fallacy-free perception and communication of what the object of cognition is, and bias means that some other factor, such as irrelevant preconceived notions,

---

[11] See above, "Drop Errors and the Trouble with Peer Review," p. 123.
[12] David F. Horrobin, "Opinion: Something Rotten at the Core of Science?," February 2001, dml.cs.byu.edu.
[13] Richard Smith, "Opening up BMJ Peer Review," December 31, 1998, europepmc.org.

whether formed by emotion or by reason, interferes with this perception and communication. Lack of objectivity stems from a failure to perceive reality accurately.

Neither blind nor open peer review can guarantee this accuracy. Indeed, anonymity removes the need for care and responsibility when commenting on someone else's work. How many ill-mannered or ill-thought-out remarks would be made about submitted papers if reviewers knew that the papers' authors will know their names and how to contact them? Being allowed to hide behind anonymity is an invitation to scurrilous behavior. This is why the objectivity of legal systems in free societies demands that witnesses, whether supporters, accusers, or expert testifiers, be identified. Contrary to the conventional wisdom of peer review, objectivity requires at minimum that the process be open.

Objectivity, at root, is an epistemological concept and the failure to perceive and communicate accurately is a function of how one uses one's mind in the processes of perceiving and communicating. Neither anonymity nor openness will improve this. The most important requirement of objectivity while reviewing someone else's work is a constant awareness of one's preconceived notions. The most significant one to watch out for is "This is not how I would have written the paper; it should therefore be changed to . . ."

As one journal editor said, no doubt with some exaggeration, all of his reviewers of so-called empirical papers recommend rejection and those of theoretical papers insist that the papers be "recreated in the reviewers' own images." And another editor[14] complained that reviewers have turned into wannabe co-authors, requiring extensive revisions and writing comments that are sometimes as long or longer than the original articles. Clearly, decentering, to use Piaget's term,[15] meaning the ability to consider other points of view or to appreciate the perspectives of others, is needed by some, perhaps many, reviewers.

Once it has been established that a paper meets a journal's editorial guidelines and philosophy, that is, that the topic of the paper

---

[14] Tyler Cowen, "Economic Inquiry Has a New Policy," July 26, 2007, marginalrevolution.com.
[15] "Jean Piaget," wikipedia.org

is appropriate for the journal, then it is the author's objective that should guide evaluation. Decentering in reviewing, or editing or criticism, means accepting the premises of the author and recommending improvements in execution. The reviewer's personal preferences on the topic, including agreement or disagreement with the author's basic premises, should be set aside. The author's paper is the reality to be adhered to in the reviewing process; interference from irrelevant, previously formed emotional associations and intellectual beliefs destroys the objectivity of the process.

A reviewer, of course, may strongly disagree with the editorial guidelines and philosophy of a journal or with the objective of a paper, but then such a reviewer should either decline to be a reviewer or come to terms with the principle of objectivity. Much suppression of innovation in the peer review process probably stems from the failure of reviewers to distinguish their personal philosophies and preferences from those of the authors they are reviewing. When reviewer and author disagree, the reviewer either demands conformity or recommends rejection.

The issue of objectivity in reviewing (or editing or criticizing) is similar to the so-called problem of taste in art. Is this work of art bad art or is my reaction to it just my taste? Artists have an aim for their art and their execution of that aim makes it either good or bad art. Whether one likes a particular work of art, though, depends on many other factors, including emotional associations and intellectual beliefs. Therefore, as Ayn Rand[16] points out, it is not a contradiction to say "This is a good work of art, but I don't like it," and vice versa. The same can be said in reviewing scholarly work, namely, "I don't like or agree with this paper, but it is well done."

The reviewer, editor, or critic who can make this last statement is one who exhibits objectivity. When looked at from the standpoint of epistemology, whether the process is blind or open is beside the point.

(October 24, 2007)

---

[16] "Esthetic Judgment," aynrandlexicon.com.

2008-09
Because the Stakes are So Small

IN ACADEMIA THERE IS AN ADAGE that says disputes among professors are bitter precisely because the stakes are so small. The statement has been attributed to various people, including Henry Kissinger and Woodrow Wilson. The more general conception is known as Sayre's law of social motion[17] (as formulated by Issawi), specifically: "In any dispute the intensity of feeling is inversely proportional to the value of the stakes at issue. That is why academic politics are so bitter." I question the generalization that high-stakes issues lack intense feeling, but the more significant point is what exactly is the nature of the stakes that the adage refers to and whose stakes are we talking about?

Much has been written by academics about why the disputes are so bitter and the answer generally is the golden handcuffs of tenure. Working in a profession that lacks tangible rewards, professors crave status and recognition, but they are cooped up like rats or chickens with the same coworkers for decades. "Married without the possibility of divorce," says one commentator,[18] "angry faculty members exhaust themselves in petty battles over ancient personal resentments that pretend to be principles."

The protection of tenure and academic freedom, says another,[19] gives some professors "license to behave with little regard for civility or collegiality." In business, this writer points out, one can move on to another company, thus minimizing the irritation of disagreements with fellow workers, but in academia, where the ease of going elsewhere becomes more difficult with the number of years beyond tenure, the distress of every resentment and annoyance grows until it erupts into volcanic acrimony. To outsiders a dispute over who gets a new $100 office chair may seem small, hence the expression, but to the participants in the dispute the stakes loom large. Why?

The disputes are not often over tangibles, such as new office chairs. They may be over class scheduling, the elimination of a favorite course, or, more seriously, who gets hired, promoted, or tenured. This last brings

---
[17] "Sayre's Law," wikipedia.org.
[18] Thomas H. Benton, "The 7 Deadly Sins of Professors," May 12, 2006, chronicle.com.
[19] John P. Frazee, "Why We Can't Just Get Along," April 1, 2008, chronicle.com.

up comparisons of competence. The willingness to hire, promote, or tenure someone who is better than oneself—for example, in teaching, service, or scholarship—requires a strong, self-sufficient ego.

The following statement by former General Electric chief executive officer, Jack Welch, and his wife, Suzy Welch, former editor of the *Harvard Business Review*, is one not shared by many academics:

> Seek out people who are better, smarter, and in every way more talented than you are. They'll push the organization to new heights of performance. And we guarantee your career will follow [from the Welch's *Business Week* column, apparently no longer available].

Instead, rationalization upon rationalization, if not outright hostility, will be flung into the discussion to justify why such a person is not qualified. The rigors of scholarly logic disappear where personnel and other administrative decisions are concerned. Protecting one's turf—and frail ego—becomes paramount. A frail ego with low self-esteem cannot tolerate the prospect of a better colleague gaining (perceived) position and power. The stakes, psychologically speaking, have become huge. This does not take into consideration the fact that the stakes for the person being considered for employment, promotion, or tenure are equally huge. The adage about academic life is ambiguous in this respect.

Not every academic, of course, suffers such a low level of self-esteem, but enough seem to populate campuses around the world to justify the expression. The disputes of the academic world have no tangible effect on tenured professors. To outsiders, therefore, the privileged professors are still tenured and still have their jobs; so what if they have to teach a different schedule or work beside colleagues who are better than they? It is impossible for an outsider to think anything other than that the stakes are small. Psychologically, however, the privileged ones find it intolerable to have anyone change their comfortable schedules or to have someone new come in and expose their shortcomings. Envy, jealousy, and resentment move to the forefront, while rationality goes out the window.

So if one has sufficient self-esteem not to get upset over a schedule change or over colleagues who are better than they, how does such a person cope with those who fling the rationalizations and hostility and, more generally, throw tantrums in department meetings? Ms. Mentor, a.k.a. Emily Toth, columnist for the *Chronicle of Higher Education*, encourages young and old professors alike to view the events of academia from a literary perspective, as a play, as it were, albeit with "atrociously bad actors":

> There are serfs; there are dragons; there are definitely bats in belfries. Ideally, you find teaching exciting and mind-stretching (if you don't, you should leave the profession). But sometimes the longitudinal study of your colleagues—Oliver Awkward, Sara Surreptitious, Barnaby Bluster—is the most entertaining, and the longest-lasting show of your life.
>
> Ms. Mentor urges you not to miss a minute of it.[20]

It is this perspective, I admit, that I need to work on!

(April 14, 2008)

The Ethics of Accreditation

EDUCATIONAL ACCREDITATION IS UNETHICAL because it is government-initiated coercion to control the production and distribution of education. In the United States the control is indirect; in many other countries it is direct. Accreditation also infringes academic freedom, though that concept itself is a mixed product of government involvement in education.

Accreditation is the process of certifying a minimum level of quality in schools and colleges. A first, simple question arises. Who accredits the accreditors? Who certifies the certifiers? Or, as Ayn Rand[21] and others have put it more generally: who protects us from our protectors? The statist assumption is that experts in the government know what is best for us because they are not motivated by the selfish profit motive. As consequence, they should have the final say on quality. This ignores that Adam Smith's invisible hand metaphor applies equally, albeit inversely, to bureaucrats who proclaim their goals as serving the "public interest"

---

[20] Ms. Mentor, "Bored by Department Meetings," September 19, 2005, chronicle.com.
[21] "Consumerism," aynrandlexicon.com.

when in fact the behavior invariably is led "as if by an invisible hand" to benefit the special interests that lobby them.

The first one hundred years of American public education were dominated by one special interest, white Anglo-Saxon Protestants, at the expense of Catholics, Jews, African-Americans, and, often, women, plus other ethnic groups and religious and philosophical persuasions. Today, public education is dominated by the special interests of political correctness. And it has always been dominated by the premise that the omnipotent government[22] knows best.

Who determines quality in the free market? The market! That is, all the people who participate in the process of producing, buying, and selling goods and services. Ultimately, it is determined by the value judgments of consumers through their repeated buying of products they like and abstention from buying of products they do not like. Entrepreneurial competition and the pursuit of selfish profit over time leads to better and better products that meet the needs and wants of consumers. The same would apply in a free market in education, if such existed.

Accreditation[23] at the university level in the United States consists of seven "natural monopolies" that regulate higher education in a particular region of the country and many specialized agencies that govern specific programs, such as health or business education. Accreditation is "voluntary" (and therefore indirect) in the sense that no school or program is required to go through the approval process, but not having such approval severely restricts the availability of government money for student loans and other uses. All accrediting agencies must be approved by the US Department of Education. This is what puts them into the government-initiated coercion category. "Cartel"[24] and "licensing monopoly"[25] are appropriate descriptions that come to mind. That most education is provided by the government reinforces the ethical issue. Privately funded and controlled education in other countries is extremely rare, if non-existent altogether.

---

[22] Ludwig von Mises, *Omnipotent Government*, mises.org.
[23] "Accreditation in the United States," ed.gov.
[24] Arnold Kling, "Accreditation of Colleges," April 2, 2006, econlib.org.
[25] S. David Young, "Occupational Licensing," econlib.org.

In contrast, the Good Housekeeping Seal of Approval[26] originated in the late nineteenth and early twentieth centuries as a market-based means of validating the quality claims of the magazine's advertisers. Very early, however, the Seal of Approval came under the watchful eye of government oversight. Similarly, Underwriters Laboratories[27] began as a market-based testing and certifying organization, but today its operations must be approved by the Occupational Safety and Health Administration.

Academic freedom is a pretense at protecting free-speech rights. In a free-market—in education or anything else—the entrepreneur has the right to hire and fire at will anyone he or she disagrees with. The fired employee is then free to hang out his or her own shingle to start a new business. In the practice of government-owned and -controlled educational institutions, academic freedom means the freedom to speak and write within the narrow confines of what the government approves. Accreditation contributes to this narrowness by specifying the requirements of "academic qualification," such as the possession of certain degrees or diplomas and the publication of a certain number of papers within a certain period of time. That the entire process is one of bean counting and hypocritical is readily acknowledged. That it ignores that science does not progress strictly through one flawed form of publication, such as the peer-reviewed journal article,[28] or in five-year cycles is shrugged off as irrelevant.

In practice accreditation is a good ol' boy network of deans and retired professors. Universities court them, produce enormous mounds of paper every five years, and jump through hoops to win their anointments. Being accredited keeps the government money flowing. That is what accreditation is all about.

(June 23, 2009)

---

[26] "Good Housekeeping," wikipedia.org.
[27] "UL (Safety Organization)," wikipedia.org.
[28] See above, "Drop Errors and the Trouble with Peer Review," p. 123.; see above, "The Ethics and Epistemology of Peer Review," p. 130.

Ignorance versus Dishonesty

A LINE FROM THE 1980 MOVIE *Coal Miner's Daughter* has the young and upcoming country music singer Loretta Lynn saying something like "I'm ignorant, not stupid." The distinction—lack of knowledge versus lack of intelligence—is significant not just for the ignorant person's self-esteem and confidence to move up in the competitive world, but also as a matter of justice in how others, especially the more highly educated, view such a person who arises from humble beginnings. Unfortunately, some of the more highly educated who themselves have come up from within the ranks do not maintain the distinction when judging their former peers who have not become so accomplished.

A similar distinction can be made between lack of knowledge and knowingly and willingly lying or cheating. A similar lack of perspective—or quickness to condemn—among the more highly educated can also be observed when judging the actions of the less knowledgeable. This became clear recently in a discussion thread among professors in response to a *Chronicle of Higher Education* news blog about plagiarism. The post reported how one university is instituting a grade lower than F, the "FD," for academically dishonest students. Over 90% of the 46 comments gleefully cheered the toughness and alleged justness of the act, including one, protected only by internet anonymity, suggesting that the firing squad be brought back.

Whether this last was sarcasm, steam letting, or internet silliness is not worth dwelling on, as most comments ignored the possibility that some or many students just might not know how to cite, quote, and paraphrase properly when writing papers. This indeed is the conviction of Brian Martin, who wrote in the *Journal of Information Ethics*,[29] fall 1994, "Students are apprentices, and some of them learn the scholarly trade slowly." Martin's conviction quickly became mine several years ago when I began using an internet-based plagiarism detection service. Students who say, "You mean a reference is needed even though I put the material in my own words?" and "I didn't know that that needs to

---

[29] Brian Martin, "Plagiarism: A Misplaced Emphasis," Fall 1994, bmartin.cc.

be in quotation marks," are not dishonest. Far from using the service to catch cheaters, I now use it to teach techniques of the "scholarly trade."[30]

My students may be a special case because many are first-generation college students. They are not as worldly-wise as those who come from more highly educated families, which means many are ignorant of the ways of citing, quoting, and paraphrasing. Not knowing how to do something, however, and proceeding to do it incorrectly does not make one dishonest. That students should have learned the skills, as professors are quick to point out, in some previous course and did not, perhaps earning a passing grade of D- , does not make them knowledgeable and therefore dishonest in the present. It often means that professors are frustrated over not having students who are as knowledgeable as they are and instead of exhibiting the patience to teach them, some professors go on the offensive to condemn.

Such attitudes of professors remind me of the cartoon showing a boy holding a report card with an F on it and saying to his teacher, "Which one of us has truly failed?" In a free market sales reps are graded by their customers, not the other way around. And since in a free market in education teachers would be sales reps of knowledge and ideas (or peddlers of ideas[31]), the message of the cartoon is accurate. Teachers need to be teachers, rarely moralists.

There are many reasons why someone may not know what is right or wrong in a particular situation. The bureaucratic state that we live in today, including the state-run schools and universities, erects all kinds of unnatural barriers and confusion to the accomplishment of our goals. Its myriad rules and regulations make it nearly impossible to know what is right according to the bureaucrats, and students are caught in the middle of the kaleidoscope.

Throw in psychology, whether it be rationalization or evasion, selective memory and selective perception, exaggeration or literal mindedness, along with the entire cumulative nature of the formation of character, and you have a very difficult task of discerning willful, knowledgeable deceit from ignorance. The ignorance may be self-created, as

---

[30] Jerry Kirkpatrick, "Teaching Acknowledgement Practice Using the Internet-Based Plagiarism Detection Service," spring 2006, cpp.edu/faculty/jkirkpatrick.
[31] See below, "Peddlers of Ideas," p. 159.

in a life of evasion, but how can the judge know in the present what is the cause of an action or statement? Due diligence in gathering information and patience before passing judgment seem to be the sensible response.

Someone may step on my toe by accident or on purpose. Either way I am likely to yell. Prudence calls for patience before further judgmental action is taken.

(July 20, 2009)

2012–15

The Flawed Environment of Academic Research

My previous post[32] discussed how mistaken thinking about research evidence in nutrition has led to a misleading or even false understanding of how we should approach and maintain our health. A broader question than the argument-from-uncertainty fallacy arises: what is it in the nature of scientific investigation that makes these kinds of errors possible? The short answer is that there is no free market in science that would facilitate the quick awareness of both innovation and error. What we have today is government domination of research that deflects attention away from concern for the constituents the science is intended to serve, for example, doctors and their patients in medicine, to compliance with the rules of grantsmanship and peer review the ultimate aim of which is publication for tenure and promotion in the cloistered academic world.*

Though data fabrication and other frauds do occur, the most important cause of flawed research is the "what do we have to do to get the money and then the publication" attitude. This expedient in the protected environment of academia leads to conventional, uninspired, and sometimes substandard, politically biased, and irrelevant work, much of it amounting to useless minutia. I don't mean to imply that there is a willful disregard for truth or facts on the part of researchers, though again that sometimes does occur, but that the system in which academics compete for money and accolades predisposes them to pursue conventional lines of inquiry.

---

[32] See below, "Nutrition and the Argument from Uncertainty," p. 301.

"The problem in science," states the chief medical officer[33] of the American Cancer Society, "is that the way you get ahead is by staying within narrow parameters and doing what other people are doing. No one wants to fund wild new ideas." Except profit-making private companies like Revlon. And peer review does not encourage originality or novelty. As British medical researcher David Horrobin[34] pointed out in 1995, the acceptance of eighteen medical innovations was either delayed or thwarted by the process. The system is also notorious for not publishing findings that are negative, that is, studies that do not produce significant findings, on the alleged assumption that what works is more important and interesting than what does not.

In my 2007 posts[35] on peer review I argued that fear of the new governs and that the process is no guarantee of objectivity. This last has been demonstrated by studies retrospectively analyzing the results of published work. How so? "Miscalculation, poor study design or self-serving data analysis," in the words of *Wall Street Journal* science writer Robert Lee Hotz.[36] The pressures of publication cause sloppiness and cherry picking of the data—data mining or data massaging, as researchers call it, to find something publishable. (Selection bias was the term used in last month's post.[37]) All of this then brings about a recurrent lack of replication[38] of the original study. Failure to replicate puts the science back to square one. Often it is the private, profit-making companies, using the double-blind[39] research technique, who cannot replicate the work of the academics, because academics frequently fail to double-blind their experiments.

---

[33] Gina Kolata, "Grant System Leads Cancer Researchers to Play It Safe," June 28 2009, nytimes.com.
[34] David Horrobin, "The Philosophical Basis of Peer Review and the Suppression of Innovation," March 9, 1990, jamanetwork.com.
[35] See above, "Drop Errors and the Trouble with Peer Review," p. 123.; see above, "The Ethics and Epistemology of Peer Review," p. 130.
[36] Robert Lee Hotz, "Most Science Studies Appear to Be Tainted by Sloppy Analysis," September 14, 2007, wsj.com.
[37] See below, "Nutrition and the Argument from Uncertainty," p. 301.
[38] Gautam Naik, "Scientists' Elusive Goal: Reproducing Study Results," December 2, 2011, wsj.com.
[39] "Blinded Experiment," wikipedia.org.

Horrobin's solution to the screening and gatekeeping process of peer review was to divide the research money equally among researchers, then let the researchers be guided by their own interests in choosing what to study. This would remove the rule-bound, paper pushing requirements of the bureaucracy and free scientists to do what they do best, namely research. Horrobin pointed out that research money was distributed in precisely this way prior to 1960 in Great Britain and resulted in more medical innovations then than since. Of course, the grant money Horrobin was talking about was from the government. Remove government involvement in research and let more retained earnings of profit-making businesses be made available and you will see more responsiveness to the market, that is, to the consumers of the research.

Bureaucrats—anyone who works for or is excessively regulated by the government, including college professors who are most of the researchers I am talking about—answer only to the requirements of the bureaucracy. Profit-making businesses, on the other hand, have a huge incentive to innovate, to increase their profits; if they make mistakes, they pay dearly, and not just in lost sales or return on investment. The bureaucrat's response to anyone who complains about the conventionality or mistakes of present-day research is to say, "I just follow the rules. We have a process to follow if the rules need to be changed. It may take time, but that's the way it is."

Entrepreneurial innovators and innovative researchers don't hesitate to go outside the conventional box, which means they don't follow rules. Their attitude is, "What can we do to push back the frontiers of business or science?" To do that, they break rules.

* Two-thirds of the roughly $65 billion (in 2011) spent on research in universities[40] is financed by the federal, state, and local governments, 63% by the US government alone.

(January 20, 2012)

---

[40] "Higher Education R&D Expenditures, by Source of Funds: FYs 2011–18," nsf.gov.

Challenging the New McCarthyism

ASSAULTS ON FREE SPEECH IN ACADEMIA are not new. As Ludwig von Mises pointed out seventy years ago, academic freedom in European universities meant freedom to teach, and agree with, the government's viewpoint.[41]

It has always been a little risky for students to disagree with their professors' ideas, unless the disagreement is done within the narrow confines, defined by the professors, of what is considered "reasoned debate." This is what happens when the government is in charge of education; the government's agents dictate what is acceptable speech, leaving its customers little choice or opportunity to take their business elsewhere.

A recent survey,[42] however, starkly demonstrates the silencing of dissent on college campuses today: thirty percent of college seniors and less than twenty percent of faculty agree that it is safe to hold unpopular positions.

The cause is McCarthyism from the left, speech and harassment codes that are blatantly nonobjective and violate First Amendment protections. As in the original McCarthyism these codes and their enforcement use "unfair allegations" and "unfair investigative techniques," such as Star Chamber[43] (secret) proceedings, "to restrict dissent or political criticism."[44]

The history of political correctness[45] has been chronicled in a number of books.[46] The latest is Greg Lukianoff's *Unlearning Liberty: Campus Censorship and the End of Academic Debate*.[47] Lukianoff, president of the Foundation for Individual Rights in Education (FIRE),[48]

---

[41] Ludwig von Mises, *Bureaucracy*, pp. 81–83, mises.org.
[42] "Engaging Diverse Viewpoints: What Is the Campus Climate for Perspective Taking?," 2010, accu.org.
[43] "Star Chamber," wikipedia.org.
[44] "McCarthyism," dictionary.com.
[45] "Political Correctness," wikipedia.org.
[46] Alan Charles Kors and Harvey A. Silverglate, *The Shadow University*, amazon.com; Jonathan Rauch, *Kindly Inquisitors*, amazon.com; Donald Alexander Downs, *Restoring Free Speech and Liberty on Campus*, amazon.com.
[47] Greg Lukianoff, *Unlearning Liberty*, amazon.com.
[48] The Foundation for Individual Rights in Education (website), thefire.org.

details hundreds of cases his organization has defended on college campuses in the last fourteen years. FIRE initially writes to administrators citing First Amendment law and urges them to dismiss the cases they have against students and professors. When discussion fails, FIRE takes the cases public and helps victims litigate. FIRE to date has won all such cases. Very few universities, however, have apologized for almost wrecking a student's or professor's future.

Orwellian-style thought control is used to re-educate students in the political correctness ideology. Code violators face threats of expulsion, disciplinary blemishes on their records, and even criminal arrest. They often are "graciously" offered to have their records cleansed if they recant their sins (Galileo style?), apologize to the offended and write papers on the "correct" ideology, and attend mandatory counseling (Soviet style?) with a psychologist or other person well versed in the PC dogma.

The way speech and harassment codes work is that they equate words and actions; they declare fully protected offensive and hurtful speech to be nearly as harmful as assault and battery. Thus, racial or sexual epithets may be in violation of the codes because they are considered "hostile acts." Sexual harassment is determined by the perceptions of recipients and may be as innocuous as a mild flirtatious comment saying "you're beautiful." If the recipients *feel* harassed, harassment has occurred. The codes are overbroad and vague,[49] and the intent of speakers, in opposition to the First Amendment legal record, is irrelevant.

Indoctrination begins in first-year orientation in which students may be made to line up in order of skin color or by sexual leaning, for the purpose of demonstrating how racist, sexist, and homophobic certain privileged races, genders, and social classes are. One-on-one "therapy" sessions—or rather, invasions of privacy—may be required with a resident assistant to probe a student's (incorrect) sexual attitudes and orientation. Ideological loyalty oaths are not uncommon, especially in fields such as social work where students must sign statements of agreement with their professors' ideas about sex.

---

[49] "What Does It Mean When A Law Is 'Void For Vagueness' Or 'Overbroad'?," court.rchp.com.

Other examples range from the comical to the reprehensibly serious. The comical includes dampening of the allegedly offensive decades-old tradition of Harvard and Yale students trading barbs over their annual football game and umbrage taken by Harvard's Information Technology Department over a satirical cartoon lampooning the department's computer glitches (Lukianoff, pp. 81 and 87–88).

The serious includes threats of arrest—for disorderly conduct of a professor who put a poster on his door of a sci-fi television hero saying, "If I ever kill you, you'll be awake. You'll be facing me. And You'll be armed." The message means "I play fair." The university guardians of peace and harmony assumed he was threatening violence (Lukianoff, pp. 138–39).

The upshot of the codes is that anyone who *feels* hurt, *feels* criticized, or *feels* threatened—regardless of objective legal criteria spelled out in multiple court decisions—may file a complaint and be backed up by the weight of modern bureaucratic PC-ness to crush (or scare the living daylights out of) the student, professor, club, newspaper writer, or Facebook poster who "inspired" such feelings.

The uniqueness of Lukianoff's organization is that FIRE is bi-partisan. Lukianoff describes himself as a lifelong Democrat and environmentalist. FIRE's founders are Alan Charles Kors, a "conservative-leaning libertarian professor," and Harvey Silverglate, a "liberal-leaning civil rights attorney." Other members of the staff include "liberals, conservatives, libertarians, atheists, Christians, Jews, Muslims" (Lukianoff, p. 13). What they all have in common is a commitment to the First Amendment and freedom of speech.

Where has this PC lunacy come from? Marxism, of course. The new McCarthyism is a coercive application of political correctness to the regulation of behavior—everyone's behavior, student as well as professor. It is not about being nice and respectful to historically disadvantaged and discriminated against races, genders, and sexual orientations. It is about old Marxism dressed up in modern cloth, using the historically disadvantaged groups as pawns in the continued political agenda to disparage capitalism.

The bourgeoisie are no longer the oppressors of the proletariat, especially since the working classes have moved up in the world under capitalism and in some cases now make more money than college professors! Today, the oppressors are white, Anglo-Saxon males and other allegedly privileged groups who are subjugating the historically disadvantaged. In true Marxist, revolutionary fashion, so goes the canon, some liberties must be sacrificed to make amends. Free speech and equality before the law must be sacrificed to the goal of social equality, that is, the goal of equalizing those historically disadvantaged races, genders, and sexual orientations even if it means harming the privileged classes and restricting their speech.

The source of this new McCarthyism is that Marxist darling of the 1960s, Herbert Marcuse and the virulent absolutism of his postmodern[50] followers. Marcuse advocated in unmistakably plain language "the systematic withdrawal of tolerance toward regressive and repressive opinions and movements" and endorsed revolutionary violence.[51]

As serious as the present state of censorship on campus currently is, organizations like FIRE and tireless writers and speakers like Lukianoff promise a freer future in what the Supreme Court has acknowledged is—and should be—a truly *diverse* marketplace of ideas.

Postscript: Read Lukianoff's *Wall Street Journal*[52] response to the latest federal government attempt, through the harassment codes, to restrict and punish speech on (and off) college campuses. Prior restraint is also involved in the feds' attempt.

(May 17, 2013)

Trigger Warnings

JONATHAN RAUCH, STRONG SUPPORTER of the Foundation for Individual Rights in Education (FIRE[53]) and author of *Kindly Inquisitors: The New Attacks on Free Thought*[54] argues sarcastically—but also

---

[50] See above, "Postmodernism and the Next Failure of Socialism," p. 33.
[51] Quoted in Alan Charles Kors and Harvey A. Silverglate, p. 71, *The Shadow University*, amazon.com.
[52] Greg Lukianoff, "Feds to Students: You Can't Say That," May 16, 2013, wsj.com.
[53] The Foundation for Individual Rights in Education (website), thefire.org.
[54] Jonathan Rauch, *Kindly Inquisitors*, amazon.com.

seriously—that the following "trigger warning" should be put on the first page of every college catalogue:

> Warning!
>
> At this university, students could be exposed, at any moment, without warning, to ideas, comments, readings, or other materials that they find shocking, offensive, absurd, annoying, racist, sexist, homophobic, discriminatory, or generally obnoxious.
>
> We call this education.[55]

I can think of a couple of other sarcastic warnings: "Most of the ideas you will hear at this university are 100-plus-year-old dusty variants of Marxism that have been well-demonstrated to be hazardous to your health, and, especially, to civilization's health."

And in my fantasies: "What you will hear and learn at this university will likely upset your foundational ideas, that is, everything you have been taught about the nature of knowledge, values, psychology, and political philosophy and economy. It will raise your consciousness in a way you never will have thought possible. You will be challenged to confront the ideas of such writers as Ayn Rand and Ludwig von Mises. Be forewarned!"

Trigger warnings are a new form of campus censorship in which professors are supposed to give notice to students, before anything is said, about possibly offensive or hurtful speech. In practice, this means ideas the students may not have heard before or, especially, ones they might consider to be a cause of pain.

They are called "triggers" because the ploy is packaged with post traumatic stress syndrome (PTSD[56]). Symptoms of PTSD can be produced or triggered by specific words, memories, or incidents.

Thus, if a professor states in class that the average wages of men and women are virtually the same when adjusted for marriage and motherhood, or that several African American intellectuals have decried

---

[55] Jonathan Rauch, "Knowledge Starts as Offendedness," January 13, 2015, youtube.com.
[56] "Post-Traumatic Stress Disorder (PTSD)," mayoclinic.org.

affirmative action because of its effect on self-esteem, he or she must let the poor babies—the students—know that their feelings might get hurt by what is going to be said!

Fortunately, the American Association of University Professors (AAUP[57]) has nailed the issue: "The presumption that students need to be protected rather than challenged in a classroom is at once infantilizing and anti-intellectual." The chilling effect on freedom of speech in the ivory tower is unmistakable, as the professors' thought process becomes, "Maybe I shouldn't discuss this issue or idea because it might be offensive to some students."

Concerning the red herring of traumatic reaction, "The classroom is not the appropriate venue to treat PTSD, which is a medical condition that requires serious medical treatment. Trigger warnings are an inadequate and diversionary response."

And, finally, the American Library Association has called the labeling and rating of ideas or speech, such as "hurtful" and "offensive," "an attempt to prejudice attitudes" and "a censor's tool" (quoted in AAUP).

"Trigger warnings" are the radical Marxist left's latest ruse to silence discussion of anything that does not fit its manifesto. The proletariat in the industrialized world are no longer an oppressed class; today, they all drive SUV's and live in four-bedroom homes.

The good campus Marxists, as a result, must now find other oppressed groups to exploit: women, African Americans, and the LGBT community.*

These "classes" constitute the new proletariat. Marxist ideology marches on.

* Though, of course, many in these groups—classes?—are not exactly downtrodden and oppressed, since they, too, drive SUV's and live in four-bedroom homes.

(June 23, 2015)

---

[57] "On Trigger Warnings," August 2014, aaup.org.

Crybullies, Non-Negotiable Demands, Micro-Totalitarianisms, Academic Fascism . . . and *Cabaret*

"It is nothing! Children on their way to school. Mischievous children! Nothing more!"—from the Broadway musical *Cabaret*.

The words are spoken by Herr Schultz, the Jewish fruit shop owner whose window has been smashed by a brick. The setting of the story is the eve of Hitler's rise, 1931 Weimar Germany.

Too strong a comparison to make to the "children" on today's college campuses?

Is it?

Roger Kimball, author of the 1990 book *Tenured Radicals: How Politics Has Corrupted Our Higher Education* (2nd ed. 2008)[58] has called protesting students *crybullies*.[59] Those are the ones making non-negotiable demands for trigger warnings[60] lest certain words or ideas they disagree with hurt their feelings.

The mothers of present-day crybullies apparently did not teach their children the familiar rhyme about sticks and stones . . . versus words.

Thomas Sowell[61] prefers to call the new "micro-aggression" buzzword *micro-totalitarianism*. "Macro-aggression" supposedly means blatant physical force, including the battery of unwanted touching. But hurtful, offensive words are said to be small coercions that, if allowed, can accumulate to become just as bad as the macro ones.

More correctly, Sowell argues, the micro-censorships that the Marxist left is pushing are moving us "even if by small steps" more and more toward the macro silencing of dissent. This is the last step to dictatorship and total control.[62]

The list of the left's no-no's[63] that must be censored has now climbed to at least 80 and were it not such a serious issue would qualify for theater of the absurd. For example, "American is the land of opportunity," "I

---

[58] Roger Kimball, *Tenured Radicals*, amazon.com.
[59] Roger Kimball, "The Rise of the College Crybullies," November 13, 2015, wsj.com.
[60] See above, "Trigger Warnings," p. 146.
[61] Thomas Sowell, "Micro-Totalitarianism," June 16, 2015, creators.com.
[62] "Dictatorship," aynrandlexicon.com.
[63] Scott Jaschik, "Escalating Demands," December 3, 2015, insidehighered.com.

believe the most qualified person should get the job," and "Where are you from or where were you born?" are said to be racist micro-aggressions that should be banned from the home of academic freedom.

Violators of these prescriptions, the protesters demand, must be reprimanded, suspended, required to attend sensitivity training classes, or, preferably, forced to resign. Students at Emory University[64] are demanding that course evaluations rate professorial micro-aggressions—the predictable ones that might offend (Marxist) class identities.

Walter Williams[65] calls the current atmosphere on college campuses academic fascism:

> From the Nazis to the Stalinists, tyrants have always started out supporting free speech, and why is easy to understand. Speech is vital for the realization of their goals of command, control and confiscation. Free speech is a basic tool for indoctrination, propagandizing, proselytization. Once the leftists gain control, as they have at many universities, free speech becomes a liability and must be suppressed. This is increasingly the case on university campuses.

Williams cites one English professor who in the process of expressing his opposition to what the left calls *Israeli Apartheid*[66] said we must "not be guided by cardboard notions of civility."

The phrase means what it sounds like. Says Williams: "That professor's vision differs little from Adolf Hitler's brown-shirted thugs of the paramilitary wing of the Nazi Party in their effort to crush dissent."

The resurrection of 1960s-style intolerance is not lost on older professors, including Sowell[67]: "Storm trooper tactics by bands of college students making ideological demands across the country, and immediate preemptive surrender by college administrators—such as at the University of Missouri recently—bring back memories of the 1960s...."

---

[64] Catherine Sevcenko, "Emory Students Demand Course Evaluations Include Rating for Microaggressions," December 11, 2015, thefire.org.
[65] Walter Williams, "Academic Fascism," August 12, 2015, creators.com.
[66] Saree Makdisi, "Does the Term 'Apartheid' Fit Israel? Of Course It Does," May 17, 2014, latimes.com; Benjamin Pogrund, "Israel Has Many Injustices. But It Is Not an Apartheid State," May 22, 2015, theguardian.com.
[67] Thomas Sowell, "A Resurgence of Intolerance," December 1, 2015, creators.com.

That is to say, non-negotiable demands followed by administrator capitulation are not new.

Not every university administration from the 1960s era, however, gave in. The University of Chicago (and my alma mater, the University of Denver) expelled and suspended numerous students who staged sit-ins at campus buildings.

Just mischievous children?

Some are ignorant, but the leaders are neither ignorant nor mischievous.

One classmate circa 1968–69 gave an impromptu speech at a protest crowd on the steps of my alma mater's administration building. His voice boomed about struggle and revolution and his fist pumped.

The chilling thought that went through my mind was this: in 1917 St. Petersburg this classmate would have been on the front lines of Bolshevism.

Today, please, let us not stick our heads in the sand as did Weimar culture in interwar Germany.

Not seeing, or wanting to see, what was on the horizon of Germany's future is the theme of *Cabaret*. Go see it, or if you have seen it, see it again.

(December 12, 2015)

3

Education

2007–08

Go Fish!

No, not the card game. I occasionally use this phrase—he or she needs to go fish—as metaphor for what some so-called problem children in elementary schools should be allowed to do.

My source for the phrase is Daniel Greenberg's Sudbury Valley School,[1] which is located on a ten-acre estate in Massachusetts. One of the essential features of the school is that the children, ages four to nineteen, are free to do whatever they want, including fish all day in the property's pond, instead of attend classes. Indeed, classes are offered only at the request of students; education in the formal or traditional sense is entirely optional. The other essential feature is that large areas of the school's social and operational behavior, including the hiring and firing of staff, are regulated by democratic vote.

Precursor to this type of school is the much older Summerhill in England,[2] founded by A. S. Neill and now run by Neill's daughter. At Summerhill, though, traditional classes are regularly scheduled,

---

[1] Sudbury Valley School: Expect Excellence (website), sudval.org; "Sudbury Valley School," wikipedia.org; Daniel Greenberg, *Free at Last*, amazon.com.

[2] A. S. Neill's Summerhill (website), summerhillschool.co.uk; "Summerhill School," wikipedia.org; A. S. Neill, *Summerhill School*, amazon.com.

albeit optional, and somewhat more control, including the hiring and firing of staff, is maintained by the owner. Grades, exams, and standard diplomas are absent from both schools. Students who seek higher education are responsible for taking and passing high-school equivalency and college entrance exams.

Whatever one thinks of these two schools—and the opinion is not devoid of emotion—they have proven successful in educating students, or rather, as the proprietors are more likely to say, the students have educated themselves.

Sudbury Valley boasts that eighty percent of its graduates have gone on to college. It also has challenged several chestnuts of the educational establishment, such as the age at which children should learn to read and the length of time required to learn elementary-school arithmetic. Students at Sudbury have become competent readers as young as four and as old as eleven, with some early readers never continuing to read much after that and some late readers becoming voracious at the task. And six years of elementary-school arithmetic was learned by a dozen nine- to twelve-year-olds in twenty contact hours over twenty weeks.

The significance of the fish metaphor is that it represents the peace and quiet of getting completely away from the stresses of modern life, but, more specifically, it represents freedom from one major source of stress in young children's lives: the coercion of compulsory, government-run education. It also represents a reprieve from the nagging coercions of adults, whether they be parents or teachers.

The guiding premise of both schools, best stated by Greenberg when asked by a new student for advice about going to college, is: "You can do anything you want to do." You can, in other words, play cards all day, cook all day, take walks, read books, ask staff for a lesson—or fish. The causes of so-called problem children vary, but many are just plain bored of sitting at a desk in a classroom and are sick of having adults lord their size and power over them.

The choice of "doing nothing," which is "nothing" only in the eyes of adults who think young people should be sitting in traditional classrooms, enables children to relax and become more at peace with themselves and others. When they are ready, they can, if they so desire, choose to pursue other forms of learning and eventually think about what they want to do the rest of their lives. One boy at Sudbury Valley who fished nearly every day for several years became interested in computers at age fifteen. At seventeen he and two friends founded a computer sales and service company; he then went on to college and a career in computers. One boy at Summerhill who had never attended classes taught himself in his last year at the school to pass the university exams.

Equal dignity, or equal respect between adult and child, is what both Sudbury Valley and Summerhill offer their students. That is probably the appeal and success of the democratic meetings for which they are well known. Every member of the staff has only one vote, while the students run the meetings. Empowerment is not too strong a word to describe the effect this has on the students at all age levels. Self-directed, self-responsible young adults are what both schools produce.

Know any children who cannot sit still in a traditional classroom or who are always getting into trouble by being disruptive? My answer to those in charge is that for some of these children the answer may be: let them go fish.

(September 26, 2007)

On Judging the Quality of Today's Students

A FAVORITE PASTIME OF TODAY'S TEACHERS, especially college professors, is the trashing of their students.

"My students are terrible," is the common complaint. "They can't write, they can't calculate, and they can't think. They are woefully ignorant! They just don't measure up to the standards of the good old days when I was a student." And those "good old days," depending on the age of the critic, could be the 1940s, the '60s, or the '80s. Exaggeration aside, the complaint is that students today are not receiving the education that their predecessors did.

The facts, however, are a little more difficult to discern. Consider first of all that teachers have always complained about their students—"shop talk" style not unlike the complaints of sales representatives about their customers or employees about their bosses. Harvard Business School faculty in the 1950s complained about the math skills of their liberal-arts trained graduate students and a Harvard report in 1894 complained about grade inflation.[3]

I, too, have expressed complaints about my students' skills, especially the handling of decimals, but my A students do know where the decimal point goes and the others have a variety of reasons why they don't know or don't care to demonstrate that they do know. Interest or desire, after all, is a major factor in determining what people learn. Some, perhaps many, students just may not be interested in the subject of the complaining teachers' courses.

In my "good old days" of elementary school in the 1950s, it was common to have Jesuitical style contests at the chalkboard to see who could solve arithmetic problems the fastest. I was usually in the top three, but in a class of thirty-five students that leaves thirty-two who did not handle the math as well. Similarly for spelling. So what? Well, almost all of those thirty-two students at the time likely did not go on to college and some may not have graduated from high school; today, most of their counterparts are sitting in college classes.* Whatever one thinks of the normal curve as it applies to intelligence (or motivation), the lower ends of the curve are now in college and probably affecting test scores and grades (not that I think much of either) and demonstrating lesser knowledge and skill than I had back in those good old days.

This phenomenon could explain declining SAT scores (not that I think much of the SAT—it's no longer referred to as an aptitude test[4] and is not a strong predictor of college success[5]), as well as the lack of broad scale grade inflation that everyone assumes to exist. If grade inflation exists, it probably has occurred at the more elite institutions, the greater influx of weaker students in less prestigious schools keeping the grade point averages level or even declining.[6] As education and

---

[3] Cited in Alfie Kohn, "The Dangerous Myth of Grade Inflation," November 8, 2002, alfie.kohn.org.
[4] SAT, wikipedia.org.
[5] Francesca Fulciniti, "Does the SAT Predict Your College Success and Income?," September 21, 2015, blog.prepscholar.com.
[6] "Principal Indicators of Student Academic Histories in Postsecondary Education, 1972–2000," www2.ed.gov.

social critic Alfie Kohn[7] has said, "No one has ever demonstrated that students today get A's for the same work that used to receive B's or C's. We simply do not have the data to support such a claim."

What about the change in curricula? Curricula change all the time. Teaching and understanding of the Greek language in ancient Roman schools declined in the latter part of the Empire (and, no doubt, teachers of Greek back then complained that their students didn't know anything!). In the early nineteenth century US, the university core curriculum consisted of math, Latin and Greek language and literature, and a strong dose of protestant Christianity. Science and history did not appear until the last third of the nineteenth century. And western civilization courses did not appear until the 1920s. (Term projects, the attempt to give students some individual choice and initiative in education, are products of the progressives.)

I would, of course, like my students to be better informed about American and world history, but then again, I took two American history courses in junior and senior high school and at least one course on world history, but I only remember what I learned in college—when I was much more interested in the topic. And, oh yes, I was also taught, among other myths that George Washington chopped down a cherry tree[8] and threw a silver dollar across the Potomac River.[9] When I finally saw the Potomac as a young adult, I concluded, "Man, the Kansas City A's sure could have used GW's arm!"

And then there's the "cacophony of teaching" that Lawrence Cremin[10] (pp. 51–83) talked about in 1990. Teaching is everywhere, not just in the classroom. More so today with the internet. That Shakespeare's *Hamlet* in the early 1960s[11] (p. 35) was seen on television by more people in one night than had seen it since it was first performed in 1600 should make English teachers everywhere praise television, not just condemn it.

---

[7] Alfie Kohn, "The Dangerous Myth of Grade Inflation," November 8, 2002, alfiekohn.org.
[8] "George Washington Mythology," mountvernon.org.
[9] "First in War, First in Peace, First in Sports?," mountvernon.org.
[10] Lawrence Cremin, *Popular Education and Its Discontents*, amazon.com.
[11] Frank Stanton, *Great Issues Lecture: Mass Media and Mass Culture*, amazon.com.

158 • *Applying Principles*

Bottom line: it's not easy to compare today's students with their grandparents, especially when most of the grandparents did not attend college (or have television or the internet) and may have quit high school to go straight into a blue-collar job. (And most of my students' grandparents attended school, if at all, in Mexico, China, or Vietnam.) It is also important for teachers to introspect about their own motivations for complaining about students. Are teachers just patting themselves on the back for being smarter than their students?** Or are they genuinely concerned about teaching and, if so, why don't they focus on the minds they are presented with and work to stretch them as far as the minds are capable. In the course of a year, one or two of the minds just might get turned on to the subject or method of the teacher and become eager to learn more.

After all, was it not one or two teachers that turned on the present teachers to become teachers? That's how it happened for me. Inspiration, interest, motivation, method. Those are the fundamentals of a good teacher, not any particular subject matter. Get the light turned on in the student first. The subject matter will follow.

* Only 2% of the US population aged 18–24 was enrolled in college in 1900, 15% in 1949, 36% in 2000, and 41% in 2017.[12] Other calculations[13] indicate that 69% of high school graduates began college studies right after high school in 2018, whereas only 52% did in 1970—the implication being that the percentages were correspondingly smaller in earlier years.

** Teachers are motivated to learn. That's why they become teachers. They love their subjects and tend to expect everyone else to love it the same as they do (an unrealistic expectation). And, because of their motivation, most were good students, perhaps very good students, but the normal curve again, in motivation, never mind intelligence, means

---

[12] Thomas D. Snyder, ed., *120 Years of American Education: A Statistical Portrait*, nces.ed.gov; "Table 302.60: Percentage of 18- to 24-Year-Olds Enrolled in College, By Level of Institution and Sex and Race/Ethnicity of Student: 1970 through 2017," nces.ed.gov.

[13] "Table 302.10: Recent High School Completers and Their Enrollment in College, by Sex and Level of Institution: 1960 through 2018," nces.ed.gov.

that many of today's students are not going to give a hoot about what the teacher is teaching. I think the critics delude themselves if they think their classmates in the good old days learned the multiplication tables or correct spelling or history, etc., as well as they did.

(January 25, 2008)

Peddlers of Ideas

TEACHERS ARE PEDDLERS OF KNOWLEDGE AND IDEAS.

Well, that's what they would be in a free market in education and that's how they should think of themselves in today's government-run and government-controlled system.

In a free market in education teachers would be sales reps for their schools. Some might even be owner-entrepreneurs who hang out their shingles and then must recruit, i.e., sell, and service their paying customers by meeting the customers' needs and wants. If they condescend, are rude to their customers, and repeatedly flunk them out, they will lose business. Their incomes will decrease; eventually, they may be out of a job and have to look for a new line of work. That's how the free market operates.

In today's semi-free private-education market, teachers at Wichita Collegiate, a K-12 private school described in Robert Love's *How To Start Your Own School*[14] (chapter 7), frequently recommended dismissal of students for a variety of disciplinary and academic reasons, that is, until the board of trustees became concerned about losses of revenue resulting from the dismissals. The board told the teachers either to find new bodies to occupy their empty desks, take a reduction in salary, or innovate to find ways of reaching those students who were having problems. The last option is what most chose to do. Innovation—product development—is what the free market encourages. It is what today's teachers, especially those in the public sector, focus on least, because there is no incentive to do so. The board of trustees at Wichita Collegiate eventually put the teachers in charge of recruitment to encourage them to stay in touch with their markets.

---

[14] Robert Love, *How to Start Your Own School*, amazon.com.

I realize that many teachers today would consider it demeaning to be called a "peddler." I consider it a badge of honor. So what are the issues?

First, the essential distinguishing characteristics of peddling, selling, marketing, advertising, etc., are *not* lying, cheating, or manipulating in order to make a sale. Yes, some peddlers, sales people, marketers, and advertisers have been known to lie, cheat, and manipulate others. But so have some parents, teachers, journalists, and, oh yes, politicians. The essence of selling is persuasive communication, the process of influencing attitudes and behavior using techniques published nearly 2400 years ago in Aristotle's *Rhetoric*[15] (book I, chapter 2). Those techniques are the appeal to emotion (to what is valuable or important to the prospect), the offer of proof (of why a particular claim is made, i.e., reasoning, evidence), and an appeal to the credibility of the communicator (to the character and knowledge of the speaker). Lying, cheating, and manipulating do not show up in these techniques.

Second, catering to needs and wants does not mean giving students easy A's, zero homework, and the freedom to do whatever they please. (All three of these—absence of grades, actually, for the first one—may be appropriate in certain types of teaching or schools or at certain age levels.) Needs are requirements for the improvement of one's life; wants are optional tastes or preferences. There are some basic needs in education, such as reading, writing, and arithmetic, but thereafter which is need and which is want for any one person depends on that person's goals in life. The quadratic equation probably would be a need for someone who wants to become an engineer, but not for someone who wants to become a photographer or musician. If a teacher/sales rep in a free market wants to teach an esoteric course on medieval literature, then he or she will have to hustle hard to find the tiny segment that really wants to learn that subject. All other prospects will vote with their feet and take their business elsewhere.

Does this mean there will be no core curriculum in a free market in education? Quite possibly. Catering to needs and wants creates wide varieties of offerings, in addition to innovation that leads to continual improvement. The concept of core curriculum is a product of education czars who think they know what is best for everyone. The government

---

[15] Aristotle, *Rhetoric*, classics.mit.edu.

today does not run the clothing industry, but if it did, the "core curriculum" in clothing would probably be the Mao tunic.[16] Instead, our free market in clothing performs extremely well in getting our bodies covered and it does so in a bountiful assortment of styles, colors, and prices.

Catering to needs and wants is the challenging task of, first, identifying the needs and wants of one's customers, then carefully crafting products that will meet those needs and wants. The teacher who does this successfully year after year is a peddler par excellence and deserves praise, just as the entrepreneur who does the same year after year deserves praise. Peddlers of knowledge and ideas care about their customers. Tenured teachers who talk rudely to their paying customers, make little or no effort to reach slower students, and, at the college level, draw the blinds of their office windows so students cannot tell whether they are in—during posted office hours—do not care much for their students. They certainly are not peddlers of ideas.

(July 17, 2008)

The Child As Small Adult

THE EDUCATION LITERATURE since at least Rousseau[17] has cautioned against viewing the child as a small adult. The meaning of the phrase, however, is not totally clear.

"Small adult" usually means that children are viewed as adults in miniature, that is, as small in height and weight and weak in physical strength, but otherwise as possessing an adult brain that is merely absent content. The job of educators and parents, then, is to fill that brain with knowledge to move the children, as they reach maturity, up to the level of educated adults.

The problem with this view is that the children obviously do not possess adult brains. And most parents and teachers have a sense that this is correct, namely that the brains of children are as immature as their bodies, that their cognitive capacities and abilities vary by age and among each other at the same age, and that pace of learning and interest determine what and how much any particular child will learn

---

[16] "Mao Suit," wikipedia.org.
[17] Jean-Jacques Rousseau, *Emile, or On Education*, amazon.com.

at any particular time. This is what the concept of "stages of development"[18] is all about.

Yet adults continue to demand that children learn the way they, the adults, think they learned, by attempting to stuff the brains of children with knowledge the children are not ready for or interested in and by expecting this learning to take place and be completed at one time. I say "think they learned" because I doubt that many adults in fact learned the way the adults expect their children to learn.

The worst mistake adults make when relating to children is to demand obedience to authority. "Learn your multiplication tables or there will be a consequence." "Pick up your clothes, or else . . ." Adults may or may not be consciously aware of acting on this premise, and sometimes it may be an act of desperation when nothing else works, but demanding obedience to authority is not nice when made either to children or to other adults. It is the demands of a dictator or authoritarian mentality; I'll assume a more innocent motivation in adults for the rest of this discussion.

A widely common mistake that adults make in relating to children is what I call "one-time learning." It manifests itself often in the (sometimes angry, sometimes exasperated) question, "What did I just tell you?" The question can be asked about anything, ranging from multiplication facts to dirty clothes on the floor to catching a softball with two hands. The assumption is that the child has been informed—the knowledge has been put into the brain; therefore, he or she should be able to instantly grasp, retain, and act on what was just "learned."

Such expectation, however, is patently absurd. Adults do not as adults, and did not as children, learn that way. Experienced teachers know that two requirements of good teaching are repetition and patience, for the variety of reasons mentioned in the third paragraph above. Some children are just not ready to learn what the adults seem to think they should be learning right now. And others are just not interested in learning that great wisdom of the adults. What the experiments of Summerhill and Sudbury Valley Schools[19] have demonstrated

---

[18] Hansa D. Bhargava, "Piaget Stages of Development," webmd.com.
[19] A. S. Neill's Summerschool (website), summerhillschool.co.uk; Sudbury Valley School: Expect Excellence (website), sudval.org; see above, "Go Fish!," p. 153.

is that children, when left free to pursue their own interests, will in fact learn to read, do arithmetic, and even go on to college, but not on the schedule that adult educators think they should be on.

This last was made obvious to me recently in my duties as assistant coach of my daughter's softball team. One of the coach's jobs is to repeatedly shout to the girls to use two hands when catching the ball, which they seldom do. A couple of weeks ago, I noticed, without my chiding, one girl (eight years old) all of a sudden was catching with two hands. Subsequently, in a game, she even made a semi-spectacular two-handed catch of a pop fly. Lesson learned, by the adult! Children march to their own drummer when it comes to learning. Something clicked in the girl's mind that I could not have predicted. One-time learning certainly did not produce the result.

On the other side of the coin, adults who treat children as small adults often fail to grant them the cognitive capacities and abilities that they in fact do have. Montessori[20] demonstrated this abundantly by teaching children to read at age four and by teaching lower elementary children geometry, algebra, and history, among other subjects that the education establishment long ago relegated to much later ages. Children desperately want to grow up and become adults, but adults have to allow them to do so, at their own pace and when they are interested enough to learn the ways of the adult.

The bottom line of the issue of viewing children as small adults is that children need to be viewed as children, not more than they are and not less than they are. And each child has to be viewed as a unique individual with unique desires and abilities. Recognizing and responding to those uniquenesses is one of the traits that separates teachers from those who would appear to be dictators.

(October 23, 2008)

2009

Interest and the Core Curriculum

IN DISCUSSIONS OF CURRICULUM over the past one hundred or so years, debate has ranged from letting children choose entirely what

---

[20] "Montessori Education," wikipedia.org.

they want to study, guided only by their interests, to forced memorization of the encyclopedia, usually called the core curriculum. "Memorizing the encyclopedia" might be a harsh characterization, but some die-hard core-curriculum advocates would not object to it.

The question is, when you take the church and state out of education and replace it with a free market, what would the curriculum be? The answer is whatever the market decides, that is, whatever the parents and students decide they want to pay money for. Just like what we find in the automobile market. The parallel question is, what would cars be like if we let the free market decide? Well, we have a (relatively) free market in automobiles today, so we have big cars, small cars, fast ones, expensive ones, cheap ones, and so on. We have an enormous variety of cars but most of us do have cars and we manage to get around town and country without much hassle. Actually, with considerable satisfaction. (Those of us who don't have cars choose other means of transportation, including walking.)

The core curriculum is a one-size-fits-all strategy and assumes that someone—an education czar or panel of education experts—knows what is best for our children. In automobiles, this strategy would give us one design, one engine, one type of tire, interior, color. Maybe a modest variety of styles—two or three at most—but none that the market actually wants, only what the "experts" think they should want. In education, thoughts of letting parents and children choose what they want unleashes panic screams from the core curriculum crowd about how parents will seek out all sorts of weird ideas, or perhaps not educate their children at all, and the children will go for easy A's and no homework. The assumption guiding the notion of a core curriculum remains that only one institution, the government, can require such a curriculum and that at the point of a gun.

A little history shows that force does not need to be brought into the curriculum debate. Hellenistic Greece is the origin of our current three-part structure broken into primary, secondary, and higher education. Governments in the ancient world rarely interfered with the educational process. Fathers paid teachers to educate their sons. The curriculum? Greeks called it *enkyklios paideia* or general education. Romans translated it at as *artes liberalis* or liberal arts. Today, we might also call this an education in western civilization. Higher education in the ancient world split into two factions that we still have to this day: professional education (rhetoric, medicine, law) versus knowledge for its own sake (philosophy). Weird ideas and easy A's? There were mystery cults but they did not dominate the education system. And there was no grading, examination, or credential system at all. That is a product of the medieval guilds and the rise of modern bureaucracy.

Another assumption of the core curriculum advocates, especially those who would require specific textbooks and lectures on western civilization, is that the students who are coerced to be in those classroom seats would actually read the book and listen to the lectures. It is obvious to anyone who teaches in the present system that many, and sometimes most, do not do this even in elective courses. The coercive, bureaucratic environment of modern education kills interest in all but the strongest, most purpose-driven students.

Let the parents decide. Let the students decide. Summerhill and Sudbury Valley Schools have amply demonstrated how wide-ranging freedom and learning guided by interest can lead to a satisfying education for one's chosen purpose in life.[21] The students' education in these schools may not match the pristine dictates of the core curriculum advocates, but it does match the students' needs and wants. That's what capitalism is all about.

And that brings us to the "weird ideas" that core curriculum advocates fear. The problem is that "weird" depends on who you are talking to. Some fear that atheism might be taught to the young. Others fear that it might be religion. Others fear capitalism and the greedy, selfish profit motive being taught. Still others fear communism will become the core curriculum.

And therein lies the heart of the issue. Core curriculum advocates want to control the minds of the young with their particular ideas. They want their ideas to rule. When enforced by the government, however, there is only one name that can be given to the core

---

[21] A. S. Neill's Summerschool (website), summerhillschool.co.uk; Sudbury Valley School: Expect Excellence (website), sudval.org; see above, "Go Fish!," p. 153.; see above, "Peddlers of Ideas," p. 159.

curriculum: censorship. It forces out or removes to the margin all other ideas. Students' and the students' parents do not get to choose.

Let the market decide.

(September 8, 2009)

The Primacy of Method

THE PROGRESSIVE EDUCATION GOAL of teaching students how to think, as opposed to teaching them a particular content, does not mean that content is omitted or ranked third, fourth, or fifth in the hierarchy. It does not even mean that content is ranked second, for as John Dewey put it in one of his occasional business metaphors, subject matter is the working capital of thought. Taken literally, a business is not viable if it does not have working capital. In Dewey's usage, the metaphor means: no subject matter, no thought.

If learning how to think conceptually—in principles and without a dichotomy between abstractions and concretes—is correctly taught, content must be included to have something to think conceptually about. The key point about primacy of method is that the content does not have to be any particular content or "core curriculum." This is in contrast to traditional education that puts curriculum first.

This is also not to say that teaching how to think is not a subject matter in its own right. It is. The principles of logical thinking, generalization, application, and the creative process are content that can and should be taught throughout secondary and higher education. The problem is that the progressive movement of the twentieth century never rigorously taught the principles of thinking. In its place it put poorly designed and controlled group projects, a barrage of failed reforms,[22] and often little if any well-organized content.

Nevertheless, the primacy of method, or teaching students how to think well, is the essential distinguishing characteristic of progressive education when it is compared to the traditional or conservative form. Indeed, the aim of the great education reformers in history, beginning with Quintilian and even including the Jesuits, was, as formulated by

---

[22] Diane Ravitch, *Left Back*, amazon.com.

Rousseau, to see the child as a child, not as a smaller version[23] of the adult. This means in particular to see the child's mind as a child's mind, hence the need for specialized techniques to develop young thought processes. It includes being nice to the child and catering to the child's interests.

"Being nice" can be viewed as symbolic of the progressive emphasis on the "whole child." The two phrases, however, mean a lot more than the clichéd versions sound. They emphasize, in addition to not physically or mentally punishing the child, the need to be aware of the child's psychology and to encourage the adoption of life-advancing self-confident premises. The extended meaning of "whole child" is the development of an unobstructed mental and emotional life that produces independent, not just sound, judgment. Content must be there in the child's brain, but stuffing it or furnishing the "empty vessel" with a prescribed core curriculum is not the primary goal of education. Teaching students sensible decision making (sound judgment) and the ability to perceive facts as facts and, more importantly, especially in the face of opposition, the willingness to act on those facts (independent judgment) is. Content follows, driven by parent and student, not bureaucratic, interest.

When parents and students are allowed to determine content by buying and abstaining from buying the services of entrepreneurial teachers who are unhampered by the dictates of educational bureaucrats, a system of progressive education can be fully achieved. It is for this reason that I would describe the theory of concentrated attention and independent judgment detailed in *Montessori, Dewey, and Capitalism*[24] as a theory of progressive education without the state. Interference of the state in education—by forcibly dictating what will be learned and how it will be learned, by forcibly expropriating funds from some to pay for the education of others, and by forcibly compelling children to attend school at all—thwarts and destroys the aim of catering to the needs and interests of the child. Only a free market in education that bans the initiation of physical force against parents, students, and entrepreneurs would make it possible for this aim to be accomplished.

---

[23] See above, "The Child as Small Adult," p. 161.
[24] Jerry Kirkpatrick, *Montessori, Dewey and Capitalism*, amazon.com.

Primacy of method means that education is aimed at the development of the mind. A mind well trained in the functions that are its distinctive nature, namely the correct perception and evaluation of the facts of reality and the guidance of behavior based on those correct perceptions and evaluations, is a mind that has been trained in method. It is one that has been taught how to think. Content is acquired and accumulated in the process but it is not primary.

(October 9, 2009)

Education and the Rent Control Model of Monopoly

EDUCATION IN THE UNITED STATES TODAY is a monopoly, as is the supply of rental apartments in many cities. Monopoly is the restriction of a portion of a market for the exclusive use of certain select sellers at the expense of other sellers who are forbidden entrance into these markets. It is a government-granted privilege.[25]

The delivery of first class mail is the most obvious privilege granted to the US Postal Service. When teenage entrepreneurs have attempted to compete with the post office, they have been ruthlessly put out of business by the feds. But monopoly does not have to be a single seller. It can be a monopoly of the many, as occurs in occupational licensing where the goal is to restrict supply in order to increase prices and therefore income for those who are granted the license.

In government-run monopolies, such as education, the goal is to keep price low and the supply widely available. Inefficiencies that result from the top-down, non-market focus of bureaucratic management[26] in turn lead to high costs that are subsidized by the government. The effect is to freeze out private-sector competition—if it is legal in the first place to compete with the government-run schools. In some countries it is not. If a private-sector system of schools is allowed to exist,

---

[25]George Reisman, *Capitalism*, chap. 10, amazon.com.
[26]See below, "On Extrinsic Motivation, Bureaucracy, and the Stage-Mother Syndrome," p. 327.

the costs of private education often require a quite high price.²⁷ This is what we have today in the United States and it is analogous to the rent control markets²⁸ in such cities as New York and Berkeley and Santa Monica, California. The only difference is that the controlled apartment buildings are privately owned. City housing²⁹ removes the need to call the comparison analogous.

The privilege granted to the operators of government-run schools consists of far more than the obvious lack of competition. It creates a guild of teachers and administrators who work primarily for the benefit of their own needs and wants, not those of their students. As Adam Smith put it over two hundred years ago, referring to publicly financed higher education³⁰:

> In the university of Oxford, the greater part of the public professors have, for these many years, given up altogether even the pretence of teaching.

And:

> The discipline of the colleges and universities is in general contrived, not for the benefits of the students, but for the interest, or more properly speaking, for the ease of the masters. Its object is, in all cases, to maintain the authority of the master, and whether he neglects or performs his duty, to oblige the students, in all cases to behave to him as if he performed it with the greatest diligence and ability.

In the privileged comfort of tenure and salary guarantees, most of today's K-12 and college teachers seldom, if ever, have to face real competition. Opposite the intended goal of a widely available supply, bureaucratic inefficiencies and indifference create large class sizes and shortages of instructors such that students bang down the teachers'

---

²⁷ "Dozens More Colleges Pass the $50,000 Mark This Year," November 1, 2009, chronicle.com. The dollar amount is for total cost of attendance, not just tuition. [Today, in 2021, the figure is more like $70,000.]
²⁸ Walter Block, "Rent Control," econlib.org.
²⁹ "Public Housing," wikipedia.org.
³⁰ Adam Smith, *An Inquiry into the Nature and Causes of the Wealth of Nations*, Book V, chapter I, part III, article II, gutenberg.org.

doors begging to get into the classes that are scheduled—not because the students want to learn from the great masters, but because they need the units. Government involvement in education creates a situation in which sellers do not have to do anything to attract customers. Some sellers—the teachers—find the door banging annoying and the students a nuisance. Niceness, cordiality, and, generally, concern for the customers' needs and wants, as a result, often go out the window. The same is true of rent-controlled apartment house superintendents.

The solution to both education and rental housing is decontrol and privatization. The privatization of the education market and the decontrol and privatization of the rental apartment market would at once increase the supply and variety of schools and rental apartments, because anyone would be free to begin offering these services and would be free to do so at a profit. The disparity between the current private and public sector prices would converge, because the abnormally high prices of the private sector would immediately drop due to the immediately increased supply (or promise of such increase).

In a free market real prices decline over time. As efficiencies and innovations emerge in the newly deregulated education and rental apartment markets, prices—in terms of the number of labor hours required to purchase a unit of the service—would also decline. Customer satisfaction would become the means to earning a profit. Niceness, cordiality, and catering to the needs and wants of the customer, not airs of guild-like smugness and superiority or indifference, would become primary.

(November 16, 2009)

Education in One Lesson

UNJUSTLY NEGLECTED, DIFFICULT-TO-FIND, and significantly influential on my own work, *The Real Academic Community and the Rational Alternative*[31] by Thomas L. Johnson is a kind of "education in one lesson." Like Henry Hazlitt's gem[32] on economics, Johnson's

---

[31] Thomas L. Johnson, *The Real Academic Community and The Rational Alternative*, amazon.com.

[32] Henry Hazlitt, *Economics in One Lesson*, amazon.com.

begins with the lesson and then illustrates it abundantly throughout the remaining chapters.

The lesson? That schools today (and since antiquity) are institutions not of learning, but of authoritarianism. Force and fear reign supreme. Administrators and instructors "are the authority figures who must be obeyed in every respect, and students, who are the 'peasants' in this establishment, must try in every way to please those who rule over them." In short, students "must please the schools, colleges or universities, instead of these institutions having to please the students." The power of the book is in its illustrations of the lesson and in the free-market alternative that Johnson proposes.

From the primary and secondary school level:

Discipline. The authoritarian setting, says Johnson, works against the possibility of order in the classroom. Students are forced to be there by law, directly in the lower grades and indirectly in the higher, by the hampering of a free market through regulation. As a result, "almost everything in the classroom is done by means of orders and threats." The students are ordered to perform certain tasks and threatened with low or failing grades if they don't comply. Cornered rats—and prisoners—rebel when squeezed too hard. Schools are scholastic prisons and teachers are the guards and wardens paid to keep order.

Drugs. In the authoritarian climate of today's schools, where the "customers" are not permitted to pursue their own interests, boredom, resentment, confusion, and low self-esteem frequently result. Drugs are seen by some students as a way to relieve their feelings of hopelessness.

Violence. "Force is the hallmark of any authoritarian establishment whether this be a state or an institution. And wherever there is force there will always be acts of violence. They are inevitable companions."

Cheating. Anyone who has been through today's school system knows that knowledge is not what is being marketed. "Students, recognizing that good grades and a diploma are what is really valuable to them, will often not hesitate to cheat in order to obtain these primary 'goods' which the teachers and schools are really selling."

At the college level, Johnson has this to say:

Degrees. "It is because institutions of learning give out diplomas or grant degrees that they operate in an authoritarian manner. It is because the students must please the teachers and professors, as well as the institutions, in their attempt to 'win' the certificates of graduation that allows the schools, colleges and universities to be the dictatorial institutions that they are.... The professor orders the students to perform certain tasks—read certain assignments, write specific papers or reports, give designated oral presentations, etc.—and the students either follow these orders, or else." Professors hold the degree up for ransom and their red ink pens are their guns.

Student Government. Why does it exist? Because students "realized that matters were often in need of change at the college or university and so they decided to band together in the attempt to see what they could do to bring about the desired changes." In a free market, dissatisfied customers can stimulate change in a supplying business rather quickly, or else a new one will soon be on the scene to meet the needs of the dissatisfied buyers. But schools are not free enterprises. "All student government could really do was to petition, that is to beg, the administration or Board for favors—like changes in rigid social rules—that would make life at a bit more bearable."

Academic Freedom and Tenure. Similar to the plight of students in an authoritarian climate, professors organized to protect themselves against administrations. They demanded and got the privilege of lifetime employment and the license to say and write whatever they please (as long as it is consistent with state or administration dogma). In a free market, employees who disagree with their employers simply leave and go elsewhere, and perhaps start their own businesses. Education, however, is not a business; there is nowhere for the professors to go.

Titles and Robes. Johnson discusses other issues, such as honor systems, academic and social probation, dress codes, hazing, and school spirit. His crowning achievement, however, is his comment on titles and robes.

"But what do titles signify?" asks Johnson, titles such as "Doctor" and "Dean." He answers:

> Titles signify power, prestige and authority, and they have always been used to instill fear in others—to con others into thinking that the titled personage is someone special

and better than others who must be looked up to and obeyed.... Titles... are almost always found where there is some degree of tyranny.

How about academic regalia—

> all those Medieval robes, caps and hoods?... It is true that certain businesses do have their employees dressed in similar outfits, or many businesses have a particular character, like a clown, dressed in a certain way and acting as a representative or symbol of the business. But one does not find, as one does in the academic community, a group of academic "clowns"—the professors, administrators, and board members—dressed in Medieval clerical garb forming and marching in academic processions that look almost identical to religious processions....
>
> Titles and robes are always found wherever one group of people is trying to lord it over another group of people. Kings and dictators get themselves up in fancy costumes and demand that they be called by an array of titles. Military and academic personnel do the same. But not businessmen. They do not, and cannot, lord it over customers. They must win the favor of customers by demonstrating their talent and ability. Talents and robes are of no help in a rational and healthy business environment.

The rational alternative to this forceful, fearful authoritarianism is a free market of educational businesses—"private, profit-making and openly competing enterprises that are only selling instruction, not grades and degrees.... There would be no entrance requirements and no prerequisites.... There would be *no grades* and *no diplomas or certificates*." (Johnson's emphasis.) The customers would evaluate the sellers much as is done in free-market businesses today. Teachers, the peddlers of knowledge and ideas,[33] would not evaluate the customers.

(December 17, 2009)

---

[33] See above, "Peddlers of Ideas," p. 159.

2010

"You Can Get It in the Book"

MANY YEARS AGO, while being interviewed by a dean for an academic position, I became engaged in a discussion of the philosophy of education. The dean tossed out as if it were self-evident: "The lecture has been obsolete for 500 years, since the invention of the printing press. Students can read the book." His assumption was that lectures were needed in the pre-printing press era when books were rare and expensive, but not today when they are plentiful.

While it is true that with careful reading and study one can "get it in the book," this neglects differences between written and oral presentations, between reading and speaking. These differences give rise to the true benefit of the lecture and explain why it has not died out in 500 years.

The average rate of reading[34] with comprehension by an adult is about 250–300 words per minute. The average speaking speed[35] is about 125 words per minute, and CBS Evening News anchorman Walter Cronkite[36] spoke at the exact rate per minute of 124 words. Casual conversation is often faster, but the point about the lecture is that formal oral presentations are delivered at half the rate, or less, of the average reading speed.

This means that less information can be presented orally in one minute than what can be read in the same amount of time. Less information in an oral presentation means essentialization. A lecture that essentializes a text makes it easier for the listener to grasp the main points of the written content. With the main points in hand, the listener can then pursue a more detailed study of the written material without first having to read and study at length to separate the essential from the nonessential. The advantage of the lecture is its efficiency; it saves time.

Whether the speaker deliberately essentializes the presentation or not, the listener hears it as essentialized, as important. The detail in the text is understood as detail. This means that it matters what gets

---

[34] "Words Per Minute," wikipedia.org.
[35] "Rate Is Speed of Speaking Measured in Words Per Minute," lumen.instructure.com.
[36] "Walter Cronkite," wikipedia.org.

selected as essential in the oral presentation. It makes the difference between good, bad, and indifferent lectures.

The efficiency of the lecture, of course, can also be achieved in conversation with an expert or mentor. The real advantage of the lecture is its ability to broadcast large amounts of essentialized material to many listeners at one time. Does this mean that everyone in the audience learns and digests the material in exactly the same way, one hundred percent? Hardly.

The comprehension and learning of listeners to a lecturer is exactly analogous to the comprehension and appreciation of listeners to a string quartet concert. One member of the quartet's audience might be tone deaf. The next might be a professional violinist from another group who frequently plays the same pieces as those being performed on stage. Similarly, some students in my classes come in with D-'s in their prerequisite courses. Others come in with A's. Most are somewhere in between. Audience members—of lectures and string quartet concerts—take away from the experience what they want, and are able, to take away.

Fine tuning may or may not be desired. In education, it usually is, which is why Jacques Barzun[37] declared, "A lecture is a sizing of the canvas in broad strokes. The fine brush and palette knife must be used close up to finish the work of art" and why Gilbert Highet[38] argued that the only two methods of teaching are the lecture and tutorial.

The purpose and value of the lecture is mass communication. The purpose and value of the tutorial is personal communication and individual attention. Though some, perhaps many, of a lecturer's audience may not absorb everything the lecturer intended, a few listeners may be motivated to study the subject in more detail, just as concertgoers may be stimulated to buy CD's of the works performed and listen to them many times over in order to learn them thoroughly.

The lecture is part of the division of labor in education. The tutorial is the other part.

(January 22, 2010)

---

[37] Jacques Barzun, *Teacher in America*, p. 39, amazon.com.
[38] Gilbert Highet, *The Art of Teaching*, chap. 3, amazon.com.

The Factory Model of Education, Technocracy, and the Free School Movement

THE AMERICAN FREE SCHOOL MOVEMENT of the 1960s and early '70s[39] arose as a rebellion against the oppressive authoritarianism of state-run education, that is, the top-down, coercive, follow-the-rules and -rubrics mentality that dictates from on high what has to be done in the classroom. Various writers have referred to this authoritarian system, among other terms, as a technocracy and a "factory model" of education.

That is to say that business and capitalism usually take the blame for the authoritarianism. The last thing that free school advocates would propose is a free market in education. Yet there is much to be admired in the work of the founders of free schools: their emphasis, in particular, on decentralized organization and catering to the needs and interests of the child. Democratic management of the schools, which no doubt empowers the children, may or may not flourish in a free-market system.

The notion of free schools goes back at least to the work of a young Leo Tolstoy,[40] who disliked the rigidity and sterility of the European schools. The proponents of the idea, however, are mistaken about the role of business and capitalism in producing the authoritarian atmosphere they are rejecting. The factory model of education, for example, has a badly misunderstood history. Some say that the entire American public education system, dating from its beginnings in the 1840s, was modeled on the factory system. Students, it is said, are products produced assembly-line style, then sold to the highest bidder in the labor market.*

The factory model, however, is an early twentieth-century phenomenon, coexistent with the rise of progressive education but not an essential characteristic of it. Labor productivity and efficiency were the focus of so-called scientific management.[41] These ideas—many of them needed at the time, as management of any kind was not well understood as a skill or taught—were transferred to the administration of public schools.

---

[39] "Free School Movement," wikipedia.org; Ronald J. Miller, *Free Schools, Free People*, amazon.com.

[40] "Leo Tolstoy," wikipedia.org; Bob Blaisdell, ed., *Tolstoy as Teacher*, amazon.com.

[41] "Scientific Management," wikipedia.org; Raymond E. Callahan, *Education and the Cult of Efficiency*, amazon.com.

The problem was (and is) that public schools are bureaucratic, top-down, coercive institutions. Businesses are not. Businesses operating in a free market have a built-in measure of efficiency: profit earned through customer satisfaction. Bureaucracies measure their success by reference to the higher authorities in government who set the rules, laws, and budget. That is the source of the authoritarian atmosphere of public education. The factory model is bad analogy. The product of education is knowledge, values, and skills; the students are paying customers.

Technocracy[42] was a movement in the 1930s that advocated using scientists and engineers to run government (and, therefore, the control and regulation of business). It gave us the phrase "social engineering." The free school movement of the 1960s brought the term back to refer to the authoritarian nature of public education. This is not incorrect because technocracy is a species of bureaucracy and bureaucrats, whether expert scientists and engineers or not, call the shots over their subordinates. It is unfortunate that the free school advocates do not see the connection between technocracy or bureaucracy and governmental coercion. It is only the free market that would fully allow them to pursue their goals without further authoritarian influence from outside.

Indeed, John Holt[43] did come to the conclusion that the only valid form of education safe from corrupting influences is home schooling, an autarchic withdrawal from the world at large. Holt never did advocate, nor would have advocated, capitalism. Other free schoolers think that their model of small, decentralized child-centered schools should become the model of public education, replacing the current authoritarian behemoths. They fail to see that any cooperation with the coercive apparatus of bureaucratic government requires compliance to rules and laws. Even charter schools that supposedly are freed from some of those rules still succumb to political football tossing and regulation. Many fail to maintain their original missions.[44]

The upshot of schooling is that schools are not factories that produce goods. They are high-traffic service firms analogous to entertainment

---

[42] "Technocracy Movement," wikipedia.org.
[43] "John Holt (Educator)," wikipedia.org.
[44] Timothy Egan, "Failures Raise Questions for Charter Schools," April 5, 2002, nytimes.com; "Charter School," wikipedia.org.

businesses. Some entertainment companies, such as concert halls and sports stadiums, provide their services to thousands of people at one time. Others provide individual services, one customer at a time. There is no reason to assume that a free market in education would not provide its services on a similar scale. The methods of delivery would be the lecture and the tutorial. Customers would be free to choose which services, as described, in combination, or in other variations, they would like to buy. The market would decide. No authority would oversee, control, or regulate.

* I have heard college professors refer to their students as work in progress. When the students graduate, they are finished goods. A better description of environmental determinism—the molding of the child's clay mind by an outside authority—could not be given. Hopefully, such professorial comments are bad metaphor, rather than serious descriptions.

(February 15, 2010)

Teaching versus Learning versus Doing

MUCH INK HAS BEEN SPILLED for decades over the concepts of teaching, learning, and doing, producing such commonplaces as "learning by doing is the best way to learn" and "let's focus on learning, not teaching." A couple of clarifications, however, need to be made about both of these remarks.

Consider the first one. Learning and doing, epistemologically and psychologically, are two different mental processes. They never occur precisely at the same time. Learning is the acquisition of knowledge, doing is application. Acquisition is generalization, application is deduction from the general to employ the deduction in a specific concrete situation. A child learns the generalization of balance, of shifting one's weight, when riding a bicycle. The child applies that knowledge in practice to perfect the skill. Learning comes before doing, perhaps from a parent or older sibling who is teaching the concept of balance or through trial-and-error learning. Sometimes it might occur a split second before the doing but it still comes before.

Trial-and-error learning proceeds in this manner. Try one thing. It doesn't work. Try something else. It doesn't work. But there may be similarities in the two actions that did not work sufficient to make a primitive generalization. Deduction from the generalization then follows to try a new action. It doesn't work perfectly, but it works better than the previous failures. More trial, error, generalization, deduction, and further trial then ensue. Some learners are quick to pick up through observation what has to be done to execute a new skill; others are not. The point, however, is that ideas—no matter how primitive or unformed, or even how unaware the actor may be of the ideas—precede action. Add to this that ingrained mental and/or physical habits may have to be challenged and changed before the skill can be developed.

The significance of teaching before doing is to save the time that can be wasted when going through repeated efforts of trial and error. It also may prevent injury that can result from uninformed trial and error, such as, without instruction, learning to ride a bicycle or operate a complicated piece of machinery. "Learn-by-doing"—when understood to mean *practice*—is essential to perfecting a skill, mental or physical, but mental understanding, even of a mental skill like logical thinking, comes first.

This takes us to the comment about focusing on learning, not teaching. To teach, however, means to effect learning, to see to it that the students understand and can apply what has been taught. Even the standard definition of teaching—the transfer of knowledge from one person to another—indicates that teaching is not achieved until learning has been accomplished.

Some of the desire, no doubt, to emphasize learning over teaching comes from distrust of the lecture[45] as a legitimate teaching method, but a well crafted lecture framed in essentials and delivered with conviction can effect a great deal of learning in its listeners. More generally, the comment most likely stems from the tired indifference to teaching and learning, not to mention overt rudeness, exhibited by many tenured teachers and professors. The state-run school and university systems do not cater to the needs and wants of their customers. Yet that is precisely what the focus on learning means.

---

[45] See above, "You Can Get It in the Book," p. 174.

In marketing—and teachers, as I have written before, are sales reps[46]—a notion called the "marketing concept" says that everyone in the company, from the president to the stock boy, should not make any decision or take any action without first considering its effects on the customer. "We are no longer in the business of selling what we make," General Electric said many years ago, "but making only what we can sell." This means, quite simply, whether one is a writer, a teacher, or a sales rep: "know thy audience." Know where the students are now in the learning process, then challenge them by stretching. But the stretching cannot go too far because that produces discouragement and it cannot be too elementary because that creates boredom. Finding the middle ground is what teaching to effect learning is all about. It is not an easy task. It requires constant observation of the students and adaptation to the their needs.

Focusing on learning is what every good teacher should routinely do. Teaching and learning are separate activities, performed by different people. The teacher teaches, the learner learns. But the teacher knows what and how to teach by first tuning into the learner. Anything else is whistling in the wind.

(March 24, 2010)

Rankism and the Well-Earned Disrespect of Some Teachers

IN THE ANCIENT WORLD, teachers were not respected. "He's either dead or else he's teaching somewhere" was a comment made in a comedy fragment about someone missing from a gathering. And Lucian [47] relegated a dethroned king to Hades to sell salt or old boots . . . or to become a teacher.[48] Making money on the market—teachers were paid a fee for their services—was disparaged. Not until the Judeo-Christian influence did teachers begin to gain respect.

---

[46] See above, "Peddlers of Ideas," p. 133.
[47] "Lucian," wikipedia.org.
[48] Cited in H. I. Marrou, part two, chap. 5, *A History of Education in Antiquity*, amazon.com.

Today, teachers are admired, not just for the service they provide to educate the young, but for their seemingly tireless dedication to long hours of preparation and their equally seemingly tireless patience to answer repetitive questions. Unfortunately, not all teachers return the admiration to their students, colleagues, and administrative assistants, which leads to sniping complaints from outsiders about privilege and long vacations.

The root of this lack of respect is what former Oberlin College president, Robert Fuller, calls rankism or the abuse of rank.[49] The disrespect is deserved, for the rankism manifests itself as expressions of power over and taking advantage of those not at the same level of authority. For example, a professor may write an email explaining why an administrative assistant should drop everything and copy his receipts from a recent academic trip. The assistant works for the chair of the department, not the individual faculty, but the professor goes to great length to explain why his time is more valuable than the assistant's—not in the least noticing that in the time it took him to compose and edit the email he could have copied his own receipts. Such manual labor, apparently, is beneath his dignity, but not that of the "lowly" administrative assistant.

Other forms of condescension by senior faculty include failing so much as to say hello to a part-time instructor or interrupting without apology a conversation between a part-time instructor and the chair of the department, with the part-timer seeing nothing but the interrupter's back. Political power play is how some might cynically or even approvingly describe the senior professor's behavior. Childish disingenuousness might be another description. Or the behavior might be characterized as the desperate quest for approval of a defensively frail ego because, as I have written before, the stakes in the academic world are so small.[50]

Rankism toward students is legion. In the absence of corporal punishment, verbal abuse has become the tool of putting students in their places. An "appalling lack of civility" is how Charles Silberman[51] in 1970 described the contempt that teachers and principals exhibit

---

[49] Dignity Works (website), breakingranks.net; Robert W. Fuller, *Somebodies and Nobodies*, amazon.com; see above, "The Market Gives Privilege to No One," p. 25.
[50] See above, "Because the Stakes Are So Small," p. 133.
[51] Charles Silberman, *Crisis in the Classroom*, amazon.com.

toward their students. Sarcasm, ridicule, and just plain rudeness seem to be the preferred means of pulling rank today, such as sternly telling a ten-year-old that she is still a child until the age of eighteen. This ignores and devalues the intelligence of the ten-year-old who knows well that one does not automatically become an adult by celebrating a birthday; it also ignores and devalues the maturity of the ten-year-old who considers a child to be younger than six. The effect of the rudeness is to deflate developing self-esteem and silence opposition or disagreement.

One of the worst forms of rankism that a teacher can pull is to talk in class negatively about others who are not present to defend themselves. Such behavior is beyond rude and childish. It is unethical. It certainly is none of the students' business what the teacher thinks about other students, teachers, or administrative assistants. But such behavior does happen in the cocoon-tenured environment of the academic world. The teacher will not be fired, but the students and administrative assistants who are talked about may be harmed. Sometimes, unfortunately, that is even the intent of the negative talk.

Fuller's campaign against rankism is to establish a new meaning of equality. It does not mean, he says, equality of ability, knowledge, intelligence, or position or rank. It means equality of dignity. It means treating others, regardless of age or rank (or race, gender, nationality, etc.), as human beings. In the military world, a soldier's general is a commander who treats those under him with care and kindness. A player's coach exhibits the same toward his athletes. Kindness and respect are what those in authority need to exude toward those in a lower rank. It means being nice.

(June 21, 2010)

2011–12

Control and Choice in Education

IN EDUCATION THERE EXISTS A CONTINUUM of how much control is exerted over students or, to put it another way, how much choice is given to them. The scale ranges from the total control and minimal choice of state-run traditional education to the considerable freedom to choose given to students of such alternative schools as Summerhill[52] and Sudbury Valley.[53] With their cleverly designed didactic materials and the choice of which materials to work on, Montessori[54] schools probably fall somewhere in between.

Teachers in all schools vary according to how much control they will exert in the implementation of their school's ideology and how much choice they will give the students. So even an American public school classroom can enjoy freedom of choice and a Montessori classroom can be tightly controlled. The question is, how much control and choice should there be in education?

One answer for the public school is given by psychiatrist William Glasser:

> We are pushing for drug-free schools. We need to push even harder for coercion-free and failure-free quality schools because it is the alienation caused by coercion and punishment that leads young people to turn seriously to drugs.[55]

"Quality school"[56] is Glasser's term for a B or above mastery learning,[57] failure-free environment for all students. Replacing coercive external control psychology,[58] says Glasser, with kind and attentive teacher-student relationships will enable students to develop success identities. Glasser's approach includes getting rid of the rewards-and-punishment system of grading and punitive detention and principal's office "solutions" to disruption. Students will then become motivated through the friendly relationships with their teachers to achieve educational goals.

Glasser demonstrates in detail how his coercion-free, failure-free approach to schooling was accomplished with so-called learning disabled students in a Cincinnati middle school (*Choice Theory*, pp. 259–69). Smothered with kindness and attention, one hundred

---

[52] A. S. Neill's Summerschool (website), summerhillschool.co.uk.
[53] Sudbury Valley School: Expect Excellence (website), sudval.org.
[54] "Montessori Education," wikipedia.org
[55] William Glasser, *Choice Theory*, p. 255, amazon.com.
[56] William Glasser, *The Quality School*, amazon.com.
[57] "Mastery Learning," wikipedia.org.
[58] See above, "Choice Theory and Capitalism versus Dictatorship,"p. 49.; see below, "Standing Down from External Control," p. 221.

forty-eight overaged, "left behind," probably destined-for-jail middle school students transformed themselves and learned what was required to move on to high school. Removing structural control over the students, adjusting to their pace of learning, and giving them choice in their education led to this success. Removing coercion removed failure.

The ultimate in coercion-free, failure-free schooling is that of Summerhill and Sudbury Valley, where nearly everything is optional—especially courses and class attendance—and the students are given wide control of the schools through the democratic process. The question remains, though, how much control and choice should be left to the students.* This question cannot be answered without understanding that the main structural control in education today is the state's monopoly over schooling, achieved through compulsory attendance laws, expropriation of funds to pay for the system, and curricular and methodological dictates through the state's regulatory power. The framework of education is that control and choice are denied to both parents and students.

In the absence of state involvement, that is, in a free market in education, the issue of control and choice becomes a little less clear. If by "control" one means a prescribed curriculum that all students must study, and the parents agree to send their children to such a school, then it is the parents' legal right to do so. Psychologically, however, one can still argue that greater control and choice be given to the child. Adjusting to pace of learning and catering to interests are two of the most important methodological requirements of a good school. Responding to students as human beings by building Glasserian friendships helps them acquire the confidence to flourish.

Traditional public education denies the legitimacy of control and choice in the classroom and through its coercive bureaucratic framework makes both impossible to maintain for any length of time. It is this context of coercion that makes the likes of Summerhill and Sudbury Valley appealing and probably has contributed to their success. (Indeed, in 1969 or so, when I read the first *Summerhill*[59] book, I longed to be a student there. I would have thrived.)

---

[59] A. S. Neill, *Summerhill*, amazon.com.

As parenting requires guiding in the process of becoming a mature adult, formal education also probably requires at least some guiding in the acquisition of knowledge, values, and skills to achieve independence. Learning to think conceptually, for example, is not automatic and may require direction from an adult. But does this learning have to take place on the adult's schedule? In the Summerhill/Sudbury model the instructor waits until lessons are requested by the students. Guidance, yes, but not coercion. As responsible parents quickly discover, they cannot force anything into their child's brain. Children must be won over by persuasion. So, too, with students in education.

* My question presupposes the principle of rights, namely that the students should not be given control or choice to harm others or their property.

(March 18, 2011)

Group Projects: The Bell Has Tolled

A RECENT *NEW YORK TIMES* ARTICLE[60] exposed group projects in business schools as the frauds they have always been. When four or five students are assigned to produce one paper, the outcome should be obvious: at most one-fourth or one-fifth of the learning results, as opposed to the one-hundred percent learning of one student producing the entire paper. Many in groups who defer to others to do the work learn less. This is all done in the name of the division of labor and a simulation of the real world workplace. When I was in graduate school, some fellow students who were currently teaching, or ready to begin teaching, bragged about how the group project reduced their work load: eight papers to grade, say, as opposed to forty. (I also heard this expressed favorably at an academic conference.)

The *Times* article exposes other sins of business schools besides group projects, such as students not reading the text (or in some cases not even buying it) or skipping class except for exams. But as usual all of these issues have extenuating circumstances that need to be

---

[60] David Glenn, "The Default Major: Skating Through B-School," April 14, 2011, nytimes.com.

elaborated. Most of my students work twenty, thirty, or forty hours a week to pay for their union card while at the same time carrying a full load of courses. Some bright students who know they will do well in business explicitly say that they don't give a hoot about grades—nor do I. And I sometimes tell my students I wish I could give them all A's for the course on the first day of class, then anyone who wants to come back for the rest of the term to learn would be welcome. The college degree as union card is precisely what it is. All else is pretense.*

The group project, of course, also has its extenuating circumstances that need to be elaborated. It's not as collectivistic as it sounds. It falls within the theory of cooperative learning[61] and some form of it was used at the Dewey Laboratory School[62] in the late nineteenth century and has been used routinely in nearly all Montessori[63] schools for over a hundred years. The formal theory blossomed after World War II. If structured as a teaching and learning interaction among the participants, everyone can benefit, especially the weaker students.

In a setting where grades are required, the group process must be well structured and highly controlled by the teacher. The comments I hear from my current and former students, and my own experience as a member of groups when I studied for my MBA degree, testify that structure and control by the teacher are nearly always absent. In one class when I was a student, the instructor spent time balancing his checkbook while the students "worked" in their groups. On another occasion, the same instructor went home leaving us by ourselves to continue working on our group projects. After he was comfortably home, we students assumed, the lights of New York City went out for the second time in history—the blackout of 1977[64] had hit the Big Apple. Is "fraud" too strong a word for this kind of professorial behavior?

The group project in no way simulates real business experience. Most significantly absent in business are the head pats and chastisements known as grades. Further, there exists a division of labor within

---

[61] "Cooperative Learning," wikipedia.org.
[62] Katherine Camp Mayhew, *The Dewey School*, amazon.com.
[63] "Montessori vs. Mainstream: An Educational Comparison," amiusa.org.
[64] "New York City Blackout of 1977," wikipedia.org.

the groups, or "teams," as they are usually called, with clearly established authority and skill-levels. Five students in a college classroom who have never met before have none of that. They are thrown into the fire and expected without guidance to survive. Typically, everyone in the group gets the same grade. And teams in business? Often the high performers are rewarded with raises and promotions. No educational system can offer such benefits.

In Montessori schools there are no grades. Younger, less experienced children learn from the older, more experienced ones. They learn by observation and imitation, and from instruction. The older children learn by leading, by setting good examples and by teaching. The process, as business people would say, is "win-win." There is no complaint about slackers in the group. Slower students may take longer to digest the material with faster students enjoying the process of helping them. An "A," a "B," or a "C" does not depend on anyone's behavior. Learning, not jumping through a hoop to get a biscuit, is the aim of Montessori's cooperative learning environment.

Group projects and group cooperative learning have their place in education. Just not in the bureaucratically credentialed and grade-driven schools we have today.

* See pp. 159ff. in *Montessori, Dewey, and Capitalism* for more on bureaucracy-based credentials.

(May 24, 2011)

Educational Innovation from Outside the Establishment

INNOVATION FROM OUTSIDE WELL-ESTABLISHED ORDERS is not unusual. Just think the work of college dropouts Steve Jobs and Bill Gates or, more generally, the rise of capitalism and the astounding accompanying increase in longevity and standard of living that we have enjoyed as a result.

Innovation from the government-run education bureaucracy is almost non-existent, despite much lip service to audio-visual aids in the

1950s and distance learning in the past decade. Charter schools have been a feeble attempt to encourage innovation from within but the vise of bureaucratic rules eventually checks their freedom.

In light of this, three educational innovations from outside the government-run system are well worth mentioning. Take first the growth of the for-profit higher education market.

Trashed vehemently and repeatedly by the academic establishment, the Kaplans,[65] Capellas,[66] and DeVrys[67] of the country, among many others, cater to a unique market segment: older working adults often seeking a career change. The story of the for-profits is told unapologetically in *Change.edu*[68] by Andrew Rosen, chairman and CEO of the Kaplan organization and himself a product of the old-line East Coast establishments, Duke and Yale Law.

The for-profits, Rosen points out, are the third of three disruptive innovations in the last 150 years. Land-grants, despised by the elite as "workingmen's colleges," were the first. Community colleges, despised as overgrown high schools, were the second. And now the for-profits are the third, despised for measuring their success by money and customer satisfaction rather than, as Rosen pointedly and with considerable data observes, by the number of new buildings constructed on the resort-like campuses of traditional nonprofit and state-run universities.

The hullabaloo[69] over the high proportion of student loans and high tuition at for-profits? Caused by de facto government price fixing. Recent innovation? The start-up for-profit New Charter University [now Bottega University][70] is offering as many classes as a student can complete within one semester, all for $796 (or $199 a month), plus a try-for-free plan. Do I hear snarky indignation from the establishment?

The second innovation from outside government channels is the rise of many entrepreneurial and parent-funded private schools in the slums

---

[65] Welcome to Kaplan (website), kaplan.com.
[66] Capella University (website), capella.edu.
[67] DeVry University (website), devry.edu.
[68] Andrew S. Rosen, *Change.edu*, amazon.com.
[69] Kelly Field, "Attorneys General Take Aim at For-Profit Colleges' Institutional Loan Programs," March 20, 2012, chronicle.com.
[70] Marc Parry, "No Financial Aid, No Problem. For-Profit University Sets $199-a-Month Tuition for Online Courses," March 29, 2012, chronicle.com; Bottega University (website), bottega.edu.

of India and Nigeria.[71] Up to sixty percent of the elementary schools in these areas are private, with as many as thirty-five percent of them unrecognized by the government's statistics. The schools are run by sole proprietors and cost perhaps five or ten dollars a month or about twenty-five percent of a typical parent's income. Parents prefer these "greedy, profit-making" schools because their quality is much better than that of the free ones run by the government.

Not an entirely a new phenomenon, Estelle James and Gail Benjamin[72] in the 1980s and '90s demonstrated that private education, whether in less or highly developed economies, will arise spontaneously when the government system fails to meet the needs—in quantity, quality, and price—of the market. The recent discovery of these schools in India and Nigeria reminds me of the work and success of Chicago teacher Marva Collins[73] who taught her "retarded" public-school rejects to quote Shakespeare.

The third innovation coming from outside the establishment is an idea remarkably similar to what I suggested in *Montessori, Dewey, and Capitalism*[74]: mass lectures followed up with individual (not two- or three-person) tutorials. Salman Khan posted several math videos on YouTube[75] designed to help his cousin only to find that many people around the world were benefitting from his ten-minute, easily digestible chunks of internet-based learning. Now he heads the Khan Academy[76] with 3100 (and counting) brief educational videos ranging from K-12 math to science to finance and history. Schools—public and private—are using the videos to communicate the basic fund of knowledge, which students access and watch at home, while class time is used to troubleshoot and individualize the learning.

My idea was to make a free market in education economically viable. Salman Khan seems to have beaten me to the punch. Now if we can only get the government completely out of the way!

---

[71] "TED Goes to School," cato.org; James Tooley, *The Beautiful Tree*, cato.org.
[72] Estelle James, "Why Do Different Countries Choose a Different Public-Private Mix of Educational Services?," summer 1993, jstor.org; Estelle James and Gail Benjamin, *Public Policy and Private Education in Japan*, amazon.com.
[73] "Marva Collins Biography," notablebiographies.com.
[74] Jerry Kirkpatrick, *Montessori, Dewey, and Capitalism*, pp. 172–79, amazon.com.
[75] Khan Academy Featured Channels, youtube.com.
[76] Khan Academy (website), khanacademy.org.

It will be interesting to see how long before the public-school bureaucracy corrupts the use of these videos. After all, are all those teachers really necessary now? Ah yes, I can see the Luddites warming up their sledgehammers.

My description of these three innovations, incidentally, in no way means that I think the intellectual or political climate is softening toward the idea of a free market in education. In the near or distant future, I still do not see the idea on the horizon.

(April 22 2012)

Look It Up, Look It Up: The Open-Book Test

Remember what teachers would often say when they were unable to answer your question? "Why don't you look it up." If there is one skill that pays rewards far beyond the school years, it is the ability to find answers on one's own to questions that arise, when and as they arise.

I used to tell my students, "There isn't any question you can come up with that you cannot find an answer to, or at least a good approximation of an answer to it, in the library." In the past fifteen years, I changed the location of those answers to the internet, since nearly everything in written form is rapidly being digitized. In the past year, I have been saying to my students, "I look up most answers to questions I have on my pocket computer." And then I hold up my smartphone. "Look it up" is how we all educate ourselves beyond the school years.

Why do we have to memorize so much in school? Because that's how schools have been run for millennia. A score or grade must be produced and memorization is said to be the key to that score or grade. But is it? The world does not work that way. Yes, memory is used in most jobs in the real world, but it is the memory of habit built up over weeks, months, or years of experience. When memory fails, the world says, "look it up."

William Glasser makes this point in his 1969 book *Schools Without Failure*.[77] The closed-book, memory-measuring examination, he states, is based on the "fallacy that knowledge remembered is better

---

[77] William Glasser, *Schools without Failure*, amazon.com.

than knowledge looked up" (p. 72, emphasis omitted). "I would hate," Glasser continues, "to drive over a bridge, work in a building, or fly in an airplane designed by engineers who depended only upon memory." Good surgeons halt surgery to look up key steps in a procedure; the not-so-good ones—products apparently of "too many closed-book tests," Glasser observes—rely on memory, sometimes "to the extreme detriment of the patient."

The world says "look it up." School says "memorize it," even though decay rates after testing, without further use of the material, are exceptionally high. So why not use open-book testing in the schools? This is precisely what Glasser advocates, to teach students how "to use reference material quickly and efficiently." It is what I have been doing over the past sixteen months . . . and no ivory-towered walls have come a-tumblin' down.

In three different courses I have given ten open-book, open-notes exams (both midterm and final). Average scores have been higher than with the closed-book versions, but the grade distributions are not unusual; advanced study is still required to be successful at taking an open-book exam. My students certainly prefer open-book testing, though all or nearly all have never been exposed to it before and, as in all test-taking, a certain strategy has to be learned. I told my students to go through the test initially as if it were a closed-book exam, then go back to look up specific answers lest they run out of time looking up an answer to one question and find themselves unable to finish the test.

As Glasser concludes, "Faced with a problem in life, we marshal all of the facts we can; we don't rely on our memories unless we have to." Open-book tests teach us "to give thought to necessary reference material, and to utilize facts to solve problems, develop concepts, and explore issues. Closed-book tests defeat all of these objectives."

Then there is the artificial and false nature of testing. As I have written before:

> Testing is a contrived situation that seldom corresponds to the reality it is supposed to represent. Supermarket shoppers in one study performed arithmetic calculations far more accurately in the store than on a formal test. . . . And one boy, considered the dumbest in his class, was discovered by his teacher to be a paid scorekeeper in a bowling alley,

simultaneously tracking the progress of two teams of four players each. The teacher promptly created word problems, requiring students to calculate scores for games of bowling. The boy could not do the problems.[78]

Time to inject education with a little reality.

(June 18, 2012)

2013–14

On Killing Creativity

TO CREATE SOMETHING means to come up with something new, to rearrange existing objects or ideas and put them into a form that has not been done before. Everyone is creative because learning is the process of acquiring new knowledge, values, and skills by rearranging what we already have in our minds and integrating that content with what we are acquiring. When we learn, we craft new concepts, principles, values, and skills.

How creative each of us is varies and the process can be, and often is, stunted and destroyed. Some cultures are known to be more creative than others. For example, the Japanese education system produces students who score higher on standardized tests than Americans, yet American students and American culture are said to be more creative. How has this come about?

Ken Robinson, in a 2006 TED[79] talk and, later, in his book *The Element*,[80] argues admirably that creativity should be just as important an objective of education as literacy and that our current one-size-fits-all system destroys it. This is the progressive idea of focusing on and stimulating the individual's interests and therefore the individual's imagination and inventiveness. It is this progressive influence in education and, no doubt, the overall non-authoritarian atmosphere of American culture that has allowed Americans to be more creative.

Robinson, however, like the progressives, erroneously clings to the government as supplier of education and blames the rise of

---

[78] Jerry Kirkpatrick, *Montessori, Dewey, and Capitalism*, p. 158, amazon.com
[79] Ken Robinson, "Do Schools Kill Creativity?," February 2006, ted.com.
[80] Ken Robinson, *The Element*, amazon.com.

"one-size-fits-all" on the so-called factory model.[81] Yet, it is precisely the government and all forms of authoritarian control that arrest and prevent imaginative thinking.

Government bureaucracy, using government guns as its means of control, only knows one-size-fits-all. In education, that calls for a core curriculum[82] and both types of grading: evaluation and age-sequencing. Catering to needs and wants is something governments cannot do, or do very well.

As discussed in last month's post,[83] any type of physical force, trauma, neglect, or emotional abuse, severely hampers the development of self-esteem and independence. Without high degrees of self-esteem and independence, children and adults become fearful of risk-taking experimentation—that is, they fear making mistakes that might be disapproved of and vilified by those who have been forcing, traumatizing, neglecting, or emotionally abusing them.

It was progressive educator Maria Montessori who realized that choice was crucial in the development of self-esteem and independence Her method of education, as a result, allows a maximum of choice in a structured environment. Montessori children who move on to more traditional schooling are known for their confidence and creativity.

Freedom to choose, which means freedom to make mistakes without fear of criticism or denigration, is the key to encouraging original thinking. Dictating to children—whether by parents, teachers, coaches, tiger moms, or stage moms[84]—what the children must think and do is nearly as stunting and destructive as hitting or beating them.

In organized youth sports, the fear of making mistakes and lack of creativity and imagination has been pointed out by former National Hockey League star Wayne Gretzky.[85] Lamenting today's excessive control and domination by adults, Gretzky finds the origin of hockey creativity on the adult-less pond of yesteryear. In the current

---

[81] See above, "The Factory Model of Education, Technocracy, and the Free School Movement," p. 176.
[82] See above, "Interest and the Core Curriculum," p. 163.
[83] See below, "The Root of Dictatorship," p. 258.
[84] See below, "Tiger Mom or Stage Mom?," p. 332.
[85] James Christie, "Gretzky Stresses Creativity," October 24, 2000, theglobeandmail.com.

environment, he says, if kids are sent to the ice to play a scrimmage, the first thing a child will ask is, "What position do you want me to play?" The pond, Gretzky's point being, as was the sandlot in the earlier days of baseball, was what taught kids how to make their own decisions. Today, they must bow to the dictates of the adults in charge, lest they be criticized for going against a coach's system. The quality of play becomes cautious and mediocre, and often not fun.

The killing of creativity can be subtle and performed by apparently well-meaning adults. The premise of demanding obedience to authority can be expressed quietly and without obviously abusive techniques. It stems from the denial of choice. A parent, teacher, or coach who criticizes a child's mistake and singles the child out as an example to others is demanding obedience to authority. The message to children under such a leader's watch is that cautiousness, not imagination and creativity, is the path to the adult's approval.

The well-meaning adult thinks that such criticism is what teaching is all about. But allowing mistakes and, as Montessori demonstrated, saving the correction for another time when a new teaching moment arises, are what build the foundation of creativity: namely confidence, self-esteem, and independence.

All forms of demands for obedience to authority, whether physical or mental, blatant or subtle, must be rejected.

(February 22, 2013)

Plagiarism—Beyond a Reasonable Doubt

PLAGIARISM IS THE UNACKNOWLEDGED, intentionally deceptive use of another's words or ideas. It is not easy to prove.

Those who seek to punish guilty parties—teachers, in particular—need to be aware of the difficulties of proof, lest they become guilty of committing injustices to their students.

The mere fact that a paper "looks better than it should be," considering the student who wrote it, or "looks like it was copied from someone else's paper" does not provide prima facie proof of wrongdoing.

In my early years as a professor, I read a paper by an international student. I thought is was too good to have been written by someone whose first language was not English. I told my chair and he immediately said, "Throw the book at her." So, I did, and got vocal protests and tears in return. I went back to my chair who then suggested that the student write something in his office, which meant she would not be able to copy her words from another source. My chair read the girl's writing and said, "Well, she could have memorized it."

The verdict was guilty. A student review committee convened the following fall, but I had left the school in the spring to work in business. I never heard what happened to the girl and, as a result, have felt guilty every since! I hope she was exonerated.

In contrast to this case, I have caught two other, and only two, students red-handed with papers copied from elsewhere—one source in a book that I had in my office, the other a previous student's paper inadvertently attached to the current (copied) one submitted to me for the assignment.

No, I did not turn the students over to any drill-sergeant morality board. I simply flunked them for the course. My experience with such plagiarism-police boards is that they share my former chair's penchant for summary judgment: throw the book at 'em, punish 'em, draw blood. Evidence? It's the board's judgment against theirs. The board has PhD degrees and the student does not.

Such an attitude is old-fashioned authoritarianism in the classroom. Knuckles use to be rapped with rulers and disobedients were made to kneel on raw peas. Many teachers today still seem too trigger happy to punish, rather than to understand and teach.

When it comes to plagiarism, none other than Mark Twain wrote the following in a letter to Helen Keller about her alleged plagiarism of a short story:[86]

> The kernel, the soul—let us go further and say the substance, the bulk, the actual and valuable material of all human utterances—is plagiarism. For substantially all ideas are

---

[86] Quoted in Maria Popova, "All Ideas Are Second-Hand: Mark Twain's Magnificent Letter to Helen Keller about the Myth of Originality," brainpickings.org.

second-hand, consciously and unconsciously drawn from a million outside sources.

And he is not alone in expressing this sentiment. Oliver Sacks[87] eloquently addresses the role of a not always accurate memory in the process of creating. A Google search of the statement, "We are all plagiarists,"[88] produces many a lively discussion of the topic of borrowing and excessive similarity.*

Intentional deception is still the issue and determining that this has occurred in the classroom is not easy. Throw in other little details about our modern educational system and one can see the difficulty of presenting a foolproof case. Like:

- Our credential system, as I argued in *Montessori, Dewey, and Capitalism*,[89] encourages cheating. When the union card is what is important, the attitude becomes: do whatever is required to get the credential.

- The cultural values[90] and therefore attitudes toward plagiarism of international students can differ considerably from those of Americans, such as considering it a form of respect to repeat verbatim without acknowledgement someone else's words.

- The group project[91] encourages collaboration but forbids copying from others. Seriously, teach? How exactly is that supposed to happen, especially when collaboration usually means discussing and editing each other's words and ideas? On the next individual assignment, will the student understand that this means no discussion or editing of others' words or ideas?

---

[87] Oliver Sacks, "Speak, Memory," February 21, 2013, nybooks.com.
[88] Robert Mankoff, "We Are All Plagiarists," November 8, 2013, newyorker.com; Lionel Beehner, "Sorry, We Are All Plagiarists," May 25, 2011, huffpost.com; "We Are All Plagiarists Now!," March 14, 2011, drownthatpuppy.wordpress.com.
[89] Jerry Kirkpatrick, *Montessori, Dewey, and Capitalism*, pp. 166–67, amazon.com.
[90] Niall Hayes and Lucas D. Introna, "Cultural Values, Plagiarism, and Fairness: When Plagiarism Gets in the Way of Learning," June 2005, researchgate.net.
[91] See above, "Group Projects: The Bell Has Tolled," p. 185.; see above, "Ignorance versus Dishonesty," p. 138.

- The internet-based plagiarism detection services, such as turnitin.com,[92] are often used as clubs or threats, rather than as learning tools, as I and others have suggested they be used.[93]

Less fear and more education[94] is the solution to the "plagiarism problem." Teachers must take responsibility for teaching, not policing.

This was captured best by the *Wall Street Journal* cartoon,[95] showing a teacher and little boy with an F on his paper. The boy says, "Ah, Miss Brimsley, I ask you: Which one of us has truly failed?"

* To avoid even the hint of plagiarism, one of my graduate school professors advised, "Cite cheek by jowl." Hence, the many references in my blog posts!

(February 17, 2014)

Filling the Swiss Cheese Holes

A MAJOR PROBLEM with our current one-size-fits-all education is the gaps that occur in learning. Thirty or forty kids are presented with material at one time. They may work on some problems or research one topic, but then the instructor moves on. Those who don't get it fall behind. Even those who do get most of the material, move on with what Salman Khan calls Swiss-cheese-like holes in their learning.

Khan has the solution for filling the holes. It is a technological solution, as many before him have promoted, but this one may stick in certain subjects.

In his book *The One World Schoolhouse: Education Reimagined*,[96] Khan describes his vision for inexpensively achieving full, 100% mastery

---

[92] Empower Students to do Their Best, Original Work (website), turnitin.com.
[93] Jerry Kirkpatrick, "Teaching Acknowledgement Practice Using the Internet-Based Plagiarism Detection Service," spring 2006, cpp.edu/faculty/jkirkpatrick; Carl Straumsheim, "Turnitin Put to the Test," February 6, 2014, insidehighered.com.
[94] Scott Jaschik, "Plagiarism Prevention Without Fear," January 26, 2010, insidehighered.com.
[95] Cartoon Collections, cartooncollections.com/cartoon?searchID=WJ900492.
[96] Salman Khan, *The One World Schoolhouse*, amazon.com.

learning in a mixed-age environment with minimal in-class lecturing and maximum special attention.

His technology is short, ten- to fifteen- minute video lectures and an elaborate tracking software both to indicate student progress and to highlight those who might be stuck, thereby requiring further tutoring. The software is also designed to motivate students with immediate awareness of how much they have accomplished.

With thousands of videos now available from the Khan Academy,[97] mostly in math and science, teachers are flipping their classrooms,[98] that is, assigning the video lectures as homework, releasing class time for troubleshooting and special attention. Khan's notion of mixed ages goes with his strong belief in the need for self-paced learning, regardless of age.

Adult learners have flocked to his videos and praised Khan for the ease with which they can fill gaps in their decades old learning.

A big chunk of Khan's book is a chronicle of how he stumbled on this idea. And "stumble" is the correct word here, as it is with many innovations that go through much trial and error.

His story has been told in many places.[99] Khan, a hedge fund manager, took on the task in 2004 of tutoring his younger cousin in math, first by long-distance telephone and occasionally with in-person visits. Other family members soon became his long-distance "tutees," as he called them, but the process was cumbersome. It was a friend who suggested that he make videos and put them on YouTube, a thought he considered ridiculous.

He did make a few videos and they became a hit, not just with his relatives, but initially with hundreds, then thousands and thousands of other people all over the world.

Khan at the time was working out of a converted walk-in closet. He decided to form a non-profit corporation so the videos could be made available without charge. However, he had no money. He quit his day job and at one point, as he put it, was burning through $5000 a month

---

[97] Khan Academy (website), khanacademy.org.
[98] "Flipped Classroom," wikipedia.org.
[99] Claudia Dreifus, "It All Started with a 12-Year-Old Cousin," January 27, 2014, nytimes.com; Sal Khan, "Let's Use Video to Reinvent Education," March 2011, ted.com; see above, "Educational Innovation from Outside the Classroom," p. 187.

in savings. Finally, one donor offered him $10,000, then upped the ante to $100,000 when she learned he was working out of his closet. Then Google offered $2 million to translate his videos into the ten most popular languages and the Gates Foundation offered even more.

Khan's notion of a "one world schoolhouse," he says, is an updated version of the one-room schoolhouse. Mixed ages with time for special attention. His videos and software, he argues, can make education inexpensively available to everyone in the world. No one should or need be left behind, as occurs in our one-size-fits-all system, because his software tracks progress and reveals the students who need that extra attention.

He is strongly opposed to the bad kind of bureaucratic tracking that takes students who are, say, stuck on a particular type of problem and then branded as slow. Such a student needlessly gets left behind, and, long-term, may even be tracked out of a college education.

As a firm believer in mastery learning, he also thinks grades and scores should be dumped.

Khan does suffer from a number of conventionalities. For example, he makes no mention of Montessori or her use of mixed age classrooms with special attention from the teachers. And he trashes the classroom lecture, ignoring the fact that his videos are just that. And like many bright students who seem to think they can get it all in the book,[100] he vehemently denies that the lecture can have any value at all in the classroom.

The worst conventionality is that he is not anywhere close to thinking of or mentioning a free market in education. This is unfortunate.

Nevertheless, if anyone can make a stab at tearing down today's educational shibboleths, it may be Salman Khan and his software-driven self-paced learning videos.

(March 28, 2014)

---

[100]See above, "You Can Get It in the Book," p. 174.

4
Psychology

2007
Describe, Don't Evaluate

"SUPERLATIVES BELONG TO THE MARKETPLACE," says David Ogilvy,[1] founder of the Ogilvy and Mather advertising agency, not in "serious advertisement; they lead readers to discount the realism of every claim." The same could be said about praise given to others: superlatives should come from the recipient of the compliment.

What Ogilvy means is that describing what a product can do for the customer, that is, explaining its benefits, is the essential requirement of good advertising copy. Hyping a product with evaluative "s-t" words—best, greatest, most wonderful thing since sliced bread—is seller's puff and is devoid of the information prospects need to help them make a purchase decision. (Puffery is extravagant praise, a combination of exaggeration and evaluation.) If a "we" is included in the copy—we are the best, most wonderful, etc.—the advertising is called "brag and boast." Evaluation, preferably of the positive superlative type, should come from the customer after product use.

This principle—describe, don't evaluate—has broad application and includes relationships not just of sellers to customers, but also of parents to children, teachers to students, and employers to employees, among

---

[1] David Ogilvy, *The Unpublished David Ogilvy*, amazon.com.

others. The principle is recommended as a replacement for negative criticism: "The milk spilled!" (describe) as opposed to "I don't believe you did it again! How could you!" (evaluate). Name-calling, sarcasm, threats, berating, and the like, undercut self-esteem and cause defensiveness by attacking the other person's character or personality.

Factually describing the incident helps the other person (child or student or employee) avoid drawing negative conclusions about him- or herself. The recipient of the criticism is then allowed to regroup and correct the situation. "Constructive criticism," child psychologist Haim Ginott[2] in *Between Parent and Child*[3] says, "confines itself to pointing out what has to be done, entirely omitting negative remarks about the personality of the child" (or, by extension, student or employee).

Ginott goes on to apply this principle to the extravagant praise that is often heaped on children, such as the ubiquitous "Good job" or "We're so proud of you." Says Ginott, "Direct praise of personality, like direct sunlight, is uncomfortable and blinding. It is embarrassing for a person to be told that he is wonderful, angelic, generous, and humble. He feels called upon to deny at least part of the praise. . . . [and he] may have some second thoughts about those who have praised him: 'If they find me so great, they cannot be so smart.'"

The same applies to the puffery heaped on students and employees. The *Wall Street Journal*[4] said as much recently when it chronicled the current praise-inflated culture of schools and employers. One such employer, said the article, dishes out praise every twenty seconds. Concerning the praise mania, one might ask, as does John Holt, "Is not *most* adult praise of children a kind of self-praise?"* Certainly the schools that issue bumper stickers saying "My child is an honor student at XYZ school" are bragging and boasting about themselves.

So what is the proper way to express compliments to another person? For Ginott the principle remains: describe effort, accomplishment, or effect on you; let the other person draw the evaluative conclusion. "Thank you for washing the car, it looks new again." is one of Ginott's examples of what

---

[2] The Work of Haim G. Ginott (website), betweenparentandchild.net.
[3] Haim G. Ginott, *Between Parent and Child*, amazon.com.
[4] Jeffrey Zaslow, "The Most-Praised Generation Goes to Work," April 20, 2007, wsj.com.

he calls helpful praise; "I did a good job; my work is appreciated" is the child's possible conclusion. "You're an angel," says Ginott, is not helpful. Note that it is the child who concludes "good job," not the adult who says it.

The phrase "effect on you" must be qualified and used carefully. "We're so proud of you," for example, can be an appropriate emotional response to a child's accomplishments, but it often is heard as an evaluation, meaning "You are worthy of us." To a child this is worse than direct sunlight, because the implication is that sometimes the child is not worthy. Properly described accomplishments should produce pride in the recipient.

"Thank you" is an appropriate expression of effect, when used in moderation. Some companies in today's age of excess apparently overdose on thank you notes, according to the *Wall Street Journal* article mentioned above. Unfortunately, the *WSJ* confusingly lumped accolades and thank yous together. The bitter irony of the praise culture is that strokes are supposed to promote self-esteem, but disbelief and the perception of being manipulated, as well as a defensive need for more praise, are often the result.

Now the praise culture of superlatives poured on a product is not quite the same as extravagant praise gushed on a person, but those "s-t" words have the same effect on the prospect, as does praise on a child, student, or employee. Superlatives produce a big "why?" in the mind of the prospect. "Why do you say that? Why should I believe you? The sunlight is so blinding," to use Ginott's analogy, "that I can't see the product or its features in order properly to evaluate it."

Just as prospects need the space to pronounce for themselves that a product is "the best, greatest, most wonderful thing since sliced bread," children, students, and employees must be given the freedom to judge themselves as someone who is doing good work and as someone who is good.

* John Holt is author of *How Children Learn*, *How Children Fail*, and *The Underachieving School*, among others.[5] The quote is from *How Children Fail*, p. 79, Holt's emphasis.

(May 3, 2007)

---

[5] All available from amazon.com.

Curiosity for Subtle Detail

As a young man I accepted the wisdom of doctors and their prescriptions without question, never bothering to learn the names of the drugs they ordered. After reading Jerome Groopman's book *How Doctors Think*,[6] I am not so sure I want to go back to a doctor! The ten to fifteen percent error rate in diagnosis and similar percentage in the misreading of x-rays and MRIs does not give one confidence in the medical profession. The nearly socialized nature of the medical market today does not help and no doubt contributes to the penchant of doctors to interrupt patients after only eighteen seconds and decide on a diagnosis within twenty. Add to this the failures to probe or to consider alternative, possibly subtle, explanations of symptoms, the stereotyping of patients, the worshipping of averages, the "this is how we've always done it" mentality, and the pressures to conform and not order more tests—and you have a prescription for bad medicine.

But Groopman's book is not just about how doctors think—or rather, do not think; the errors apply equally to teachers and other professionals, as well as to anyone who has a problem to be solved or person to be judged. The arrogance, for example, that doctors are sometimes accused of is not the prerogative of medicine. Groopman's parents were told by his fifth-grade teacher that he was "not college material" and an Ivy-League-trained first-grade teacher of the son of one of my colleagues predicted that the boy would become a high school dropout. (The colleague's son is now applying to graduate school.) What are these errors and how can they be avoided?

Groopman's book is a work of epistemology and psychology that describes how everyone tends to think at one time or another. Better thinkers, though, as Groopman points out, do not often make the mistakes he discusses. They do make, more importantly, concerted efforts to learn from their mistakes. One doctor for example, that Groopman mentions keeps a log of each mistake he makes and analyzes why the error occurred. Bad thinkers are not usually aware that they have committed any such errors, or if they are, choose to do nothing about them. I would

---

[6]Jerome Groopman, *How Doctors Think*, amazon.com.

characterize the essential mistake described in Groopman's book as a mental passivity that lacks curiosity for subtle detail.

Curiosity is an eagerness to know, and knowing subtle detail requires the ability and willingness to make fine distinctions or to delve deeper and deeper beneath surface appearances. Not many people seem willing, or perhaps know how, to go this distance. The curiosity does not require a college education. I recall a garage door repairman who told me about a difficult-to-diagnose malfunction; he finally figured out that the sun's reflection off the car that was frequently parked in front of the garage interfered with the electric eye controlling the door. With an eager glint in his eye, the repairman said, "That was an interesting problem!" This man certainly did not have a college education and possibly not a high school degree, but he did have what I would call a curiosity for subtle detail.

Judging other people—as doctors must judge their patients; as also parents must judge their children, teachers their students, managers their employees; as everyone must judge others with whom they come into contact, whether friend or foe—is not an easy task. It requires effort to gather data—facts—about the other person. Failure to gather one fact can change a negative evaluation to a positive, or vice versa. Omniscience is not possible, so rules-of-thumb based on past experience help us make decisions. The better the past experience the better the rules-of-thumb. This means that accumulated knowledge is a factor in making sound judgments, but interest and desire to go beyond what too often become comfortable rules-of-thumb are what cause one person to see facts that another does not. Continued observation, not contentment, and a determined search for clues that might solve a problem or explain a behavior are what separate good thinkers from bad. And, further, as new evidence arises, the additional information is acknowledged by the good thinker and revision of a previous judgment, if necessary, is gladly made.

Curiosity for subtle detail is a commitment to observation, the commitment of a scientist in all areas of one's life. It is a commitment to spot the relevant in the mass of data that daily confronts us and sometimes a commitment to stand in opposition to the conventional wisdom that might ignore or silence us.

(July 27, 2007)

Sound or Independent Judgment?

SOUND JUDGMENT MEANS SENSIBLE—i.e., rational or considered, not impulsive—decision making. Many parents and teachers value this process as a primary skill that children and students should possess upon reaching adulthood.

In contrast, independent judgment, which presupposes sensible decision making, is not often cited as a valued goal of either education or adulthood, yet this is the personality and character trait that should be exhibited by all citizens of a fully free society. Independent judgment, and its practical consequence, independent action, should be a fundamental aim of both parenting and education. What is independent judgment and why is it not encouraged by parents and teachers?

Independence is the more common term that parents and teachers use to describe what they think children should achieve as adults, but this usually means the ability to pay one's own bills, by providing one's own food, shelter, and clothing without parental help. The mental act of asserting something as fact and doing so entirely on one's own is independent judgment. The willingness to act on what one has judged to be right, in the face of disapproval and opposition, is independent action. True independence is the ability and willingness to see and say that the emperor has no clothes.

In history, both Socrates and Galileo exhibited this true independence, both to their detriment. Socrates[7] could have bowed to the will of the majority and stopped upsetting the Athenian elite, but he chose not to and was put to death for his independence. Galileo[8] did capitulate to the Inquisition, but nonetheless was put under house arrest for the remainder of his life. In literature, Henrik Ibsen's Dr. Stockmann in *An Enemy of the People*[9] stood steadfastly to his judgment while one by one losing nearly all who were supposedly his friends. Independent judgment and action are not well tolerated by those who are not themselves independent.

---

[7] "*Apology* (Plato)," wikipedia.org; *Crito*, wikipedia.org.
[8] "Galileo Galilei," wikipedia.org; "Galileo Is Accused of Heresy," history.com.
[9] "An Enemy of the People," wikipedia.org; Henrik Johan Ibsen, *An Enemy of the People*, amazon.com.

Some advocates of sensible decision making may argue that Socrates, Galileo, and Stockmann, by stirring up the hornet's nests in which they were trying to work, were not being reasonable. But there are two issues here: are the advocates of sensible decision making saying that these three men should have given up their judgments in order to conform to the majority? or are they saying that independent judgment does not require sacrifices when under duress? The principle of self-defense indeed does say that it is morally equivalent to fight or flee when threatened with force. Rejecting self-sacrifice as a noble ideal, as I do, Socrates probably should have escaped to live in exile. Ibsen's Stockmann remained to fight partly because he assumed that many of his so-called friends were on his side but mainly because fighting was the right thing to do. Giving in as a pretense, which is what Galileo did, is a third option. Abject conformity or sacrificing one's independent judgment was not considered by any of these men.

The problem with sound judgment as a goal of education is that it often becomes interpreted as conformity or conventionality. A free society requires rebels—people like Socrates, Galileo, and Stockmann whose independence leads them to see and say what the majority cannot. People with independent judgment are the innovators and entrepreneurs who move economies and societies forward. They rock boats, not necessarily on purpose, but because they see things others do not. The challenge is, can independent judgment be taught? and can every person possess such a trait? My answers are: indirectly and yes.

Independent judgment is first and foremost the correct perception of reality that is not influenced or contaminated by the perceptions of others. Misinformation is not a goal of education, so teaching facts is a start, but encouraging children and students to pursue their own goals and ideas without commands, criticism, and ridicule is better. This will enable them to develop the conviction that they can do anything they set their minds to—regardless of what others say or do. Freedom and nurture in the learning process, not coercion or neglect, are two requirements for instilling an independent and confident spirit in the child and student.

So can everyone in adulthood possess this childlike independent and confident spirit that says "the emperor has no clothes"? Why not?

That many adults today do not possess such a spirit indicates only that something is terribly wrong with our educational system such that it kills the spirit.

By about the fifth grade, according to John Holt.[10]

(December 26, 2007)

2008

Rules vs. Principles

IN CHAPTER 4 OF *MONTESSORI, DEWEY, AND CAPITALISM*, I wrote: "Rules are commands to act or not act a certain way. Obedience may be rewarded; disobedience is certainly punished." The context was the regulation of child and student behavior and my point was that "rules have no place in a theory of nurture." Rules call for obedience to authority. Principles, on the other hand, teach abstract thought and lay the foundation for independence.

This is not to say that rules to protect young children from harm or to help them respect the rights of others are not ever a good idea. Young children, including those up to the age of adolescence, have not yet acquired the skill of abstract reasoning. Guidance from adults cannot always be made in the form of rational argument, nor is the young child likely to understand such reasoning. A screamed "Stop!" when a three-year-old is about to run into the street is appropriate, as is the command "Don't step off the curb until I get there to take your hand." The latter is a rule, but when the added explanation "Cars can do bad things to little children" is provided, the groundwork for reasoned thought is being laid. Repeated explanations on similar occasions lead to understanding and eventual grasp of the principle of observation and self-protection. Absence of the added explanation, or worse, punishment for something the young child cannot possibly know or understand sends only one message: "Obey."

Elementary-aged children, roughly from six to twelve, pose an interesting challenge for adults. Logical thinking is noticeable in children of this age but it is concrete thinking, the "period of concrete operations,"

---

[10] John Holt, *How Children Fail*, p. 263, amazon.com.

as Piaget[11] calls it. Broad abstractions, formed and retained over time, are difficult and rare. Yet elementary-aged children exhibit a highly active and rambunctious behavior that is often not to the liking of adults. The easiest solution is a barrage of rules, such as "Don't run," "No talking in class," "No eating after 7PM," etc. Such rules, to be effective, must be enforced with stern consequences, ranging from confinement to withdrawal of possessions or privileges to spanking; if the rules are not enforced, or meekly enforced, they will be ignored and children will run amok and have what some would say is a lowered respect for the adult. Lowered fear of the adult would be a more correct description.

Teaching principles means giving children a full explanation, for example, of why running is not advisable on the patio: they might stumble and hurt themselves or others, who have just as much right to be there as they do, and the running might interrupt or destroy the other children's enjoyment. Such explanations require more words than a simple rule and there is no guarantee that the children will grasp and remember what was just said and implement a change of behavior to become the perfect angels that adults want them to become. Repetition of the explanation is required; so also is repetition required to enforce rules, unless the coercive consequences of breaking rules are so stern that the children get the message immediately. But then, what price has been paid in the psychological development of such coerced children?

Rules presuppose coercion. Principles presuppose teaching. A lot of it. But teaching principles requires patience, understanding, and, especially, fast thinking (of the right thing to say) that many adults—parents and teachers—do not have when trying to regulate and influence the behavior of elementary-aged children. Distractions and demands too often preclude the use of these three traits.

The middle ground between rules imposed from above and principles taught repeatedly (and exasperatingly) might be the democratic meeting in which children make and enforce their own rules. This is the solution adopted by the Summerhill School in England and Sudbury Valley School in Massachusetts.[12]

---

[11] "Jean Piaget," wikipedia.org.
[12] See above, "Go Fish!," p. 153.

A variation of this advocated by Jane Nelsen, author of *Positive Discipline*[13] and *Positive Discipline in the Classroom*,[14] is the family and class meeting. The purpose of such meetings is to brainstorm for solutions to problems and agree on the solutions either by vote or consensus. To be effective, the adults must reduce themselves to equal participants, rather than act as lecturers or moralizers.

Having children take responsibility for their own behavior through discussion, brainstorming, and democratic voting or consensus frees adults from having to play cop and peacemaker and enables them to spend more time being the long-term thinkers and leaders that children need. Until the perfect handbook is written and published on how to teach children to become perfect angels, this technique will probably have to do.

(May 16, 2008)

Ensuring That Disposition Trumps Situation

As I argue in a previous post,[15] independent judgment, the ability and willingness to perceive facts as facts and to respond to them regardless of what situational factors—especially, other people's approval—may dictate, should be a fundamental aim of parenting and teaching.

Independence means that one's psychological disposition, i.e., one's self-esteem, integrity, and courage, should be sufficiently strong to resist outside pressures for conformity. Instilling this trait in children and students is a large order for both parents and teachers to fill. And Philip Zimbardo's 2007 book *The Lucifer Effect: Understanding How Good People Turn Evil*[16] provides ample evidence that situations all too often trump disposition, leading too many people to conform to the requirements of the situation rather than to resist the external pressure and judge for themselves what the right course of action should be.

---

[13] Jane Nelsen, *Positive Discipline*, amazon.com. See also Positive Discipline: Creating Respectful Relationships in Homes and Schools (website), positivediscipline.com.
[14] Jane Nelsen, *Positive Discipline in the Classroom*, amazon.com.
[15] See above, "Sound or Independent Judgment?," p. 206.
[16] Philip Zimbardo, *The Lucifer Effect*, lucifereffect.com.

Zimbardo was principal investigator in the 1971 Stanford Prison Experiment,[17] which had been scheduled to last for two weeks but was stopped after six days because of the frighteningly realistic submissiveness and depression of the "prisoners" and aggression and sadism of the "guards." All participants were randomly assigned college students, tested to be "normal" on the psychological tests of the day.

The Lucifer Effect provides the most detailed chronicle to date of the events of that experiment. It also reviews the literature on the power of situation over disposition, including the Milgram[18] obedience-to-authority experiments in which participants, at the request of an experimenter, repeatedly increased the voltage of electrical shocks to a subject. The book, in great detail, also discusses the unnerving similarities between the events and behaviors of the 2003 Abu Ghraib scandal[19] and the Stanford Prison Experiment.

Zimbardo is a social psychologist, which means he emphasizes the power of situation over disposition, but it is obvious from the prison experiment and other examples of situational influence that some participants did strive to maintain their values and dignity. And Zimbardo acknowledges this, so in the final chapter of his book he does discuss techniques of resisting external pressures and provides examples of true heroes who did not allow situations to trump their dispositions. Alas, Zimbardo's suggestions for resisting situational influence, such as "assert your identity and individuality," do not go deep enough into the conscious and subconscious mind.

Now I am not claiming to have *the* solution to the problem of teaching disposition over situation, but the key to developing strong convictions and the willingness to act on them lies in our subconscious premises about ourselves, other people, and the world. An adolescent, for example, who believes deep down "I'm no good—I just want to get along with others" is ripe for influence from those others who say, "A few beers won't affect your driving" or "This drug will help you loosen up. Come on. I want to help you." And such an adolescent may appear

---

[17] Stanford Prison Experiment (website), prisonexp.org.
[18] "Milgram Experiment," wikipedia.org.
[19] "Researcher: It's Not Bad Apples, It's the Barrel," May 21, 2004, cnn.com; "Abu Ghraib Torture and Prisoner Abuse," wikipedia.org.

on the surface to be healthy and even independent in a conventional sense. In later years, working in business, the situational pressure may become, "Tell 'em the order's on the truck; what the client doesn't know won't hurt 'em!"

The appearance of ordinariness is a point much emphasized by Zimbardo in both prison cases and in all of his examples of situational influence. But it is the pressures of the situation—the outside influencers—that tap into the adolescent's (or adult's) premise of wanting to get along, thus crumbling any chances of resistance.

An alternative premise of self-worth and confidence to make one's own decisions without caving to external pressure would lead to a different outcome. Such premises, or conclusions, about oneself, others, and the world are formed in our earliest years and reinforced frequently thereafter. The challenge for parents and teachers is how to encourage the formation of correct premises and how to uncover and correct false or harmful ones. This puts psychology, specifically psychological self-awareness and the art of introspection, at the center of education.[20]

To ensure that disposition will triumph over situation, introspection as a scientific method for acquiring data of reality—inner reality—needs to be welcomed back after its one-hundred-year exile from science. Further, logic, the method by which we assess the mental processes used in perceiving the outer world, needs to be recognized as an introspective art. It also needs to be acknowledged as the method by which we assess the mental processes for perceiving our inner world. The conclusion "I'm no good" or "I want to get along with others at all costs" is a logical fallacy and should be corrected as much as the conclusion "The earth is flat."

Disposition consists of conclusions we have made over the years and hold in our minds, usually subconsciously. If the conclusions are correct, that is, logical and free of fallacies, self-esteem, independence, integrity, and courage will develop. If the conclusions are not logical, but contain falsehoods and fallacies, then varying amounts of situational influence will take hold. And strange or harmful behavior may

---

[20] See Edith Packer, *Lectures on Psychology*, esp. chap. 1 and 8, amazon.com.

result, even though such a person outwardly may appear completely ordinary or normal.

Such is the power of the subconscious to influence conscious behavior. The successful parent and teacher will find a way to nurture better subconscious premises.

(August 12, 2008)

Faking Your Way Through Life

WHEN I FIRST CAME UP WITH THE TITLE FOR THIS POST, I thought I should google it to see if anyone had done anything similar. Sure enough. *Phony!: How I Faked My Way Through Life*,[21] a confessional memoir, was just published. I have not read the book, but the publisher's blurbs say it is the story of a young woman who lied about not having a college degree and rose to high positions in business. Degrees and diplomas do not impress me as qualifying anyone for anything, but I was taught that it is not nice to lie.

My interest in the subject is not so much why people fake reality in a big way like the author of this book, but why do they fake reality at all? Why do people misperceive the most obvious facts? Why do they exaggerate and embellish them? Why do they have selective memories? Why do they fake reality in the smallest of ways when, to an outside observer, a simple statement of truth would be so easy and anxiety-free to make?

As creatures of habit, we learn much of our behavior from others, especially by example from our parents and other admired adults. Sometimes, those lessons are not the best ones to learn. For instance, an attendant at the ticket booth of a tourist attraction, where children under six were admitted free, related this story. One parent said that his daughter was under six, but the daughter, proud of her recent birthday, shot back with an "I'm six!" Lesson learned and seed planted? Fake your way into paying events and, when generalized, fake your way through life, such as saying you have a college degree when in fact you do not. Why would the father say such a thing? Affordability

---

[21] Andrea Stanfield, *Phony!*, amazon.com.

aside (the ticket price was trivial), he presumably learned it at an earlier time from his admired others.

This line of thought only leads to an infinite regress. At some point, someone must have decided on his or her own, absent outside influence, that something is not true or completely true and yet went on to recite the falsehood. The standard motivations[22] offered to explain lying are fear and glory. Fear of being caught for having done something wrong and glory of enhancing one's image in the eyes of others. And children are known to exhibit both motivations. When children become adults, however, some follow the straight and narrow of truth-telling, others do not. Among the others, some become self-aware fakers; the rest fall into that fuzzy middle ground and become BS'ers,[23] all the while insisting that they are completely honest. Why?

The answer has to be some combination of influence from the outside and decisions made by the individual. The myriad decisions made daily, from childhood to adulthood, about the myriad influences that come into our minds from the outside ultimately determine how we go about living our lives. A commitment from early on to perceive facts as facts and to state facts as facts, without regard for the consequences of getting caught or for an unearned image in the eyes of others is the path to developing a mind that will find faking of any kind anathema to living a decent life. A lesser commitment leads to fudging, guessing, and being susceptible to the influence of fear and the siren calls of glory. A lesser commitment leads to the adult who, in a seemingly confident and oh-so-precise manner, asserts in a meeting that the vote two years ago was nine to nine to one, when in fact there was no vote at all.

The result of these decisions and commitment is what Ayn Rand called psycho-epistemology,[24] the mental habit built up over time that determines each individual's unique way of perceiving reality. This is not determinism in the philosophical sense that we have no genuine alternatives in life because every decision and action is causally preformed

---

[22] "Lie," wikipedia.org.
[23] Jerry Kirkpatrick, "On Marketing Bull----," April 2006, cpp.edu/faculty/jkirkpatrick; see below, "The Dangerous Admiration of BS," p. 293.; "Bullshit," wikipedia.org.
[24] "Psycho-Epistemology," aynrandlexicon.com.

and could not have been otherwise. Our decisions and actions could have been otherwise because of the myriad decisions we have made since childhood. The cause of our behavior is the decisions we have made, and continue to make, about outside influences. We make them every minute of our waking lives. That the results of the decisions have become entrenched premises in our subconscious minds since childhood only makes changing them as an adult difficult, but not impossible. It is in this sense that our behavior is self-caused.

This means that the policy of faking one's way through life could have been and, in the present, can be otherwise. Changing a psychology at an advanced age can be achieved, though it can be challenging—and painful—to go against the years or decades of prior decisions. Preventive medicine calls for making correct, reality-focused decisions in one's early years. The task of parents and teachers is to be especially alert to these decisions and encourage their children and students by example and instruction to see facts as facts and then to communicate the facts as facts. Nothing more or less.

(December 23, 2008)

2009–10
The Von Domarus Principle and the Nature of the Subconscious Mind

AS I STATE IN *MONTESSORI, DEWEY, AND CAPITALISM* (p. 86), Freud was first to identify that we possess a dynamic, integrating subconscious mind, "dynamic" meaning continuously active and making connections whether we are awake or asleep. Thus, when we are asleep, our subconscious mind is constantly operating, connecting our many experiences of the previous day, week, or years, oftentimes manifesting the connections in dreams. But dreams are notoriously illogical and sometimes bizarre. What is the actual nature of the subconscious mind and what is its mode of operation?

We have a sense of how the conscious mind works. We direct attention to specific facts or events, identify and evaluate those facts or events, and as a result of the evaluation experience a favorable or unfavorable emotion. The knowledge, evaluations, and emotions then are stored in our memories, that is, in our subconscious minds for later retrieval and use. Thus, the subconscious is a valuable storehouse of all of our previous experiences. How well the storehouse is organized determines how easily or difficultly we can retrieve and use what is there. It is the conscious mind that directs this organization.

But how does the subconscious operate when it is not being controlled by the conscious mind, such as in our sleep or when we are focused elsewhere? Psychiatrist Eilhard von Domarus, in describing the thought processes of schizophrenics, posed a fascinating hypothesis about how the subconscious might operate. Because schizophrenics seem to have lost conscious control of their minds, they apparently exhibit raw, subconscious reasoning. And that reasoning is exemplified by the fallacy of undistributed middle,[25] the error in thinking and form of overgeneralization that holds that if two subjects possess the same predicate, they are then the same. For example, dogs and cows both are four-legged animals, therefore all dogs are cows. The thinking is illogical and requires the attention and control of the conscious mind. The less educated, of course, commit the same error, but a major objective of education is to increase the child's and adult's conscious control over thought processes. When left uncontrolled, the implication is that the illogical processes of the subconscious take over, making less than rational connections. The illogic of this "von Domarus principle" would explain our more bizarre dreams.[26]

The von Domarus principle has been criticized as the result of subsequent studies,[27] but most of those experiments conclude only that schizophrenics do not exclusively use undistributed middle and/ or that healthy people also commit the same fallacy. The more general conclusion to be drawn from the von Domarus principle is that if schizophrenics are left defenseless with no control over their behavior by the conscious mind, then their mental functioning may well represent the

---

[25] "Fallacy of Undistributed Middle," wikipedia.org.
[26] Eilhard von Domarus, "The Specific Laws of Logic in Schizophrenia," in J. S. Kassanin, ed., *Language and Thought in Schizophrenia*, pp. 104–14, amazon.com.
[27] Charles G. Costello, ed., *Symptoms of Schizophrenia*, p. 105, books.google.com; Phillipa A. Garety and David R. Hemsley, *Delusions: Investigations Into the Psychology of Delusional Reasoning*, p. 32, books.google.com.

raw expression and operation as prototype of the subconscious. Obviously, more thought and study is needed to fully describe the subconscious mind. That the psychological profession today does not even acknowledge the existence of a subconscious mind indicates how far the science of inner reality must go to explain its subject.

Knowledge of the subconscious mind would enable us to harness its dynamic, connection-making powers by understanding not just its operation in sleep or mental illness, but also its role in aiding and influencing our everyday mental functioning. The more intelligent person, for example, is generally acknowledged to be the one who sees and understands connections among ideas before others who are slower. How does this happen? Is it a better organized subconscious mind than that of the slower thinker? Is it greater interest in the topic that drives the subconscious to look for specific connections? The more intelligent do not always possess greater knowledge about a subject than the less intelligent when hitting upon new connections. What is the role of the amount of knowledge one possesses in leading to quick links? And, of course, is there a genetic component in intelligence and how does this contribute to the efficient and effective operation of the subconscious? These are the questions that a science of the subconscious, if such existed, should be studying.

The dynamic subconscious is a powerful mental tool that can and should enable us to enjoy life by means of a well-ordered mental structure, a conscious mind interacting without obstacles or inhibitions with the subconscious to guide us smoothly to the achievement of our goals. Lack of knowledge of how this interaction takes place makes it more difficult for many of us to move forward without unnecessary extra effort to correct the organization of our minds. It is psychology that needs to give us this knowledge.

(January 20, 2009)

The Courage to be Patient

COURAGE IS BEING TRUE TO YOUR VALUES in the face of danger, fear, or other difficulty. Sometimes it is considered a willingness to undertake challenges others would not, but everyone in fact possesses the capacity to take such actions. Confidence in one's abilities, cultivated over many years, is often a precondition of courage, as in the brave calmness exhibited by a performer standing before thousands of people and not revealing the slightest stage fright. Other times, courage is prompted spontaneously by the conviction of strongly held values, as in the case of a mother racing into a burning building to save her child. In either situation, action in the face of difficulty is the essence of courage. Inaction, nevertheless, in the form of patience is occasionally called for as an expression of courage. How can this manifest itself?

I am talking about a pause or mental inaction that calls for active thought before jumping to a conclusion. Quickness to condemn as dishonest,[28] for example, when in fact ignorance may be the explanation, is a behavior that requires the courage to be patient, to search for evidence and examine arguments before speaking up to pass judgment. While temperament, no doubt, plays a role, it is psychology that determines whether or not one can be patient in a variety of situations. Just as a child caught in a burning building can trigger a mother's strongly held values, stress of a hectic work schedule or a perceived attack on one's child can trigger insecurities that unleash hasty actions or judgments.

The demands of work—urgent phone calls, deadlines for reports, disagreeable customers or colleagues, etc.—can sometimes fray the judgment and cause us to give hasty and incorrect approvals or disapprovals. The question is, why does this happen? Hecticness by itself is not the answer, since many successful business people can and do maintain their composure under pressure. Stress, as in the example of the mother racing into a burning building, taps deep-seated inner urges. Those urges may be solidly formed values or defenses built out of self-doubt caused by anxiety. The result of acting on a defense is an inappropriate response to the situation triggering the urge. Hence, the hasty and incorrect approval or disapproval. A pause to reflect before making the decision, that is, patience, can help us regain a more objective perspective by facing the anxiety and thereby allowing us to find the solidly formed values that normally guide our actions.

Perceived criticism, neglect, or other alleged negative treatment of our child by a teacher or other authority figure can also tap inappropriate

---

[28] See above, "Ignorance versus Dishonesty," p. 138.

inner urges. A parent in an attempt to right the apparent wrong may hastily lash out at the authority figure with anger or hostility. The key words here are "perceived" and "hastily." The negative treatment may not be negative at all because the parent's immediate response prevents a more considered—and patient—exploration of the facts leading up to the treatment. An appropriate inner urge that could be tapped here is protection of our child from harm, but another urge may also be tapped: distrust of authority figures built up over many years of experiences in which the conclusion "you treated me (or mine) unfairly" was repeatedly drawn. These conclusions may have thereby created expectations of being slighted and the expectations can easily be transferred to our child's treatment. The alleged negative treatment may then trigger those expectations and cause rash judgment.

Courage to be patient in this instance is the courage not to act on what our psychology is prompting us to do, but to hold off and inquire about the facts of the situation. There are other reasons why parents may feel their child is slighted, such as accepting without question every negative word the child says, but this, too, requires patience to investigate before passing judgment.

Courage to be patient is the courage to face anxiety, to endure it, while calmly exploring a more rational response to the trigger. Courage to be patient means, when angry, counting to ten before speaking or acting.

(April 27, 2010)

Questions about Independent Judgment

THE BOY IN THE HANS CHRISTIAN ANDERSEN TALE of "The Emperor's New Clothes"[29] is often admired for his independent judgment, that is, for his courage to speak a truth that the adults feared to acknowledge openly. Two questions, however, can be asked about independent judgment as a virtue. One, can everyone really practice it (besides naive children) or is it the province of true creators and innovators, such as Socrates and Galileo? And, perhaps giving rise to doubts expressed in the first question, a second asks, how does one handle the dangers of

---

[29] "The Emperor's New Clothes," wikipedia.org.

independent judgment, that is, the prospect of offending other people, sometimes resulting in death (Socrates) or house arrest (Galileo)?

Independent judgment is correct perception of the facts of reality and the courage to acknowledge and assert them. The two questions above arise because of complicating factors; intelligence and interest can affect the initial perception and other people can affect both the initial perception and the assertion of it. Psychology plays a role throughout.

Great innovators, especially those who challenge centuries of convention, are highly intelligent. They also are extremely interested and motivated in their areas of innovation. Those of us who do not possess the same intelligence or interest, whether college professor or blue collar worker, can nevertheless use our intelligence in our areas of interest to perceive and assert what we do see. Intelligence combined with interest determines who is likely to see ahead of others, and those of us who do not see initially can learn from those who do, but intelligence is not a prerogative of the highly educated. Independent judgment can be practiced equally by a garage door repairman[30] as by a scientist.

So why don't more people practice independent judgment? Which is to ask, why are they so afraid to join the boy in the tale of "The Emperor's New Clothes"? The answer is fear, real or imagined, of what might happen to them. The real fear of death or incarceration that can result from speaking one's mind poses a needless moral quandary. We have no moral obligation to drink hemlock, as Socrates did, in order to preserve our independent judgment. Many in the Soviet Union managed to maintain theirs by expressing it to family and trusted friends, sometimes speaking in a foreign language to prevent nosy neighbors from overhearing their conversations and reporting them. They were conventional on the outside, in public, to preserve their lives, but independent on the inside, at home, to preserve their self-esteem.

Most of us do not face the real fears of a Socrates, Galileo, or citizen of the Soviet Union. Our fears of expressing independent judgment stem from what others might think of us. Disapproval, maybe rejection, is the worst that might happen, yet the anxiety caused by the fear can be so strong as to blur our perception of the facts, thus preventing any expression of an independent judgment. When choices based on fear

---

[30] See above, "Curiosity for Subtle Detail," p. 204.

build up over time, habits of perceiving reality through clouded lenses become established patterns of behavior. Seeing the world through the eyes of others, whoever those significant others may be, becomes the norm. Conventionality is the result.

Can independent judgment be taught? Yes, but from an early age. Children need, of course, to be given love and support, but they also need to be given freedom, within limits appropriate to their maturity, to choose their own values. And they need to be allowed to learn from their mistakes. Most parents are loving toward infants, but when the children move into their "terrible twos," parents begin controlling and in some cases hitting. Often, the controlling continues throughout childhood and becomes a constant in traditional schools. Choice and self-assertion are seen as signs of disruption and disobedience to authority. In reality, they are signs of developing self-esteem and personal identity.[31] When they are erased by the controlling, authoritarian behavior of adults, children quickly get the message that getting along means going along. It is a rare child who matures as an adult with independent judgment intact. Perhaps this is why we tend to think that only certain people can fully achieve it.

Independent judgment is a fundamental requirement of the free society. Unless every adult citizen possesses a significant amount of self-esteem expressed as independent judgment, such a society cannot last.

(August 17, 2010)

Standing Down from External Control

In economics the principle of unilateral free trade[32] holds that everyone benefits when one country by itself, ignoring what others may do, eliminates all tariff and non-tariff barriers to trade. Cheap imports increase the standard of living both at home and in the exporting country. The historical experiment and demonstration of this principle

---
[31] Edith Packer, *Lectures on Psychology*, chap. 9, amazon.com.
[32] Richard Ebeling, "Free Trade, Peace, and Goodwill Among Nations: The Triumph of the Free Trade Movement In Great Britain," cobdencentre.org; Jacob G. Hornberger, "The Case for Unilateral Free Trade and Open Immigration," November 1, 1994, fff.org; "Richard Cobden," wikipedia.org.

was the repeal of England's Corn Laws[33] in 1846. Other countries followed England's lead and for a brief time peace, the natural consequence of free trade, was achieved.*

In human relationships psychiatrist William Glasser, whose choice theory[34] I discussed in a previous post,[35] offers a similar principle: in spite of what others may do (assuming the absence of physical abuse or attack), eliminate all habits of external control psychology from one's own behavior. The result will be less stress—from trying and failing to control the other person's behavior—and may even bring about a sense of calm. And the other person, says Glasser, may notice your change leading to a discussion of internal control psychology and new ways of relating to one another. Peace within the relationship may be achieved.

This strategy of unilateral refusal to use external control tactics is especially effective with teenagers, but works well in all relationships. Teenagers are not yet fully mature and can therefore afford guidance from parents, but they also want to be independent of their parents and resist attempts at control. Parents in the meantime instinctively practice all of Glasser's deadly habits—criticizing, blaming, complaining, nagging, threatening, punishing, and bribing, plus many variations—and protest that if none of these are used the child will not learn or mature or become responsible, etc. But parents in Glasser's practice who have stood down from using the external control habits have found their teenagers coming back to them, opening up, and even asking for advice. "When you stop controlling," as Glasser says,[36] "you gain control." The strength of the relationship is what gives the parent influence. The deadly habits erode and destroy both.

The value of eliminating external control tactics with students, a relationship that is not unlike that of parents to teenagers, has been demonstrated abundantly by Glasser in numerous books.[37] Other factors may complicate matters in couples and work relationships. A mature adult can choose to walk away from either or both. And a boss

---

[33] "Corn Laws," wikipedia.org.
[34] William Glasser, *Choice Theory*, amazon.com.
[35] See above, "Choice Theory and Capitalism versus Dictatorship," p. 49.
[36] William Glasser, *For Parents and Teenagers*, chap. 1, amazon.com.
[37] William Glasser, *The Quality School*, amazon.com; William Glasser, *Every Student Can Succeed*, amazon.com.

or spouse may not be willing to try to make the relationship work. Nevertheless, one-sided abandonment of external control, notably the "CBC's" (criticizing, blaming, and complaining), can work wonders in improving a relationship. Criticizing, says Glasser, is the most corrosive habit one can use in any relationship, but it is particularly harmful in marriages. Caring, trusting, listening, supporting, negotiating, befriending, and encouraging—Glasser's connecting habits—bring people closer together.[38]

Work relationships sometimes pose a challenge if the employee feels stuck and cannot move to a new job. The boss should be practicing what Glasser calls lead management, the application of choice theory to managing employees, but what if the boss is external control to the point of being almost drill-sergeant harsh? What can the employee do? Abandoning external control and practicing the connecting habits are a must, but offering an occasional compliment might melt some of the insecurities that seem to motivate such a boss. And reminding yourself that you are choosing to remain in that position can help; you may be choosing to stay for the benefits, for example, or to stay until economic conditions improve. Internal control means choosing one's own behavior. Knowing that builds confidence and contentment.

The connection between internal control psychology and free trade is simple. The former is a theory of human relationships, of how people get along with one another on a personal basis, whereas the latter is a theory of human relationships occurring within the social institutions of business and society. The latter is the implementation of the former and there is no place for external control in either relationships or trade.** This is why advocates of capitalism argue that the monolithic and historical practitioner of external control, the government, should be prevented permanently from intruding into all aspects of our personal and business lives.

---

[38] William Glasser and Carleen Glasser, *Getting Together and Staying Together*, amazon.com; William Glasser and Carleen Glasser, *Eight Lessons for a Happier Marriage*, amazon.com.

* "If goods don't cross borders, armies will" is a phrase attributed to French economist Frederic Bastiat.[39] It emphasizes the connection between free trade and peace.

** Indeed, Ayn Rand calls the trader principle[40] the foundation of all rational human relationships, because it is the principle of justice.

(September 14, 2010)

Theory of the Big Mouth

IT IS WITH GREAT TREPIDATION that I write this post. Not ever having been one to talk a lot, I know from experience that if I dare to talk back to a talker I will be talked into the ground. Talkers do not suffer comment lightly, especially when the comment comes from quiet people. Talkers are experts at having the last word, and if they do not like what I say in this post, I am certain that they will tell me.

The theory of the big mouth has a simple premise. The world is run by people who talk a lot. The trouble is that 99.9% (well, some large percentage—I have not conducted a survey) of the talkers do not know what they are talking about. I sometimes fantasize that the world would be a better place if the talkers were to take a holiday one day a month and say nothing for twenty-four hours. Having been a shy, quiet person all my life, I have been on the butt end of many a talker comment. Also, by not talking a lot I have been able to observe much talker behavior. What follows are my comments to talkers, my turn at talking back to them.

The butt end of talker comment is the unsolicited and often rude and ill-mannered advice given to quiet people. "Speak up kid," "bite your tongue kid," "you're going to have to learn to speak up or you won't survive in this world," and that gem of the reverse golden rule given to me as fatherly advice when I was a young man working in business: "you're going have to learn to do it to others before they do it to you." Variations on these comments go on ad nauseam. I have often wondered

---

[39] Thomas J. DiLorenzo, "Biography of Frederic Bastiat (1801–1850): Between the French and Marginalist Revolutions," August 1, 2007, mises.org.
[40] "Trader Principle," aynrandlexicon.com.

why it is okay for a talker to give unsolicited advice to a quiet person, but rude and ill-mannered for a quiet person to talk back to a talker, for example, by saying something like, "you're going to have to learn not to talk so much" or "you need to stop and think before speaking." When any attempt is made like this, the talker usually responds with an indignant "how dare you talk to me that way." Funny, I always thought advice-giving was a two-way street.

My observations of talkers have shown that many talkers are oblivious to psychology, especially the psychology of the person they are talking to. Often they are just oblivious, unable to see or acknowledge the obvious boredom on the faces of their listeners. It is especially sad, though, to see a parent feeling embarrassed for the behavior of a shy child when, say, the child speaks an inaudible "thank you" or "goodbye" or does not speak up at all. Haranguing children in such situations will not help them become comfortable in the company of other people and encourage them to speak up; it may drive them to become quieter and more withdrawn. Addressing their fears and discomfort is the correct aid. Besides, shyness does tend to decrease with age and maturity. It did for my father, a quiet man most of his life, and today even I, in my older years, talk to strangers!

The "theory of the big mouth," of course, is an unfriendly designation. In me it renders an image of the bigmouth bass, a fish. What I am really talking about is a variant of Glasser's external control psychology, best captured by this quote:

> The seeds of almost all our unhappiness are planted early in our lives when we begin to encounter people who have discovered not only what is right for them—but also, unfortunately, what is right for us. Armed with this discovery and following a destructive tradition that has dominated our thinking for thousands of years, these people feel obligated to try to force us to do what *they know* is right (Glasser's emphasis).[41]

And talkers seem to be the ones who know what is right for everyone else, especially those pesky quiet types. It is in the elementary school years when children become aware of right and wrong. As they discover

---

[41] William Glasser, *Choice Theory*, p. 4, amazon.com.

what is right, they often conclude that whatever they do is not just right for themselves but also for everyone else. They fail to acknowledge, and need to be taught, the existence of options, the wide range of behavior that is not the same as theirs, but still is right. If not corrected, this premise can lead to rankism[42] and BS'ing,[43] or worse.

It is not a sin (or disadvantage) to be shy. Remember the western cowboy heroes? They all spoke few words. Indeed, psychologists[44] have found that many people, including the gregarious and famous, feel shy at some times and in some areas of their lives. The entertainer and comedian Johnny Carson several times said that he often felt shy at cocktail parties. The advantage of being a quiet type is that we can sit back and observe what is going on in the world around us and then write about it—as in a blog like this one. And I don't think I've been a failure in life.

So talk on you talkers. I'll just write about you!

(November 5, 2010)

Follow-up. In a short 2003 essay in *the Atlantic*[45] titled "Caring for Your Introvert: The Habits and Needs of a Little-Understood Group," Jonathan Rauch quotes silent Calvin Coolidge as saying, "Don't you know that four fifths of all our troubles in this life would disappear if we would just sit down and keep still?" A flood of responses from readers led to this interview: "Introverts of the World, Unite!"[46] Rauch must be on to something!

(February 13, 2012)

---

[42] Dignity Works (website), breakingranks.net; see above, "The Market Gives Privilege to No One," p. 25.; see above, "Rankism and the Well-Earned Disrespect of Some Teachers," p. 180.
[43] See below, "The Dangerous Admiration of BS," p. 293.
[44] Philip G. Zimbardo, *Shyness*, amazon.com.
[45] Jonathan Rauch, "Caring for Your Introvert," March 2003, theatlantic.com.
[46] Sage Stossel, "Introverts of the World, Unite!," February 2006, theatlantic.com.

2011
The Primacy of Psychology

IN A PREVIOUS post,[47] I argued that method is primary in education, not content. By method I meant teaching students how to think conceptually. In the process of learning how to think, content would follow. In the current post, I would like to broaden this theme to the primacy of psychology, to teaching the effective use one's mind in controlling and guiding behavior.

The primacy of psychology means cultivating the development of the child's independent, uniquely individual self, that is, cultivating the growth of a strong conviction of worthiness and efficacy sufficient to guide the child to acquire the knowledge, values, and skills necessary to live a happy life without making compromises to please others. As I often find myself telling my students, "That last sentence was a mouthful. Let's break it down into a few digestible chunks."

First, "worthiness and efficacy" refer to the child's self-esteem.[48] Not the watered-down superficial stuff that the government schools promote, such as awarding bumper stickers to children for being first in their class for attendance or getting all A's. This is a comparative award that makes children feel superior to all the others, not loveable or competent. Feeling worthy means "I am loveable, capable of being loved." It is a deep conviction that begins in the relationship with the children's parents (and relatives) and continues to develop (or become thwarted) in their relationships with teachers. Positive experiences from such friendships promote worthiness, negative experiences degrade it.

The same is true for the development of efficacy, which is a sense of competence, of being able to do things in the world. Children need frequent senses of accomplishment, whether it be learning the multiplication tables or whittling the image of a dog on a piece of pine. What children accomplish does not matter as long as they keep feeling that sense of accomplishment. Worthiness and efficacy influence and reinforce each other. The feeling "I can't do it" often leads to the feeling "I'm no good" and the "I'm no good" feeling often leads to and encourages

---
[47] See above, "The Primacy of Method," p. 166.
[48] Nathaniel Branden, *The Psychology of Self-Esteem*, amazon.com.

the "I can't do it." Self-esteem is prerequisite for and concomitant to the acquisition of an education.

"Knowledge, values, and skills" are the content of education. Because life is action, all education in essence is the acquisition of skill. And skill is the application of knowledge and values whether it be the technique and importance of performing a good car wash, a good weld, a good sale, a good lecture, a good design, or a good moral decision. Everything we do in life is a behavior, driven by what we know and value in the performance of the task. The aim of education, then, is to ensure that we possess sufficient self-esteem to acquire the knowledge and values necessary to pursue our chosen tasks in life. Those tasks may not be reading English literature or solving quadratic equations. They are what the child wants to pursue, not what the teacher wants to teach. Demanding that children study certain subjects in order to be "well-rounded" or exhorting them to acquire "knowledge for its own sake" is a prescription for many to drop out. Control and choice[49] in their own education is what children require for both their self-esteem and their future.*

Finally, "without making compromises to please others" refers to independence.[50] Because government-run schools demand the opposite, as do many parents and other adults, independence is the least understood and least taught of psychological skills. Some few children are naturals at standing up for themselves. Most need guidance in understanding that they do not have to go along with their peers or significant adults if they do not agree with what is being asked of them. High self-esteem and a strong sense of personal identity are required to be able to say that the emperor has no clothes. Independence—independent judgment and independent action—can be taught, but educators today have a long way to go before they begin to understand what is required to achieve this feat.

---

[49] See above, "Control and Choice in Education," p. 182.
[50] See above, "Sound or Independent Judgment?," p. 206.; see above, "Questions about Independent Judgment," p. 219.

* As I discuss in *Montessori, Dewey, and Capitalism*,[51] "well-roundedness" is probably a slap at egoism, because it is "selfish" to concentrate in only one area of interest, and acquiring "knowledge for its own sake" is a hobby of privileged elites.

(April 19, 2011)

On Hitting . . . Dogs and Children

HITTING IS NOT NICE. I'm talking about the non-self-defensive kind, the initiation of the use of physical force to get your way. Its goal is submission. Just think thief with a knife. If you don't hand over your wallet, that is, submit to the thief's wishes, you may suffer the physical force of a knife or fist.

Why are dogs and children hit? "Smacking" is a word one still hears today as a recommended teaching method for both. Pre-teen children are not usually known to be aggressive, requiring self-defensive restraint, though some dog breeds have the reputation of being aggressive and unpredictable. And it's not uncommon to hear something like, "A Rottweiler can bite your nose off. You have to teach him who's boss. Be the alpha dog!"

Well, let's take that comment first. I probably could bite a nose off if provoked in the right (or wrong) way, and I suspect many a small dog could do the same. Indeed, in the very act of making a friendly overture, I have been bitten by a small dog. Does dog training require hitting? Does a dog that jumps up on the bed have to be smacked?

Consider the similarities between dogs and children. They both have minds. They both can learn. They both want to please their parents or owners. They both experience (sometimes strong) emotions, which means they can feel confident or insecure, happy or sad, eager or listless. Inappropriate methods of relating to a child or dog by using, say, force and fear can result in insecurity, which in turn leads to compensating behavior. In older children, this can lead to depression, drugs, alcohol, or crime. In dogs, it can lead to uncontrolled aggression.

---

[51] Jerry Kirkpatrick, *Montessori, Dewey, and Capitalism*, pp. 56, 144–46, amazon.com.

Teaching, whether of dogs or children, requires positive motivation,[52] not negative. The alpha dog notion is a myth.[53]

What about the original sin, or rather, the alleged aggressiveness of certain breeds, such as Rottweilers,[54] Doberman Pinschers,[55] German Shepherds,[56] and the notorious Pit Bull Terrier?[57] Uninformed hysterics aside, these dogs all have pleasant temperaments,[58] if trained properly. Hit a dog—or me—and you might be surprised by the attack mode we each quickly move into. As with child rearing, pet ownership requires teaching and is the responsibility of the adult.

Of course, dogs are protective of their families and territory, but again the adult is responsible for the dog's behavior, just as the adult is responsible for the child who hits a playmate or takes a playmate's toy without permission. Dog bites are common among unsupervised children.[59] The responsibility of the adult is to teach the child how to approach and relate to animals, not to leave the child alone with a pet. Pulling a tail or ear will certainly generate a response from a dog. Just try pulling my ear and see what will happen!

Higher-level mammals that possess a consciousness also possess a psychology. They are not stimulus-response[60] black boxes. Their psychologies must be acknowledged and interacted with supportively. This does not necessarily mean that your dog should be allowed to sleep on all the furniture in the house or that your child should be allowed to eat ice cream anywhere he or she desires. Teaching, not hitting, which means positive communication and reinforcement, along with the nurturing of a warm relationship, is key to training an animal. This is not much different from what is required for raising a healthy child, except that the techniques used for the child must be more sophisticated in order

---

[52] "Positive Reinforcement Training," humanesociety.org.
[53] Jeninne Lee-St. John, "Dog Training and the Myth of Alpha-Male Dominance," July 30, 2010, time.com.
[54] "Rottweiler," wikipedia.org.
[55] "Dobermann," wikipedia.org.
[56] "German Shepherd," wikipedia.org.
[57] "American Pit Bull Terrier," wikipedia.org.
[58] Dog Temperament (website), dogtemperament.com.
[59] "Young, Unsupervised Children Most At Risk for Dog Bites, Study Shows; Dogs Often Target a Child's Face and Eyes," November 12, 2010, sciencedaily.com.
[60] "Behaviorism," wikipedia.org.

to be appropriate to the higher level of consciousness. Even then, the techniques used must match the child's stage of development. This means, for example, not treating the child as a small adult.[61]

Wild horses, unfortunately, are sometimes still broken by tying them to a tree, letting them kick and fight until they give in, that is, are "broken,"[62] so they will finally let a rider get on its back. Come to think of it, human slaves have also been treated the same way. Breaking the spirit is the goal of any initiation of the use of physical force; it is the goal of hitting. Dogs and children do not deserve to be treated this way. Their behaviors, with a little awareness, are predictable and understandable.

Smacking is the tool of a slave owner.

Postscript. As an undergraduate, I shared a basement with two Dobermans. (I had my own apartment; they had their own space.) They were two of the sweetest dogs I've ever met. And contrary to its reputation, the American Pit Bull Terrier can be used as a therapy dog.[63] Are service dogs[64] and all the exotic animals[65] used in the entertainment industry trained by using negative motivation? I don't think so. Check the sources in this post.

(June 23, 2011)

Follow-up. "With the popularity of *The Dog Whisperer*[66] television show, books and products, the controversy over which methods are the most humane and effective ways to address behavior problems in dogs is dividing dog lovers all over the world.

"While animal behaviorists, trainers and other dog professionals recognize that the show is exposing dog owners to the possibility that their dogs' behavior can be changed (and indeed, business is booming), the concern is that the show gives the false impression that behavior

---

[61] See above, "The Child as Small Adult," p. 161.
[62] Jeffrey Rolo, "The Fatal Flaw behind Horse Breaking," alphahorse.com.
[63] "Trainer Turns Pit Bull into Therapy Dog," June 21, 2008, npr.org.
[64] "Assistance Dog," wikipedia.org.
[65] "Animal Training," seaworld.org.
[66] "Dog Whisperer with Cesar Millan," wikipedia.org.

can be changed within a matter of hours and that the methods used are known to incite or increase aggressive behaviors."[67]

(December 3, 2011)

Should Spanking Be a Felony?

IN MY PREVIOUS post[68] I argued that hitting a child or dog is neither nice nor necessary. Positive motivation and the desire and willingness to develop a warm relationship are what generate influence to channel behavior in appropriate ways. The implication about hitting a child is that it transgresses legal boundaries.*

Indeed, spanking would seem to violate child abuse laws and some judges[69] have concurred. Current law says that any marks or bruising left as the result of physical contact constitutes abuse.[70] In most states, however, the law exempts "reasonable disciplining," though precisely what that means is not always clear. The trend is unmistakably in the direction of banning spanking.

Whether it leaves a mark or not, spanking is the initiation of the use of physical force. Its purpose is to cause pain and to command obedience to the will of the adult. Its consequence is usually humiliation. In light of modern theories of child psychology and child rearing, such adult behavior is unacceptable. Whether every spanking parent should immediately be arrested is an issue of the implementation of new law. A long and unquestioned historical context of using physical force as a teaching technique calls for education of the populace and gradual, not impulsive, execution of the new principle. Uninformed parents can be well-meaning when spanking their children. The complications of parental and child psychology call for a grace period.

Consider the young father of a toddler I observed a number of years ago. I was having my hair cut and the toddler was supposed to

---

[67] Lisa Mullinax, "Behavior: What a Dog Does, Not What a Dog Is," May 16 2017, 4pawsuniversity.com; Fanna Easter, "The Real Reason Dog Trainers Dislike Cesar Millan," March 24, 2016, dogtrainingnation.com.
[68] See above, "On Hitting . . . Dogs and Children, p. 229.
[69] "Pastor Charged with Felony for Spanking Son," October 28, 2008, wnd.com.
[70] "Child Abuse," wikipedia.org; "Child Welfare Information Gateway: Factsheets Series," childwelfare.gov.

be obediently crawling into the barber chair across the way, but he was not cooperating. The father became exasperated and swatted the child on the behind. The boy cried and obediently sat in the chair. What struck me about this incident were the emotional expressions of the father: embarrassment, probably because his child in public view was not "minding" him, and guilt, probably for having had to resort to force. The father's behavior was not mean-spirited or felonious. He just needed to learn better ways of relating to his son.

In contrast, our daughter's first experience with a haircut was completely pleasureful. Before getting her near the barber's chair, her talented hair stylist bounced her on his knee for a few minutes and said funny things to make her laugh. Her haircut was a pleasant success—no need for physical force. Bottom line: it's all in the technique. Teaching method is everything. The hair stylist used the fun theory[71] of behavioral influence.

The most significant emotion present in all spankings, including the young father's behavior above, is anger. To be angry enough to inflict pain, one must feel that an injustice has been committed, which then is allegedly righted by the spanking. This is the absurdity of spanking. Has the child committed an injustice? Has he robbed a bank? No, he refused to sit quietly in a barber's chair! When parental anger in the twenty-first century rises to the level of using an implement, such as a paddle, stick, belt, hairbrush, or wooden spoon, etc., the intent is mean-spirited and sometimes vicious. I do not sympathize with anyone who calls this "reasonable disciplining."

Psychologies are complex, though, and parents have reportedly cried after using such implements on their children, saying they didn't mean to or couldn't help themselves. Is such behavior criminal? Some murderers have regretted their killings and said they couldn't help themselves. What's the difference between these two kinds of behavior? One has thousands of years of cultural tradition behind it saying that it is okay to hit children, the other has the same number of years of tradition saying that it is wrong to kill another human being. Saying that it is okay to spank because of our historical tradition is cultural relativism. Other cultures have equal numbers of years of tradition saying that it

---

[71] Stuart Wickes, "The Fun Theory," November 25, 2018, familyadventureproject.org.

is okay to hit women and mutilate their genitals. Historical context is only relevant in putting the new law into practice.

Spanking should be a felony because behavior is controllable, and whether or not a mark or bruise is left on the body, physical force has been initiated by a big, powerful adult against a small, helpless child. The issue here is one of fairness to the young father with the toddler in the hair salon. Throwing him in the slammer or putting him on probation would not help him become a better dad. As always, the issue is one of education, of the adult.

* In spite of what animal rights advocates say, dogs are property and rights belong to the owner. Children are human beings and their rights derive from that nature as such.

(July 25, 2011)

Follow-up. From A. S. Neill[72]: "Is it right or wrong to spank? It is not a question of right or wrong; in a way it is a case of cowardliness, for you are hitting someone not your own size. I don't suppose you hit your husband when he is being a nuisance. Is it because you wouldn't dare? He might strike you back. Of course, you're perfectly safe hitting your child of three. She can't strike you back.

"Spanking is an outlet for adult rage and frustration and hate. . . . Happy mothers do not spank."

(December 3, 2011)

Look at Your Premises. Look. Look. Look!

THE FUNDAMENTAL METHOD OF SCIENCE is observation, so nineteenth century naturalist Louis Agassiz[73] stressed its importance in teaching and learning. As he told one student, "Take this fish and look at it." Hours later, when the student wanted to know what to do next, Agassiz replied, "Look at your fish." And still later, "Look, look, look." For three days the student looked at the fish, then on the fourth, Agassiz

---

[72] A. S. Neill, *Freedom—Not License!*, pp. 99–100, amazon.com.
[73] Lane Cooper, *Louis Agassiz as a Teacher*, pp. 40–48, amazon.com.

presented him with a new specimen. Observation means using our senses to perceive the world. Figuratively, it means opening our eyes and looking at it. The more one looks, Agassiz was encouraging his student, the more one sees.

In the human sciences, psychology in particular, observation is also the fundamental method of acquiring knowledge. It means not just looking at human behavior, but more importantly at the mental content of human beings. Introspection, as I have argued before,[74] is a legitimate method of science, actually a form of observation. Looking at the premises people hold in their minds, that is, their beliefs, values, and emotions, is key to understanding why they act the way they do.

The word "premise" refers to a thought or proposition assumed to be true that supports a later conclusion. In the face of an apparent contradiction—such as, on the one hand, the attacks made on McDonald's and Walmart as less than virtuous companies and, on the other, the amazing job creation of the former[75] and wonderful, inexpensive products of the latter[76] made available to the masses—Ayn Rand's line to "check your premises" comes to mind. Look deep, as Rand would urge, at all conclusions that lead to other conclusions and go all the way down to the starting points of one's beliefs, values, and emotions.

Thus, when critics of McDonald's and Walmart are pressed for their reasoning, their response might be something like this. "McDonald's and Walmart are just seeking profits; the profit motive and customer satisfaction, after all, are opposed to each other." Why are profits bad? "Because profit seeking is selfish." But eating and drinking are selfish; why is the pursuit of self-interest when it doesn't hurt others bad? "People can't be left free to pursue their own interests; the poor especially don't know what's good for them. They aren't able to distinguish good food and good products from the bad. The government has to regulate business and guide the poor in their choices." Don't the poor have free will and the ability to reason out their own choices? "We're all controlled by our environment and reason can only go so far; it's limited." How

---

[74] See above, "Ensuring that Disposition Trumps Situation," p. 210.
[75] Jeffrey A. Tucker, "McDonald's as the Paradigm of Progress," June 27, 2011, Mises.org.
[76] William L. Anderson, "What Is Walmart's Crime?," June 27, 2011, Mises.org.

do you know? "We can't really know anything with certainty. In fact, people who claim certain knowledge are dangerous, potential dictators. We have to talk things over and let the majority vote for the best alternatives."

Although many additional lines of questioning of these critics could be pursued, this example demonstrates the many premises (in this case, false ones) underlying a simple concrete conclusion. The more one looks at the premises people hold, the more one sees and comes to understand.

The same process can be performed on personal psychology. Although nothing in psychology is simple, consider the relatively uncomplicated phenomenon of stage fright,[77] such as the anxiety an actor feels before going on stage or a speaker before delivering a lecture. Premises behind the fear might range from the thought "I can't do it, I don't want to do it, I'm going to be a failure and be humiliated, I have to get out of it" to "I hope I don't make too many mistakes, I know I can do a good job, I'll just keep working on my craft to polish it, I know that once I'm out there I will begin to relax." Or something in between. Deeper exploration might find connections to similar premises that operated in similar situations in one's early, formative years and might also reveal how choices made then produced feelings of anxiety that still operate. Looking at these earlier premises provides fuller understanding of how personal psychology develops, the role of choice in that development, and the role of choice in making corrections in the present—in this case, taking a deep breath, walking on stage, and delivering one's lines or lecture.

Looking at a mind or looking at a fish, the process is the same. Observation is the method of science and the more one looks, the more one sees. Indeed, a modern-day Agassiz working in the human sciences might say to his or her students, "Look at your psychology. Look. Look. Look."

And, of course, this directive applies not just to students, but to all of us. If we unfailingly "look, look, look" into our souls, we might be surprised by what we see.

(August 29, 2011)

---

[77] "Stage Fright," wikipedia.org.

"Children Don't Have Disorders; They Live in a Disordered World"

THE TITLE OF THIS POST comes from psychiatrist and attention-deficit/hyperactivity-disorder (ADHD) critic Peter Breggin.[78] It's a variation of Maria Montessori's[79] line to "control the environment, not the child." For Montessori, children develop healthy psychologies—become "normalized," to use her term—by being left free to pursue their own interests and choose their own educational work, provided the surroundings of the classroom are made safe and stimulating. Drugs are a cruel and totally unwarranted control of the child.

Most children who exhibit the well-known ADHD symptoms[80] are simply failing to handle the boredom, confusion,* or authoritarianism, or all three, of school, home, and other environments in which they live and play. They are not diseased kids, possessing neurological or biochemical imbalances, who require addicting, cocaine-like stimulants to cow them into submission. They are youngsters trying to learn, and have fun in the process, but their world is complex and often the opposite of fun, especially school. What they desperately need is to be left free as much as possible to pursue their own interests and, when they request it, one or several adults to be their friends, to pay attention to them, to listen to their pleasures and worries, and to be their coach and confidant. What they most decidedly do not need are William Glasser's seven deadly habits[81]: criticizing, blaming, complaining, nagging, threatening, punishing, and bribing. All of these habits, of course, are staples of their world, and ours, but many children do not know how to cope with them. What they also most definitely do not need is to be made to feel stoned or spaced out.

Labeling children with ADHD stigmatizes them as inadequate and, as a result, induces unearned guilt, because the adults who recommend the drugs are actually blaming them for their behavior even though

---

[78] Peter R. Breggin, "The Hazards of Treating 'Attention-Deficit/Hyperactivity Disorder' with Methylphenidate (Ritalin)," 1995, Breggin.com.
[79] "Montessori Education," wikipedia.org.
[80] "Symptoms and Diagnosis of ADHD," cdc.gov.
[81] William Glasser, *For Parents and Teenagers*, p. 13, amazon.com.

the theory behind the whole psychotropic drug mantra is materialism[82] and determinism.[83] A child who acts up in class, or who does not pay attention, according to the adults, must be controlled. Something, so the adults say, is wrong with the child, not with the adults' methods of relating to the child. The message is clear. Donna Bryant Goertz[84] says that medication today is the new spanking.

The evidence for a physiological basis of ADHD behavior does not exist. The experimental studies do not uphold the belief. This is especially confirmed when the ADHD researchers themselves admit that the children improve during summer vacation and when taught in smaller, more attention-focused classes. Indeed, when looking at the psychiatric professions[85] nine symptoms of inattention and the nine symptoms of hyperactivity-impulsivity, I can say that I have often exhibited everyone of them—today, when I was a child, and in all the years in between. I also know too many highly successful people, and have heard of many others, who, if the medicines had been available when they were children, would have been drugged to the hilt and probably had their futures destroyed.

The criteria to look at concerning ADHD are Glasser's[86]: if your child can watch and understand television, play video games, and use a computer, do better for some teachers than for others, do better in one subject than another that requires the same level of reading and understanding, and has good friends he or she enjoys being with, then it is highly unlikely that there is anything wrong with your child.** Glasser piercingly and humorously puts the issue in perspective when he says that the worst attention deficit disorders in the world are husbands and wives, because many of them so often do not listen to each other!

As I have said in these pages before, the solution to helping so-called problem children is to let them go fish[87]: "Many are just plain bored of sitting at a desk in a classroom and are sick of having adults lord their size and power over them." Going fishing, though literally possible at

---

[82] "Materialism," wikipedia.org.
[83] "Determinism," wikipedia.org.
[84] Donna Bryant Goertz, *Children Who Are Not Yet Peaceful*, amazon.com.
[85] "Symptoms and Diagnosis of ADHD," cdc.gov.
[86] William Glasser, *Choice Theory*, p. 256, amazon.com.
[87] See above, "Go Fish!," p. 153.

the Sudbury Valley School,[88] is metaphor for getting adults off their backs and more generally for removing confusion and authoritarianism from their lives.

* I say "confusion" because some parents today who have rejected the authoritarianism of their parents and grandparents have nevertheless failed to provide structure and consistency for their children. Similar behavior can result. Some schools can also provide this confusion.

** I've simplified these criteria. See pp. 255–59 in *Choice Theory* for a fuller understanding of Glasser's analysis of the so-called learning disabilities. Glasser calls psychotropic medicines "brain drugs," refusing to grant them the honorific "medicine," and refers to their side effects as effects. There's nothing secondary or "side," he says, about the effects of brain drugs.

(September 21, 2011)

Statements of Independence

INDEPENDENT JUDGMENT is both a personality trait, a distinctive way of thinking and acting, and a character trait, a moral conviction in the face of opposition or indifference to stand by one's beliefs and values. A number of writers in their own nuanced ways have captured the gist of these traits.

The late Steve Jobs, co-founder of Apple Computer, offers in his Stanford Commencement Address of 2005[89] an eloquent statement of independence:

> Your time is limited, so don't waste it living someone else's life. Don't be trapped by dogma—which is living with the results of other people's thinking. Don't let the noise of others' opinions drown out your own inner voice. And most important, have the courage to follow your heart and intu-

---

[88] Sudbury Valley School: Expect Excellence (website), sudval.org.
[89] David Ewalt, "Steve Jobs' 2005 Stanford Commencement Address," October 5, 2011, forbes.com; "Steve Jobs' 2005 Stanford Commencement Address," youtube.com.

ition. They somehow already know what you truly want to become. Everything else is secondary.

Follow your own thoughts and emotions, Jobs is saying. Don't give in to the edicts and requests of others.

Psychiatrist William Glasser in *Positive Addiction*[90] ties independence to happiness:

> As we grow, we should learn to judge for ourselves what is worthwhile, but it takes a great deal of strength to do what is right when few people will agree with us for doing it. Most of us spend our lives in a series of compromises between doing what we believe in and doing what will please those who are important to us. Happiness depends a great deal on gaining enough strength to live with a minimum of these compromises.

It is these compromises to please others, Glasser says, that create unhappy relationships and lead us to seek compensating behaviors, such as anxiety and depression, or worse. Strength to say "yes" to ourselves and "no" to possibly too-demanding and probing others is the path to happiness.

Daniel Greenberg, founder of the Sudbury Valley School,[91] ties independence to the free society[92]:

> Dependence, not independence, is the quality most suitable to authoritarian states.... The hallmark of the independent man is the ability to bear responsibility. To be responsible and accountable for one's actions. To do, and to stand up for what one has done. Not to hide behind "superior orders," not to seek shelter in group decisions, and to take strength from some heroic figure—but to be one's own man.

The self-reliant and self-responsible individual, Greenberg is saying, does not unquestioningly take orders from authority. The citizen of a free society exhibits a healthy distrust of anyone in power.

---

[90] William Glasser, *Positive Addiction*, p. 3, amazon.com.
[91] Sudbury Valley School: Expect Excellence (website), sudval.org.
[92] Sudbury Valley School, *The Crisis in American Education*, p. 54, amazon.com.

Ayn Rand, by way of Galt's speech in *Atlas Shrugged*,[93] places the source of independent judgment in one's own mind:

> Independence is the recognition of the fact that yours is the responsibility of judgment and nothing can help you escape it—that no substitute can do your thinking, as no pinch-hitter can live your life.

No one, in other words, can get inside our heads to make us do our own thinking or, for that matter, make us not think. Perception, judgment, decision making, and action all originate within our minds. Control of our lives, then, is internal. Letting others "pinch hit" for us is to allow them to do our thinking.

What encourages us to become independent? How can our children develop it? Perhaps Summerhill School[94] founder, A. S. Neill, states the conditions best[95]:

> Free children are not easily influenced; the absence of fear accounts for this phenomenon. Indeed, the absence of fear is the finest thing that can happen to a child.

By "free child," Neill means one whose rights as an individual are respected by other children and adults in both home and school, and one who respects the rights of other children and adults in both home and school. Otherwise, the child is free to do whatever he or she desires, that is, is free of authoritarian edicts and bossing and bullying by others. Not surprisingly, Neill also ties independence to the free society as an essential requirement.

Independence and happiness require freedom because freedom produces independence. And independence makes happiness possible.

(November 4, 2011)

---

[93] Ayn Rand, *Atlas Shrugged*, p. 1019, amazon.com.
[94] A. S. Neill's Summerhill (website), summerhillschool.co.uk.
[95] A. S. Neill, *Summerhill*, p. 9, amazon.com.

2012

Introversion, Quiet Persistence, and the Tortoise

FOR MUCH OF MY ADULT LIFE I have thought of myself as the tortoise in the Aesop fable of "The Tortoise and the Hare." Many "hares" at various times have run circles around me—secured promotions before me in business, published articles or books before me in academia, and, of course, given me all kinds of advice about how I needed to speak up and become more gregarious if I wanted to survive in this world.[96] Labeled as shy by those hares, I nevertheless felt that if I kept plugging away at what I was doing, success would follow. As it has turned out, I have beaten a few of those hares, not that I viewed my life as a contest against them, but my quiet persistence has won the day.

And quiet persistence is precisely what Susan Cain describes in her book *Quiet: The Power of Introverts in a World That Can't Stop Talking*[97] as key to the introvert's success in today's extrovert-driven world. An introvert herself and former Wall Street attorney and negotiator, Cain reviews the considerable research on introversion and extroversion and provides in the process a liberating manifesto for introverts everywhere.

Careful to distinguish shyness from introversion—"shyness is the fear of social disapproval or humiliation, while introversion is a preference for environments that are not overstimulating" (p. 12)—Cain refutes the claim of the psychiatrists' *Diagnostic and Statistical Manual*[98] (DSM-IV) that fear of public speaking is pathological. Citing the likes of Eleanor Roosevelt and Mohandas Gandhi, among many other famous introverts who were terrified of speaking up in a crowd, she goes on to report the research that shows introverts to be more creative, artistic, empathic and better at problem-solving than extroverts.

Introverts are more cautious, that is, we look before leaping, or rather, think before acting, and they crave solitude: rather than go to

---

[96] See above, "Theory of the Big Mouth," p. 224.
[97] Susan Cain, *Quiet*, amazon.com; Susan Cain, "The Power of Introverts," February 2012, ted.com; Quiet Revolution (website), quietrev.com.
[98] "Diagnostic and Statistical Manual of Mental Disorders," wikipedia.org.

a party on a Saturday night, we often prefer to spend the time alone reading a book. Deep discussion one on one is the desired method of socializing by an introvert; small talk may then occur after the two have gotten to know each other, but not before.

Crowds are generally avoided because they are a main source of the overstimulation Cain is talking about. Groupthink and group projects[99] of the type that are required so routinely on college campuses today produce conventionality and suppress imagination. It humiliates members of the Asian culture who, by western standards, are unfortunately viewed as shy by nature; the irony is that Asian culture views fast-talking extroverts as weak and insecure!

Solitary persistence is our source of innovation. "It's not that I'm so smart," as Albert Einstein, a tortoise-introvert and not-very-good student in our conventional schools, put it. "It's that I stay with problems longer" (quoted in Cain, p. 169).

It is the din of crowds that shuts down the minds of introverts. At crowded dinner tables where three or more conversations may be going on at once, I confess, if someone is trying to talk to me, to pretending to hear what they say, guessing at their words. Usually, I prefer to remain silent.

So how is it that introverts can become great speakers, actors, comedians . . . or college professors? This of course is a question only an extrovert could ask! Cain says that a certain amount of "pseudo-extroversion" can be developed, but I think of it, assuming extensive preparation has been completed, as being in control when I am in front of a class. The fear is then minimized, not that I wasn't terrified the first time I did it or that I don't still feel an edge thirty years later. Spontaneous or extemporaneous speaking by introverts is not likely to happen many times or be performed very well.

To the surprise of the hares of the world, quiet persistence is the path to success, not just in the performing arts but also, as Cain illustrates, in personal selling and entrepreneurship. For thirty years I have been telling my students that they do not have to be a back-slapping, plaid-wearing Herb Tarlek[100] in order to become a successful salesperson or

---

[99] See above, "Group Projects: The Bell Has Tolled," p. 185.
[100] "Herb Tarlek," wikipedia.org.

entrepreneur. Both can be and at times are introverted. Persistence, the confidence to pursue one's goals in the face of opposition and discouragement, eventually wins.

To close this post, I think it is only fitting to cite a familiar text to demonstrate Susan Cain's accomplishment. Paraphrasing the text:

> Introverts of the world, read this book! You have nothing to lose but your chains.
>
> The chains of guilt and humiliation that there is something wrong with you because you would rather not speak up in front of a crowd or would rather read a book than go to a party. Let the extroverts of the world find some other way to entertain themselves than by telling you what they think you should be doing!

(March 16, 2012)

The Barbarity of Modern Psychiatry

IT IS NO ACCIDENT THAT Thomas Hobbes[101]—the "solitary, poor, nasty, brutish, and short" guy—advocated dictatorship. He was a materialist, the philosophical notion that consciousness is an illusion, at best an effect or non-causal by-product of the brain. Materialism denies free will and therefore assumes that all of our behavior is determined either by internal bodily functions or by external environmental events. The mind plays no role in influencing behavior. To avoid living in a nasty, brutish, anarchical society, says Hobbes, we need a strong, controlling central government to tell us what to do.

Today, the field of psychiatry is dominated by the theory of materialism. As a result, most of its practitioners have no qualms about imprisoning people against their will, then equally forcibly giving them electro-convulsive shock treatments or neuroleptic (psychotropic) drugs or performing surgery on them. The coercion is considered good medical practice, made possible by the government-sanctioned licensing and patent monopolies, the government socialized and cartelized medical-insurance system, and the laws regulating state-run mental hospitals and

---

[101] "Thomas Hobbes," newworldencyclopedia.org.

wards. The effects of the treatments are not cures for so-called mental illness ("biochemical imbalances"). They amount to total control over unwanted behaviors and their ultimate consequences often are irreversible brain and body damage.

The story is exhaustively documented in Peter Breggin's 1991 book *Toxic Psychiatry*.[102] The culprit is the "medical model" that says psychological problems such as anxiety, depression, and paranoia are physiologically based and must be treated medically, with electroshock, drugs, or surgery. Yes, psychosurgery of the Ken Kesey[103] type is still practiced today[104] in the twenty-first century. Courses on psychotherapy, Breggin points out, are no longer taught in most medical schools that train psychiatrists. The outrage of it all, he demonstrates, is that there is no scientifically valid evidence for the physiological cause of any of these problems.*

In page after page, chapter after chapter, Breggin cites researchers, many of them psychiatrists, who acknowledge that no causal connection has been demonstrated between brain physiology and psychological problems. Quite the contrary, evidence of brain damage due to electroshock, drugs, and surgery is abundant. For example, tardive dyskinesia[105] and brain shrinkage are two common effects of the typical "treatments." The terms "chemical straitjacket" and "chemical lobotomy" are used to characterize the results of some drug use and the immediate, short-term effect of drugs (and shock and surgery) is described as "blunting the personality," "flattened affect," and "subdued behavior." The patients, in other words, look and act drugged.[106]

The treatments are instruments of restraint, especially of the hyperactive type that may occur in prisons and mental wards . . . and in schools.[107]

---

[102] Peter R. Breggin, *Toxic Psychiatry*, amazon.com.
[103] Ken Kesey, *One Flew over the Cuckoo's Nest*, amazon.com.
[104] "Psychosurgery Page," breggin.com.
[105] "Antipsychotic Drugs and Tardive Dyskinesia Resources Center," breggin.com.
[106] "Dr. Peter Breggin's Antidepressant Drug Resource & Information Center," breggin.com.
[107] See above, "Children Don't Have Disorders; They Live in a Disordered World," p. 237.

Yet, as William Glasser says, so-called schizophrenics are "just lonely people." And, as Breggin concurs, the root of the problems most often is family abuse (verbal and physical) or neglect.** The solution is Carl Rogers' "unconditional positive regard"[108] and nurturing talk therapy. Safe houses run by uncredentialed amateurs, psychiatric survivors[109] in some cases, produce far better results for schizophrenics than any of the shocks, drugs, or surgeries of psychiatrists.

Why do establishment psychiatrists persist in using the medical model when the evidence for using it continues to pile up? Materialism, of course, is no small theory that blinds them to the contents of consciousness and possible psychosocial causes of mental stress. As academic researchers, some do what other academics have been known to do when discovering embarrassing facts: they bury them in tiny footnotes (found by Breggin) or relegate their confessions and cautions to post-research interviews (all again found by Breggin) long after the headlines of supposed drug success have played out in the press. And then there's the blatant conflict of interest, acknowledged by too few psychiatrists, of the millions of pharmaceutical company dollars that are fed to the profession.

"Modern psychiatry," as Breggin[110] puts it, "is not about counseling and empowering people. It's about controlling and suppressing them." Its history dates to the seventeenth century but its tactics too often over the years have been those of the Inquisition: subjugating "behaviours unacceptable or inconvenient to those in power."[111] Mental hospitals of the nineteenth century, and even of the twentieth, have been called snake pits[112]; inmates then, and still today, were and are treated as objects, not people with problems to be resolved.

Consider the eugenics programs of the 1920s and '30s in both the United States and Nazi Germany. Both were promoted in the name of science by psychiatrists; hundreds of thousands of people were sterilized

---

[108] "Unconditional Positive Regard," wikipedia.org.
[109] "Psychiatric Survivors Movement," wikipedia.org.
[110] Peter R. Breggin, "The Fort Hood Shooter: A Different Psychiatric Perspective," May 25, 2011, huffpost.com.
[111] John Read, Loren R. Mosher, and Richard P. Bentall, eds., *Models of Madness*, p. 14, amazon.com.
[112] "Snake Pit," thefreedictionary.com.

or killed during that time and the death houses of the Nazi psychiatrists became the models of concentration camp gas chambers.[113] (In the United States compulsory sterilizations[114] continued well into the 1970s.) And let us not forget the political abuse of psychiatry[115] in the Soviet Union, the incarceration of political dissenters. Abuse? Yes. Surprising? No, given the philosophical premise of materialism. (And China?[116])

Consider also the 1992 federal Violence Initiative of the National Institute of Mental Health. It proposed psychiatric interventions to identify and treat children allegedly biologically and genetically predisposed to violence. Presumably the targeted children would have been treated with drugs. Because there is no evidence whatsoever of a genetic connection to crime or violence and because most victims and perpetrators of violence in the United States today are African Americans, accusations of racism quickly quashed the plan.[117]

But again, this is what materialism can lead to. Total domination. Consciousness is irrelevant. Psychosocial causes of behavior are only an illusion.

Thomas Szasz[118] likened the questionable science of modern psychiatry to alchemy and astrology. Perhaps it should be called totalitarian science.

* In the twenty-one years since the publication of *Toxic Psychiatry*, evidence against the shock-drug-cut approach to helping distressed people has only increased. See Breggin's web site[119] for detail.

---

[113] "Eugenics in the United States," wikipedia.org; Peter R. Breggin, "Psychiatry's Role in the Holocaust," 1993, breggin.com.

[114] Lutz Kaelber, "Eugenics: Compulsory Sterilization in 50 American States," uvm.edu.

[115] "Political Abuse of Psychiatry in the Soviet Union," wikipedia.org.

[116] Shannon Lafraniere and Dan Levin, "Assertive Chinese Held in Mental Wards," November 12, 2010, nytimes.com.

[117] Vernelia R. Randall, "Violence as a Public Health Issue," udayton.edu; Peter R. Breggin and Ginger Ross Breggin, "A Biomedical Programme for Urban Violence Control in the US: The Dangers of Psychiatric Social Control," 1993, breggin.com; "US Hasn't Given Up Linking Genes to Crime; How We Inspired Nazis," September 18, 1992, nytimes.com; Philip J. Hilts, "US Puts a Halt to Talks Tying Genes to Crime," September 5, 1992, nytimes.com.

[118] Thomas S. Szasz, *The Myth of Mental Illness*, amazon.com.

[119] Psychiatric Drug Facts (website), breggin.com.

** Glasser and Breggin, both psychiatrists who heroically stand up to the authoritarianism of the profession, are not the only practitioners who talk and work in this manner to help so-called schizophrenics. See, for example, the authors of *Models of Madness*. Chapter 5 explains why I keep saying "so-called" about schizophrenia; John Read argues that it is an invalid concept.

(July 17, 2012)

Kindness versus "Hard Science"

IN MY PREVIOUS POST[120] I cited Peter Breggin's *Toxic Psychiatry*[121] as evidence to call modern psychiatric medical science both dictatorial and devastatingly harmful. Robert Whitaker's very readable 2002 book *Mad in America*[122] provides a great deal more detail about how the insane have been cared for in US history.

In the eighteenth century, for example, the insane were not considered human; they were wild beasts that had to be tamed. Hence the prison-like atmosphere, restraints and beatings, the blood-letting, the spinning chair, the dunking in water to the point of nearly drowning, and the administration of powerful emetics. These techniques were used repeatedly, day after day, sometimes for months. The aim of the mad-doctors,[123] as psychiatrists were called prior to the late nineteenth century, was to terrorize patients, to break their will and supposedly knock the insanity out of them.

The twentieth century, as I mentioned in last month's post, had its eugenics episode, and it is chronicled in detail by Whitaker, but the century also gave us shock therapies: insulin-coma, metrazol (camphor), and electro-convulsive. Administered perhaps hundreds of times, the purpose was to induce seizure, to supposedly shock the delusions and hallucinations out of patients. "Brain-damaging therapeutics" (Whitaker, p. 96), as these techniques were called, produced effects similar to brain trauma. (All subsequent page references are to Whitaker.)

---

[120] See above, "The Barbarity of Modern Psychiatry," p. 244.
[121] Peter R. Breggin, *Toxic Psychiatry*, amazon.com.
[122] Robert Whittaker, *Mad in America*, amazon.com.
[123] "Psychiatrist," etymonline.com.

Transorbital lobotomy, performed with ice picks in the 1940s by the flamboyant Walter Freeman,* was called "surgically induced childhood" (p. 122). And because masturbation was still believed to be a cause of insanity, clitoridectomy was performed until 1950 (p. 79). In 1954 the drug era then began with the introduction of Thorazine.

But what happened in the nineteenth century? To be sure, many of the same cruel and inhumane techniques continued to be used. The Quakers, however, had a better idea, one that spawned the "moral treatment" movement in mental health (pp. 30–38). Recognizing that mental illness was not physiological, that it resulted from being overwhelmed by certain life events, they insisted that kindness, attention, listening, and talking were key to helping the mentally ill.

Fed well and allowed to sew, garden, read, write, and play games, the patients in the Pennsylvania Hospital that opened outside of Philadelphia in 1841 enjoyed a "pastoral comfort." The hospital included a dining room, a greenhouse, a library, and a museum. The patients were encouraged to develop friendships, dress well, and rethink their behavior. They were urged to exercise free will and, not unlike Glasser's *Choice Theory*,[124] choose to be sane. Needless to say, they were neither chained nor beaten.

By 1890 all trace of moral treatment of the mentally ill was gone. The explosive growth of state-run, i.e., bureaucratic, hospitals made it impossible to train attendants in the spirit of kindness and empathy. What really killed moral treatment, though, was the ridicule and condescension put forth by medical doctors, especially the neurologists. They all considered themselves to be "men of hard science" and the moral treatment advocates were just old-fashioned, religious "gardeners and farmers" (p. 37). In the name of science straitjackets and cruelty were brought back; kindness and empathy were out.

The short-lived pastoral comfort of moral treatment brings to mind the "one brief shining moment" phrase from the title song in the Broadway musical *Camelot*.[125] Somewhat similar to King Arthur's humanitarian moment in legendary history, moral treatment was eclipsed. It was stamped out by "hard science."

---

[124] William Glasser, *Choice Theory*, amazon.com.
[125] "*Camelot* (Musical)," wikipedia.org.

Robert Whittaker is an award-winning investigative journalist. Before writing *Mad in America*, he subscribed to the conventional wisdom that psychiatry, especially the use of modern neuroleptic drugs, was good for the mentally ill. That is, until he stumbled on "symptom-exacerbation"[126] experiments, conducted well into the 1990s, in which psychiatric researchers were giving patients drugs (such as ketamine, chemical cousin of angel dust[127]) in order to *worsen their psychotic symptoms*. After this discovery, Whitaker in earnest began researching his book.

Psychiatric reviewers of *Mad in America*, not surprisingly, were unhappy campers. The reviews in fact were so negative that Whitaker's editor advised him, if he wanted to make a living as a writer, to stay away from the field of psychiatry. He did so for awhile, writing two unrelated books, but psychiatric survivor groups kept contacting him. As a result in 2010 he wrote *Anatomy of an Epidemic*,[128] the story behind the tripling of mental health disabilities from 1987–2007—this tripling despite increased usage of the alleged miracle drugs.

I have not yet read Whitaker's latest book, but in a podcast interview[129] about it with Peter Breggin, Whitaker relates three attempts by the psychiatric profession to silence him with ad hominem attacks and character assassinations. Here's his response[130] to one of the attempts. The profession, he stated in the interview, has succeeded in keeping him out of magazines where he used to write regularly.

This is how privileged "men of hard science" react when their monopoly and livelihood are threatened by facts. Fortunately, Whitaker has had the courage and independence to press on.

Many years ago William Glasser was denied a position at UCLA because he refused to buy into the medical model. In the 1980s Peter Breggin was threatened with having his license revoked because of comments he made on an Oprah Winfrey television show. (He won his

---

[126] Robert Whittaker, "Testing Takes Human Toll," November 15, 1998, thejabberwock.org.
[127] "Phencyclidine," wikipedia.org.
[128] Robert Whittaker, *Anatomy of an Epidemic*, amazon.com.
[129] "The Dr. Peter Breggin hour—06/04/12," podbean.com.
[130] Robert Whittaker, "Answering the Critics: Massachusetts General Hospital Grand Rounds," December 2, 2011, madinamerica.com.

case in court.) From outside the psychiatric establishment, Whitaker now joins this admirable pair.

Gentlemen, I raise a glass to you.

* It is worth noting that prior to taking up the ice pick, Freeman analyzed 1400 autopsied brains and found no differences between the normal and the schizophrenic (p. 115).

Postscript. One of the many tragic ironies in the history of science is the story of Ignaz Semmelweis[131] who discovered the significance of and recommended—futilely in his lifetime—the use of antiseptic procedures in childbirth.

Semmelweis died a brutal death in an insane asylum.

Suffering in 1865 either from a breakdown because none of the "men of hard science" would listen to him or from Alzheimer's disease or from syphilis, he was deceptively lured to a mental hospital. When he tried to leave, he was severely beaten, put in a straitjacket in a dark cell, doused with cold water, and given castor oil. Two weeks later he died . . . of septicemia, or blood poisoning, which he had argued was the cause of childbed fever and that the poisoning could readily have been prevented by washing the hands with chlorine.

(August 16, 2012)

The Science Isn't There

IN MY DECEMBER 2011[132] POST on "Nutrition and the Argument from Uncertainty" I cited and applauded the work of science writer Gary Taubes[133] for unearthing the truth about nutrition science. The upshot was that the science just isn't there for the conventional wisdom recommending a low fat diet and lots of exercise to protect us against obesity, diabetes, and heart disease. The science instead shows sugars and starches to be the most likely villains.

---

[131] "Ignaz Semmelweis," wikipedia.org.
[132] See below, "Nutrition and the Argument from Uncertainty," p. 301.
[133] Gary Taubes (website), garytaubes.com.

In a remarkable similarity of investigative journalism, science writer Robert Whitaker, in *Anatomy of an Epidemic*,[134] demonstrates that the science isn't there either for the chemical imbalance theory of biopsychiatry. In fact, the evidence in the psychiatric profession's own literature shows that drug usage for depression, anxiety, and schizophrenia causes more harm than help. In place of a genetic or chemical imbalance theory, Whitaker cites numerous studies supporting psychosocial issues as the causes of psychological problems and psychosocial treatment as the preferred technique to help victims of such problems improve.

To begin the presentation of Whittaker's argument, let me repeat a point from last month's post (see above) in which I reviewed his earlier work *Mad in America*[135]: in the pre-drug era of the 1930s and '40s analysis of 1400 autopsied brains found no differences between the normal and the psychotic. Given this statement as a sort of prelude, what does Whittaker's new book say about the chemical imbalance theory?

The theory for both depression and schizophrenia, as it has been tendered by the psychiatric profession, is quite simple. For depression, there is too little serotonin in the brain; for schizophrenia, there is too much dopamine. The drugs, therefore, according to the theory, should increase serotonin to combat depression and reduce dopamine to treat schizophrenia. Measurement of these neurotransmitters in cerebrospinal fluid is the benchmark for both existence and cure of alleged chemical imbalances.

What does the science show? For depression (pp. 71–75 in Whittaker's *Anatomy**):

- Studies in 1969 and 1971 revealed no significant difference between serotonin levels of normal and depressed subjects.

- In 1974, serotonin levels were normal for unmedicated depressives.

- Similar results were found repeatedly in subsequent years, leading to this statement (in *PLoS Medicine*, 2005) by Stanford psychiatrist David Burns: "I spent the first several

---

[134]Robert Whittaker, *Anatomy of an Epidemic*, amazon.com.
[135]Robert Whittaker, *Mad in America*, amazon.com.

years of my career doing full-time research on brain serotonin metabolism, but I never saw any convincing evidence that any psychiatric disorder, including depression, results from a deficiency of brain serotonin."

- And this pointed conclusion by psychiatrist David Healy (in a *PLoS Medicine* news release, 2005): "The serotonin theory of depression is comparable to the masturbatory theory of insanity."

A comparable pattern occurred in the studies of schizophrenia (pp. 75–79):

- No difference between normal and schizophrenic dopamine levels (1974) and no abnormal level of dopamine in unmedicated schizophrenics (1982).

- Similar results were found repeatedly in subsequent years, leading Steve Hyman, neuroscientist, former National Institute of Mental Health director and former provost of Harvard University, to conclude: "There is no compelling evidence that a lesion in the dopamine system is a primary cause of schizophrenia" (in *Molecular Neuropharmacology*, 2002).

- And: "The evidence does not support any of the biochemical theories of mental illness." Elliot Valenstein, U. of Michigan neuroscientist, in *Blaming the Brain* (1998).

How do the psychotropic drugs work? They "create perturbations in neurotransmitter functions." The brain tries to compensate by doing the opposite of what the drug is striving to do. After a few weeks, the attempts at adaptation break down. The brain becomes "qualitatively as well as quantitatively different from the normal state." Steve Hyman, *American Journal of Psychiatry* (1996). The drugs, in other words, make the brain abnormal (Whittaker, pp. 83–84).

The drugs also worsen long-term outcomes. In schizophrenics relapse rates of psychosis increase when neuroleptics are stopped.

When on the drug, the brain becomes supersensitive to dopamine, furiously trying to produce more. Upon sudden drug withdrawal, out-of-control, rapid firing of dopaminergic neurons in both the basal ganglia and limbic areas of the brain produce tics, agitation (sometimes leading to thoughts of violence or suicide), and psychotic relapse. The drug then must be brought back. Continued long-term use, however, at some point makes the wild firing of neurons irreversible. Tardive dyskinesia, frontal lobe shrinkage, and permanent psychosis result. (Guy Chouinard, physician, McGill University, in various psychiatric journals 1978–1991, cited in Whittaker, pp. 105–07).

Whittaker does not stop at depression and schizophrenia. He meticulously documents similarly flawed science and destructive outcomes of drugs for anxiety (the benzodiazepines, such as Valium and Xanax), bipolar disorder (Lithium), and so-called ADHD (Ritalin and its relatives).

Evidence for psychosocial causes of mental illness and the effectiveness of psychosocial treatment?

- World Health Organization cross-cultural studies in 1969, 1978, 1997 have shown that medicated schizophrenic patients in the US and five other developed countries fared much more poorly—short term and long term—than the mostly unmedicated patients in India, Nigeria, and Columbia (Whittaker, pp. 110–11).

- In the pre-drug era, the majority of first episode schizophrenics were dismissed from their hospitals within a year, 50 percent as cured, 30 percent as relieved. Twenty percent or fewer needed continual hospitalization. Today, the recovery rate is 36 percent and patients over a ten-year period require three times as many hospitalizations as their counterparts a century ago. The mentally ill die 15–25 years earlier than normal and their death rate has dramatically increased in the last 15 years (Whittaker, p. 335).

- In Tornio, Finland (western Lapland), "open-dialogue" family-centered therapy has reduced first-episode schizophrenia by 90% since the 1980s. Psychotic symptoms often retreat within a month. Drugs are seldom used; if necessary, they are used in modest dosages and short term. One ward of the hospital is empty because schizophrenia is disappearing from the region! (See more here[136] and in Whittaker, pp. 336–44.)

Bottom line: the science is not there for biopsychiatry. And the above is merely the tip of Whittaker's iceberg of evidence.

The science is not there for biopsychiatry, just as it is not there for low fat diets. But nor is it there for zero-rate interest and "quantitative easing" in economics as cure of our current Great Recession. What bothers me in particular about psychiatry is the immediate and concrete self-evidence that the drugs cause harm, such as flattened affect, subdued behavior, and the appearance in patients of looking and acting drugged.

One can argue that economic thinking is abstract and the chains of reasoning long. Therefore, failure to understand its arguments may be excused (despite the harm caused by the boom/bust cycle of the 2000's). But psychiatry, where the effects of the practitioners' actions are immediately evident? Where the effects of a legal drug show little difference from the effects of an illegal one? That I do not understand.

Whittaker has performed profound service to science by writing *Anatomy of an Epidemic*. As with the work of Gary Taubes, I urge you to read Robert Whittaker for the science he has uncovered, for the meticulousness of his method, that is, for his epistemology, and for his courage to expose a profession that refuses to examine itself.

* All subsequent page references are to Whittaker's *Anatomy*. Full journal citations are in Whittaker's notes. For a listing of source documents in both of Whittaker's books, see this web page.[137]

(September 19, 2012)

---

[136] "Study on Five-Year Outcomes from Open Dialogue Approach in Finland for 'Schizophrenia,'" July 27, 2010, mindfreeedom.org; "Open Dialogue," wildtruth.net; Daniel Mackler, "Finnish Open Dialogue: High Recovery Rates Leave Many Psychiatric Beds Empty," March 21, 2011, beyondmeds.com.
[137] "Mad in America: Source Documents," madinamerica.com.

"Men of Hard Science" and the Denial of Animal Emotions

IN A PREVIOUS POST[138] ABOUT PSYCHIATRY I put the phrase "men of hard science" in scare quotes to contrast these alleged experts with the more sensible and scientific kindness movement of nineteenth century mental health. In all fields, the "hard science" culture, which today of course includes some women, gospelizes philosophical materialism and the "if it's not quantitative, it's not scientific" approach to intellectual rigor.

It also preaches that ascribing human traits, such as consciousness, thoughts, or emotions, to the likes of dogs and cats is unscientific anthropomorphism, because materialism precludes the use of such terms when describing animal (or human) behavior. And "anthropomorphism" is used as a club to disparage anyone who uses such language.

Jeffrey Masson,[139] Sanskrit scholar turned psychoanalyst* turned bestselling author of books on the emotional life of animals, challenges the "hard science" approach to biology. Indeed, he points out in *When Elephants Weep*[140] that women for many years were considered by their male colleagues to be too emotional, and therefore more likely to be anthropomorphic, to work directly with animals.

Yet none other than Charles Darwin[141] and, more recently, Donald Griffin[142] and Jane Goodall have championed the scientific study of animal consciousness and Goodall (*Elephants*, p. 3) has defended anecdotal evidence, that scorned lay technique "hard scientists" would never touch.**

The anthropomorphism charge stems from our alleged inability to know "with certainty" what goes on inside an animal mind. We don't even know, the hard scientists say, if animals feel pain when they are being shocked or locked in isolation from all other animals and humans.

---

[138] See above, "Kindness versus 'Hard Science,'" p. 248.
[139] Jeffrey Masson (website), jeffreymasson.com.
[140] Jeffrey Moussaieff Masson, *When Elephants Weep*, p. 33, amazon.com.
[141] Charles Darwin, *The Expression of the Emotions in Man and Animals*, amazon.com.
[142] Donald R. Griffin, *Animal Minds*, amazon.com.

But it is an unjustified leap to conclude that we can know nothing about the contents of an animal's consciousness and therefore require all descriptions of behavior to be mere responses to external stimuli. For example, if a lay person were to say that a dog is feeling left out and wants attention, the "proper" scientific jargon of hard science would be: the dog "is performing the submissive display of a low-ranking canid" (*Elephants*, p. 31).

Behavioristic reasoning such as this can be pushed to a solipsistic extreme by saying that all we can really know *with certainty* is the contents of our own mind, not that of other human beings or animals. And torture of humans, which fortunately no hard scientist today would agree to, can be justified on grounds that no one can know *with certainty* whether the victim is really feeling pain when whipped and stretched on the rack (*Elephants*, p. 39).

The term "with certainty" above is in scare quotes because it is both a redundancy and an equivocation; probable knowledge, which we can obtain by observing and interacting with animals, is a percentage of certainty, so any knowledge we have is certain knowledge, just not one hundred percent certain. To know anything, even as a probability, is to know it with certainty.

And one of those interesting ironies of probable knowledge, Masson points out, is that animals may sometimes be *zoomorphic* in relation to their human companions, such as the cat that deposits a tasty morsel of gopher innard under the lady of the house's desk (*Elephants*, p. 44).

The bottom line of the anthropomorphism argument is not that some people improperly ascribe human qualities to animals. It is the contradiction and hypocrisy of the "hard scientists" who use animals to test hypotheses about human pain and depression (*Dogs Never Lie about Love*[143]). And more significantly, but not surprising to those who work in the academic world, it is the cowardice of those scientists who secretly believe that animals have emotions, but will never say so in their published work and may even criticize those who do (*Never Lie*, p. 17). Courage and "hard science" do not necessarily go together.

The further contradiction of the hard scientists—and tragedy and disgrace—is their failure to examine and acknowledge the similarities

---

[143] Jeffrey Moussaieff Masson, *Dogs Never Lie about Love*, p. 20, amazon.com.

the human animal shares with its lower brethren. It is this failure that allowed mad doctors[144] of the eighteenth and nineteenth centuries to describe the insane as wild beasts and, as a result, chain and beat them because animals were assumed not to feel pain.

Little progress, unfortunately, has been made today among the "men of hard science."

* Masson[145] became director of the Freud Archives in 1980. While in that position he discovered unpublished letters that shed light on Freud's repudiation of his 1890's seduction theory. Masson subsequently wrote *The Assault on Truth: Freud's Suppression of the Seduction Theory*,[146] arguing that Freud lacked moral courage to stand up to professional indifference and cultural hostility to his claims of child abuse as the cause of patient hysteria. Children at the time were viewed as considerable distorters of the truth and respectable males, especially fathers, were beyond reproach. Masson's payment for his courage and independence to publish these letters[147] and his book was to be fired from his job and dismissed from all psychoanalytic societies.

** The validity of anecdotal evidence in science rests on the assumption that universals exist. A good scientist using sound epistemology needs only two or three observations, not a probabilistic sample of 500, to make a generalization.[148]

(December 7, 2012)

2013

The Root of Dictatorship

In *Montessori, Dewey, and Capitalism*,[149] I gingerly suggested that the root of dictatorship is the parent/child relationship. The simple

---

[144] See above, "Kindness versus 'Hard Science,'" p. 248.
[145] "Jeffrey Moussaieff Masson," wikipedia.org.
[146] Jeffrey Mouissaieff Masson, *The Assault on Truth*, amazon.com.
[147] Sigmund Freud, *The Complete Letters of Sigmund Freud to Wilhelm Fliess, 1887–1904*, amazon.com.
[148] See Jerry Kirkpatrick, *In Defense of Advertising*, pp. 153–59, amazon.com.
[149] Jerry Kirkpatrick, *Montessori, Dewey, and Capitalism*, p. 117, amazon.com.

reasoning was that if one thinks it is right to coerce children, then it must also be right to coerce adults. (Restraining children who are about to harm others or themselves is not counted here as coercion.)

It seems, however, that my comment was too tame and needlessly cautious. At least that is my conclusion after reading works by Alice Miller, Lloyd deMause, and Bruce Perry.

Miller,[150] a Swiss psychologist (and former psychoanalyst), provides the strongest link in her book *For Your Own Good*,[151] in which she quotes the untranslated German text *Schwarze Pädagogik*,[152] a collection of extensive excerpts from child-rearing and educational guidebooks of eighteenth- and nineteenth-century Germany. "Black pedagogy" is the literal translation of this work, but Miller refers to it as "poisonous pedagogy."*

The upshot of advice from this period is to break the child's will, to beat the wickedness—which usually means the budding assertiveness and independence—out of the child, and to command strict, unquestioned obedience to authority (of the parent, teacher, and other adults).** In the course of enduring this brutality, shame, and humiliation, children are expected to thank their tormentors for the "discipline" and in some cases to kiss the hand that has just viciously beaten them. It is, after all, for their own good. (Even without these demands, Miller points out, abused children defend and cling to their abusive caregivers, because the small amount of caregiving they have received is all they know.)

Hitler and all the leaders of the Third Reich, says Miller, suffered this "pedagogy" and proudly passed it on to their children and subjects. Hitler often bragged of not flinching when his father repeatedly beat him. In *For Your Own Good* and elsewhere[153] Miller cites D. G. M. Schreber, whose nineteenth-century book on child-rearing went through some 40 editions and preached self-renunciation and self-denial. When his nanny fed his child before herself, Schreber fired the nanny on the spot, thus sending a message to all of Germany that the

---

[150] Alice Miller Child Abuse and Mistreatment (website), alice-miller.com.
[151] Alice Miller, *For Your Own Good*, amazon.com.
[152] Katharina Rutschky, *Schwarze Pädagogik*, amazon.com.
[153] Alice Miller, "The Political Consequences of Child Abuse," Fall 1998, psychohistory.com.

goal of child-rearing is to harden children and rid them of alleged weakness. They must learn to sacrifice from the first day of infancy on, said Schreber. With this kind of upbringing, asks Miller, is it any wonder that the German people became attached to Hitler as a father-substitute and were only too glad to obey his commands?

Lloyd deMause,[154] psychoanalyst and founder of the *Journal of Psychohistory*,[155] traces the bleak history of childhood, concluding that it "is a nightmare from which we have only recently begun to awaken."[156] While his psychoanalytical jargon can become a bit much, his historical facts are shockingly accurate and well documented, for example, the extensive infanticide, usually of baby girls, practiced in ancient Greece and Rome and the *legal right* of Roman fathers to kill their children.[157] Brutalization, terrorization, and sexual abuse were common throughout history, gradually improving over the centuries such that the descriptions in the above paragraphs are actually an advance over the past!

Although traumatic childhoods per se do not trump free will and deterministically turn children into dictators or sacrificial lambs, those experiences certainly make recovery difficult, and it would require an unusual child to break free of the circumstances. Bruce Perry,[158] neurobiologist and psychiatrist, specializes in childhood trauma and neglect. He acknowledges (without endorsing free will or volition outright) that children do make hundreds, perhaps thousands, of decisions while growing up.[159] It is those decisions, not genes or environment, that ultimately determine whether one neglected child (such as an infant left home alone every day for hours in a dark room) becomes a psychopathic killer and another an emotionless, socially awkward adolescent.

To be sure, Perry insists, early discovery and non-drug, empathetic psychotherapy are the remedies to such disturbances. Trauma of any

---

[154] "Lloyd de Mause & Psychohistory," psychohistory.com.
[155] "The Journal of Psychohistory & Abstracts," psychohistory.com.
[156] Lloyd deMause, *History of Childhood*, p. 1, amazon.com; Lloyd de Mause, "On Writing Childhood History," Fall 1988, psychohistory.com.
[157] Carl A. Mounteer, "Roman Childhood, 200 B.C. to A.D. 600," Winter 1987, psychohistory.com.
[158] The Childtrauma Academy: A Learning Community (website), childtrauma.org.
[159] Bruce Perry and Maia Szalavitz, *The Boy Who Was Raised as a Dog*, pp. 119–20, amazon.com.

kind—and this includes spanking[160] by hand—overloads the brain's stress response systems, causing a loss of felt control and competence by the victim. That is, the trauma prevents or erodes the development of self-esteem and independence. It does not have to be physical force. Trauma can be emotional abuse brought about by raging insults, name-calling, and belittling, or the lack of nurturing warmth, hugs, and empathetic understanding. Neglect, Perry points out, is not the prerogative of the poor and uneducated. There are also many uncared for infants, children, and adolescents among the educated well-to-do.

For as far back as we can go in history, children—at least those that have been allowed to live—have been beaten by their caregivers, abused, manipulated, and commanded to obey authority. Obedience and independence are opposites. A parent/child relationship that commands obedience from the child is one that prepares the way for dictatorship. A free society thrives on independence; it requires a healthy disrespect of authority, which is acquired through nurturing, warm, and affectionate caregiving. Coercion of any kind, physical or emotional, in the parent/child relationship must be eliminated.

* "Alice Miller is well known for her first book *The Drama of the Gifted Child*,[161] also published under the more correct title *Prisoners of Childhood*. Its thesis is that childhood experiences, many of which are traumatic, influence our adult behavior, trapping us in the futile pursuit of infantile needs that were not satisfied by our parents.

** "The only vice deserving of blows is obstinacy. . . . Your son is trying to usurp your authority, and you are justified in answering force with force in order to insure his respect, without which you will be unable to train him. The blows you administer should not be merely playful ones but should convince him that you are his master. . . . this will rob him of his courage to rebel . . ." J. G. Krüger, 1752, quoted in Miller, *For Your Own Good*, pp. 14–15.

(January 23, 2013)

---

[160] See above, "Should Spanking Be a Felony?," p. 232.
[161] Alice Miller, *The Drama of the Gifted Child*, amazon.com.

In Praise of Quitters and Failures

"What are you? A quitter??"

These warm words of support, heard by many children, adolescents, and even adults who have dared to vacate an activity, speak volumes about the speaker, not the quitter or failure. The activity left behind may have been the Boy Scouts or Girl Scouts, a sport, a college, or a job.

Quitting and failing is a natural part of life. Bill Gates quit; so did Steve Jobs and Mark Zuckerberg, to mention three notable quitters. And entrepreneurs are notorious failures, failing many times at ventures before, during, and after their successes.

Quitting and failing mean you have been testing many values to find the ones that fit your unique talents and interests, the ones that identify you as you. Staying with one activity that is not enjoyable is a prescription for misery and over the long term can lead to a profound sense of failure in life. Quitting and failing, especially in the early years, helps maintain psychological health.

The self-appointed experts on success in life who denigrate quitters and failures with name-calling and labeling are just the garden variety authoritarians who think they know what is best for the other person. A label that often accompanies the quitter and failure comments is "You're so lazy."

For a parent to call a child lazy is the ultimate insult and is in fact a sign of failure as a parent. It also probably means the parent at some point quit trying to learn how to improve as a parent, falling back on traditionally authoritarian techniques of the parent's parents or grandparents. Learning in the adult has stopped and rather than allowing oneself to feel like a quitter or failure the parent projects this feeling onto his or her children.

Children are not lazy. They often are bored because they have not been taught how to entertain themselves, whether through reading, music, sports or other activities. If allowed and encouraged to freely choose activities, children will not often be bored. If repeatedly told what to do by an adult, however, and punished when "disobedient," creative and independent thinking eventually shuts down. Action stops while children wait for the next marching order from the parent or teacher. The adult calls this laziness, but it is the adult who has caused the lack of action.*

What children need is not name-calling, but understanding and guidance that they are voluntarily allowed to accept. The grain of truth in the statements about quitting and failing is that children do need to think about what they want to do and if they suffer a misstep must develop resilience, by learning to work hard either to see something through to fruition or to start over again. But resilience is not acquired by being called a quitter or a failure. Quite the opposite is likely to occur.

Hence, quitting and failing are healthy. Sticking to something one does not like and taking unwanted actions to avoid the appearance of a lack of success are not healthy options.

When an adult quits a job, sometimes the boss feels rejected, especially if the employee is valued and a personal relationship has developed over months or years. Technically, psychologists would probably tell us that the boss should not feel rejected, but this is a natural part of the process of moving on to pursue other values. Children should be taught this lesson and be encouraged to act with impunity, following their own choices.

From the standpoint of ethics, it is no one's moral duty to stick to something he or she does not like, though many think it, especially those who call others quitters and failures. This also is what is behind the labels. Repeating as an adult what one heard in childhood is all too common.

Questioning what one heard in childhood, or better yet, questioning and analyzing in childhood what one is currently hearing from adults, is a sign of an active mind and a growing independence.

But then again, adults have to let these buds blossom. They have to want to encourage independence. Many do not want that.

* Hyperactivity also often results from this type of adult treatment. That, unfortunately, sends children down the path of becoming ADHD drug addicts.[162]

(August 6, 2013;)

---

[162] See above, "Children Don't Have Disorders, They Live in a Disordered World," p. 237.

Parents: Be Your Children's Friend—Give Them the Easy Life

"It's not our job to be our children's friend and make life easy for them," so states a mom blogger[163] recently. She is apparently responding to the modern disease known as "helicoptering,"[164] the parental behavior of hovering over one's children to make sure they suffer no pain in life.

Many issues are raised in the above false dichotomy. Let me focus on friendship and the easy life.

A friend, according to *Webster's*,[165] is "one attached to another by affection or esteem." Presumably, we feel affection for our children, so what is the objection to being a friend? Plenty, according to a quick Google search.[166] We should not use our children as confidant, we should not obsess over getting them to like us, we need to set limits—after all, we can't let them run out into the street or hit other kids at the playground—and, in short, we need to make sure they obey us.

While there are valid points in some of these statements, the last is root of the friend-parent debate. Friends do not lord it over their friends, do not tell them what to do, and certainly do not scream at them to "mind what I say, or else." As William Glasser[167] has pointed out, we would not have many friends left if we acted that way.

Authoritarianism is what the anti-friend advocates are talking about. Or, external control psychology, as Glasser called it. Demanding obedience to authority is the centuries old mantra[168] of what it allegedly means to be a good parent.*

---

[163] Carson Walker, "Mom's Blog about Bullying Draws Praise, Ire," November 14, 2013, today.com.
[164] "Helicopter Parent," wikipedia.org.
[165] "Friend," merriam-webster.com.
[166] Liz Hull and Sarah Harris, "Why, as a Parent, You Should Never Be Tempted To Treat Your Child as a Friend," July 20, 2012, dailymail.co.uk; James Lehman, "Your Child Is Not Your 'Friend,'" empoweringparents.com; Stephanie Metz, "Why My Kids Are NOT the Center of My World," October 25, 2013, themetzfamilyadventures.blogspot.com; Joanne Stern, "Parent or Friend: Do I Have to Choose?," March 7, 2011, psychologytoday.com.
[167] William Glasser, *Choice Theory*, amazon.com.
[168] See above, "The Root of Dictatorship," p. 258.

Discouraging the easy life also goes along with authoritarian parenting. After all, in days not too long ago, kids, beginning as soon as they could walk, had to milk cows, pluck chickens and scoop the poop in the chicken coop, pull weeds and hoe long rows, and perhaps even help out with the castration of farm animals. This was in addition to walking one to several miles to school every day. For such children, life certainly was not easy!

In short, what the anti-friend advocates are calling for is to "toughen up" our children, to make sure they don't end up a bunch of "weaklings." And they expect them to stand up to bullies like real men (or real women).

This machismo life is, or should be, ancient history.

To be sure, some less than honest helicopter parents have overreacted to the point of doing their kids' homework and writing their college application essays. Others just lobby hard with their kids' teachers, principals, and employers to make sure the children do not have to face any hardships, such as taking a course in school from a teacher one disagrees with or having to "pay dues" in a job to work one's way up the corporate ladder.

Parents, aside from being loving nurturers, are, or should be, teachers of values and principles,[169] not dictators who issue rules and commands. Among the most important values to teach the young are responsibility, independence, and, in their relationships with others, the principle of individual rights. Children, after all, do have rights. Ordering them to obey—to take out the trash or to wash the dishes, for example—is not teaching. Explaining, demonstrating, encouraging, and especially being an admirable role model are what teachers do.**

Friends do the same thing. Not every friend is a confidant and we certainly shouldn't be discussing our sex lives with our children—except perhaps in general terms to let them know that we do have sex and that it is not dirty, bad, or something to keep secret. Critical judgment and discretion is required to be a good parent.

But so is good judgment as to which hardships your children should be allowed to endure in the process of growing up. Removing the need for effort to acquire values is counter to learning responsibility and independence.

---

[169] See above, "Rules vs. Principles," p. 208.

Giving children everything without having to work for it produces a needy dependence. This is what the authoritarians correctly see in the hoverers. Denying your children the advances of modern civilization, however, is equally bad. Today, we don't have to pluck chickens to have food on the table; we buy our chickens dead, cut up, seasoned, and well done.

There is nothing wrong with enjoying the easy life. As Maria Montessori[170] observed, poor children who play with stick horses may be exercising their imagination, but what they want are real horses. Wealthy children may have the real thing but their responsible parents should still expect them to exert effort to learn to ride and care for the animals.

The easy life has its responsibilities just as the difficult life did.

The essence of good parenting is teaching principles and values, not making dictatorial commands or doing everything for one's kids.

Come to think of it, plucking chickens isn't all that bad. A handful of wet feathers has an interesting texture. Modern parents should try it sometime!

* "When you stop controlling, you gain control" was Glasser's recommendation, especially for teenagers.[171]

** Parenting is a twenty-plus year contract signed when children are conceived. Terms are to raise the children to adulthood in good mental and physical health. Coercing them to do menial tasks that their parents dislike (i.e., chores) only makes them hate work and feel guilty in adulthood when trying to enjoy genuine leisure.[172] Children are not "weaklings" who have to be "toughened up." These terms are modern synonyms for original sin and doing one's duty.

(December 21, 2013)

---

[170] Maria Montessori, *Spontaneous Activity in Education*, p. 258, amazon.com.
[171] William Glasser, *For Parents and Teenagers*, chap.1, amazon.com.
[172] Jane Smiley, "The Case against Chores," spring 2004, harpers.org; also here: jkirkpatrick.net/chores.pdf; Rebecca Lang, "Why I Don't Make My Kids Do Chores," August 15, 2016, parent.com.

2014
Thoughts, Not Environmental Conditions, Cause Criminal Behavior

FOR OVER FORTY YEARS, clinical psychologist Stanton Samenow has been interviewing criminal offenders for the courts.[173] His conclusion is that criminals are not criminals because of their upbringing or environment, or because of what they see on television or in movies.

Criminals are who they are because of the thoughts they hold, and have held, in their minds from an early age.

When many people walk into a crowded room, they think about who they would enjoy talking to. The criminal first checks escape routes, then looks for items to steal or weak targets to intimidate, swindle, or rob (i.e., pick their pockets). Criminals go to great lengths, sometimes using a considerable intelligence, to plan their crimes.

The criminal mind enjoys, or gets a jolt of excitement, as Samenow puts it, by doing what is wrong and getting away with it. "If rape were legalized today," said one offender[174] "I wouldn't rape. But I would do something else." The criminal act has to be illegal, otherwise the criminal would not experience the excitement.

When criminals get caught, they blame themselves for being stupid and careless. When interviewed by the courts and Samenow, they either never admit to their wrongdoing or blame their behavior on external circumstances, such as upbringing or environment. They insist that they are good human beings and find no contradiction in "praying at ten and robbing at noon.[175]

Some even express disgust at child abusers, then find no difficulty robbing and murdering someone else who, according to their way of thinking, "deserved it."

---

[173] Stanton Samenow, *Inside the Criminal Mind*, amazon.com; Stanton Samenow, *Before It's Too Late*, amazon.com; Stanton Samenow, *The Myth of the Out of Character Crime*, amazon.com.

[174] Stanton Samenow, "An Expanded Concept of 'Criminality,'" April 2006, samenow.com.

[175] Stanton Samenow, "Pray at Ten O'Clock, Rob at Noon," March 2014, samenow.com.

Samenow repeatedly insists, and demonstrates with many examples, that criminals are not victims of family abuse or unpleasant surroundings. Criminals come from all walks of life and include the highly educated and intelligent. They all have siblings and other relatives who grow up in the same family cultures and situations and do not turn out the way they did.

What they have in common is lying as a way of life, and it starts young. A child of five or six may lift a friend's or sibling's toy and get a thrill out of it. Denying guilt or blaming someone else—and getting away with the theft—provides another thrill and encourages further, more daring behavior.

People who follow the rules, according to such a young child, or adult thief, are suckers. Their lives are boring. "My life of crime," thinks the criminal, "is exciting." It is these thoughts that drive the criminal mind to plan the next "exciting" caper.

Criminals do not have friends, because they trust no one; they see other people as targets to manipulate. They do nonetheless gravitate to each other so they can share illegal adventures and plan bigger and bigger payoffs. They have nothing in common with the child or adult who lives a quiet, law-abiding life. Criminals envy the nice things in life, such as a home, car, or expensive computer, but they cannot conceive of working to attain these values. They would just rather take them.

Can criminals change? Not easily. Those who try to settle down in a job to make money for a car or home often succumb to their urges for the excitement of crime. Samenow does describe two success stories of criminals who changed, but they both went through long processes of catching the criminal thoughts midstream, challenging them, and struggling to substitute better ones. The process required is not unlike the will power of recovering alcoholics who must repeatedly check their desires for a drink.

In addition to dispelling the myth of environmental determinism as cause of criminal behavior, Samenow demonstrates that there is no such thing as a "crime of passion," the so-called out-of-character crime.

The reason, again, is the thoughts the criminal holds. A sudden and gruesome knifing, Samenow reveals, is not so surprising and out of character when one discovers the hostile thoughts, resentments, and perhaps even fantasies of stabbing or killing the target that the criminal has experienced for many months or years.

Samenow states, "I have found that thinking errors are causal in every case of criminal conduct. . . .The *error* is a flaw in the thought process that results in behavior that injures others. The harm done may be minor or extremely serious" (Samenow's emphasis).[176]

Humans are rational beings, which means thought causes behavior, both good and bad.

(April 24, 2014)

The Role of Honor in Moral Revolutions

IN HER 1974 WEST POINT MILITARY ACADEMY[177] ADDRESS, Ayn Rand said, "Honor is self-esteem made visible in action." It is a sense of worthiness and competence that others can see in one's deportment. It is not pseudo-self esteem that requires praise or respect from others lest an affront occur that demands satisfaction. It is not psychological dependence.

Yet that is precisely what Kwame Appiah in his book *The Honor Code: How Moral Revolutions Happen*[178] means by honor. The book is interesting because it chronicles the role of honor, or at least what certain cultures have understood to be honor, in supporting and eventually eliminating the practices of dueling, footbinding, and slavery.

Appiah also suggests a desperately needed role for honor in bringing about an end to the modern, horrific practice of honor killing.

Unfortunately, Appiah's analysis of the concept of honor makes it into something separate from morality. Usage, both historical and current, seems to concur. Honor reflects a code of values that demands respect and praise from others because of one's position in society or family rank.

Thus, an English gentleman is verbally insulted—his honor has been disrespected. The gentleman demands satisfaction through a duel because that is the honorable thing to do. And the Pashtun father orders

---

[176] Stanton Samenow, *The Myth of the Out of Character Crime*, pp. 6–7, amazon.com.
[177] Ayn Rand, "Philosophy: Who Needs It," *Philosophy: Who Needs It*, amazon.com.
[178] Kwame Appiah, *The Honor Code*, amazon.com.

his daughter killed, because the daughter disobeyed him by seeking to divorce her abusive husband. Honor to the Pashtuns means loyalty to kin; it is strictly and brutally enforced.

Conventional morality in the cultures discussed, points out Appiah, and often even the law, disapprove of the honor practices. Dueling in eighteenth century England was disparaged by many writers as barbaric and was illegal. Similar sentiments and laws are present against honor killings in today's Pakistan.

What ultimately led to the elimination of the historical honor-code practices was a changed conception of honor that incorporates modern notions of a civilized morality. A gentleman in the middle of the nineteenth century demands a duel. His opponent responds, "Seriously? No honorable man engages in a duel today!" And then laughter and ridicule may follow. What was once honorable became dishonorable.

This, in essence, is Appiah's conclusion about how moral revolutions occur. And it is what he says must occur if honor killings are to be eliminated.

For a thousand years it was a badge of honor for Chinese aristocrats to marry young women whose feet as little girls had been broken and bound until permanently deformed. In the early twentieth century, the practice was laughed at and disappeared within a generation.*

The one example of Appiah's that does not quite fit those above is the abolition of the slave trade throughout the United Kingdom in 1807. Appiah's narrative projects a strong theme of dignity and respect for manual labor and the working classes. Black African slaves performed manual labor and were a working class. Hence, national honor in England came to mean dignity and respect for the African slave. The slave trade in the name of honor had to be abolished.

It is this last example that best depicts the correct meaning of honor, especially as defined by Ayn Rand. Self-esteem is the result of a process, as psychologist Stanton Samenow[179] describes it: an outcome or accomplishment that does not depend on what others think of you. Productive work, whether manual or intellectual labor, is a key source of that sense of worthiness and competence.

---

[179] Stanton Samenow, "Self-Esteem—What Is It?," June 2002, samenow.com.

The emotional product of self-esteem is pride, and pride helps generate the desire to do the right thing, that is, to act, as did the English abolitionists. Honor becomes the outward manifestation of one's self-esteem. It is individualistic, not social. It is not a contest for status as it was thought of in much of the past.

The conventional conceptions of honor that Appiah outlines confuse genuine self-esteem with pseudo-self-esteem[180] and perhaps should be called pseudo-honor. In pseudo-honor there is a pretense of accomplishment, but the sense of accomplishment derives from one's station in society, tribe, or other social group. It does not derive from earned effort.

At root pseudo-honor is a tribal concept and is derived from rank within the tribe.

Genuine honor is what the abolitionists felt and expressed.

* One can only hope for one more moral revolution to eliminate the likes of altruism and socialism. A conversation might go something like this: "Seriously? You think we should sacrifice ourselves to others and expect the government to control our lives and economy? No honorable person would believe such ideas or act on them!"

(May 31, 2014)

A Neoconservative's Defense of Pseudo-Honor

The origin of the concept "honor," along with its two historical meanings, can probably be traced to battle.

James Bowman in *Honor: A History*[181] cites a line from the movie *Black Hawk Down*[182] that suggests this. When the bullets start flying, paraphrasing a key character, politics and everything else go out the window. "It's about the men next to you."

The two meanings are the praise, respect, fame, and glory that derive from your peer group (the men next to you) or the value you place on human life—yours and the men's next to you—such that your egoistic

---

[180] "The Psychology of Self-Esteem," wikipedia.org.
[181] James Bowman, *Honor*, amazon.com.
[182] *Black Hawk Down*, 2001, imdb.com.

pride propels you to do whatever is required to accomplish the objective of battle, namely, to kill the enemy before he kills you.

In such a situation, it would be nice to have others at your side who share the same value. But your honor does not derive from the good opinion of your foxhole mates.

The former meaning is what in my previous post[183] I called pseudo-honor, the latter genuine honor. Samuel Johnson's eighteenth century *Dictionary of the English Language*[184] recognized the two meanings, but Bowman and much of history have interpreted honor as a social concept.

More specifically, Bowman identifies the essence of honor as manliness in men, exemplified historically as bravery, and chastity or fidelity in women. It is the group—family, tribe, ethnic background, culture, etc.—that sets the rules of honor and provides the accolades when followed or shame when not.

Honor, Bowman says, has not changed for millennia in most of the world, including the Middle East. Islamic jihadists care more about maintaining the appearance of power and control—the manliness of honor—than strict adherence to their religion that condemns killing innocent people. It is the "insults" of the US and other western countries that motivated the jihadists to act, on 9/11 and at other times, to preserve their honor and to avoid shame.

In the West, however, honor underwent a transformation, beginning in the eighteenth century and culminating with what Bowman calls the "Victorian accommodation" of the nineteenth century. The change was brought about in part by the decline of aristocratic privilege through democratization, economic liberalism, and equality before the law for everyone.

But what Bowman means by Victorian accommodation is the Christian rejection of reflexive honor behavior that calls for an eye for an eye, along with the retention of respect for, and deference to, certain elites. This he admires and longs to return to.

In contrast, I would say that his history shows the concept of honor in the eighteenth and nineteenth centuries moving away from its socially

---

[183] See above, "The Role of Honor in Moral Revolutions," p. 269.
[184] "Honour," Samuel Johnson's *Dictionary of the English Language*, vol. 1, amazon.com. Also at archive.org.

dependent meaning to what Ayn Rand described as the more genuine, egoistic expression of self-esteem and individualism. Bowman does not buy this interpretation because he cites the self-esteem movement as a product of the political left and nearly synonymous with egalitarianism.

Even individualism is seen by him in this light, as a form of egalitarianism, and he disparages the loner in literature and movies that has been prominent in the arts since the end of World War II.

To be sure, the current shallow self-esteem movement as practiced in the public schools is too focused on appearances and praise, but this is not what self-esteem means in serious psychological research.

The upshot of Bowman's book is that honor in the West as an important social motivator collapsed in the twentieth century and has all but disappeared from personal and public discourse in the twenty-first. The collapse began with the public's recognition that the slaughter of World War I was fought on both sides over honor, with some leaders viewing the whole thing as a game. Honor came to be viewed as a pretentious and hypocritical obsession with image.

The left (Bowman's foil throughout) picked up the harangue against honor by eliminating the military draft, allowing legal abortions, and promoting the radical feminist agenda that there are virtually no differences between men and women. All of this then means that we—the US and the West—are no longer willing to make the altruistic sacrifices necessary to defend Christian values.

"Without honor," says Bowman,[185] "we have no fight in us, and thus no more will to survive."

To reclaim honor's place in the world and to fight for our future against the ancient honor culture of the terrorists, Bowman argues, we must praise and respect (i.e., honor, in his sense of the word) our political and military elites, and they must demand respect and deference from us. We must debunk the celebrity worship that dominates today. (Bowman speaks nostalgically about the good old days when the profession of acting was viewed as less than honorable!) We must acknowledge inequality and the media must stop being the handmaiden of the left.

---

[185] James Bowman, "Viele Feinde, keine Ehre," June 4, 2006, jamesbowman.net. Google Translate: "many enemies, no honor."

Bowman is not optimistic that his brand of honor will ever make a comeback, because no one today is willing to make those Christian sacrifices.

In short, he apparently sees us as weak and cowardly, possessing too little Victorian honor to go forth and become martyrs.

Genuine honor, however, does not require sacrifices. It requires genuine self-esteem to produce courage and integrity. This sometimes motivates ordinary people to perform extraordinary feats, which is the source of heroism, in war or anywhere else.

Bowman's book is extremely erudite, so much so that it is sometimes difficult to follow key points, though the last hundred pages make it clear that he is a neoconservative[186] and does not like the left.

What he does not acknowledge or hardly mention is the political and economic tradition of classical liberalism that eliminates the need for sacrifice of any kind by endorsing voluntary consent in all relationships, personal, as well as public.

Such ideas are expressed eloquently and persuasively in the works of Ayn Rand and Ludwig von Mises.

But conservatives, neo- or otherwise, have never been big fans of either writer.

(June 14, 2014)

Fixed vs. Growth Mindsets

IN 1964, MINNESOTA VIKINGS FOOTBALL DEFENSIVE END, Jim Marshal,[187] picked up a fumble and ran 66 yards the wrong way, into his own end zone, causing his team to suffer a safety, or loss of two points.

To many, a faux pas such as this could result in humiliating embarrassment and a devastating blow to self-esteem. Marshall, however, realized he had a choice: either sit in his misery or do something about it. In the second half of the game he caused a game-winning fumble that was picked up by his teammate and carried to the correct end zone for the score.

---

[186]"Neoconservatism," wikipedia.org.
[187]"Jim Marshall (American Football)," wikipedia.org.

This incident in essence illustrates the difference between the two mental habits or, more technically, psycho-epistemologies,[188] described in psychologist Carol Dweck's book *Mindset: The New Psychology of Success*.[189]

A fixed mindset is a set of beliefs that one's skill and ability are innate, something we are born with that cannot be much improved with learning and practice. The tendency of the fixed mindset is to be a perfectionist, so when perfection is not achieved, self-doubt and diminished self-esteem result. Perfection, the fixed mindset assumes, is supposed to be easy.

The growth mindset, on the other hand, believes that concentrated thought and effort can improve skill and ability in whatever endeavor one happens to be participating in. Mistakes to a growth mindset are a sign that more effort and practice are needed. Perfection is not the standard; accomplishment is.

The seemingly effortless, silky-smooth moves of dancer Fred Astaire, for example, were attained not through an innate talent but an astounding number of hours in rehearsal.

Dweck's concepts of fixed and growth mindsets result from years of research on students, athletes, managers, parents, teachers, and coaches. The former two are learners, the latter four are teachers of one type or another.

In studies of students, as Dweck found and many a teacher can attest to, fixed-mindset students who get bad grades, such as a C or D, conclude that that is who they are, a C or D student, and that they can do nothing to change. Growth-mindset students who get a bad grade do not "sit in their misery"; they do something about it, as did Jim Marshall. They work harder to improve their next grade.

Fixed mindsets do not believe that effort can affect their skill or ability. Either you have it or you don't, they think.

Unfortunately, many of Dweck's four types of teachers can exhibit a fixed mindset in themselves and in turn assume the same to exist in their learners. A rude and offensive teacher will tell a C student, "That's who you are; you're a C student!"

---

[188] "Psycho-Epistemology," aynrandlexicon.com.
[189] Carol S. Dweck, *Mindset*, amazon.com.

A fixed-mindset manager may resent criticism from subordinates and may even fire them, because the boss is the one who supposedly knows best and his or her sense of worth depends on being right. Dweck provides many examples of fixed-mindset managers, such as Lee Iacocca (of Ford and Chrysler), and contrasts them with their growth-mindset counterparts: Alfred P. Sloane of General Motors and Jack Welch of General Electric, who both welcomed criticism as an essential part of their learning and growth process.

Welch was known for rolling up his sleeves and going to the production floor to ask workers what they thought would resolve a problem.

Emphasizing that fixed mindsets can be changed, Dweck appeals to child psychologist Haim Ginott[190] and cognitive therapist Aaron Beck.[191] Changing thoughts and beliefs that constitute the fixed mindset are what are needed to change the mental habit.

In relation to children, labels, such as "you're dumb" or "you're a C student," and extravagant praise, such as "you're awesome" or "you're so smart," must be dumped. *Describe* the incident, as Ginott insisted, *don't evaluate*.[192] Let the child draw the evaluative conclusion based on the description.

All of us, says Dweck, maintain a running account of what events mean to us and how we should react to them. These are the beliefs that control our lives. To change, say, from that of a fixed to a growth mindset, we must introspect and change those entrenched beliefs. This is not an easy task, but with a commitment to effort and practice, it can be done.

What is missing from Dweck's book, as it is from many contemporary psychological works, is any mention of the subconscious mind, defense mechanisms, or defense values. Such terms, no doubt, are avoided like the plague by modern psychologists for fear of being accused of being a Freudian.

Freud, nonetheless, did make contributions to the field.

The evidence provided by Dweck in her book is that the fixed mindset is a defended mindset, meaning that one's self-esteem is on

---

[190] Haim Ginott, *Between Parent and Child*, amazon.com.
[191] Aaron T. Beck, *Cognitive Therapy and the Emotional Disorders*, amazon.com.
[192] See above, "Describe, Don't Evaluate," p. 201.

the line every time one takes a test in school, performs on the athletic field, or makes a decision in business. This performance anxiety must be defended against through denial, role playing, and other defensive maneuvers, lest one experience the humiliation of failure.

But it's not a humiliating failure. It's just a bad grade on a test, a wrong play on the field, a decision that may have cost the company some time and money.

It was an educational experience.

For more on the significance of the subconscious in psychotherapy and the relevance of defense mechanisms and defense values in explaining motivation, see psychologist Edith Packer's book *Lectures on Psychology*.[193]

(July 28, 2014)

"They'll Be Fine"—Two Takes on Indifference to Psychology

THE CHIDING PHRASE "they'll be fine" can be found abundantly on the internet aimed, deservingly so, at the hysterically paranoid helicopter parents who hover endlessly over their children.

In a different way, the phrase is also used dismissively when, say, a child must be away from the family.

Consider the helicopter parents first.

The anxious, and now self-righteous, helicoptering has become so pronounced that some hoverers use the law to have working moms arrested if they dare leave their nine-year olds alone to play in a crowded park.[194]

One such nine-year old left in a park was sent to foster care and the mother went to jail. How good is that for the child (or mother)?

---

[193] Edith Packer, *Lectures on Psychology*, amazon.com.
[194] Conor Friedersdorf, "Working Mom Arrested for Letting Her 9-Year-Old Play Alone at Park," July 15, 2014, theatlantic.com; Lenore Skenazy, "Mom Jailed Because She Let Her 9-Year-Old Play in the Park Unsupervised," July 14, 2014, reason.com.

And four children,[195] ages five to ten, were recently taken from a widow who left the children home alone while the mother pursued her college education attending night classes; the children were split up by social services, bounced around, and possibly even abused in the bureaucratically indifferent and incompetently run foster care system.

Power over others, as this mother observed, not empathy or protection, is what the busybody hovering is all about.

The hoverers also ignore that since time immemorial, older children, sometimes as young as six or seven, have cared for the younger ones.

My derisive and acerbic emotional response to such totalitarian and tyrannical motivations is to say to these busybody[196] hoverers: "Why don't you just have the secret police (the local SWAT team[197]) arrest these evil parents in the middle of the night and then shoot them?!"

Never mind that kids under five in the 1950s were five times more likely to die than their counterparts are today, or that child-abduction is no more likely now than sixty years ago. Injury or even death from riding in a car is far riskier.[198]

Facts don't matter.[199]

Psychological harm by being left alone? Please. These are not infants or two-year-olds. Independence is what the above children are learning.

Police-state spying and informing are what the modern puritans are promoting.

Scolding the coercively minded hoverers by saying "the children will be fine" seems too mild. "Back off and mind your own business" might be more appropriate.

On the other side of the coin the expression "they'll be fine" sometimes is used to dismiss concerns over sending a child to daycare while the parents work.

"It won't hurt 'em" is the reply to objections.

---

[195] Conor Friedersdorf, "This Widow's 4 Kids Were Taken After She Left Them Home Alone," July 16, 2014, theatlantic.com.

[196] See below, "Virulent Absolutism in an Age of Relativism," p. 304.

[197] See above, "Return of the Blackshirts?," p. 71.

[198] "Relax, Your Kids Will Be Fine," July 26, 2013, economist.com; "Crime Is Lower Today Than When Most Parents Were Growing Up," freerangekids.com.

[199] See below, "Facts Don't Matter, Or: The Art of BS," p. 307.

At first this usage may seem to be opposite the excessive concern of hoverers. However, both hoverers and dismissives ignore the importance of psychology in the development of a child. Both are looking only at the physical side of things, the former at the threat of physical harm, the latter at physical safety, which seems to be all that matters to a dismissive.

Children who are subjected to long hours of daycare can feel hurt and can and do feel abandoned by their parents. No, physically they do not appear to be damaged—"they seem fine"—but the conclusions children draw about themselves and others when parents leave and do not come back for a long time influence their subsequent development.

Conclusions such as: "My parents are not coming back." "What did I do wrong to make them put me here and go away?" Or, "Adults like my parents are too busy to spend time with me; I must not be very important to them."

These conclusions, unless checked and discussed by the parents with their children, become entrenched guides to future personality growth and subsequent behavior.

To be sure, most parents need to work, requiring them to leave their children behind in the care of others.

Awareness and acknowledgement of the psychologies involved—that is, careful and serious discussion with the children of the issues and alternatives, not dismissiveness—is what is required.

Hoverers fear the children might die. Dismissives say they will not. The evidence speaks otherwise, challenging these two extremes.

The facts of psychology especially call for more attention to the mental and emotional sides of children, not just the physical.

Postscript. There are also plenty of hoverers and dismissives in relation to the family pet. Hovering dog owners, for example, never go anywhere without the dog and may even give up an enjoyable vacation to keep the dog from experiencing separation anxiety. Dismissives, on the other hand, insist that "it won't hurt 'em" to kennel the dog while the family goes away.

Contrary to what the "men of hard science"[200] say, higher-level animals, especially dogs, do have minds and psychologies and can suffer hurt similar to that of a child. They can also be taught to tolerate staying alone or in a kennel. Or, in the case of separation anxiety,[201] a well-known phenomenon among competent animal trainers, they can be taught not to chew up the family's prized possessions!

Awareness of what might be going on in the mind of the family's best friend and doing something to reduce possible anxiety can go a long way toward preventing those unwanted welcomings upon returning home.

(September 29, 2014)

The Bureaucratic Personality: Similarities to the Criminal Mind?

THE CRIMINAL PERSONALITY enjoys manipulating and intimidating others. Excitement from lying and getting away with the forbidden is a way of life.

Intimidation includes verbal abuse and physical harm (robbery, assault, murder), which means bullies[202] are potential criminals, actual when they get physical. Power over others is what the criminal thrives on. Lack of empathy for victims and lack of conscience are nearly total.

Criminals, according to Yochelson and Samenow in their fifteen-year study *The Criminal Personality*,[203] get away with substantially more crimes than they are ever arrested for—200,000 for one offender over 40 years with the only arrest sending the criminal to a mental institution, along with a "no criminal record" statement in his file.

Criminality, the authors point out, is a continuum of irresponsibility ranging from hardened psychopaths to less extreme arrestable criminals to a category they call "non-arrestable criminals," the type

---

[200] See above, "'Men of Hard Science' and the Denial of Animal Emotions," p. 256.
[201] "How To Ease Your Dog's Separation Aniety," webmd.com.
[202] Stanton Samenow, "Bullying: A Sign of a Developing Criminal Personality?," March 2011, samenow.com.
[203] Samuel Yochelson and Stanton Samenow, *The Criminal Personality*, vol.1, amazon.com.

of persons who on the surface look like responsible citizens but under cover of family and job lie, cheat, manipulate, and intimidate everyone they come in contact with.

Non-arrestable criminals seek the same power over others the hardened criminals do, as well as the jolts of excitement from getting away with the forbidden (in this case, getting away with what is considered unethical, rather than what is illegal).

Given this description of non-arrestable criminals, a startling question arises. Does bureaucracy provide protection for criminal personalities and therefore attract them?

Yochelson and Samenow state that many criminals are attracted to law enforcement and the military—both bureaucracies. And some former soldiers in the authors' research admitted that they enjoyed shooting unarmed civilians.

What is it in bureaucracy that might attract the criminal mind? The answer has to be the coercion that is bureaucracy's distinguishing characteristic. "The management of coercion" is Ludwig von Mises's[204] concept of bureaucratic management, which he carefully distinguished from the profit management of business.

Everything bureaucrats do derives from the laws and administrative rules created by the state. Force backs up the bureaucrats' behavior. Violation of laws and rules requires punishment, which means coercion. No private business that is not highly regulated by the state has this kind of power.*

What is the signature of bureaucrats? "Rules are rules, fella; I don't make 'em. I just enforce 'em." Or, as Victor Hugo's Javert[205] put it, paraphrased: "The law is the law and it must be obeyed."

Bureaucratic personalities enjoy creating and enforcing laws and rules to impose on others. They are indifferent to the needs, wants, and genuine concerns of consumers and other constituents. (Think no phosphates[206] in laundry detergent and no plastic bags[207] in grocery stores, just to name two recent, dictatorial edicts.)

---

[204] Ludwig von Mises, *Bureaucracy*, mises.org.
[205] "Javert," wikipedia.org.
[206] Jeffrey A. Tucker, "Why Everything Is Dirtier," May 5, 2011, mises.org.
[207] "Plastic Bag Ban," huffpost.com.

Bureaucrats assume they know what is just and have the right to impose those judgments on others. Lying, stretching the truth, selective memory, shoddy research, sins of omission, BS'ing[208] and, in today's political climate, spin, which means fabrication, may be justified in the creation and execution of such laws and rules.

Coercion is available to the bureaucrats and they will not hesitate to use it. Obedience to authority is the essential requirement of a successful bureaucracy.

How many bureaucrats are like this? I don't know, and the cover of job and respectability—especially the respectability of working for the "public good"—makes it difficult, if not impossible, to identify such less-than-savory mentalities.

I must hasten to emphasize that not every bureaucrat is so motivated. Yours truly, of course, is a bureaucrat. I have been a college professor in state-run universities for nearly thirty years, and my red ink pen, as I said in *Montessori, Dewey, and Capitalism*,[209] is my gun. I wrote this not as a joke or an exaggeration. It is literal, in the nature of bureaucracy.

Sometimes, as a card-carrying bureaucrat, I do have to tell students that "rules are rules." If the rules are really stupid, and I can do so, I gladly ignore them to help out. I do this knowingly, but I also could be punished for such a transgression. The punishment could be a hand slap, but far worse has happened in the academic world.

In my thirty years, I have seen competent colleagues forced into retirement with no explanation given. I have also seen colleagues kept on the payroll, neither teaching nor seemingly doing much of anything else. Star Chamber[210] (secret) proceedings and gag orders are not uncommon.

Selective memory of something that to me one could not possibly have forgotten occurs frequently, along with BS'ing, stretching the truth, sins of omission, denial of well-deserved tenure, and many other unkind things done to others, all of which are often dismissed as "just politics."

---

[208] See below, "Facts Don't Matter, Or: The Art of BS," p. 307.
[209] Jerry Kirkpatrick, *Montessori, Dewey, and Capitalism*, p. 162, amazon.com.
[210] "Star Chamber," wikipedia.org.

To me, though, I must ask this question, "How can these people be sincere?"

The criminal of the non-arrestable type does help explain such personalities. It is no secret in the non-criminal world that there exist people who are hostile, mean, manipulative, and seem to enjoy their callousness. And it is no secret that human psychology exists along a considerable continuum.

Yochelson and Samenow's non-arrestable criminal personality provides a possible foundation for understanding the type of person who enjoys lording it over others.

To what extent does this apply to elected politicians? Job and respectability, again, make it difficult, if not impossible, to know.

Cover of family and job, Yochelson and Samenow emphasize repeatedly, is a favorite ploy of some hardened criminals, and it certainly is also of the non-arrestable ones.

* As I have written before,[211] the popular conception, derived from the work of Max Weber,[212] is that a bureaucracy is a large, hierarchically structured organization, implying that big business and big government are both bureaucracies. Weber's conception, however, is a package deal, uniting two fundamentally different types of organizations. Consequently, Mises defines bureaucracy as the government's method of managing its affairs. Businesses become bureaucratic only to the extent that they are regulated, which effectively turns them into bureaus of the state. An unregulated business does not have the political power to force anyone to do anything; it only has the economic power to satisfy consumer needs and wants.

A tech radio show host recently captured the difference succinctly: Google only has the power to put annoying ads on your search pages; the NSA[213] has the power to arrest you.

(November 19, 2014)

---

[211] See above, "It's Just Being Turned into a Business," p. 31.; see above, "The Whistleblower: An Indictment of the Mixed Economy and Bureaucracy," p. 77.
[212] William P. Anderson, "Mises versus Weber on Bureaucracy and Sociological Method," July 30, 2014, mises.org.
[213] "National Security Agency," wikipedia.org.

2015–16

On Hitting Dogs and Children . . . and Prisoners of War

The supposed aim of hitting dogs, children,[214] and prisoners of war[215] (POWs) is a change of behavior, which may include in the latter two the acquisition of information.

To be sure, change of behavior does result—cowering, rebellion, or a combination of the two.

The initiation of the use of physical force does not produce confident and loving dogs; confident, loving, and independent human adults; and accurate, reliable counterintelligence. The psychological principle is the same in all three cases. Talk, which means use reason, don't hit. Advocates of torture, mostly Republican conservatives, seem to be the same ones who also have no qualms about kicking their helpless dogs or smacking their helpless children.

In the twenty-first century, considering what we know today about psychology, there is no excuse for the torture of incarcerated POWs.

(January 12, 2015)

Defending Hate Speech and Satire against the Criminal Mind

Because the criminal suffers a far greater deficiency of self-esteem than anyone else—"I am a nothing" was a frequent confession to criminal personality researchers Yochelson and Samenow[216]—and because he cannot tolerate the thought of being injured or maimed . . . a not uncommon fantasy is that of a grand flourish in which the criminal shoots everyone in sight and is then killed himself (p. 260).

---

[214] See above, "On Hitting . . . Dogs and Children," p. 229.
[215] Alexandra Jaffe, "McCain Makes Passionate Defense for Torture Report's Release," December 10, 2014, cnn.com.
[216] Samuel Yochelson and Staton Samenow, *The Criminal Personality*, vol. 1, amazon.com.

When criminals actualize their fantasies, they produce Columbine,[217] Sandy Hook,[218] and now *Charlie Hebdo*.[219]

The enemies of free speech are criminals who just happen to latch on to some ideology as a front, cover, or alleged justification.

Je suis Charlie.[220]

(January 12, 2015)

From the Stick Motivation Department: Chores

THERE ARE MANY WAYS in which adults lord their size and power over children.

It usually begins with spankings of a disobedient toddler by, say, a towering six-foot-plus dad who leers, yells, then hits the helpless tot. (See related posts.[221])

Why? Aside from the excuse that "that's the way my parents treated me and their parents treated them," etc., ad infinitum, the most common rationalization is that children have to learn to mind, lest they run out into the street and get killed, or turn into juvenile delinquents, or become criminals.

"Didn't hurt me none" is the less than introspective response of some adults when asked why they did not question their parents' stick-motivation techniques.*

The assignment of chores to kids so they allegedly will learn how to work hard and become responsible citizens of society is another form of stick motivation.

Webster's Unabridged and the *Oxford English Dictionary* both define "chore" as a tedious task that must be performed regularly, such as washing the dishes or hoeing long rows. The *OED* also says the word is a colloquial Americanism.

---

[217] "Columbine High School Massacre," wikipedia.org.
[218] "Sandy Hook Elementary School Shooting," wikipedia.org.
[219] "Charlie Hebdo Shooting," wikipedia.org.
[220] "Je Suis Charlie," wikipedia.org.
[221] See above, "The Child as Small Adult," p. 161.; see above, "Should Spanking Be a Felony," p. 232.; see above, "On Hitting Dogs and Children . . . and Prisoners of War," p. 284.

What astounded me when examining these two reference works was the absence of any mention that chores are not optional. Yes, adults sometimes do refer to their own monotonous tasks, such as brushing their teeth twice a day, as chores, but the origin of the term in American culture surely is coercion of the young.

Chores for children are almost never voluntary. Just ask a child what happened the last time he or she refused to do one!

Fortunately, novelist Jane Smiley,[222] writing in *Harper's Magazine*, has put the kibosh on the supposed benefits of this favorite of coercive parenting.[223]

Smiley was born with a silver spoon in her mouth, so she never had to clean her room or wash the dishes. She did have a horse and, as she puts it, through her love of and interest in the animal learned to work hard to groom and feed it and clean its stall, which meant removing the poop.

Smiley's husband, on the other hand, grew up in Iowa, less than wealthy, and was forced to do chores—mixing concrete with a stick at age five and, later, pushing wet, heavy wheelbarrow loads of it across the yard.

Guess which one, Smiley or her husband, enjoys life more today?

Smiley's husband feels guilty playing golf when there is always more work—chores—to be done at home; when doing the chores, his motivation is to get them over with as quickly as possible.** He was taught well. Chores are tedious drudgery, which means work is drudgery.

And that's because parents give kids the dirty work as chores. Says Smiley, "Mom cooks and Sis does the dishes; the parents plan and plant the garden, the kids weed it."

In addition to teaching the "value" of work, Smiley points out that another apparent purpose of chores is to make sure the children contribute to maintaining the family, by sharing the work that needs to be done. Smiley comments:

> According to this rationale, the child comes to understand what it takes to have a family, and to feel that he or she is an important, even indispensable member of it. But come on. Would you really want to feel loved primarily because you're

---

[222] "Jane Smiley," wikipedia.org.
[223] Jane Smiley, "The Case against Chores," harpers.org. Also available at jkirkpatrick.net/chores.pdf.

the one who gets the floors mopped? Wouldn't you rather feel that your family's love simply exists all around you, no matter what your contribution? And don't the parents love their children anyway, whether the children vacuum or not? Why lie about it just to get the housework done?

Why lie indeed? It is really a threat to withdraw love if the child is not obedient, similar to the withdrawals of love for disobedience that result in time outs and being sent to one's room.

Smiley concludes: "It's good for a teenager to suddenly decide that the bathtub is so disgusting she'd better clean it herself. I admit that for the parent, this can involve years of waiting. But if she [mom] doesn't want to wait, she can always spend her time dusting."

Parenting, after all, is a twenty-plus year contract chosen and signed by the parents. Children are not their slaves.

Presumably, the American concept of chores originated on self-subsistent farms, where there certainly was a lot of heavy, tedious work to be done to maintain the homestead.

The "justification" of requiring pre-school children to lug heavy pales of milk and to pluck chickens, however, is not the assumed necessity of a division of labor in the family. It is the value system of nearly all American farmers, absorbed by their citified descendants, of Puritanism. American culture still today is highly Puritanical.

And what might that value system be? The duty ethics of Christianity reinforced by philosopher Immanuel Kant. As one middle American farm-raised father said not too long ago: "You do your job because it is your duty, not because you enjoy it."

As Kant said, never act from inclination, but always in accordance with duty. Fun and pleasure are out. Chores are in.

In contrast, visit a Montessori school to see how children are taught without coercion to love work, to associate pleasure with it, and to learn the skill of intense concentration.

* Corporal punishment[224] in all settings, which includes spanking by hand in the home, is now banned in sixty-one countries[225] of the world.

---

[224] End Violence against Children (website), endcorporalpunishment.org.
[225] "Progress," endcorporalpunishment.org.

The United States is not one of them. Sweden was the first, in 1979, and surprise, surprise, those children who were not smacked or beaten did not turn into juvenile delinquents or criminals![226]

The website corpun.com[227] archives a large number of video clips from around the world of both adult and child corporal punishment. I could only stomach watching one: a Sri Lankan military trainer hitting female recruits with a long stick.

** Stemming from the same value system, this is the motivation for children who eat their peas first to get the disgusting stuff out of the way so they can enjoy the good-tasting meat and gravy last! (Guess who did that as a child.)

(May 4, 2016)

From the Stick Motivation Department, Part Two: Class Participation

IN LAST MONTH'S post[228] I discussed the coercive parenting technique of assigning chores to children. The alleged lesson of such coercion is to teach children the value of work, though it likely teaches them to hate it.

Coercive teaching contributes a number of techniques to the stick motivation department. Let's take a look at class participation.

For middle and high schoolers, and even college students, teachers feel obliged—and claim the unquestioned right—to coerce quiet members of the classroom to "come out of their shells" lest they fail to succeed in life or live up to their potential; grades based on class participation, by as much as fifty percent, I have heard, is the brass knuckle approach to teaching this lesson.

---

[226] Jamie Gumbrecht, "In Sweden, A Generation of Kids Who've Never Been Spanked," November 9, 2011, cnn.com.
[227] World Corporal Punishment Research (website), corpun.com.
[228] See above, "From the Stick Motivation Department: Chores," p. 285.

Five to ten percent, perhaps as extra credit, may have some instructional value. But fifty percent? These classes of twenty to forty students are not courses in public speaking.

And grades, after all, are the carrots and sticks by which teachers maintain control of their charges. I'm not the first to suggest that grades be dumped from the classroom entirely.

In the old days, the traditional (and coercive) recitation technique of class participation required students to summarize the content of their reading assignment, or, frequently, to recite something from memory. If not accomplished to the liking of the teacher, the kids would have their knuckles rapped with a ruler, or worse. In ancient Rome, they were beaten with a stick.

The modern version is a mixture of old-style recitation and analysis. The former, as the new schoolmarms are wont to say, should be kept to a minimum, because "we have all read the assignment." Memorization, of course, is scorned as authoritarian and having no place in school. The latter, analysis, can include putting the reading material into different words, evaluation, and, too often, the spewing of undefended opinion.

According to education school "edubabble," such discussions will help teach students how to think. It usually degenerates quickly into BS sessions. And some of the more talkative students have mastered the technique of impressing teachers by their glibness; the quiet ones are then marked down.*

In recent years, some class participation teachers have discovered—and have experienced revelations when discovering—that their heavy-handed approach to getting those pesky and resistant-to-talking quiet kids to speak up in class may not be the best thing for them.

This has come about largely due to Susan Cain's 2013 book *Quiet: The Power of Introverts in a World That Can't Stop Talking*[229] and her subsequently established website Quiet Revolution.[230] (See related posts.[231])

---

[229] Susan Cain, *Quiet*, amazon.com.
[230] Quiet Revolution (website), quietrev.com.
[231] See above, "Theory of the Big Mouth," p. 224.; see above, "Introversion, Quiet Persistence, and the Tortoise," p. 242.

Jessica Lahey is one such reformed class-participation tyrant. Writing in *The Atlantic*,[232] she firmly defended her conviction that quiet kids must be forced to speak up. When she received an "avalanche of angry comments," many of which, to put it mildly, declared her "uninformed," she wrote a softened article[233] on Cain's website. Lahey acknowledges that she was influenced to alter her teaching by Cain's book and other articles on the topic (See especially Schultz[234] and Cain[235] for examples of teaching quiet kids without putting them on the spot.)

The upshot of "class participation reform" is that introversion and shyness are not the same and that any behavior can be motivated by multiple causes, not just what the extroverted teacher assumes is operating in the quiet kid.

"Shyness is the fear of social disapproval or humiliation, while introversion is a preference for environments that are not overstimulating."[236] A room filled with twenty to forty classmates can produce considerable overstimulation for an introvert. Extroverts prefer the stimulation.

And most extroverted teachers assume shyness and introversion are identical. They also do not recognize that quiet kids may be actively listening to the other talkers, waiting for the moment to speak up when they have formulated what they would like to say. They also might be taking notes, say, for a subsequently required paper. Or, something extroverted teachers usually do not want to hear or acknowledge, the student may not like the teacher or the class, or both.** Certainly, there are other motivations.

But just as not voting in an election is participation in the political process, so also is not speaking up in class a form of participation. Teachers need to respond to, and find techniques of, reaching all personality types sitting in their desks.

---

[232] Jessica Lahey, "Introverted Kids Need to Learn to Speak Up at School," February 7, 2013, theatlantic.com.
[233] Jessica Lahey, "Class Participation: Let's Talk about It," quietrev.com.
[234] Katherine Schultz, "Why Introverts Shouldn't Be Forced to Talk in Class," Februaray 12, 2013, washingtonpost.com.
[235] Susan Cain, "Help Shy Kids—Don't Punish Them," February 12, 2013, theatlantic.com.
[236] Susan Cain, *Quiet*, p. 12, amazon.com.

A "one size fits all" approach to teaching, such as the assumption that speaking up in class is good for everyone, invariably brings out the specter of stick motivation.

* I must point out one more time that John Dewey, the alleged father of progressive education—"alleged" because he gave the epithet to Francis W. Parker[237]—lectured when he taught, expected excellent memorization from his students, and wrote a book in 1938 to repudiate many progressive techniques used in his name, such as the necessity of class discussion to teach students how to think. For Dewey, subject matter was fundamental, because it is the "working capital" of thought.

The premise of many teachers today, as one colleague said to me years ago, is that "we teachers talk too much as it is. We have to get the kids talking." I took that to mean less work for the teacher, something that was explicitly stated by my grad school classmates as justification for group projects[238]: one paper to grade instead of four or five.

** Yes, I know there are teachers who brag about how they don't care whether or not students like them or their courses. But they should.

(June 12, 2016)

---

[237] "Francis Wayland Parker," wikipedia.org.
[238] See above, "Group Projects: The Bell Has Tolled," p. 185.

5

Epistemology

2007–11

The Dangerous Admiration of BS

WHY IS BS'ING ADMIRED, almost to the point of being "cuddly and warm," as philosopher Harry Frankfurt put it, whereas lying is considered morally repugnant?

Frankfurt examined BS in his 2005 monograph *On Bullshit*[1] (BS) and distinguished it from lying. The liar, Frankfurt argued, is focused on facts so he or she may state the opposite, but the BS'er is an entertainer or artist who uses words and sophistical arguments to manipulate others. Individual statements of the BS'er may be true, but their truth or falsity are irrelevant. The "show" is what counts. A sales rep, thus, puts pressure on a prospect by saying, "buy now, because I already have two firm offers." The rep may or may not have two other offers; those particular words were chosen because they provide the most persuasive language.

Frankfurt's discussion seems to imply that the creative and imaginative skills of the artist are what people admire in BS'ers and lead many to make comments about BS'ers to the effect "He's good" or "She's clever." Such comments may be made about anyone. Politicians, of course, are often consummately admired spinmeisters, as are many

---

[1] Harry Frankfurt, *On Bullshit*, amazon.com.

lawyers and sales and advertising practitioners. Some admiration may stem from the challenge a BS'er must overcome, such as a sales person confronted with the objections of a particularly difficult prospect. A well-crafted story, not entirely based on fact, to convince the prospect to buy can produce the above accolades.

Expectation of truth is doubtless the reason we are offended by the liar, but why not the same for the BS'er? After all, the overall impression made by the BS'er is false, even though individual statements made by such a person may be true. BS, as I suggested in a conference paper,[2] is a species of lying, the two behaviors occupying opposite ends of a continuum.

In a post-publication interview,[3] Frankfurt named marketing (of course) and, perhaps surprisingly, democracy as causes of the preponderance of BS in our culture today. Marketing, because salesmanship and advertising are falsely assumed to mean lying in order to separate consumers from their hard-earned dollars. And democracy, because in such a system we are obligated to have an opinion about everything; since we cannot know everything, says Frankfurt, our opinions amount to BS.*

One consequence of the connection between democracy and BS, Frankfurt continued, is that the highly educated, because they have the linguistic skills with which to express their opinions and the arrogance to neglect facts in the process, are more prone to BS than their lesser educated counterparts. Does this "democratic skill" cause admiration of others who exhibit the same?

Rationalization abounds to justify BS, such as "everyone does it," "everyone knows it's done this way," and "that's how business (or politics) is conducted." Not "everyone" does know it, however, and if everyone did know *it*, how would that justify departures from the truth? Storytelling belongs in the art of fiction, not in business, politics, or daily conversation. Justifying fabrication in negotiation and salesmanship is precisely what gives capitalism a bad name.

The danger in admiring BS, and not carefully distinguishing it from the creative fiction of a true artist, is that habits of mind become

---

[2] Jerry Kirkpatrick, "On Marketing Bull----," April 2006, cpp.edu/faculty/jkirkpatrick.
[3] Harry G. Frankfurt, *On Bullshit*, press.princeton.edu. Scroll down for video.

established and human relationships end up being built out of little more than BS. Perception of the truth becomes nearly impossible, because every statement is for show, not a description of facts. Politics has become almost entirely a BS show, with honest intention seemingly nonexistent.

Worst of all, parents can encourage this habit in children at an early age. Smiling approval of a less-than truthful statement can communicate a "you're clever" message to a child. For example, a boy who wants to get his way makes something up that will please his mother. The mother plays along, knowing fully that the gambit is less than genuine. A pattern of behavior has just been sanctioned by the mother.

Commitment to facts and truth, when such encouragement is continued throughout childhood and adolescence, goes out the window. Of course, parents who exhibit the same behavior become their children's models. The BS habit becomes ingrained in the child's subconscious and he or she may not even be aware that anything is wrong. "My parents do it. Everyone around me does it. Politicians do it. It must be right."

From this beginning in the home, we derive a culture of BS.

* The fundamental cause is altruism, specifically the premise that self-interested behavior, which is required in our daily lives, is opposed to character and morality.

(August 30, 2007)

Dewey in Context

IN MY BOOK *MONTESSORI, DEWEY, AND CAPITALISM* I treat favorably a number of ideas from philosopher John Dewey, which may come as a surprise to admirers of Ayn Rand. The key to understanding why I do so is to see Dewey as an Aristotelian who rejects intrinsicism without resorting to skepticism or subjectivism.

During his years at Columbia University, Dewey came under the influence of Aristotelian scholar F. J. E. Woodbridge,[4] major figure in the early twentieth century school of realism and naturalism. When

---

[4] "Frederick James Eugene Woodbridge," jwood.faculty.unlv.edu.

Dewey was asked by students how he should be classified, he replied, "That is easy. With the revival of Greek Philosophy."* Intrinsicism is Ayn Rand's term for the doctrine that essences and values inhere intrinsically—eternally and immutably—in concretes, and that the mind is a passive mirror or spectator of these essences and values. The doctrine originated in Greek thought and has plagued philosophy ever since. Both Dewey and Rand reject it. Reality, for Dewey, is the Darwinian world of evolutionary change, not the Greek or medieval world of immutable, eternal forms or essences (or biological species) that exist intrinsically in reality. Knowledge—forms, essences, concepts—are constructions of the mind based on the human animal's participations in, or interactions or transactions with, the world in which he or she lives. When Dewey speaks of the "spectator theory," he means the doctrine of intrinsicism.

With this background in mind, I would like to demonstrate in this post how two quotations of Dewey in *The Ominous Parallels*[5] by Leonard Peikoff take on a different meaning when put into full context. On page 124 of the paperback edition, Peikoff states that, according to Dewey, we cannot know facts "antecedent" to the mind, that it is not a function of the mind to know facts, and that the mind is not a "spectator." Knowledge in particular, quoting Dewey, is not "a disclosure of reality, of reality prior to and independent of knowing. . . ." (from *The Quest for Certainty*.[6]

These statements and quotation sound quite subjectivist, but the full context is the so-called problem of value created by physical science's failure to find anything resembling value-in-itself or intrinsic value. Here is the context; the original quotation is italicized:

> There are two rival systems that must have their respective claims adjusted. The crisis in contemporary culture, the confusions and conflicts in it, arise from a division of authority. Scientific inquiry seems to tell one thing, and traditional beliefs about ends and ideals that have authority over conduct tell something quite different. The problem of reconciliation arises and persists for one reason only. As long as the notions persist that knowledge is *a disclosure of reality, of reality prior to and independent of knowing*, and that

---

[5]Leonard Peikoff, *The Ominous Parallels*, amazon.com.
[6]John Dewey, *The Quest for Certainty*, p. 35, amazon.com.

knowing is independent of a purpose to control the quality of experienced objects, the failure of natural science to disclose significant values in its objects will come as a shock. Those seriously concerned with the validity and authority of value will have a problem on their hands. As long as the notion persists that values are authentic and valid only on condition that they are properties of Being independent of human action, as long as it is supposed that their right to regulate action is dependent upon their being independent of action, so long there will be needed schemes to prove that values are, in spite of the findings of science, genuine and known qualifications of reality in itself. For men will not easily surrender all regulative guidance in action. If they are forbidden to find standards in the course of experience they will seek them somewhere else, if not in revelation, then in the deliverance of a reason that is above experience.

Rephrasing Dewey in terms of the doctrine of intrinsicism: "As long as the notions persist that knowledge is a disclosure of [intrinsic essences], of [intrinsic essences] prior to and independent of knowing, . . . the failure of natural science to disclose significant [intrinsic] values in its objects will come as a shock." It should be noted here also that Dewey uses the term "value" as presupposing a "to whom and for what purpose," as does Ayn Rand.

The next quotation in *The Ominous Parallels* immediately follows the previous one: "The business of thought is not to conform to or reproduce the characters already possessed by objects" (*Quest for Certainty* p. 110).

This quotation arises in the context of the premise that all knowledge is experimental or operational in origin. "The test of ideas, of thinking generally, is found in the consequences of the acts to which the ideas lead, that is in the new arrangements of things which are brought into existence. Such is the unequivocal evidence as to the worth of ideas which is derived from observing their position and role in experimental knowing" (pp. 109–10). In other words, all knowledge and thought is for the sake of action. Photographs of intrinsic essences, however, since intrinsic essences do not exist, provide no guidance for action. The full context reads, with the original quotation again italicized (pp. 110–11):

> In the previous chapter, we saw that experimental method, in reducing objects to data, divests experienced things of their qualities, but that this removal, judged from the standpoint

> of the whole operation of which it is one part, is a condition of the control which enables us to endow the objects of experience with other qualities which we want them to have. In like fashion, thought, our conceptions and ideas, are designations of operations to be performed or already performed. Consequently their value is determined by the outcome of these operations. They are sound if the operations they direct give us the results which are required. The authority of thought depends upon what it leads us to through directing the performance of operations. *The business of thought is not to conform to or reproduce the characters already possessed by objects* but to judge them as potentialities of what they become through an indicated operation. This principle holds from the simplest case to the most elaborate. To judge that this object is sweet, that is, to refer the idea or meaning 'sweet' to it without actually experiencing sweetness, is to predict that when it is tasted—that is, subjected to a specified operation—a certain consequence will ensue. Similarly, to think of the world in terms of mathematical formulae of space, time and motion is not to have a picture of the independent and fixed essence of the universe. It is to describe experienceable objects as material upon which certain operations are performed.
>
> The bearing of this conclusion upon the relation of knowledge and action speaks for itself. Knowledge which is merely a reduplication in ideas of what exists already in the world may afford us the satisfaction of a photograph, but that is all. To form ideas whose worth is to be judged by what exists independently of them is not a function that (even if the test could be applied, which seems impossible) goes on within nature or makes any difference there. Ideas that are plans of operations to be performed are integral factors in actions which change the face of the world.

Rephrasing: "The business of thought is not to conform to or reproduce the [intrinsic essences or properties] already possessed by objects but to judge [the objects] as potentialities [to serve the purposes of my professional or personal life] through an indicated operation."

Dewey did not like the term "pragmatism" and did not use it to refer to his philosophy. He preferred "instrumentalism," in the sense that thought is an instrument of action. Dewey, indeed, was no Objectivist, nor was he a capitalist, but he does have interesting ideas. Admirers of Ayn Rand who carefully read Dewey as an Aristotelian should be repaid for the effort.

* Walter B. Veazie, "John Dewey and the Revival of Greek Philosophy," *University of Colorado Studies, Series in Philosophy*, no. 2, 1961, p. 3. Raymond Boisvert (in *Dewey's Metaphysics*, amazon.com.) has analyzed Dewey's metaphysics and concluded that it is Aristotelian.

(March 16, 2008)

The Epistemology of Ethics, Salesmanship, and Basket Weaving

IN A PREVIOUS post[7] I said that teachers are peddlers of ideas who must sell their wares as much as any other sales rep or entrepreneur. The process by which soap and ideas are sold is essentially the same. The method is persuasive communication and the purveyors of both can be honest or dishonest. There is nothing unique to the theory of salesmanship that makes sales reps more prone to dishonesty than teachers, and teaching in a free market is salesmanship.

In this post I would like to make a similarly iconoclastic statement about three apparently disparate fields, namely that ethics, salesmanship, and basket weaving are all applied sciences. The first anomaly, according to many hard core philosophers and scientists, is that I would dare to call any of these fields a science. The second is that I would dare to lump them together with equal epistemological standing. Let me take these one at a time.

In its broadest sense, science studies reality—not just the physical, but also the mental—and aims to describe it accurately and provide guidelines for human choices and actions. In this sense philosophy is the science of all sciences, because it identifies the broadest abstractions about reality and provides the broadest guidelines for the rest of the special sciences. The special sciences, whether physics, engineering, medicine, or basket weaving, must be consistent with the more general sciences, but they in turn describe their own areas of

---

[7] See above, "Peddlers of Ideas," p. 159.

reality and provide guidelines for choice and action to achieve specific goals in those realms.

To explain and predict are said today to be the two aims of science. Explanation, however, implies prediction. If a ball is described as round, for example, the description predicts that the ball will roll. This positivist view of science as explanation and prediction leaves values out completely. Values are guides to action. If a ball is to be thrown accurately to a target, then it is valuable for the hand, arm, and rest of the body to move in a certain way. A scientist of ball throwing prescribes which actions have to be made in order to achieve the goal of hitting a target. To live a healthy and moral life, scientists of nutrition and ethics also prescribe certain actions that must be taken to achieve the respective goals. There *are* two aims of science, but they are to explain and guide.[8] Guidance specifies a goal and the actions necessary to reach the goal. All value theories are sciences of guidance. This applies equally to ethics, salesmanship, and basket weaving. (For doubters about basket weaving as a science, a Google search generates millions of hits and refers the searcher to an enormous literature describing the principles of basket weaving.)

Value theories are applied "how to" sciences and are just as factual as any so-called hard or descriptive physical science. Value theories describe how to get things done. Ethics describes how to live the good life, salesmanship describes how to sell products, and basket weaving how to make baskets. Nothing could be more factual than that, which makes all of these fields as scientific as physics, chemistry, or biology.

For that matter, epistemology is also a how-to discipline, since its aim is to describe how we know what we know and then, on the basis of that knowledge, to prescribe how to improve our ways of knowing. As a result, there is no difference in essential methodology used by epistemology and ethics, or ethics and salesmanship, or salesmanship and basket weaving. They all use the same approach to identifying the concepts and principles that constitute their particular subjects of study. The only relevant difference among all of these disciplines is level of abstraction. The concepts and principles of epistemology and ethics are far more abstract than those of salesmanship and basket weaving.

---

[8] "Theory-Practice Dichotomy," aynrandlexicon.com.

Putting on an air of superiority simply because one works in an area of greater abstraction smacks of what Robert Fuller would call rankism.[9] Science is science and applied science is applied science. As much can be learned from blue-collar workers who love their jobs and approach them with attention to subtle detail[10] as one can learn from college professors who work in the stratosphere of theoretical concepts and principles. In many cases one can learn more from blue-collar workers than from professors, because the latter are too often caught up in their own jargon to be able to relate it to the lay person. And some professors all too often have no desire to relate their work to the lay person. But everyone today in our knowledge economy[11] holds, or should hold, equal epistemological standing in the generation and application of knowledge.

One does not pay plumbers so much for what they do as for what they know. That makes plumbers, basket weavers, sales reps, and ethicists all fellow professionals.

(April 26, 2009)

Nutrition and The Argument from Uncertainty

THE FALLACY OF THE ARGUMENT FROM UNCERTAINTY, or at least one form of it, might also be called the "it's better to be safe than sorry" argument. For example, the European Union,[12] among other inanities, recently ruled that children under eight must be supervised while blowing up a balloon, lest the children swallow or choke on part or all of the dangerous inflatable. How likely is this to occur? "Well, we don't really know for sure," the reasoning apparently goes. "We can't be certain, so it's better to be safe than sorry. An adult must be present."

The problem with this reasoning is that it is asking opponents to prove a negative. "The balloon might cause choking. Prove that it won't." In logic proving a negative cannot be done; the burden of proof is on

---

[9] See above, "The Market Gives Privilege to No One," p. 25. Dignity Works (website), breakingranks.net.
[10] See above, "Curiosity for Subtle Detail," p. 204.
[11] "Knowledge Economy," wikipedia.org.
[12] Bruno Waterfield, "Children To Be Banned from Blowing Up Balloons, Under EU Safety Rules," October 9, 2011, telegraph.co.uk.

the one who makes the positive assertion. All that can be said accurately here is that the probability of choking[13] is minuscule and parents must choose their own levels of risk tolerance. When pressure groups and their legislators tell us what to do, our freedoms and possibly our health become endangered.

This last is meticulously demonstrated in the exhaustive investigations of science writer Gary Taubes. In his two latest books, *Good Calories, Bad Calories*[14] and *Why We Get Fat*,[15] Taubes reviews over one hundred years of research on the causes of several diseases of civilization,[16] especially heart disease, obesity, and diabetes. His finding is that not only is the consensus of the past thirty to forty years wrong, but that it also was generated and is today still maintained by the argument from uncertainty (my terminology, not his).

The litany of contemporary nutrition says that we should eat a high carbohydrate, low fat—low saturated fat—diet in order to maintain our heart health, remain trim, and fend off diabetes. If overweight, we should of course exercise and cut back on the calories. Taubes found little sound evidence in the scientific literature to support these claims and indeed uncovered a wisdom that was conventional for over a hundred years, until after World War II, that said good health, including trim weight, is achieved by eating a low carbohydrate, high meat, fish, and fowl diet. That is, cut out the sugars and starches and eat as much of the rest as you want. Exercise? It makes us hungry, something from the foggy distant past that our mothers and grandmothers used to say; it does not cause weight loss. Cholesterol and saturated fat? No causal relation to heart disease. Go low carb for all three diseases.

What gives? Are today's nutritionists lying? No, just "better to be safe than sorry," so they seem to be saying. During the 1950s and '60s, the more rigorous scientific researchers said that data on fat and cholesterol in relation to heart disease were inconclusive, in particular the data of the Seven Countries Study,[17] a project notably omitting

---

[13] "Small Children—Avoiding Choking Accidents: Warning Labels and Adult Supervision Work," balloonhq.com.
[14] Gary Taubes, *Good Calories, Bad Calories*, amazon.com.
[15] Gary Taubes, *Why We Get Fat*, amazon.com.
[16] "Lifestyle Disease," wikipedia.org.
[17] "Seven Countries Study," wikipedia.org.

France and other countries that would have contradicted the study's findings. This study, the rigorous researchers said, was at most associational, not causal.

The promoters of the Seven Countries Study, however, said that lives were at stake. We can't wait for "final scientific proof" (*Good Calories, Bad Calories*, p. 23). We must inform the public and have them change their diets. This attitude partnered with the '60s hostility to McDonalds and other high-fat fast food diets and culminated in the McGovern[18] Report of 1977 that made the litany virtually gospel. In the meantime, well-controlled experiments, right up to the present, continued and still continue to disconfirm the creed. Selection bias,[19] the omission of anomalous data, is a term Taubes uses to help explain the championing of the litany.

In the course of his investigations, Taubes most importantly has liberated obese people from the tyranny of the "gluttony and sloth" argument. "You're overweight because you eat too much and exercise too little." Implication? Weakness of the will, bad character. Taubes and the more rigorous researchers? Clearly there is a genetic component to growing wide, just as there is a genetic component to growing tall. Causation indeed just may run in the opposite direction. That is, we are not necessarily fat because we overeat and underexercise. Rather, we likely eat more because we are growing and become sedentary because we are fat.

The mechanism of obesity, writes Taubes (*Why We Get Fat*, pp. 118–21), operates through the hormone insulin. The more carbohydrates we eat, the more insulin our bodies secrete, the more fat—for obese people, at any rate—is taken out of our bloodstream and stored in our fat cells. "Insulin," as Taubes puts it, "works to make us fatter.

Coercion in the public schools[20] to make children eat "right" or less has become common, just as the European Union is now making sure children are not unduly exposed to those allegedly dangerous inflatables. Aside from the issue that governments have no right to tell us

---

[18] "Dietary Goals for the United States," 1977, zerodisease.com.
[19] "Selection Bias," wikipedia.org.
[20] Dave Bohon, "Chicago School Bans Bag Lunches, Forces Kids to Eat School Fare," April 15, 2011, thenewamerican.com.

what or how much to eat, or how we should micromanage our children, how fallacy-proof is the scientific evidence that has led to these policies and near dogma about health and safety? How long before we're all compelled to eat "right" or less?

Taubes has shown us how bad science can become a new consensus and lead to policy. I hope my attempt to condense his seven hundred pages into a few paragraphs is clear and correct. *Why We Get Fat* is only two hundred pages. I enthusiastically recommend that you read it. Taubes' writing is sparklingly clear. His website is garytaubes.com.[21]

(December 3, 2011)

Follow-up. Political rumblings, of course, are now stirring to regulate or ban sugar. Scott Dailey in *The Wall Street Journal*[22] parodies this sugar-police mentality with a variety of stories. Here's one: "Excuse me, sir, could you buy me an Orange Crush?" "Sorry, kid. I could go to jail for that."

(March 16, 2012)

2013–15

Virulent Absolutism in an Age of Relativism

IN TODAY'S WORLD OF ETHICAL RELATIVISM we seem confronted with the incongruity of a militant and unapologetic self-righteousness.

This should come as no surprise. Relativism argues that there are no objective or universal moral values, because values are dependent on, and therefore relative to, such things as culture, social class, race, gender, ethnic group, or time period. Nothing is absolute and anything goes.

However, to avoid chaos, as Thomas Hobbes informs us, we need a strong central government to dictate to us what is right and harsh punishments must be enforced to maintain order.

In our present government-by-lobby mixed economy, this means the squeakiest wheel dictates the laws and rules. The legal has become identical to the moral, thus moral outrage is expressed at any violation

---

[21] Gary Taubes (website), garytaubes.com.
[22] Scott Dailey, "Get Ready for the War on Sugar," February 23, 2012, wsj.com.

of the law—no matter how inane, incomprehensible, or irrational the law or rules may be.

Rules in our K-12 schools provide an abundance of self-righteous inanities, mostly related to the schools' phobia for guns. A kindergartner[23] who brought a souvenir cap gun to school was interrogated for two hours until he wet his pants, then suspended for ten days.* A six-year-old[24] was punished and forced to apologize for bringing a gun to school made out of Legos no more than the size of a quarter. Enforcers of the rules say that intent and motive are irrelevant. Seriously? We're talking about five- and six-year-olds! "How is this not bullying?," one commenter on the forums asked.

"Well-intentioned" are words that do not come to mind when thinking of these enforcers. "Vicious" and "mean-spirited" do.

Remind me to keep my Boy Scout knife at home the next time I go to school.

The so-called zero-tolerance policies[25] have no value or foundation in fact. One couple[26] who sponsored a prom party in their home were arrested for supplying alcoholic beverages to their underage guests. Their motive—which, of course, is irrelevant—was to keep their son from attending a liquor-filled party on the beach forty miles away. Car keys were collected at the door so no one could leave until sober. The couple, no doubt, saved lives that night. Mothers Against Drunk Driving (MADD), a politicized[27] and, now, militantly self-righteous organization, was delighted over the arrest.

Then there was the mother[28] who left her sleeping infant and her five-year-old in the car while running into the store to make a quick purchase. During the nine minutes that passed, 9-1-1 was called, the mother's purse was searched, and she was taken to the police station.

---

[23] Eric Owens, "Kindergartener Interrogated Over Cap Gun Until He Pees His Pants, Then Suspended 10 Days," May 31, 2013, dailycaller.com.

[24] Lee Moran, "Lego Gun Causes Panic on School Bus; Kindergartener Gets Detention," May 29, 2013, nydailynews.com.

[25] D. C. Innes, "When Zero Tolerance Makes Zero Sense," October 21, 2013, world.wng.org.

[26] Radley Balko, "Zero Tolerance Makes Zero Sense," August 9, 2005, cato.org.

[27] Radley Balko, "Targeting the Social Drinker Is Just MADD," December 9, 2002, latimes.com.

[28] Lenore Skenazy, "The Latest Suburban Crime Wave," July 1, 2013, wsj.com.

Three visits from child-protection services warned her that next time her kids would be taken away.

The latest and most disturbing[29] of inanities was the arrest of a underage college student for buying a six-pack of bottled water. Seven of Virginia's state Alcoholic Beverage Control agents mistook the water for beer and the terrified teen and her two friends mistook the plain clothes agents for the type of people who can do bad things to young girls. They drove off brushing two of the agents who were trying to smash the car's windows. Upshot? One night in jail, two-and-a-half months' anguished torment under threat of imprisonment for five years, and the girl had to apologize for mistaking the agents.

Something is terribly wrong in the above case. The agents should be apologizing to the girls and the higher authorities should be investigating the behavior of overly zealous law enforcement officers. That's what one would expect in a free society.

My previous two posts demonstrated how overly zealous and self-righteous federal prosecutors[30] and college administrators[31] go after people with a vengeance for the slightest transgressions, if one can even call them that, of the law and university rules.

A "busybody state" is how we might describe our current situation. H. L. Mencken[32] once described puritanism as "the haunting fear that someone, somewhere, may be happy." In today's cultural atmosphere, puritanism from the right has waned a bit, but it certainly seems alive and well from the left. Perhaps Mencken's quote should be amended to read: the haunting fear that someone, somewhere, may be responsible—that is, accountable, competent, and independent.

Busybodies know what is best for everyone else and through their officious meddling they aim to make sure we do what they think is best. If we dare to deviate ever so slightly from the prescribed norms, as defined by the busybodies, the fullest power of retribution must be brought down on us.

Everything is relative? Yes, except for what the busybodies dictate.

---

[29] K. Burnell Evans, "Bottled-Water Purchase Leads to Night in Jail for U.Va. Student," June 28, 2013, richmond.com.
[30] See above, "The Sovietization of Federal Law," p. 68.
[31] See above, "Challenging the New McCarthyism," p. 143.
[32] "H. L. Mencken Quotes," brainyquote.com.

* Had the gun been loaded with caps, it would have been described as an explosive and the police would have been called.

(July 15, 2013)

Facts Don't Matter, Or: The Art of BS

ON NUMEROUS OCCASIONS in the very political world of academic bureaucracy I have been known to express dismay over less than accurate statements made by my colleagues. On almost just as many occasions one colleague and dear friend has promptly looked me straight in the eye and said, "Facts don't matter!"

The word "politics," when used in "academic politics" or "company politics" or the real-thing "political politics," means maneuvering for advantage without regard for merit or ability. It means one-upping others through connections or favors to get what the politician wants. It means acquiring unearned power over others.* With merit or ability removed from the equation, it means that facts don't matter.

Princeton University philosophy professor Harry Frankfurt has analyzed this phenomenon in his little book (originally a long article) *On Bullshit*.[33] BS'ing, says Frankfurt, is not the same as lying, because the liar is concerned with facts, or truth, in order to state the opposite. But the BS'er is focused on what sounds or looks good. Facts are irrelevant. BS'd statements may be true, but they don't have to be.

"I got four job offers," a BS'er might say. "No you didn't," a fact-oriented bubble-burster might reply. "You went to four interviews and got one offer." Saying I got four job offers, though, sounds better than admitting to only one.

"The X (famous) Rock Band played at that historic venue." Huh? Do you know that for sure? "Well, not really, but they probably did." In the absence of anything else to say, it apparently sounds better to a BS'er to make that grand statement.

Insincere? Dishonest? Maybe, maybe not. Lying and BS'ing can be thought of as existing on opposite ends of a continuum. Lying, as Frankfurt puts it, is a craft, a skill at telling non-truths, whereas BS'ing is an art. The BS'er is creative and puts on a show.

---

[33] Harry Frankfurt, *On Bullshit*, amazon.com.

Somewhere in between the two poles lies that gray area where even the speaker may not know whether he or she is speaking contrary to fact or exaggerating for effect.

Psychologies are complex and a further complicating factor is the continuum between deliberateness and carelessness. One can lie or BS by design, with forethought, or out of ignorance or habit. Forgetting is a common cause of misleading statements, as is insecurity that sometimes calls for bravado to help reduce anxiety.

But we tend most often to speak the way our mental habits developed in childhood. A family culture that lies or hyperbolizes frequently is going to produce adults who lie or hyperbolize.

BS'ing, as a result, may end up being one's habitual way of talking. That is unfortunate. Normal people rely on the truth of what liars and BS'ers say. As outside observers they cannot tell whether the liar/BS'er is being deliberate or careless.

"Yeah, our flights to Hawaii only cost $200!" Each way or round trip? It doesn't matter. A thorough search of Hawaii airfares reveals nothing close to that number. The consequence of BS'ing is its effect on listeners who know the facts, or who can readily find them. Trust and respect go out the window. Disappointment sets in.

When the BS'ing, or worse, moves into the work, academic, or political worlds, the stage is set for partisan maneuvering. "Spin" in governmental politics was coined originally to mean positioning[34] for politicians. Today it means fabrication.

Facts matter. Sticking to the facts is the essence of objectivity. Everyday life, whether in school, business, or government, is not an exercise in creating fiction. It is nonfiction.

If you are not sure whether a certain rock band performed in a certain venue, it would be more objective to say, "They may have (or likely) played there, but I am not sure."

A serious BS'er, however, unfortunately, would not make those qualifications. Saying "I'm not sure" reduces one-upmanship over others. It takes away the BS'er's power and power is what politics is all about.

---

[34]Jerry Kirkpatrick, "On Marketing Bull----," April 2006, cpp.edu/faculty/jkirkpatrick.

* Political junkies[35] may now complain that I am being unfair to those sincere, conscientious politicians working in our government-by-lobby mixed economy. Even if there is such a thing as a sincere politician, "government-by-lobby mixed economy" is the problem and cause of what I am talking about. The mixed economy with its countless laws, many of them contradictory and nonobjective,[36] is what gives rise to the rent-seeking,[37] one-upmanship behavior that pervades our society. A "zero sum"[38] assumption, means someone suffers if I gain. Well, then, I'd better get mine before those others get theirs. That's politics.

(September 16, 2013)

Polylogism, the Right to Lie, and Serial Embellishers

THE SUBJECTIVIST BELIEF that each class has its own logic, that is, that there is no universal logic that applies to all human beings, is an essential tenet of Marxism.[39] Capitalists have their logic; proletarians have theirs. Communication between the two is not possible. Therefore, the capitalist bourgeois exploiters must be controlled and, in some cases, liquidated.

This is why, in reference to the House Un-American Activities Committee, Ayn Rand said, "What those goddamned communists wanted was the right to lie!"*

If you're an enemy, facts don't matter.[40]

Today, polylogism is rampant and assumes that all kinds of groups based on race, gender, sexual orientation, nationality, religion, physical ability, etc., ad nauseam, have a unique logic that is consequently beyond rational understanding. White males in particular are typically targeted

---

[35] See above, "Politics Is a Bore (Retitled: Who Are We Going to Coerce Today?)," p. "62."
[36] See above, "The Sovietization of Federal Law," p. 68.
[37] "Rent-Seeking," wikipedia.org.
[39] "Zero-Sum," merriam-webster.com.
[39] "Polylogism," wikipedia.org; Ludwig von Mises, *Human Action*, chap. 3, "Economics and the Revolt against Reason," mises.org; Jeffrey A. Tucker, "Marxism without Polylogism," August 31, 2009, mises.org.
[40] See above, "Facts Don't Matter, Or: The Art of BS," p. 307.

as enemies, but groups in a position of power can and do declare any other opposing group persona non grata and, as a result, conclude that they owe the other groups nothing but ad hominem attacks.

One moderate liberal, Jonathan Chait,[41] recently acknowledged that his more radically left colleagues "borrowed" Marx's polylogism to establish our current virulently absolutist[42] climate of political correctness. However, Mr. Chait is mistaken. Political correctness is rooted deeply in Marxism and its proponents are the tenured radicals of the 1960's!

This means moderate liberals, as well as conservatives—most people today, in other words—have uncritically and probably unwittingly swallowed the Marxist agenda of their professors. Have they bought into the "right to lie" part of the agenda?

Probably not, though there are plenty of "serial embellishers" in all areas of our present culture.

"Serial embellishment" is an interesting new phrase that has popped up to describe repeat BS'ers,[43] such as the now less-than-esteemed NBC News anchor.[44]

When facts don't matter, fiction and fabrication become primary. The trouble with serial embellishment is that the embellishers intend listeners to take their words as true. And most listeners assume they are.

When the words turn out not to be true and the speakers are obviously not novelists or screenwriters, listeners will draw one conclusion: embellishers have adopted the right to lie.

Criminal psychologies are those that lie as a way of life. How should we classify serial embellishers?

* I am quoting from memory here, from the 1970's. Rand was answering questions of a small group of students after a lecture in New York.

(February 16, 2015)

---

[41] Jonathan Chait, "How the Language Police Are Perverting Liberalism," January 27, 2015, nymag.com.
[42] See above, "Virulent Absolutism in an Age of Relativism," p. 304.
[43] See above, "Facts Don't Matter, Or: The Art of BS," p. 307.
[44] "Brian Williams," wikipedia.org.

2016

Why Don't Facts Matter?

IN SEVERAL PREVIOUS COMMENTS I have in one way or another attempted to answer the question that titles this post.

My first encounter with the issue occurred when I complained to a colleague about other associates whose selective memories seemed beyond the pale, because I had assumed it was impossible for the latter to have forgotten what was said in a meeting not too long before the immediate incident.

The colleague gave me a dead serious glare and said, "Facts don't matter!" I briefly responded with an embarrassed "you can't be serious" chuckle, but soon realized that the glare was not going away.

Naiveté aside—I am aware that there are dishonest people in the world—I nonetheless have a hard time understanding those who seem to be honest, yet clearly are not sticking to the facts.

In 2006 I wrote an academic paper[45] about Harry Frankfurt's little book *On Bullshit*,[46] in which Frankfurt distinguishes liars from BS'ers. Liars care about facts in order to say the opposite. BS'ers, however, don't care because their goal is to impress and sway whether or not what they are saying is true. Are BS'ers dishonest?*

In my paper I argue that there are a couple of continua operating here, the relevant one ranging from the deliberately dishonest to sloppy thinkers who are unaware of their premises or where the premises came from.

This may somewhat account for those who seem to be decent people but at the same time are habitual hyperbolizers and habitually selective rememberers. But where do these habits come from?

In a 2008 blog post[47] I make the not too original point that we learn—that is, pick up habits—from our parents, teachers, and significant others, which means our significant others learned from their significant others who learned from theirs, etc. In the absence of an infinite regress, however, someone somewhere along the line had to

---

[45] Jerry Kirkpatrick, "On Marketing Bull----," April 2006, cpp.edu/faculty/jkirkpatrick.
[46] Harry Frankfurt, *On Bullshit*, amazon.com.
[47] See above, "Faking Your Way through Life," p. 213.

have chosen to embellish his or her statements and selectively ignore certain facts. Why?

Free will, of course, dictates that anyone in the present, or past, can choose to ignore facts. Is that it? Isn't there more to the sloppy thinking that many seem to exhibit?

Consider the following cases.

1. Philosopher Sidney Hook describes two instances from his travels in the mid-twentieth century.[48] In Japan, Hook relates, he was confronted by his academic hosts and the Japanese press with nothing but complaints about the US bombing of Hiroshima, yet not a single word was said about the Japanese attack on Pearl Harbor. In India, the conversation centered on US race discrimination—without mention of India's caste system. Near the end of his stay, Hook invited an academic host to dine with him at his hotel, but the host, after several evasions, finally admitted that he could not accept—because the waiters at the hotel were Muslim and the host was Brahmin.

Hook does not provide an explanation for the stark logical disconnects in either instance, other than to imply differences between Eastern and Western cultures.

My conclusion would have to specify the lack of Aristotelian logic in the East and its presence in the West. Most westerners, however precariously they may do so, cling to the notions of non-contradiction and non-fallacious thinking, which means they maintain some respect for facts that apparently the educated in the East do not.

Respect for logic means respect for facts.

2. Anthony Watts, former television meteorologist and current climate change doubter (to use the Associated Press's preferred moniker for global warming skeptics), blogs on wattsupwiththat.com,[49] a site that enjoys three to four million page views per month. Several highly qualified guest climatologists also regularly post their thorough, technical analyses of "climate change" issues.

---

[48] Sidney Hook, *Out of Step*, pp. 585–88, amazon.com.
[49] Watts Up With That? (website), wattsupwiththat.com.

Last June,⁵⁰ Watts reported the details of a meeting he had with journalist, ardent environmentalist, and staunch global warming supporter Bill McKibben. Instead of fireworks and hostility between the two, Watts described their discussion as civil and friendly. They discussed their respective agreement and disagreement on numerous climate and environmental issues.

Concluding his report, Watts said, apparently to challenge strong opinions within the denier community, "I don't think Bill McKibben is an idiot." He then added, "But I do think he perceives things more on a feeling or emotional level and translates that into words and actions. People that are more factual and pragmatic might see that as an unrealistic response."

Why don't facts matter according to the scientist Watts? Because emotion sometimes trumps facts.

3. Ayn Rand in her article "To Dream the Non-Commercial Dream"⁵¹ emphasizes the significance of emotion trumping fact. She says this about "impassioned advocates" of altruism and collectivism:

> They are not hypocrites; in their own way, they are "sincere"; they have to be. They need to believe that their work serves others, whether those others like it or not, and that the good of others is their only motivation; they do believe it—passionately, fiercely, militantly—in the sense in which a *belief* is distinguishable from a *conviction*: in the form of an emotion impervious to reality (Rand's emphasis).

Deep down, in their psychologies, it is emotion that dictates to these "sincere" people what is true. Facts don't matter because emotion says otherwise. Altruism and collectivism have become their entrenched beliefs.

Rand adds that this "depth"—the "deep down" part of these unexamined psychologies—can be "measured by distance from reality" and

---

⁵⁰ Anthony Watts, "My One-on-One with Bill McKibben," June 6, 2015, wattsupwiththat.com.
⁵¹ *The Ayn Rand Letter*, January 1, 1973, reprinted in Ayn Rand, *The Voice of Reason*, amazon.com.

that there exists a continuum, based on the distance, that runs from "sincere" to totalitarian dictator.

Rand puts "sincere" in scare quotes, which probably means she is not entirely endorsing the term, but I still have to ask: are those on the "sincere" end of the continuum . . . sincere? And honest? Who, really, after all is a bad dude?

Rand goes so far as to acknowledge that the "butcher of the Ukraine," Nikita Khrushchev, was compelled to believe the "truth" (my quotes) and magical ritual of dialectical materialism. He had to, she says, lest he "face something more frightening than death" (Rand's quotes).

This comment on Khruschev leads me to *The Criminal Personality*[52] by Yochelson and Samenow. Criminals certainly are bad dudes. They lie (and BS) as a way of life and enjoy getting away with the forbidden. ("If rape were legalized today . . . I would do something else," one offender told the researchers.)

And criminals, like Khrushchev, don't have much deep down, that is, they are considerably deficient in self-esteem. What is there, as Rand puts it, is distant from reality. "I am a nothing, a zero," several criminals confessed, but added that if they routinely thought that way, they would have to kill themselves. So they live by substitute thoughts, or rather rationalizations. Their accumulated mental habits have taught them to believe and say: "that guy deserved it" or "everything in the store belongs to me" or "she really wanted me."

Khrushchev substituted the communist mantra.

So how can these bad dudes seem "sincere"? They are liars and BS'ers. The goal of the liar and BS'er is to sound good. Most criminals are con artists, which means they are consummate liars and BS'ers to make what they say *sound good*.

The same applies to dictators. Many have been charmers at cocktail parties. Hitler was.

So would I want to be friends with someone on the "sincere" end of Rand's continuum?

---

[52] Samuel Yochelson and Stanton Samenow, *The Criminal Personality*, vol. 1, amazon.com.

Sidney Hook and Anthony Watts did not seem to find offensive the disagreements they had with their associates, but those associates were presumably not on the extreme end of Rand's scale.

I would say that friendships, whether professional or personal, depend on how distant one's contact is from reality. That is to say, on a scale of decency—by adapting Rand's continuum—honest, fact-oriented people are at the top, scummy criminals and Khruschevs are at the bottom, but most decent people, the "sincere" ones Rand was talking about, fit into the middle to upper tiers.**

The difficulty in forming professional and personal friendships is in understanding the other person's psychology and discovering that distance from reality.

Facts do matter.

* Frankfurt thinks BS'ers are worse than liars—and more likely to be found among the highly educated because of their facility with language.

** In Rand's article she was talking about a retired editor of the *New York Times*.

(February 3, 2016)

Genes vs. Environment: Anyone for Free Will?

DO GENES CAUSE BEHAVIOR? If they do, one would expect to see evidence of criminality, genius, schizophrenia, homosexuality, and evangelical Christianity in infants. All of these behaviors, plus many others, have been said to be inborn.

To expect an infant to exhibit these traits is absurd. To say that an infant has inherited the *potential* to become a criminal, or evangelical Christian, says nothing. We are all born with that potential, plus countless other potentialities.

Does environment cause behavior? The trouble with this assertion is that there are always exceptions to the good and bad things environment does to children when they are growing up.

Some children reared in crime-ridden, slum neighborhoods become criminals while others do not, even if they are siblings in the same family. The same can be said for children reared in safe, wealthy suburbs. Others raised in religious families follow their parents and become evangelical Christians, while some rebel and become atheists.

The determinism of the genes/environment axis is a self-contradiction—determinists have to acknowledge that they are determined to believe in determinism. Yet they pretend to be making a logical choice to believe in determinism.

Something other than genes or environment must be operating to cause our behavior.

Here's a novel idea. How about thought, that processor of genetic inheritance and environment that generates our motivation and directs behavior?

Thought, or more broadly, consciousness, makes errors and has to control itself in order not to make mistakes. Free will is cognitive self-regulation, which means we may choose to focus on the facts or evade them, allowing other factors, such as emotions, presuppositions, or political doctrine, to interfere with correct perception.*

Our guide to the correct perception of reality is the 2500-year-old science of thinking called logic. As the discipline and art that regulates internal thought processes, logic is the quintessential *introspective* science. The genes/environment axis, however, does not want to admit that logic is introspective, because then they would have to admit that consciousness controls behavior and that introspection is a valid method of science.

Psychologically, this means our personalities are self-created. The cause of behavior is the innumerable conclusions we have drawn—the myriad thoughts, logical or not, we have had—about our genetic inheritance and the environment in which we live, from the time we were able to process words right up to the present.

These innumerable conclusions and myriad thoughts accumulate and become the mental habits by which we live. As habits (or psycho-epistemologies[53]), many have become so automatized, buried in our subconscious with their origins largely forgotten, that they *feel*

---

[53] "Psycho-Epistemology," aynrandlexicon.com.

to us as if we were born that way, or that something external is making us act the way we do.

Lack of introspection, or more specifically, introspective skill, to examine our motivating premises—thoughts, evaluations, emotions—makes it hard to appreciate how much control we in fact have over our lives.

Habits can be good or bad, the good ones leading us to live a happy life, the bad ones not so happy. The examined life, to paraphrase Socrates, is worth living; the unexamined one leads to problems in living.

Mental habits are all learned.** We were not born knowing how to drive a car, for example, but in adulthood, adults can safely drive while carrying on a conversation and listening to music on the radio. All of our actions follow this pattern.

Certain habits, generated from core evaluations and other less fundamental but nevertheless significant evaluations, are usually acquired when very young, from toddlerhood on. We retain these early conclusions about ourselves (our sense of personal identity), the world, and other people and hold them as unquestioned absolutes.***

It is in toddlerhood that we begin to speak, which means we are beginning to think in concepts and words.

Young children do not usually form these important conclusions through explicit reasoning, but through a process of emotional generalization. At the risk of oversimplification, an emotion at this stage in life, if it could be put into words, might say something like, "That made me feel good about myself. I'll do it again." Or, "I didn't like that and I'm not going to feel it again."

Repeated many times over, the former, if based on a correct perception of reality, can lead to the development of self-esteem, the latter, which most likely includes errors, to repression and subsequent psychological problems.

If taught from an early age to look inward to identify our thoughts, evaluations, and emotions, and to correct errors we have made, we would grow up with healthy psychologies. Most of us, however, have not been taught much of anything about psychology, in childhood or adulthood.

Thus, when the genes/environment axis comes along, it makes perfect sense that our behavior is caused by something we have no control over.

The irony is that genes and environment do have an influence on us, in the sense that genes give us gender and skin color and environment can make life easy or difficult, but we are the ones who develop attitudes—conclusions, evaluations—about gender, skin color, and environment.

To help us correctly perceive and evaluate what genetics has given us and what goes on in our environment, teaching is crucial. Parents and the schools need to instruct children in the skill of applying logic to their own psychologies.

The unfortunate consequence of the genes/environment debate is that the axis devalues the environmental influence of an education in sound psychology. For that is what is required to help us use our free will to assess genetic inheritance and environment and thereby make better choices to live a happier life.

* This is Ayn Rand's theory of free will as volitional consciousness.[54]

** All habits, at root, are mental. I use "mental" here to emphasize their psychological origin.

*** The concept of core evaluations was identified by psychologist Edith Packer and presented in her lecture "Understanding the Subconscious" in 1984.[55]

(August 15, 2016)

Is Intelligence Inborn?

My IQ—THE SO-CALLED INTELLIGENCE QUOTIENT—is probably twelve. (Psst! And I'm proud of it!)

I say "probably" because I have never known my score. One day in junior high school we were all herded into the auditorium to take

---

[54] "Free Will," aynrandlexicon.com.
[55] Edith Packer, *Lectures on Psychology*, chap. 1, amazon.com.

a standardized test. After about the first page of questions, I decided, "This is stupid," and stopped answering. Hence, my presumed score. Teachers never told us what the purpose of the test was.

Intelligence, as defined by the *Oxford English Dictionary* is "understanding as a quality admitting of degree; spec. quickness or superiority of understanding, sagacity."

There are two usages here. One, "the intelligence" or "understanding" is synonym for rational faculty, which is our capacity to reason and think conceptually that distinguishes us from the lower animals. The other usage, as the *OED* says, "admits of degree." Thus, there are supposedly brighter, smarter, more intelligent people and there also are the dull and dumb.

Degree of intelligence is not the same as quantity of knowledge or retained subject matter. I have met many uneducated blue collar workers and unskilled laborers who are more intelligent than college professors!

Intelligence is supposed to be an inborn ability, not an issue of how much knowledge one has accumulated and can spew out to impress those supposedly less endowed.

Ayn Rand has variously defined intelligence[56] as "the ability to deal with a broad range of abstractions" and "the ability to grasp the facts of reality and to deal with them long-range (i.e., conceptually)."

I don't doubt that this is a component of what we think of as smart, but a genius who has a greater degree of intelligence than the rest of us, to put it in the vernacular and to relate it to the *OED*'s definition, is a "quick wit," a person who grasps an insight or makes a connection ahead of everyone else.

By analogy, an entrepreneur is someone who sees and seizes profit-making opportunities ahead of others. Some of us may also see the opportunity but we often do not act on it. The entrepreneur does.

Similarly, the highly intelligent person does not just make an unseen-before connection, but acts on it by conducting an experiment and writing a book. Some of us may have daydreamed about a "what-if" fuzzy linking but never get beyond the fuzziness.

The genius and entrepreneur both must hold in mind a great deal of knowledge related to their field, possess the ability to work with a

---

[56] "Intelligence," aynrandlexicon.com.

broad range of abstractions, and think long-range (i.e., conceptually), but it is their "quick wit" that puts them out in front of others. (And contrary to what our Marxist-laden intelligentsia may think, entrepreneurs can be highly intelligent and even geniuses.)

The problem I have with the concept of intelligence, like all the other traits I discussed in last month's post on the genes/environment debate (see above), is that other variables, such as that unmentionable one, free will, but especially *interest*, can explain what is supposedly inborn.

Interest is a desire that directs intensive and sustained attention to a particular goal or object. It is interest, when put into action as effort, that drives a five-year-old to become a concert pianist as an adult. It is interest that drives entrepreneurs to think day and night about the next profit-making opportunity. And it is interest that drives geniuses to uncover every stone until they have found that next important discovery.

Interest is a potent motivator that can separate the highly accomplished, whom we would also likely call highly intelligent, from the rest of us. Strong interest—which also has to mean here the absence of psychological inhibitions and presence of choice or free will—could well be the key variable to explain the "degree of understanding" that the highly intelligent possess.

Yes, knowledge, or a context of subject matter, is required to make great accomplishments and to make great discoveries possible, but I am convinced that anyone with a normal brain, a good teacher, and patience can learn that context of knowledge, however abstract it may be. Interest and will power, if present, can take such a student to the next level.

So is "quick wit" inborn?

Those twin studies don't prove anything. For nearly a hundred years they have attempted to prove that many traits, including intelligence, are inherited. Clinical psychologist Jay Joseph has thoroughly examined the studies of identical and fraternal twins, both reared together and reared apart,[57] (see his latest book here[58]) and has declared them

---

[57] Jay Joseph, "The Trouble with Twin Studies," March 13, 2013, madinamerica.com; Jay Joseph, "Twin Studies Are Still in Trouble: A Response to Turkheimer," November 2, 2015, madinamerica.com; Jay Joseph, "Studies of Reared-Apart (Separated) Twins: Facts and Fallacies," December 15, 2014, madinamerica.com.

[58] Jay Joseph, *The Trouble with Twin Studies*, amazon.com.

"one of the great pseudoscientific methods of our time . . . [that] will eventually be added to the list of discarded pseudosciences where we now find alchemy, craniometry, and mesmerism."

What about IQ tests? Please! Aside from the fact that these tests, along with college entrance examinations, correlate with socioeconomic status and the latter do not predict college success (high school grades are the better predictors), IQ testing is a contrived situation, as is paper and pencil testing of all kinds. Testing seldom corresponds to the reality it is supposed to represent.*

As I wrote in *Montessori, Dewey, and Capitalism*,[59] "Supermarket shoppers in one study performed arithmetic calculations far more accurately in the store than on a formal test. And one boy, considered the dumbest in his class, was discovered by his teacher to be a paid scorekeeper in a bowling alley, simultaneously tracking the progress of two teams of four players each. The teacher promptly created word problems, requiring students to calculate scores for games of bowling. The boy could not do the problems."

I think I'll go find that dumb kid and have him teach me how to score games of bowling. I never could figure that out.

No wonder my IQ is only twelve!

---

* And let us not forget that IQ testing originated in the eugenics era, designed to sort out the "dumb" and "feeble-minded" for isolation and perhaps sterilization. Today, IQ testing and college entrance examinations perform a similar function (sterilization excepted), shunting the "dumb" off to the less prestigious colleges and trade schools (and in many countries to a blue collar life that they cannot overcome). The ones who score a little better than the "really dumb" ones and live in government-created slum areas are given special favors and money to attend the prestigious universities. There, many suffer a mismatch with their classmates—and flunk out. The sorting continues.[60]

(September 11, 2016)

---

[59] Jerry Kirkpatrick, *Montessori, Dewey, and Capitalism*, note 19, p. 158, amazon.com.
[60] Walter Williams, "Academic Mismatch I," September 2, 2008, walterewilliams .com; Walter Williams, "Academic Mismatch II," September 9, 2008, creators .com; Richard Sander and Stuart Taylor, Jr., *Mismatch*, amazon.com.

Statistical Projection vs. Scientific Generalization

When my daughter was quite young, before she was able to walk, she saw a ball bounce and roll. She laughed heartily. I don't think she needed to observe a sample of five hundred round, spongy things bounce and roll in order to conclude that round, spongy things bounce and roll.

Similarly, neurologist V. S. Ramachandran, proponent of the value of individual cases to science, has remarked (quoted in Doidge .[61]

> Imagine I were to present a pig to a skeptical scientist, insisting it could speak English, then waved my hand, and the pig spoke English. Would it really make sense for the skeptic to argue, "But that is just one pig, Ramachandran. Show me another, and I might believe you!"

The skeptical scientist, typical of nearly all scientists today, insists that the only way to establish knowledge is to observe five hundred cases, or a thousand, or two thousand. Anything less is an isolated instance, often denigrated as anecdotal evidence. In the absence of a sound theory of universals—because David Hume failed to find a necessary connection between cause and effect, and logical positivism picked up the banner of science, followed by Karl Popper's notion of falsificationism[62]—statistical "generalization" is said to be the only valid method of science.

It is this premise that allows modern psychologists to dismiss the entire Freudian psychoanalytic corpus, including the concept of repression, as unscientific, or worse, as pseudoscientific. Why? Because Freud's evidence is "anecdotal" and the experimental methods of the physical sciences cannot validate his ideas. It is this premise that allows nearly all scientists to dismiss the notions of consciousness, free will, and introspection.

There is, however, a sound theory of universals: Ayn Rand's theory of concepts,[63] which I have summarized in my two books, *In Defense*

---

[61] Norman Doidge, *The Brain that Changes Itself*, p. 178, amazon.com.
[62] "Falsifiabiity," wikipedia.org.
[63] Ayn Rand, *Introduction to Objectivist Epistemology*, amazon.com.

of Advertising[64] and *Montessori, Dewey, and Capitalism*[65] Conceptualization is a process of universalization. It is based on Aristotle's formal cause, which says that an entity's actions are determined by its identity. Identifying universal relationships between entities and their actions give us principles and laws.

Concepts identify the nature of entities. Their essential distinguishing characteristics are universal. It is not that hard.

Thus, my daughter's laughter at witnessing the round spongy thing bounce and roll was her conceptualization of that entity, by observing its essential distinguishing characteristic. Of course, she did not have words to describe the process at the time, but her mind, nonetheless, was processing her perception. The same can be said about Ramachandran's English-speaking pig (assuming no tricks of ventriloquism). One does not need a sample of five hundred English-speaking pigs to conclude that something quite unusual has just happened.

Statistical projection—and the correct word is "projection," not generalization—has its place in our search for knowledge, but it does not replace scientific (inductive) generalization.

Statistical inference, as it is also correctly called, projects a finding from a sample to a population. Thus, if data in a sample of 500 American men show that two percent have red hair, and the research did not commit any flagrant methodological errors, then a projection (or inference) can be made, within a margin of error, that two percent of men in the entire country have red hair.

A projection moves from *some to some*—from two percent of the sample to the same two percent in the population.

A scientific generalization, on the other hand, when, for example, forming a concept of round, spongy things as something that bounces and rolls, or of human beings who possess the capacity to reason, moves from *all to all*.

All of the balls I have observed bounce and roll; all humans that I have observed possess the capacity to reason. Therefore, all balls, past, present, and future, by their very nature, bounce and roll. The same conclusion is drawn for all humans.

---

[64] Jerry Kirkpatrick, *In Defense of Advertising*, pp. 147–52, amazon.com.
[65] Jerry Kirkpatrick, *Montessori, Dewey, and Capitalism*, pp. 82–86, amazon.com.

The place of statistical projection? As I wrote in *In Defense of Advertising* (p. 157), "Statistics is a branch of mathematics and, as such, is a method of measurement. Statistical inference . . . is used only in contexts in which we do not know—or there do not exist—universal laws that could explain the causal relations of the variables."

Meteorology represents the former, because of the large number of unknowns and difficult-to-measure variables in constructing weather forecasts (all of which, though given many different names, are forms of statistical projection).

Predictions of people's behavior, because free will precludes the existence of universal laws governing all of our behavior, represents the latter; we make statistical projections, albeit not based on randomized samples, unless we are professional researchers, of what others will do in the future based on our current and past knowledge of them.

Statistical projection assists scientific research. It is not a substitute for it.

And one does not have to accept everything Freud said to acknowledge his accomplishments, not least of which is his presentation of the first comprehensive theory of psychology.

Freud was looking for universals, and he found a few: repression, defense mechanisms, and the significance of the subconscious to influence our present behavior.

They may not be round, spongy things, but I am laughing heartily—at my discovery of these Freudian universals!

(October 4, 2016)

6

Youth Sports

2008–12

Caterpillars into Butterflies

I DON'T KNOW WHERE I'VE BEEN for the past several decades but I had never heard the expression "turning caterpillars into butterflies" used in relation to teaching. That is, until this spring when my daughter's softball coaches used it several times to explain their goal of coaching twelve eight-and-under girls. Add to this the coaches' commitment to "no child left behind"—meaning every girl on the team, no matter how young or inexperienced, would learn how to throw, catch, and bat or, if an older veteran, how to improve these skills—and you have a heck of a model of teaching. Winning certainly was not the only thing, and most of the girls did not seem to attach any significance to it, but winning did follow from the teaching.

So what does the metaphor mean for teaching? It is a biological process that turns caterpillars into butterflies, occurring naturally with proper nurture and a minimum of interference from predators and the elements. For teaching, this means that children are natural learners and therefore do not need to be forced to learn. They need guidance and motivation perhaps more importantly than any particular knowledge content; they need encouragement, not coercion, angry yelling, or contemptuous denigration. The goal of teaching is to build confidence in the child's own ability to learn such that the child can continue to learn throughout life without need, or with only occasional need, of additional teaching. The butterfly knows how to fly and does not need additional "instruction" or development. A clipped wing, however, will destroy it.

Many years ago, when I was in high school, I played in an orchestra of extremely talented teenagers. (Almost all, I should say, were far more talented than I.) Several different conductors would direct us in weekly concerts. Only one knew how to get the butterflies to fly. He was a motivator of adolescents and young adults and was well liked. He would make exclamations like "Sound! I want to hear sound from you!" and "Brass, I can't hear you!" Which to trumpeters, trombonists, and French horn players was a call to action. Not loud noise, but beautiful, controlled, and confidently self-assertive sound that made the difference between amateurishness and near professionalism.

The keyword here is "controlled," for that is what skilled musicians exhibit—control of air stream and finger movement for wind instrument players and control of muscle movements for stringed instrument players and percussionists. Control is also what skilled athletes exhibit, in muscle movement of course, but also, as sports psychologists point out, in their thoughts about playing the game. The good motivator is the one who finds ways to make sure their students or musicians or athletes get their heads in the game and keep them there.

In contrast to the above orchestra motivator, one stern task master of a conductor succeeded in clipping the wings of the orchestral butterflies with one simple but true statement. He said, "Remember, the audience is applauding the composer as much as they are you, the performers." Message: "don't think you are so good." The statement is true about audiences and, often, their standing ovations, but to say it to teenagers was utterly deflating to their developing egos. The conductor did not ask for sound and he did not get it. Was he predator or the elements? Take your pick. Demeaning comments kill confidence and a willingness to perform.

Patience is a requirement of good teaching and the passage of time is what is required for a caterpillar to pass through the chrysalis stage to turn into a butterfly. Let me conclude this post by bringing back my daughter's softball coaches and describing their seemingly infinite patience with even the youngest, most inexperienced girl on the team, a girl who would tend to get down on herself and say "I can't do it." At one practice the assistant coach must have thrown thirty or forty balls to this girl for her to swing at, and with each swing she would fail to make contact. Periodically, the coach would stop to make an adjustment in her stance, then he would pitch more balls. On about the fortieth pitch... boom. A big pop fly went to shortstop. High fives, the coach insisted, were called for from all the other players; then he picked up the girl and said, "I don't want to ever again hear you say that you can't do it."

A week or two later, the same girl made contact with the ball in a game that helped drive in winning runs. This caterpillar metamorphosed into a beautiful butterfly and that is the ultimate payoff of good teaching.

(June 13, 2008)

On Extrinsic Motivation, Bureaucracy, and the Stage-Mother Syndrome

CARROT AND STICK MOTIVATION, especially the latter, as opposed to communication, persuasion, and appeals to inner values, are alive and well in today's world. The question is, why are such extrinsic sources of motivation so common? A number of reasons can be given.

For example, in the academic world of professorial tenure, faculty can almost never be fired. As a result, some administrators and chairs resort to stick tactics such as making meetings "mandatory," providing sign-in sheets to yield evidence that faculty attended, and reciting stories like "back when I started to work in business, I said 'yes sir!' when the boss requested something of me." None of these work and they certainly do not endear the administrators or chairs to faculty. In rare cases, professors have been docked a day's pay for not attending a meeting or returning from a conference a day late. Needless to say, this tactic is even less endearing. Why do administrators and chairs feel they must wield these sticks?

The easy answer is that people tend to do what they were taught by their parents and significant others. And extrinsic, coercive methods of motivation continue to dominate our culture. But the academic world, especially the state-run university, is bureaucratic.[1] Its management is top-down with myriad rules and regulations to guide lower-level decision making. Bureaucracy is the means by which government bureaus are run. In contrast, business management is bottom-up with policies derived from the needs and wants of paying customers and the requirements of making a profit. Employees are often viewed metaphorically as intermediate customers who perform valued services for management. Coercing and talking down to employees can lead to unhappy customers and unpleasant bottom lines. The profit motive, an extrinsic source of motivation for entrepreneurs, ironically encourages appeals to inner values in employees.

Bureaucracy encourages a legalistic, rule-bound mentality. It says, in effect, you can only do what has been codified. This leads to the generation of hundreds of thousands of rules and laws to control behavior, coupled with the impossible-to-follow proviso that ignorance of the law is no defense. This is why the bureaucratic state has become the modern form of dictatorship, a system of excessive law. A truly free society, on the other hand, says you can do whatever has not been codified, i.e., you can do whatever you choose provided you do not violate the rights of others. Rules and laws are few and they are abstract principles. Communication, persuasion, and appeals to inner values become the primary means of relating to others. Intrinsic motivation is allowed to develop.

In addition to the external structure of bureaucracy as spur to extrinsic, especially stick motivation, an insecure psychology has to be another source. Local organizations, such as youth sports leagues, that issue edicts to parents that meetings or practices are mandatory, vacations are expected to be given up for sake of the sport, and games may be forfeited if a snack-bar work commitment is not met, are certainly pushing the limit of respectful communication among adults. Not that one should issue such edicts to children either.

---

[1] See above, "It's Just Being Turned into a Business," p. 31.

The question is, why do the leaders of these organizations talk to other adults this way? The easy answer again is probably that they do not know better, as they have never learned alternative communication techniques. But for some the reason may be deeper, a psychological need to live the sport through one's children to compensate for their own failings in the sport earlier in life. It is called achievement by proxy.[2] As a result, such stage mothers[3] or fathers—little league parents—push everyone hard, especially themselves and their children, and they brook no excuses for failing to make practice or the snack bar. Nothing is more important than the sport and they assume everyone else should have the same values. They become blind to the needs of others, especially the needs of their children.

The push for longer and longer seasons for younger and younger children, along with an apparent obliviousness to youth injuries, probably stems from this compulsive psychology. But then a similar psychology also probably operates in some (or many) bureaucrats who seem to need to prove something about themselves by issuing new edicts—new rules or laws. The more rules or laws with their names on them, the better they feel. And stick motivation seems to be all they know.

Extrinsic motivation can have its place in appropriate situations, but an excessive use of it, especially the stick part, often becomes a power trip. Appeal to inner values is the better way to go.

(May 18, 2009)

Yes, There Is Crying in Softball

IN YOUTH SPORTS THESE DAYS, a favorite refrain from adults, especially male coaches, is "There's no crying in . . . [name the sport]." The phrase, taken from the 1992 Tom Hanks movie *A League of Their Own*,[4] has even come into the vernacular[5] with people now saying "there's no crying in . . . [name the profession]." Certain phrases that become common can be charming, such as "where's the beef?" or "it's time

---

[2]"Achievement by Proxy," medical-dictionary.thefreedictionary.com.
[3]"Stage Mother," wikipedia.org.
[4]*A League of Their Own*, 1992, imdb.com.
[5]"There's No Crying in Baseball," urbandictionary.com.

to make the donuts," but this one about crying is not just hurtful, its speakers are woefully unaware of psychology and the full context of the source of the phrase.

Let's take the source[6] first. Coach Jimmy Dugan, the Hanks character, screams criticism at one of his players for making a mistake. The player, a member of a World War II all-women's baseball team, cries. Coach Dugan continues to scream, this time in disbelief, and recites the famous line.

A few points about this scene need to be remembered. One is that coach Dugan, who enjoys the bottle, has a less than savory character. Another is that during the screams, Doris, a character played by Rosie O'Donnell, tells the coach to leave Evelyn (the crier) alone. Then, the umpire follows up with this advice to the coach: "Treat each of these girls as you would treat your mother." At which point the Hanks character lets out an X-rated remark to the man in blue and is promptly ejected. The scene concludes with Doris happily and proudly asserting herself by saying, "I'm in charge now." The phrase "no crying in baseball" is hardly endorsed as admirable.

So why do so many people, especially men, like to recite this line? And why do they say it to younger and younger kids, especially nine- and ten-year-old girls, playing softball? Does no one remember the 1993 movie *In The Line of Fire*[7] in which Clint Eastwood, playing a secret service agent, cries on screen? Real men, I'm tempted to say, in the late twentieth and early twenty-first centuries do seem to cry and it seems to be okay. Why isn't it okay for nine- and ten-year-old girls to cry?

The answer is that many men are embarrassed by crying. They see it as a sign of weakness and will do anything to avoid crying themselves, especially in front of anyone close to them, such as their wives, and certainly not in public. If they are in charge of a sports team and one of their players begins to cry, they become uncomfortable, worrying about what everyone else in the area—parents, opposing coaches, umpires—may be thinking of them. They feel compelled to do something, to fix the situation, hence the exhortations about not crying.

---

[6] "League of Their Own: 'There's No Crying in Baseball,'" excerpt from the movie, January 7, 2007, youtube.com.
[7] *In the Line of Fire*, 1993, imdb.com.

But crying is a sign of pain, not weakness. Striking out for the last out of the inning or making a mistake on the field can be just as painful as taking a line drive on the knee. Pain requires comforting, not rebuke. Telling anyone, especially a child, that it is wrong to feel something only encourages psychological repression, which can lead to a muted emotional life as an adult and unpleasant, angry emotions coming out at the wrong time or place.

There can be complicating factors in the situation that needs to be fixed. A shortstop or pitcher must get out on the field, but is still crying over her strikeout, and the umpire is urging the coach to keep the game moving. However, there are alternatives to rebukes and sending an upset girl to the field with the clichéd line to "shake it off." Comforting words and a request from the umpire for thirty more seconds can do wonders for the pain of the strikeout and perhaps turn coach into a hero of a ten-year-old girl, maybe even of some of the parents in the stands.

There are also other ways of responding to the "no crying in baseball" line of coach Dugan's. Why is it just crying that should not be a part of baseball? Why not other emotions, such as laughter or anger? I'm tempted to approach coach Dugan and say something like the following, in disbelief, of course: "Hey coach. Are you angry? . . . You're angry?? . . . There's no anger in baseball!"

Sports, especially the youth variety, would probably be a lot more fun if adults abided by that admonition. And if the popularity of this new phrase were to spread, we would soon be saying, "There's no anger in business . . . or politics . . . or education!" And what about laughter, reducing the argument to the absurd? Can we not also say, "There's no laughter in baseball!"

The point of this post is that emotions have their place in life, which includes sports. Emotions should not be denied.

(January 14, 2011)

Tiger Mom or Stage Mom?

THE RECENT HULLABALOO over Amy Chua's *Wall Street Journal* article[8] generated at least one response[9] identifying a similar obsession in American moms. Chua, who acknowledges that her behavior is not unique to the Chinese, coerced her daughters, often punishing and shaming them in numerous and, to many Americans, shocking ways, to insure that the daughters would be the top in their classes and play the "right" musical instruments. The American version emphasizes child beauty pageants, various sports competitions, and after-school SAT courses to game the test and insure acceptance to the "right" colleges. In a previous post,[10] I touched on the achievement-by-proxy motivation of the stage-mother syndrome. Both kinds of parental behavior go by the old-fashioned name of authoritarianism.

The "stage mother" concept illustrates the possible consequences of such an overbearing parent and the Broadway musical *Gypsy*[11] eloquently dramatizes what can happen. In the musical Rose, the mom, drags her two daughters, June and Louise, from city to city to perform in vaudeville shows. Disliking the pressures of the business, June elopes. Later, as vaudeville begins to wane, Louise stumbles onto a talent for striptease, taking the name and becoming the famous Gypsy Rose Lee.[12] The mom is devastated and in real life—the musical is based on the memoirs[13] of Gypsy Rose Lee—becomes estranged from her two daughters for many years.

The psychological consequence of authoritarianism is either rebellion or submission. Rarely is there anything in between. In *Gypsy*, June and Louise reflect the former reaction to the coercion of their mother. Submission means going along, losing one's independence and individuality, seldom being able to pursue one's own interests because of the

---

[8] Amy Chua, "Why Chinese Mothers Are Superior," January 8, 2011, wsj.com.
[9] Hilary Levey Friedman, "American 'Tiger Moms' Obsess in Other Ways," January 21, 2011, usatoday.com.
[10] See above, "On Extrinsic Motivation, Bureaucracy, and the Stage-Mother Syndrome," p. 327.
[11] "*Gypsy* (Musical), wikipedia.org.
[12] "Gypsy Rose Lee," wikipedia.org.
[13] Gypsy Rose Lee, *Gypsy*, amazon.com.

demands of the activity and parent. Burnout in sports is well known, usually occurring in high school after years of pressured practices, perhaps year round, that began at the age of six. Parents of these pressured kids assume that nothing is wrong, because the child seemingly goes along with all of the practices and tournaments. The parent may even claim that his or her child is having "so much fun." An outside observer, however, may be compelled to raise an eyebrow and ask, "Is she?" Objectivity may be lost even on well-meaning parents in today's pressure-cooker life.

There are, of course, exceptions to this overbearing parental control. My brother is a professional musician who began playing the piano at age five, gave a solo recital at age eleven, and practiced something like six hours a day in high school, at one point getting two hours of practice in before school in the morning. I don't recall a single time in which he was forced by our parents to practice. So did his talent and drive come from our parents? No, we were a blue-collar family and our parents' musical talent amounted to singing hymns as members of the church congregation. My brother's motivation was all internally generated. (This is not to say that our parents were not authoritarian. They were, but in other areas of our lives.)

In addition to the strident obedience to authority that the tiger-mom, stage-mom syndrome exhibits, the values pursued are insipidly conventional. Why only piano or violin, as Amy Chua insisted? There are great tuba players in the world and they perform the great tuba concertos. Would it be so terrible if your child played the tuba? Or the banjo? Or did not want to learn a musical instrument at all? The answer is that it would be terrible . . . to the parents' pseudo-self-esteem. And that is what this hubbub is all about.

The "right" musical instrument, the "right" sport, and the "right" college are *right* only if the child, not the parent, given family finances, chooses them. The parent may be consultant, cheerleader, and chauffeur, but not dictator over what the child should pursue. Independence and individuality require making one's own choices and pursuing one's own chosen values, sometimes in the face of opposition or expressed doubts of others. Success, accomplishment, and self-esteem all result from having done it "my way."

Playing the "right" musical instrument, the "right" sport, or getting into the "right" college are doing it the Jones' way. Keeping up with the Joneses[14] and fearing what the Joneses might think are what the tiger-mom, stage-mom parent is most concerned about. This is a prescription for dependence.

(February 17, 2011)

There Are More Important Things in Life Than Softball

THE IMPETUS FOR THIS POST is once again my daughter's softball. She is currently playing in what is called "travel," as opposed to "recreational," ball and the seemingly endless string of practices and games almost every weekend tempt me to recite the title of this post to other parents. Not that I want to take anything away from my daughter's talent and desire to excel in a fun sport, nor the same of the other parents' daughters, but a sense of perspective may be in order, especially considering the low odds of winning an athletic scholarship[15] to college, the risks of injury[16] and burnout[17] before even getting to that point, and the studies[18] that now show multiple sports experiences and deliberate (unorganized) play develop better perception and decision making than the single, year-round specialization many young athletes today endure. Sports, of course, are not the only activity of youth in which a nearly 24/7 pressure-cooker atmosphere exists. Music, dance, and drama teachers, and the children's parents, not to mention the

---

[14] "Keeping Up with the Jones," wikipedia.org.
[15] "Recruiting—The Scoop on College Softball Scholarships," softballexcellence.com.
[16] Stop Sports Injuries (website), stopsportsinjuries.org; Mark Hyman, *Until It Hurts*, amazon.com; "The Most Expensive Game in Town," youthsportsparents.blogspot.com.
[17] "Overtraining Syndrome/Burnout," rchd.org.
[18] Jason Berry, Bruce Abernethy, and Jean Côté, "The Contribution of Structured Activity and Deliberate Play to the Development of Expert Perceptual and Decision-Making Skill," December 2008, nih.gov.

academic teachers, can also lay it on thick; the term "stage mom"[19] that comes to us from the theatre keeps coming to mind.

Part of the obsession many coaches, teachers, and parents have about sports, or the arts and academics, stems from a misunderstanding of the differences between the less accomplished and the more accomplished, or between "amateur" and "professional." By "professional" here I mean only a greater degree of skill and dedication, not "paid professional," though the young persons may be aiming for professional careers in sports or the arts or science and the coaches and teachers may be grooming them for that goal. In softball the difference is between "recreational" and "travel" ball and in the arts it may be the difference between performing in the local community and attending a select arts high school. The assumed differences between these two levels, as stated by one youth baseball organization (link no longer active), include the possibility of failure and rejection in travel ball, but not in recreational; the alleged life lesson to sacrifice leisure to hard work so success will follow; and the supposed lack of need for instruction at this "nearly professional" level. There are kernels of truth in all three of these differences, but these kernels get distorted when coaches, teachers, and parents lose perspective, forgetting about the whole of life.

Take the difference about the possibility of failure. Even at a lower level of skill, such as in a marching band or softball, not everyone participates one-hundred percent of the time. Only some band members may perform in the pep band at basketball games and even fewer in the swing band. Soloists at the spring concert may be fewer than a handful. The same is true for softball; not everyone can be pitcher. More important, not achieving an initial goal need not be a viewed as failure. A clarinetist, for example, who transfers from a small-town marching band to an arts high school orchestra may not earn one of the top four positions in the orchestra. This eye-opening awareness of the greater skill of others should be experienced as motivator, not a threat to success or happiness. There is no more important attitude to cultivate than seeing others' achievements as an inspiration.

---

[19] See above, "Tiger or Stage Mom?," p. 332. see above, "On Extrinsic Motivation, Bureaucracy, and the Stage-Mother Syndrome," p. 327.

To say that youth should sacrifice leisure to hard work so success will follow is misleading, especially if it is presented as "we expect you to give up your vacation" for the sake of softball, or music, etc. Paid professionals do not do this, except on occasion, mainly because they know their schedules well in advance. The problem with youth sports is that communication, advance or otherwise, is often lacking, leading to surprises in the schedule. Hard work, yes; and all children who enjoy an activity, whether it be sports, the arts, or a business or science club will, if not hampered by authoritarian adults, devote long hours of concentrated attention to improving their knowledge and skill. This concentrated attention is sometimes, unfortunately, interpreted by adults as "sacrifice" in the sense of giving up a higher value for the sake of a lower one. "Dedication" and "self-motivation" would be better descriptors.

The notion that higher levels of skill do not need instruction stems from the term "director," such as the director of a play or conductor of an orchestra. Some coaches claim the same prerogative for their advanced teams. But direction means guiding the skills of others to produce the effect the director envisions. That in itself is teaching, and all directors, including conductors and coaches, provide a variety of instructions to their performers to accomplish what they want. That coaches at the highest level of professional sports are teachers became obvious during the 1982 National Football League strike[20] when secondary players were hired as substitutes to play games while the stars were walking picket lines. Much commentary was made about the expert teaching abilities of various coaches. When a coach, or conductor or director, says that he or she assumes a certain skill level and is not there to teach, I would beware that blind obedience is what is wanted, as in "I expect you to have the discipline to do what I say." "Discipline," however, means acting in accordance with one's own self-imposed guidelines. It is the mark of an advanced skill. Even at an advanced level, coaches, teachers, and conductors should aim to help turn caterpillars into butterflies.[21]

Total commitment at the expense of everything else—spending every weekend and a few week nights on one's sport or art, because

---

[20] "National Football League Players Association," wikipedia.org.
[21] See above, "Caterpillars into Butterflies," p. 325.

"that's the way we do it here" or because "that's the only way to get a scholarship"—is obsession of the stage parent type. When the commitment does not originate in the child, injury or burnout or even parental estrangement can result. Perspective on why an activity is being pursued needs always to be kept in the forefront of parents' minds.

(October 7, 2011)

"Miniature Adults," the Marketing Concept, and a Montessori Approach to Organized Youth Sports

BEING AWARE OF AND CATERING to the needs and wants of customers is the essence of marketing. The textbooks call this the "marketing concept" and emphasize that everyone in a business, from the president down to the lowliest stock person, should not make any decision or take any action without first considering the effects of the decision or action on customers. Contrary to what Marxists and leftists of all types say, it is through customer satisfaction that businesses earn their profits.

But the marketing concept applies to any organization that has constituents—nonprofits, as well as governmental agencies. The broader principle says simply: acknowledge and, to the extent possible and appropriate, satisfy the needs and wants of the person with whom one is interacting. This is not some self-sacrificial duty. Rather, it is the good manners of recognizing another person as an individual human being.

The problem is that many people, to use a popular expression, "get so caught up in themselves and their own egos" that that they become incapable of seeing life from another person's perspective. The consequence of this type of behavior is inconsiderateness and disrespect. The problem is especially prevalent among parents and teachers in relation to young children, exemplified in acute form by adult attitudes in organized youth sports.

Bob Bigelow,[22] former professional basketball player, has nailed this phenomenon in his book *Just Let the Kids Play*.[23] As the title implies, the rise of elite or select teams in organized youth sports—those teams that hold tryouts and cut less effective players when better ones are found—has robbed youth not just of the fun of playing a sport, but also the chance of developing into a talented athlete later in adolescence.

With astute turns of phrase, Bigelow states: "The worst thing we adults do in youth sports is to forget that these players are not miniature adults or high school stars in some kind of larval stage. They are children, with bones that have yet to develop, with minds that are not thinking the same way that we are thinking" (pp. 107–08). And, because these teams are all organized and managed by adults and often include travel out of town, out of state, and perhaps even across the country to play games on a schedule that would exhaust an adult professional team, Bigelow quips: "Parental egos and a full tank of gas—a frightening combination" (p. 111). Some of these teams consist of children as young as five!

The notion that children are not small adults[24] comes from developmental psychology and was championed by Maria Montessori. Children have needs and wants that vary widely by age and most particularly differ from those of adults. The Montessori approach to education adapts learning to the appropriate developmental stage while giving the child as much independence and control in the learning process as possible. Bigelow, without any mention of Montessori in his book, urges the same approach in youth sports.

As Montessori hands over much of the teaching and learning to the children, Bigelow recommends the same for youth sports. For example, recalling the days on sandlots where no adults or coaches were present, children played, made up their own rules, and coached each other on the field. To bring this spirit back into organized youth sports, Bigelow recommends that baseball and softball players up through sixth grade should be the coaches on first and third bases, an idea that would turn most adult coaches today apoplectic!

---

[22] Bob Bigelow (website), bobbigelow.com.
[23] Bob Bigelow, *Just Let the Kids Play*, amazon.com.
[24] See above, "The Child as Small Adult," p. 161.

His main point is that adults need to back off because development in athletics does not really blossom until after puberty. (Former National Basketball Association star Michael Jordan did not make his varsity high school team until junior year.) Playing on an elite team at five or eight or ten does not give anyone an advantage, but getting cut from such a team at five or eight or ten sends a clear message to the child that he or she is not good enough. Nothing could be further from the truth. Many a coach, as Bigelow points out, has seen uncoordinated freshmen and sophomores become stars in their junior and senior years.

It is a myth and a shame, as he puts it, that so many adults think "more, more, more" at a younger and younger age means better. It does not. It may mean overuse injuries and burnout. It may mean, as one young man told Bigelow about his experiences with youth hockey, "[It] stole my childhood." The young man started learning to play hockey at age three and quit at thirteen because he hated it. Subsequently he became estranged from his father who had driven him to every practice and game.

Bigelow's book zeroes in on what I have examined before: the stage parent syndrome.[25] Stage parents push, that is, coerce, their children to do what the parents think their children should be doing. Often, the parents live vicariously through their children's accomplishments. What parents are unaware of in this process is their children's physical, cognitive, and emotional needs. The adults' actions are all about the adults.

Not that adults do this deliberately or in a mean spirit. Most think they are doing what is best for their children . . . but the science isn't there.[26] Multiple sports experiences and free (unsupervised and unorganized) play produce better perception and decision making among elite athletes. The needs and wants of youth are to have fun. Just as fun should be the goal of any career one chooses to pursue, fun should

---

[25] See above, "On Extrinsic Motivation, Bureaucracy, and the Stage-Mother Syndrome," p. 327. see above, "Tiger Mom or Stage Mom?," p. 332. See above, "There Are More Important Things in Life than Softball," p. 334.
[26] Jason Berry, Bruce Abernethy, and Jean Côté, "The Contribution of Structured Activity and Deliberate Play to the Development of Expert Perceptual and Decision-Making Skill," December 2008, nih.gov.

be the goal of all sports, whether at the high school, college, or professional level, but especially at the youth level.

Youth sports is about the kids, not the adults.

(October 12, 2012)

2013

Life Lessons from Sports: What about the Sixty Years after College?

IN ANCIENT ROMAN SCHOOLS, boys who failed to learn their lessons were beaten on their bare backs with a ferula,[27] a long piece of flat wood. Fast forward to the twenty-first century and we rarely hear about corporal punishment in the classroom, even of the kind I recall from childhood, like the paddle, knuckles rapped with a ruler, or kneeling on raw peas. Treatment of this type by a teacher today would be called assault and battery.

Yet in collegiate sports a coach who shoves his player[28] "to motivate" him merely gets a mild rebuke from the university administration. Another coach,[29] who threw basketballs at his players' heads and knees, kicked them, and called them insulting names, has recently been fired ... but only after the smoking gun of video went viral on the internet.

Life lessons from sports? To be sure, quite a few life lessons are being learned by the victims of these coaches. What it's like to be abused by a caretaker would be one. And, paraphrasing Menander,[30] the lesson that you haven't been trained unless you've been flogged. Sadly, many of the players, typical of abuse victims, defend their abusers by saying "it was for my own good."

Remove the physical abuse from consideration and a dictatorial drill sergeant mentality,[31] which would not likely be tolerated in a

---

[27] A. S. Wilkins, *Roman Education*, p. 4, books.google.com.
[28] "Pac-12 Reprimands Mike Montgomery," February 18, 2013, espn.com.
[29] Tom Canavan, "Rutgers, Pernetti Fire Rice After Video Release," April 3, 2013, espn.com.
[30] Frank Richard Cowell, *Life in Ancient Rome*, p. 43, books.google.com.
[31] Ken Reed, "Old-School Coaching Model Needs to Be Mothballed," May 16, 2014, leagueoffans.org.

classroom teacher, still dominates coaching in sports. The mentality is often defended under the blather of providing valuable "life lessons." Dependent robots and obedience to authority are what these coaches want and get.*

Independent thinking is the life lesson kids most desperately need to be learning—at home, in the classroom, and in sports. They need to be thinking about what they will do with their lives after the sports end, and the sports will end in college, if not sooner, for nearly all of them. What happens then? Get a job stocking shelves at Walmart?

Half of all college athletes[32] after they graduate make less money than their non-athletic counterparts. Why? Because they don't have the work experience and internships to put on their resumes that the non-athletes have. Athletes are expected by their drill sergeants to spend up to 45 hours[33] per week on their sport. Throw in two hours of homework for every hour in class and not much time is left in the week. The "solution," of course, for college athletes is to take fewer units and perhaps not ever graduate, or take puffcake courses like billiards, bowling, and water color painting.

Walmart is a fine place to work, but working there after college is not why one gets that degree.

If the words "fraud" and "exploitation" come to mind in relation to amateur sports, there is good reason. The National Collegiate Athletic Association deserves the epithets the most. Fraud because, as scathingly chronicled with analogies to slavery by civil rights historian Taylor Branch,[34] there is nothing amateur—in expertise and, especially, money—about today's sports. And exploitation, because the kids never see a penny of the billions they earn for their universities.

Scholarships are payment, no? No. The so-called full ride, contingent on not getting injured, still leaves an average of $3200 a year [in 2013 dollars, according to one link no longer available] to cough up out

---

[32] Daniel J. Henderson, Alexandre Olbrecht, and Solomon W. Polachek, "Do Former College Athletes Earn More at Work?," 2006, jhr.uwpress.org.
[33] Justin Pope, "NCAA Athletes Work Long Hours, Survey Says," September 4, 2009, diverseeducation.com; Ken Reed, "Q's & A's with Notable Sports Figures: Taylor Branch," March 9, 2012, leagueoffans.org.
[34] Taylor Branch, "The Shame of College Sports," October 2011, theatlantic.com.

of pocket, leaving some of the kids from poor families without grocery money or bus fare home for spring break. Another life lesson learned!

The obsession that parents and coaches in youth leagues have over landing a scholarship to college is, to put it mildly, absurd. Aside from the minuscule chance of being granted one, scholarship is still not necessary in most states to get a college education.**

In my thirty-plus years as a college professor, I have had my share of athletes in the classroom. One Division 1 football player told me his practices were from 2:00 – 6:00PM. My class started at 6:00, so he was always late. After four or five weeks, I never saw or heard from him again.

Another football player (at a different school) attended my class just after completing his first season in the National Football League. He made two pointed comments to me about why he was in that seat. One, that unlike his teammates he was determined to finish his degree. The second was his observation that when playing in the NFL you are just a highly paid blue-collar worker. Meaning there was no way he was going to remain a blue-collar worker (or become a stock clerk at Walmart) when his playing days were over. This student went on to a successful career in the NFL and now has an equally successful career in business.

Projecting and setting goals beyond sports. That's a good life lesson.

* "Legal, even celebrated child abuse" in Olympic gymnastics and figure skating was exposed by Joan Ryan in her 1995 book *Little Girls in Pretty Boxes*.[35] "Absolute subservience" is how she described the demands of certain famous coaches.

** This assumes that education is what these parents and coaches really care about, as opposed to bragging rights about the child getting a scholarship to a Division 1[36] school. Twenty percent[37] of students in the California State University system [2016–17] receive no financial aid at all. Most do not receive scholarships. These students earn their education the old-fashioned way, going to community college for two

---

[35] Joan Ryan, *Little Girls in Pretty Boxes*, amazon.com.
[36] "NCAA Division I," wikipedia.org.
[37] "Financial Aid FAQ," calstate.edu.

years, then working 20–40 hours a week to earn the rest at a Cal State. And California is no longer among the least expensive states in which to attend college.

(April 9, 2013)

The Obsession with Scholarships

OUR FAMILY HAS NOW COMPLETED its first full year of 12U travel softball—98 games, 26 weekends plus two week-long tournaments. This does not include weekends and school nights in which there were practices but no games. I did not keep track of expenses, though StatsDad[38] spent $11,704 on three kids in 2011.

Our daughter has turned thirteen and will be moving up to 14U soon, but in the five years of recreational and club ball, plus other school sports, that she has played, we have developed more than a few concerns about the direction youth sports today is headed. Parents and coaches do not seem to have many facts correct and we are concerned that some of what we see in youth sports is not good for the kids. For starters...

The obsession with scholarships is misplaced. Aside from the tiny odds* of landing even a partial college athletic scholarship, *scholarships are not necessary to get a college education* in most states in the US.

College, in today's world of budget crunches and annual tuition increases, is *still affordable*.[39] Twenty percent of students in the California State University system receive no financial aid at all, mostly non-scholarship aid. Twenty-five states in the US charge a lower rate of tuition and fees at public 4-year institutions than the Cal States. California and New Mexico charge the least for community colleges.

The path to a college education is simple. Two years of community college, then 20–40 hours a week working at a job to pay for the rest at a four-year state institution. Your son or daughter may not get the degree in four years—it may take five or even six years and he or she will be complaining that one foot is in the grave—but the degree will be obtained.

---

[38] "Youth Sports Costs," statsdad.com.
[39] "Trends in College Pricing and Student Aid 2020," p. 18 and throughout, collegeboard.org.

And as I have pointed out before (see above) the non-athletic students will likely earn more money upon graduation than the athlete, because the non-athlete will have accumulated work experience and internships that look good on resumes when applying for jobs. Athletes are often too busy with their sport, spending up to 45 hours per week on it, to gain work experience.

If your child does well in high school (and this does not have to mean "straight A's"), he or she will do well in college. If he or she does well in college, the same will be true in graduate school. Getting a college education is not rocket science . . . well, unless your child decides to major in rocket science!

Now we're not saying you should pass up a scholarship if it is offered. You should apply for everything when considering college, especially the academic and need-based grants (but minimize the loans—$20–25,000 maximum for the entire college career). College is doable without the scholarship, no matter how humble your situation.

So parents and coaches, relax. Enjoy the game.

And coaches, please don't mislead parents into thinking that anything in the scholarship area is a shoo-in.

The so-called full ride scholarship is quite rare, except perhaps at some top football and basketball schools and for a very few elite athletes in other sports. A 50% scholarship at a $50,000 a year private university still leaves a lot of money for mom and dad to fork over. And this may not include the $12–14,000 for room and board, plus books, transportation, and personal expenses. Tuition and fees at Cal States is currently about $7500 per year for in-state students and at the University of California schools $14,000. Rates in other states for public institutions are similar, though higher in some states.

Athletic scholarships also, as few parents seem to know or understand, are not four-year contracts. They are for one year at a time and can be taken away for poor grades, poor performance, or injury. California did pass a law recently providing protections and benefits for athletes at certain well-heeled institutions, but all parents of an athlete who are now, or soon will be, negotiating with a coach and university should print out and keep handy the College Athlete Protection[40] guarantee suggested by the National College Players Association.

Getting informed is your best protection.

* The stats, of course, depend on who you read. Cindy Bristow[41] [2007] says the chances are one in 500 for all girls currently playing softball to win an NCAA scholarship. Scholarshipstats.com[42] provides these numbers:

- Only 8.5% of high school softball players went on [in 2020] to play college ball.

- Fewer than 1% of high school players received a Division 1 scholarship.

- One out of two women, though, on a brighter note, who made it on a college team did receive some financial aid from softball.

(August 6, 2013)

Not-So-Good Life Lessons from Sports

YOUNG PEOPLE LEARN a great deal by imitation of what adults say and do. Some may reject what they hear and see, saying to themselves, "I'm not going to be like that," but repeated comments and behaviors often become difficult to dismiss.

In a previous post[43] I presented a few less than savory life lessons for young athletes, concluding that one of the best lessons learned by a former student was to think way beyond college, and even professional sports, to project a fulfilling career to pursue for the rest of one's life.

---

[40] "Download Free Players' Contract," ncpanow.org.
[41] Cindy Bristow, "Recruiting—The Scoop on College Softball Scholarships," softballexcellence.com.
[42] "Odds of a High School Softball Player Competing in College 2020," scholarshipstats.com.
[43] See above, "Life Lessons from Sports: What about the Sixty Years after College?," p. 340.

Sports for nearly all young athletes, after all, are a recreational pastime that sooner or later end.

Here are additional life lessons observed or heard about in our family's five years of recreational and travel softball. Fortunately, we have not observed physical abuse or violence, such as the Junta manslaughter[44] or the Picard assault,[45] and we have enjoyed numerous positive experiences of coaching, sportsmanship, and camaraderie, but the influences below that many coaches and parents exhibited in front of their children are not good.

Such as:

1. Coaches and parents scream from the dugout or sideline at the umpire about a pitch, at a vantage point from which they could not possibly see the true path of the ball.

> Comment: Yes, most officials are paid to take the heat and some have a skin that is too thin, but come on, parents, isn't it time for a reality check?

2. A coach screams from the dugout, "Can't anyone out there make a play? What's the matter with you!"

3. A first base coach fails to get an interference call on a play at first base. He then yells to his player, "Hit her harder next time!"

4. A coach's negative, humiliating comments brings a talented, hardworking catcher to tears after three hot, dusty games. Her sin? A single mental mistake, on the last play of the third game. Another girl who made an error is told to drop and do ten pushups in front of everyone.

5. After a line drive third out to right field, the batter rounds first base and knocks down the second base player who was heading for the dugout. The second base player had to leave for the ER with a bloody, possibly broken nose. The umpires talked at length with the offending coach. We could hear the coach vehemently protesting, "There was no way that was on purpose." Okay, coach, but what we did not hear either from you or your player was an apology. The game was a late bracket

---

[44] Alex Duncan and Jessica Reaves, "Person of the Week: Hockey Dad Thomas Junta," January 11, 2002, time.com.
[45] "Teacher Charged in Beating of Daughter's Coach," May 19, 2005, boston.com.

game in an end-of-the-year tournament. The teams represented major organizations.

6. We have heard of, though not experienced first hand, coaches swearing at their players.

> Comment on the above gems of role modeling: As former Los Angeles Laker coach Phil Jackson said, "Anger is the enemy of instruction," and as many a good teacher has recognized, "Punishment stops learning." Both comments are backed up thoroughly by twenty-first century psychological research. As for the cursing, child-protective agencies would probably call it emotional abuse.

7. A physical therapist reports that nearly all young people come to him with overuse injuries. One high school softball pitcher had a shoulder and elbow so sore that he could hardly touch her. The therapist asked the girl's father how much, especially pitching, she was doing every week. The father replied that she was spending a few hours a day on her game. How many pitches? "Only four or five per week." "Hundred?" the therapist asked. No, the father meant four or five thousand!

8. A recreational softball league asks parents of all stars: "Are you willing to change your vacation, or simply give it up this year?" Travel ball coaches don't ask. They seem to assume you should be willing to give up vacation for the sake of their sport. One 12U team lists its schedule on the web as year round, with two weeks off in December and two off in August.

> Comment: Gee thanks, coach. You're so generous with our free time! The National Athletic Trainers Association,[46] ever cognizant of overuse injuries, urges kids through age 12 to take "2 to 3 nonconsecutive months away from a sport if they participate in that sport year round" (p. 208). Comparable research-based

---

[46] "National Athletic Trainers' Association Position Statement: Prevention of Pediatric Overuse Injuries," 2011, nata.org.

recommendations, adjusted for age and stage of development, are made for older players.

9. At an out-of-town tournament, coaches and parents drink beer until 3AM—many nights, actually, but especially the night before an early game.

<u>No comment</u>.

10. Then there is the cost of elite club and travel sports. Minimum $1500 a year for softball, $2500 for soccer, $3500 and up for volleyball (and cheerleading—$3500 for cheerleading?!). [2013 dollars]

<u>Comment</u>: Quite a lesson for low and middle income families. Maybe—maybe—one child can be supported in a sport, but not two. We've met the families and heard the stories.

Sports are about having fun and learning life lessons. Adults need to be careful what they say and do lest the wrong lessons be picked up by their children. We've observed too many of the wrong kind in our short tenure with youth sports.

A question for coaches and parents: what would you be doing in youth sports if there were no college athletic scholarships? Would your behavior differ?

Ken Reed at leagueoffans.org[47] and Walter Byers, former NCAA Executive Director, have both called for the elimination of college athletic scholarships.

An interesting thought experiment!

(September 3, 2013)

---

[47] Ken Reed, "League of Fans Proposes Eliminating Athletic Scholarships to Help Restore Integrity on College Campuses," March 25, 2011, leagueoffans.org.

More, More, More Does Not Mean Better

PRACTICES FOR RECENTLY RETIRED JOHN GAGLIARDI,[48] the winningest college football coach ever, were no longer than ninety minutes a day. No tackling and his players wore shorts or sweats. In games, his quarterbacks called their own plays.

John T. Reed[49] in the 1992 season did not hold any batting practice for his youth baseball team. Batting average for all kids combined was .320. Slugging average was .463 and on-base percentage .590. Reed also seldom held pitching or ground-ball fielding practice. His teams, he says, were at or near the top of those categories.

Accomplishment requires innate talent plus practice. How much practice is required to bring out the talent to achieve expert status?

A much ballyhooed number these days is the 10,000 hours reported by psychologist Anders Ericsson[50] at Florida State University. Ericsson's original studies were of musicians. The first thing, however, a musician will tell you is that it is not a question of how many hours you practice, but how you practice in the one hour you have available. Deliberate, focused practice with goals to achieve every session is what is required. Just putting in the hours won't cut it.

Besides, the 10,000-hour rule is an average. In chess the average is 11,000, and the amount of time required to become a master player[51] ranges from 3000 to 23,000 hours. Some, though, have never achieved that hallowed standing after more than 25,000 hours of practice.

Years, meaning maturity with age, is in certain respects a better measure. Kids who begin playing a musical instrument[52] in 4th grade and those who start in 8th are often even in skill by 9th. Reed observed that his teams improved more with age than anything else. Basketball

---

[48] "John Gagliardi," wikipedia.org; Pat Borzi, "After 489 Wins, Coach Chooses Retirement," November 19, 2012, nytimes.com.
[49] John T. Reed, "Having Almost No Batting Practice Is Better," September 27, 2015, johntreed.com.
[50] K. Anders Ericsson, Michael J. Prietula, and Edward T. Cokely, "The Making of an Expert," August 2007, hbr.org.
[51] Robert A. Cutietta, *Raising Musical Kids*, amazon.com; Bryant Urstadt, "Book Review: 'The Sports Gene' by David Epstein," August 1, 2013, bloomberg.com.
[52] In Robert A. Cutietta, *Raising Musical Kids*, amazon.com.

great Michael Jordan,[53] after all, did not make varsity until his junior year in high school and Cy Young baseball pitcher Orel Hershiser[54] did not make a name for himself in college until his third year—after he grew, gained weight, and, as a result, was able to increase the speed of his fastball.

Quantity, in other words, to quote an old and perhaps trite proverb, does not make quality.

So why so many hours every week in youth sports and so many games? The answer we hear on the fields is that it is necessary to get your child ready to be selected by those Division I coaches, which allegedly means full-ride scholarships.

Cancel the obsession with scholarships[55] and what is left?

Fewer hours spent on a single sport, one would hope, which could and should mean fewer overuse injuries and more diversity of athletic experience. That would then mean rest for overused body parts from the single sport and development of other body parts from other sports.*

It could and should mean more time to spend on homework and other after school activities. We are not fans of school-night practices, especially those that go until 9:00 or 10:00pm and emphatically not of those that start at 5:00am, and earlier, in such sports as hockey.**

There is of course a curve to learning. Some quantity is required to acquire basic skill and more is required to make finely tuned professional adjustments. But too much quantity, as in a four to six hour practice, sometimes after a long week at school, or in the wee hours of the morning, stops learning and can even degrade it.

And team practices that often do not acknowledge or cater to individual differences accomplish little. Not every pitcher needs to throw hundreds of pitches every week and not every batter needs to hit hundreds of balls off a tee. Some chess players, remember, only need 3000 hours to achieve master status. Requiring such a "one-size-fits-all" regimen produces fatigue, overuse injuries, and burnout.

---

[53] "Michael Jordan Didn't Make Varsity—At First," October 17, 2015, newsweek.com.
[54] "Orel Hershiser," wikipedia.org.
[55] See above, "The Obsession with Scholarships," p. 343.

What about the number of games played today in youth sports? Research[56] clearly shows that greater learning takes place in practices, for the simple reason that that is the time in which all kids get their hands (or feet) repeatedly on the ball and their hockey sticks on the pucks. Comparable times in a game may only be a few seconds, if at all.

Games are for the adults because that is what the adults enjoy—and for the kids who get to play; they are not much fun for the bench warmers.

Are so many games good for the kids?

Baseball hall of famer Cal Ripken, Jr.,[57] agrees with the European soccer clubs whose ratio of practices to games is about three to one. Fewer games are better for development.

With so many games—80–120 a year not uncommon in club or travel sports—what kids learn to do is to pace themselves in order to endure the marathon. That's not exactly what coaches have in mind.

But screaming at the kids to give 110% in every game—say, a fourth or fifth game of the day—grossly misunderstands childhood. The only thing "toughened up" in such a marathon is adult ego.

* Georgia Soccer[58] recommends that its elite players take "4–8 weeks of off-season rest each year, for regeneration and recharging."

** High school and college teams practice in the afternoons, completing everything by 5:00 or 6:00pm. This leaves the evening for rest and homework or, for college students, night classes. We know why youth sports teams practice in the evening: facilities are not available and amateur coaches cannot make it to an afternoon practice. Is this good for the kids or good for the adults?

(October 23, 2013)

---

[56] "Practice vs. Game: Which Is Better for Development?," georgiasoccer.org; Tom Turner, "Practice vs. Games: The Impact on Individual Player Development," September 2009, leagueathletics.com; "Hockey Practice vs. Hockey Game," howtohockey.com.
[57] Cal Ripken, Jr., "More Games May Not Be the Answer," coaching-youth-baseball.blogspot.com.
[58] "Practice vs. Game: Which Is Better for Development?," georgiasoccer.org.

And Now, the Concussion Issue

Sportswriter Frank Deford has predicted[59] that interest in football will eventually degenerate to a status similar to boxing, or "reach a point like smoking where it no longer can be justified."

The reason is concussions. Youth participation[60] in football, according to a National Sporting Goods Association study, has declined thirteen percent in the last two years. Even professional athletes today don't want their kids to play football.

But football is not the only sport that puts our kids at risk; ice hockey, with its body and head checking, is right up there. Non-collision sports also produce concussions. Wrestling (from slams to the mat), soccer (from heading) and volleyball (from being on the receiving end of a spike) cause their share of trauma. Any collision—with another player or with the ground or floor—can cause concussion. Thus, basketball, baseball, and softball are not exempt from the matter.

Concussions and Our Kids[61] by neurosurgeon Robert Cantu and sports journalist Mark Hyman provides everything one needs to know about concussions. A knock to the head, for instance, is not required to suffer one. The rotational forces of whiplash effect that result from hard hits to the shoulders or neck can sometimes bring about even more severe concussions.

How so? The brain floats in cerebrospinal fluid and the skull is not smooth. A concussion occurs when the brain crashes into the skull, often resulting in tears to brain tissue. Resulting symptoms are headache, nausea, dizziness, depression, sleep disturbance, and cognitive impairment (such as difficulty concentrating). Treatment is physical and cognitive rest. The latter can mean no reading, electronics, TV, or even school. Missing school, in some cases, has lasted as long a year.

Repeated concussions put athletes at serious risk. Second impact syndrome—caused by a second blow, or more, can result in death.

Concussions are deadly.

---

[59] Ken Reed, "Q & A with Legendary Sportswriter Frank Deford," January 27, 2013, leagueoffans.org.
[60] Frank Deford, "Why Has Football Become So Brutish?," November 13, 2013, npr.org.
[61] Robert Cantu and Mark Hyman, *Concussion and Our Kids*, amazon.com.

If the athlete survives his or her playing years, chronic traumatic encephalopathy (CTE) may greet the player in older age. Originally called dementia pugilistica to describe the brutalizing effects of boxing, CTE is a degenerative condition that mimics the symptoms of Alzheimer's and other diseases.

Indeed, it has been suggested[62] that Lou Gehrig, beaned many times by baseball pitchers but also known as an active brawler when the dugouts cleared, may not have died of the disease that carries his name. CTE can also mimic the symptoms of ALS.[63]

Recommendations? Cantu says tackling should not be allowed in football until age fourteen, when bodies and minds of children have at least matured to a point where the kids can begin to protect themselves from violent hits. Checking in hockey should be banned (and, of course, so should fighting, which goes without saying). Cantu even recommends that "hit counts" be used in football and hockey in the same way and for the same reasons that pitch counts are now used in baseball.

This means that drill-sergeant mentalities who call themselves coaches of youth and who tell youngsters to "play through the pain" and not complain lest they be ridiculed as weaklings or sissies—need to be removed from sports.

It means that hockey coaches who ignore medical advice[64] and send kids with well-defined symptoms of head trauma back on the ice . . . well, let's just say that sports psychologist Alan Goldberg[65] would call that coaching abuse, which is another name for the criminal behavior known as child abuse.

It is impossible today for anyone, coach or parent, not to know about the concussion issue. Abundant information is available on the internet and anyone who has a pocket computer (that is, a smartphone), can readily access it.

---

[62] Alan Schwarz, "Study Says Brain Trauma Can Mimic A.L.S.," August 17, 2010, nytimes.com.
[63] "Amyotrophic Lateral Sclerosis," wikipedia.org.
[64] Jeff Z. Klein, "Report Urges 'Cultural Shift' as Hockey Coaches Defy Concussion Specialists," November 30, 2012
[65] Alan Goldberg, "Coaching Abuse: The Dirty, Not-So-Little Secret in Sports," May 28, 2015, competitivedge.com.

If we care about the health of our kids, we must park the ego that wants to win at all costs and put fun back into youth sports as the primary goal.

The need to win that causes or allows harm to our children must go.

(December 10, 2013)

2014

Overuse Injuries—What the Experts Are Saying

THE STATISTICS ON OVERUSE INJURIES are astounding.

- Half of all pediatric sports medicine injuries[66] are due to overuse. [2018]

- Thirty percent of college athletes[67] suffer overuse injuries, with 62 percent going to women. Low contact sports, such as rowing, softball, volleyball, cross country, and track and field, have the highest rates of overuse injury. [2012]

- Overuse injuries drastically increasing in youth.[68] [2020] Highly specialized athletes[69] 18 percent more likely to suffer overuse injuries than moderately specialized ones. [2018]

- Shoulder and elbow injuries[70] in young baseball and softball players have increased five times since 2000, with 45 percent of 13- and 14-year-olds[71] suffering arm pain in a typical baseball season (and these are not just pitchers who get the arm pain).[2014]

---

[66] "Overuse Injuries in Young Athletes," sparcctucson.com.
[67] "Nearly 30% of All College Athlete Injuries a Result of 'Overuse,'" April 12, 2012, edwp.educ.msu.edu.
[68] "Overuse Injuries Drastically Increasing in Youth," February 24, 2020, middleearthnj.org.
[69] Lisa Rapaport, "Sport Specialization Tied to Injuries in Kids and Teens," August 22, 2018, reuters.com.
[70] "Risk Factors for Elbow and Shoulder Injuries," stopsportsinjuries.org. Search "shoulder and elbow injuries."
[71] Kenan Trebincevic, "Keeping Kid Athletes Safe," residentpublications.com.

What is an overuse injury? In any physical activity, there is breakdown and buildup of tissue. When breakdown exceeds buildup, injury in the form of inflammation—the "-itis" in tendonitis—and mild pain result. The mild pain that athletes become aware of initially is not usually sufficient to make them cut back. With continued activity, the inflammation and pain increase gradually, though both may take days, weeks, or even months to become significant.

The cause of overuse is too much, too soon. Too much running, throwing, jumping, etc., before the body has had time to rebuild the tissue that was broken down by the excessive activity.

Treatment of overuse injury requires rest and physical therapy to build up strength surrounding the injury and manipulation to stimulate blood circulation.

Failure to treat overuse injury can lead to physical deformity and arthritis.[72]

The cause of these alarming statistics is generally agreed to be the rise of year-round specialization in a single sport. This in turn has meant a dramatic increase in the number of games and practices required of young, unprepared bodies.

Recommendations to prevent overuse injuries are more rest, meaning time off from the sport, and more multi-sport participation, to use different parts of the body and give rest to those parts stressed in the first sport. Time off does not mean a couple off days here and there. Depending who one reads on the subject, recommendations range from taking off two to three non-consecutive months[73] in a year to taking an entire season off.[74] The doctor-run website Stop Sports Injuries Now[75] recommends pitch counts for softball pitchers.*

Change comes slowly in almost every endeavor, but especially in sports. I recently attended a meeting sponsored by a regional softball governing body. I asked the head of the organization if anything was

---

[72] "Nearly 30% of All College Athlete Injuries a Result of 'Overuse,'" April 12, 2012, edwp.educ.msu.edu.
[73] "National Athletic Trainers' Association Position Statement: Prevention of Pediatric Overuse Injuries," 2011, nata.org.
[74] "New Research Reveals One Third of Young Athletes Sidelined Due To Preventable Injuries," April 24, 2012, safekids.org.
[75] "Preventing Softball Injuries," stopsportsinjuries.org.

being done to deal with overuse injuries and if perhaps pitch counts for softball pitchers would be recommended. His reply was a testy "We leave that to the coaches." Yet, another speaker at the meeting pointed out that "concussion training is coming," meaning training will soon be required for all coaches. My conclusion? Such organizations are not going to do anything until they are forced into it by public opinion and the media!

Leaving control over an athlete's health to coaches is unfortunate. Coaches do not read the research and at the high school and college levels, they do not listen to their athletic trainers. At the college level, coaches have the power to hire and fire their trainers, so if the trainer says an athlete is not fit to play, the coach tells the trainer to take a hike. As a result, a few colleges—too few—are moving their trainers out of the athletics departments and into health services where they will no longer be beholden[76] to the coaches, but perhaps now will be able to influence them.

I am tempted to say to some of these win-at-all-cost coaches who ignore both research and medical advice, "Sooner or later, coach, it is not just a doctor or athletic trainer who is going to be knocking on your door. The next knock just might come from a lawyer!"

* It is a myth, heard too frequently and as gospel in the softball world, that softball pitchers do not need the rest of their baseball counterparts. Shoulder and elbow pain are commonly felt by all softball players, but especially by the pitchers, plus back and neck pain. Rupture of the bicep tendon[77] has occurred in college softball pitchers due to overuse.

(February 21, 2014)

---

[76] Brad Wolverton, "Coach Makes the Call," September 2, 2013, chronicle.com.
[77] "A Long-Head of Biceps Tendon Rupture in a Fast Pitch Softball Player: A Case Report," July 27, 2016, sportssurgerychicago.com.

Year-Round Single Sport Specialization: Not Good for Kids or Skill Development, Experts Say

EXPERTS TODAY—ranging from sports researchers and sports psychologists to doctors, ex-pros, general managers of professional teams, and Division I college coaches—are all expressing the same theme: year-round, single sport specialization, and its accompanying professionalism, is not good for the kids.

More significant, contrary to what most youth coaches and parents seem to think, the year-round specialization does not produce better skill than that of those who take time off from the sport to rest and to learn, and compete in, other sports.

The recommendations for rest and multi-sport experiences are not just being made for 8- or 10-, or 12-year-olds. They are being recommended for athletes playing well into high school.

Dr. James Andrews,[78] 40-year sports medicine orthopedist, surgeon to both pros and, as he puts it, far too many 13- and 14-year-olds, makes the strongest case against specialization and professionalism—because he sees the shredded cartilage, ligaments, and tendons on his operating table every day. Some of the youth are as young as 12.

The cause is overuse due to practice and game schedules designed for 25-year-old professional athletes, not 12-, 14-, and 16-year-old amateurs. The young body, he says, was just not made for that kind of punishment. Dr. Andrews' recommendation? "At least two months off each year to recover from a specific sport. Preferably, three to four months."

Another orthopedist has said that whenever athletes feel aches, pain, or fatigue, they should stop practice or play, because that is when injuries occur. The doctor then added, "These kids aren't on multi-million dollar contracts!"

ESPN *The Magazine*[79] recently sponsored a study showing that the kids who participate in year-round sports enjoy every minute of it. After

---

[78] Dennis Manoloff, "Noted Surgeon Dr. James Andrews Wants Your Young Athlete To Stay Healthy by Playing Less," February 27, 2013, cleveland.com; Dennis Manoloff, "Dr. James Andrews on Seven Major Sports Health Myths," January 12, 2019, cleveland.Com; James R. Andrews, *Any Given Monday*, amazon.com.

[79] Eddie Matz, "The Kids Are Alright," February 21, 2014, espn.com.

all, they are the center of attention and treated like pros-in-the-making. They get to travel, stay in hotels, and, of course, do not have to pay!

But is this good for the kids, Eddie Matz, the article's author asks? Or is it ruining their childhoods?

Kids love tons of sugar, says sports psychologist Kristen Dieffenbach, but an excess of sweets is not good for them. Likewise, the year-round regimen of youth sports is not good for the kids' long-term development.

The mantra of travel and club sports is that year-round specialization is necessary to get to the next level. But is it, asks Matz?

General managers of the Pittsburgh Pirates and Toronto Raptors say that multiple sports experiences in high school make better athletes and teammates, as well as produce fewer injuries and less burnout.

John Savage, head coach of the world-series winning UCLA baseball team, says, "We like 'em cross trained. Stick with multiple sports as long as you possibly can, and people are going to see your tools." Matz then follows up with this line: "Stick with one sport long enough, and people are going to see your scars."

Five college lacrosse coaches[80] echo the importance of multiple sports experiences through high school to produce better athletes and teammates. An informal survey of National Federation of State High School Association (NFHS)[81] members also speaks to the benefits of multi-sports experiences.

Ex-pros have weighed in on the subject. Wayne Gretzky,[82] Cal Ripken, Jr.,[83] and Bobby Orr[84] say that creativity and experimentation are lacking in today's college and professional athletes. They say this is due to specialization and the absence of free play.

---

[80] Paul Ohanian, "Why College Coaches Prefer Multi-Sport Athletes," December 30, 2014, uslacrosse.org.

[81] Mike Dyer, "Trend Toward Sport Specialization Not Always Best Decision," January 13, 2015, nfhs.org.

[82] "Wayne Gretzky Says He Wanted to Play Pro Baseball," February 9, 2019, nhl.com; James Christie, "Gretzky Stresses Creativity," October 24, 2000, theglobeandmail.com; see above, "On Killing Creativity," p. 192.

[83] Ken Reed, "Youth Sports Specialization Defies Logic," October 31, 2014, huffpost.com; Cal Ripken, Jr., and Rick Wolff, *Parenting Young Athletes the Ripken Way*, amazon.com.

[84] Ken MacQueen, "Bobby Orr: How We're Killing Hockey," February 2, 2018, macleans.ca; "Orr: My Story," wikipedia.org.

Gretzky and Orr played baseball in their off-seasons and Ripken attributes his success at shortstop to the footwork he learned in high school soccer. The ponds, sandlots, and streets of yesteryear—where no adults were to be found—gave kids the freedom to experiment, to try out something new and different. This, of course, is no longer allowed in today's adult dominated, adult controlled organized youth sports.

Tommy John says the current major league epidemic of surgeries in his name is "unreal" and "crazy." The cause, he points out, is not over-pitching in the big leagues, but a buildup of overuse as a kid, especially pitching year round. And he calls it a racket the way organized youth sports today is run,[85] hyping scholarships and better performance to parents so they will spend increasingly more money.[86]

John then goes on to say that Justin Verlander is probably one of the best pitchers today in the major leagues. So he asks parents who force their kids into year-round play, "You think Justin Verlander plays baseball year-round?" The answer is a big "no."

What does sports research[87] say? Professional athletes who enjoyed plenty of free play in their younger years and participated in multiple sports show better perception, decision making, and pattern recognition than their single sport, organized and controlled counterparts. In one study these characteristics differentiated the super elite of professional athletes from the mere elite.

Most today acknowledge the importance of free play in their development as young athletes, but nearly all assume that that is a bygone era, never to return.

Bob Bigelow,[88] former NBA player and youth sports reform advocate, says otherwise. Bigelow suggests that coaches today should periodically drop their sports equipment off at the various facilities, then disappear for two or three hours. Their instructions to the kids should

---

[85] "Tommy John on Surgeries: 'Unreal,'" April 24, 2014, espn.com.
[86] Nancy Cambria, "Is It Really a Good Idea for Kids to Play a Sport All Year Round?," November 17, 2013, stltoday.com; John O'Sullivan, "Is It Wise to Specialize?," January 13, 2014, changingthegameproject.com.
[87] John O'Sullivan, "Is It Wise to Specialize?," January 13, 2014, changingthegameproject.com.
[88] Bob Bigelow, *Just Let the Kids Play*, amazon.com.

be, "Just go out and play." The kids, he says, will know what to do with the equipment!

Bigelow is not known for mincing his words about organized youth sports—he describes travel and club sports as a "caste system."

He also has said this about adult involvement in the present world of young people's recreation: "Parental egos and a full tank of gas—a frightening combination."

Note on softball. Dr. Andrews, in his book *Any Given Monday*,[89] discusses the health concerns of twenty-eight of the most popular youth sports, including cheerleading, which he says is "out of control" from the perspective of health, and dance. Here are a few comments about fastpitch softball:

"Unfortunately, softball lags behind all other youth sports in injury rate recognition and preventative safety rules. There have been very few rules regulating softball at any level and, as a result, softball injuries in young athletes are on the rise and are nearly as prevalent as baseball injuries." This includes tears in the ulnar collateral ligament of the elbow, the ligament that gets replaced with Tommy John surgery.

"These young women," Andrews concludes, "need to be protected for the sake of their long-term health, not just for their team's win-loss record."

(May 9, 2014)

Postscript 2021. Our daughter dropped out of travel ball early in her freshman year of high school. She went on to play four years of tennis and three years of school softball, the latter, unfortunately, in an uncompetitive league. In her senior year, she dropped softball to work in theater tech (as her required extracurricular activity). In her sophomore year of college (at the University of Wisconsin, Madison), she tried out for and played on the competitive club softball team—and had a blast! Why? Because it was all player coached! In the current atmosphere of totalitarian pandemic, she can't wait to get back out on the frozen ballfields of the upper midwest.

---

[89] James R. Andrews, *Any Given Monday*, amazon.com.

Sad stories heard on the travel ball circuit: one girl earned an athletic scholarship to a prominent school . . . but got pregnant before attending. End of college career. Others have been awarded scholarships in small schools on the east coast—a long ways from home. For various reasons, homesickness among them plus the expense of travel and other incidentals, at least one has returned home with no indication of attending college.

7

The Arts

2009–13

Life in Three-Quarter Time

This post is a paean to the arts, especially music, and especially the three-quarter time signature. In music, three-quarter time means that the rhythm of the music is played in a pattern of three beats to the bar, instead of the more common four, and usually with emphasis on the first. It is the rhythm of the waltz and carries with it a lilting, cheerful disposition. It is the seemingly silky smoothness of two dancers masterfully floating and turning across the floor to a Viennese waltz. To the listener and viewer, it is the expression and symbol of effortless joy.

In contrast, work, or labor, is not effortless, though it may be enjoyable. To be sure, the dancers and musicians who portray this effortless joy have spent hours and years perfecting their craft. The end result of their efforts is the effect the craft has on the consumers of music and dance. That effect is pure emotion, a child-like not-a-care-in-the-world fun. The effect of art is to enable us to experience this carefree joy and thereby to rest and refuel in order to carry on with life's labors. The three-quarter time signature in music does this to me par excellence.

In a larger perspective, life in three-quarter time represents the ability to perform the tasks of one's daily life, in both family and career, in a manner that expresses effortless joy. Not that the tasks are effortless, but that the enjoyment in performing the tasks is uninhibited by what to some appear to be enormous obstacles. These obstacles are usually mental rather than physical, such as feelings of drudgery when going to work every day or hassles and conflicts of dealing with family, bills, and chores, etc. Everyone experiences these barriers to some degree and at some times. The person who lives in three-quarter time, however, is inspired by the prospect of daily obstacles and views the challenges as opportunities with which to have more fun in life.

The impetus for this post was a recent experience my wife, daughter, and I had that enabled us to witness fifteen or so twenty-something singers, actors, and dancers who exhibited and projected life in three-quarter time. We attended a regional production of a Broadway musical and were allowed to tag along with a high school class that interviewed the performers afterward. The exhilaration and relaxed confidence of these young performers, especially right after a two-and-a-half hour staging, were obvious. Despite the fact that a show business life can be grueling with audition after audition (and rejection after rejection), every one of these performers exhibited what I call the spirit of three-quarter time. To observe it on stage and in person was a treat; it enabled us to live in three-quarter time for those few hours. That the music and memories of the performance keep playing in our minds two weeks later only adds to the experience.

It is a rare person who knows what he or she wants to do in life at an early age. It is equally rare to find someone who feels about his or her job, "I have so much fun in what I do—I'm amazed they pay me to do it!" Yet, this is precisely what these young performers exhibited and, in some cases, admitted. It is this early and untainted, anxiety-less certainty of what one wants to do in life that enables a person to overcome barriers as if they were not even there and to work tirelessly and without any evidence of labor in the many hours and years required to achieve a goal. Though actually working very hard, the appearance and, often, psychological feeling of such a person is that of floating and turning through life to a waltz.

While not everyone can regularly achieve or directly experience the spirit of life in three-quarter time, and the young performers my family and I observed may not be able to maintain it throughout their lives, nearly everyone can experience the general feeling vicariously through art, either as performer or consumer. For me it is most often achieved through music, especially the three-quarter time signature.

I do have other associations in music with three-quarter time, but they are a bit more technical: the quarter-note triplet and harmony in major thirds. They evoke in me the same feeling as three-quarter time, but perhaps they should be a topic for another day.

(March 23, 2009)

Evita: Why We Love That Musical about a Dictator

FACTS DON'T MATTER[1] . . . *in art.*

Our family recently attended a touring performance of the musical *Evita*[2] by Andrew Lloyd Weber and Tim Rice. The production debuted in London's West End in 1978 and on Broadway in 1979. The show loosely chronicles the rise and short political life of Eva Peron, wife of Argentinian dictator Juan Peron. It is an operatic rags-to-riches love story that ends with cathartic tragedy when the heroine dies of cancer at age 33. The production comes complete with Greek chorus in the form of the character, narrator-critic Che.

Heroine? Therein lies the debate. Can the wife of a dictator be admired, and therefore her artistic portrayal enjoyed, while a talented, professional cast sings and dances to beautiful music in her name?

In art the prickly factual detail of who the historical Evita was is not terribly relevant. Artistic license allows facts to be altered for esthetic purpose. If that were not the case we would have trouble appreciating animations and such science fiction classics as *Star Trek* and *Star Wars*. Indeed, the word "fiction" means portrayal of *imaginary* people and events—not factual ones. And it is precisely contrasted to the word "fact," because reports of news or historical events are supposed to be true, not creatively crafted stories.

---

[1] See above, "Facts Don't Matter, Or: The Art of BS," p. 307.
[2] "*Evita* (Musical), wikipedia.org.

In some fiction there is a phenomenon known as the loveable crook, but such characters are usually either doing a good deed, as Robin Hood stole from the thieving rich to return wealth and property to the dispossessed poor, or are, or become, reformed sinners, such as John Robie in the Alfred Hitchcock movie *To Catch a Thief.*

Eva Peron is not a loveable crook or loveable dictator. She is loved in the musical (and was in real life) by the poor, but she is (and was) hated by the military and rich. In the show, Che is ideologically sympathetic to Evita's politics, but he is a critical commentator suspicious of her methods and motivation; he makes sure the audience knows Evita may have done less than nice things. All good stories require conflict and this is it in a nutshell.

But *Evita* the musical is not about politics. As Lloyd Weber and Rice describe the show it is a Cinderella story.[3] This is the most likely reason the highly stylized musical is loved worldwide and has been a success for so many years. To see Eva Peron as a Cinderella requires a considerable feat of abstraction to dispense with the facts presented in the musical and what we think we know about her historical facts. It requires that the audience not be too literal in their understanding of the show's characters.*

The stylization of the show helps us accomplish that move away from literalness. "Stylized"[4] means a particular way of doing or presenting something that is distinctively non-naturalistic. Musicals from the get-go, with their singing dictators and dancing soldiers, are stylized. *Evita* is highly stylized because it is "sung-through,"[5] meaning there is no spoken dialogue, which makes it more like an opera, and it leaves much of the story to be told by the narrator.

In a lengthy analysis of the musical, Scott Miller[6] points out that the original New York production portrayed Che as the Marxist revolutionary Che Guevara, but the intent of the creators was different. Current productions have restored Che as an "anonymous Everyman," a phrase that stems from the colloquial Argentine meaning of the word

---

[3] Scott Miller, "Inside *Evita*: Background and Analysis," 2010, newlinetheatre.com.
[4] "Stylized," vocabulary.com.
[5] "Sung-Through," wikipedia.org.
[6] Scott Miller, "Inside *Evita*: Background and Analysis," 2010, newlinetheatre.com.

"che" as "friend," "mate," "pal," or even "dude." This stylization further removes the audience from politics and makes Che a more believable Greek chorus.

Evita the musical, therefore, becomes a quite enjoyable, polished, and integrated work of art, not a tome of history—or paean to dictators.

There are many reasons to like and dislike a work of art, but if we focus too concretely on the uprightness of main characters, we are going to have trouble enjoying certain truly great works of art.

The operas *Don Giovanni, Rigoletto,* and *La Traviata* immediately come to mind.

* As for the historical facts of Eva and Juan Peron, a considerable revisionist history[7] has portrayed them as less than the villains their enemies claimed they were during their lifetimes. "Peronism" can be described as a somewhat mild—though still not always nice—fascist FDR-ism that promoted such familiar programs as social security and pro-union labor and women's suffrage legislations. Peron himself was neither anti-Semitic nor the vicious tyrant that subsequent Argentine military leaders became.

(November 22, 2013)

---

[7] "Eva Peron," wikipedia.org; Dolane Larson, "Evita versus *Evita*," evitaperon.org.

Index

abuse of rank, caused by government, 26
academia: bitter quarrels in, 133–35, 181; Orwellian thought control in, 144; and Star Chamber proceedings, 143
academic freedom: infringed by accreditation, 135; pretense at protecting free speech, 137, 143
accreditation: and academic qualification, 123, 128, 137; as government control of education, 136–7; unethical, 135–37
administrative law, promoted by progressives, 83
advertising: need for defense of, 23–25; social and economic criticisms of, 24; subliminal, 19–21
Agassiz, Louis, "look at your fish," 234–35
age of digitization, 44, 190
altruism: and Ayn Rand, 88–90; coerced, 39; and honor, 271; and monument building, 61; as public service, 56–59; as self-sacrifice, 39–41, 88–90; and "sincere" people, 313; synonym of ethics, 38, 40, 59; theory of dependence, 61
amateur vs. professional, in sports and the arts, 335–36
American Economic Association, founded to exclude classical liberals, 111
American Medical Association, and restriction of supply, 47
Andrews, James, *Any Given Monday*, injuries in youth sports, 357, 360
anecdotal evidence, validity of in science, 258
animal emotions, and "men of hard science," 256–58
antitrust laws, and the Department of Justice, 70
Appiah, Kwame, *The Honor Code*, 269–71
application, as deductive, 12–13
applied science: nature of, 11–13, 15; as "art," 11–12
Arab Spring, and property rights, 82
Aristotle: formal cause, 323; logic, 312; *Rhetoric* and persuasive communication, 160
Arthur Anderson, and Supreme Court, 68–69
arts, the: as rest and refueling, 364; stylization in, 366; why facts don't matter in, 365
attention deficit hyperactivity disorder (ADHD): and children who are bored, 237–39; Glasser's criteria for, 238; as stigmatizing, 237
authoritarianism: and capitalism, 176;

370 • Index

authoritarianism (*continued*)
in education: 170–73; and external control psychology, 264; in parenting, 49, 239, 332; in psychiatry, 248; and relativism, 93
autonomy of individual, devalued in nineteenth century, 34

Bailey, J. Michael, Galilean personality, 92
Balko, Radley, *Rise of the Warrior Cop*, 71–74
bankers' hours, monopolistic privilege, 25
Barzun, Jacques, on lecture and tutorial methods of teaching, 175
Bastiat, Frederic: on free trade and peace, 224; seen and not seen, 24;
Beck, Aaron, and growth mindset, 276
Beckerman, Ray, recording industry vs. the people (website), 29
behavior, cause of: genes vs. environment, or free will, 315–18
beliefs, sincerity of, as measured by distance from facts (reality), 313–14
benefit corporation, new name for social responsibility, 58
Beria, Lavrenti, "show me the man, I'll find you the crime," 68
big bands, and tax on dance halls, 74–75
Bigelow, Bob: and caste system in youth sports, 360; *Just Let the Kids Play*, 338–39; on kids coaching first and third bases, 338
big mouth, theory of: danger of rankism and BS'ing, 226; and external control psychology, 224–26
Bill of Rights, as a joke, 110–11
black market, when valid products made illegal, 79
Blackshirts, and SWAT teams, 71–74
blender principle, on gift giving, 54–56
Bowman, James, *Honor: A History*, 271–74
Brecht, Bertoldt, and Sidney Hook, 101
Breggin, Peter, *Toxic Psychiatry*, 244–47
bribery, and similar but confusing terms, 45–46

BS (bullshit): dangerous admiration of, 293–95; distinguished from lying, 307–8, 311, 314–15; family culture of, 308; and the highly educated, 294; serial embellishment (habitual hyperbolizing), 309–10. *See also* Frankfurt, Harry
bureaucracy: invisible hand of, 135–36, 169; "the list had to be correct," 118; of medicine and education mimicking business, 31–33; misconceptions of, 32, 283; reductio of, 117–21; as rule-bound society, 119. *See also* bureaucratic management
bureaucratic education: as grading and sorting, 52–53, 321; institutionalized comparison, 66; obedience to authority as goal, 67; students as number on a roster, 127
bureaucratic management; and business or profit management, 283; as deflecting attention away from constituents or customers, 47–49; incentive to cheat, 78–79; loyalty to superiors, 79–80; as management of coercion, 281, 283, 328; as method of running government bureaus, 31
burnout in youth sports: lack of multiple sports experiences, 334, 358; and overuse injuries, 339, 350; and parental estrangement, 337, 339; pressure of practices, 333
business: value in knowing ethics and epistemology, 44–46; working in, as opposed to being a student, 52–54
business management. *See* profit management
busybody state, and self-righteous control of others, 278, 306–7

Cabaret (musical), on the eve of Hitler's rise, 149–51
Cain, Susan, *Quiet*, 242–44
Calvo, Cheye, mayor, botched SWAT raid of home, 73
Cantu, Robert, and Mark Hyman, *Concussions and Our Kids*, 352–54
capitalism: laissez-faire as internal control society, 50; need for defense of, 23–25; property rights and rule

of law, 83; social liberalism, history and theory of, 37; system of social cooperation, 65; unleashed productive powers of reason, science, technology, 37;
capitalism vs. socialism, in two cities hit with tornadoes, 59–61
castle doctrine, and no-knock entrance, 71–72
caterpillars into butterflies: as principle of teaching, 325–27, 336
censorship, and core curriculum, 165–66
central planning, essence of socialism, 120
Chagnon, Napoleon, as Galilean personality, 92
Chait, Jonathan, and political correctness, 310
Chambers, Whittaker: and Ayn Rand, 105; former Stalinist spy, 101
children: bored, not lazy, 262–63; developmental stages of, 162, 338–39; hovered over vs. befriended, 264–66; need to "toughen up," 265; not slaves of adults, 39, 287; not small adults, 161–63, 167, 338; psychologies of, 167
chores: and coerced menial tasks for children, 266; stick motivation, 285–88
chronic traumatic encephalopathy (CTE), effects of concussions in older age and Lou Gehrig, 353
civilization, alleged collapse of, 41–44
class participation, as stick motivation, 288–91
Coal Miner's Daughter, on ignorance vs. stupidity, 138
cobweb parties, Victorian gift entertainment, 56
coercion: advocated by social liberals and conservatives, 37–39; essence of governing, 86–87; of quiet student through class participation, 288–91
common law, better than legislation, 119–20
communist era in NYC, 101–5
competition: in animal kingdom, 22, 23; on doing well (economic) vs. beating others (defensive), 22, 65;

healthy and unhealthy, 21–23; competition, bureaucratic, 22–23
compliance to rules and regulations, essence of bureaucratic management, 32, 118–19
compulsory school attendance: like being in jail, 53–54; main structural control, 184
Comte, Auguste, on altruism, 89
conceptualization, as process of universalization, 323
concussions in youth sports: head impact not required, 352; and winning at all costs, 353–54
condescension, by the elite, 40
consciousness, naturalization of, 43
conservatism, as advocating governmental coercion, 38–39, 105
control, in skilled athletes and musicians, 326
Cook, Tim: as standing up to government, 105–9; and two *Atlas Shrugged* moments, 107
Coolidge, Calvin, "just sit down and keep still," 226
core curriculum: and interest, 163–66; as censorship, 165–66; and the Mao tunic, 160–61
core evaluations: behind stage fright, 236; of self, others, and the world, 211–13; when left in daycare, 279
corporal punishment, 287–88. *See also* spanking
correctness as conformity to an orthodoxy, 100
courage, and need to be patient, 217–19
creativity: breaks rules, 142; and experimentation in sports, 358–59; what defeats it, 192–94
criminal personality: in bureaucracy, 280–83; and crime of passion, 268–69; deficiency of self-esteem, 314; in mass killings, 284–85; and non-arrestable criminals, 280–81, 283; thinking errors of, 267–69
criticism: constructive, of Haim Ginott, 202; perceived, and need to be patient, 218–19
crying in softball, as sign of pain, 329–31

culture, likened to iceberg, 57
curiosity for subtle detail, 204–5
customer satisfaction: aim of business management, 31; attention to deflected by bureaucratic rules, 31–32

decentering, Piaget, seeing other points of view, 131–32
definition, rules of, 45–46
Deford, Frank, concussions and the demise of football, 352
DeMause, Lloyd, on history of childhood, 260
democracy vs. totalitarianism, Sidney Hook's view of political issues, 102
Democratic Party: goal to increase size of state, 63; soul-searching after 2004 loss, 36
Dershowitz, Alan: criminal law so clear it can be read while running, 82; witnesses encouraged to compose, not just sing, 69
De Soto, Hernando, extralegal poor, need for property rights and rule of law, 81–83
determinism, genes and environment, 316
Dewey, John: as Aristotelian, 295–96; rejects intrinsic essences and values, 43, 295–99; subject matter required for thought, 166, 291
dictatorship: and monument building, 61; and non-objective law, 68–70; root of, 49, 258–61; and Thomas Hobbes, 244, 304
dignity: equal, as goal in democratic schools, 155, 182, 209; and internal control psychology, 51
dishonesty and ignorance, 138–40
disposition: as one's psychology, 211–12; vs. situation, 210–13
Doctorow, Cory, giveaway of novel, 29
dogs: alpha, myth of, and positive motivation, 230
draft, military, as involuntary servitude, 39–41, 106, 108, 273
Dreger, Alice: and First Amendment, 93; *Galileo's Middle Finger*, 90–97
drill sergeant mentality, and external control psychology, 195, 223, 340–41, 353
drop error and peer review, 123–26
drugs: as cruel control of children, 237; the new spanking, 238; off-label use, 95; psychotropic, 238, 245
drug war, and alcohol prohibition, 73, 79, 84

education: control and choice in, 182–85, 228; factory model of, 176–78; primacy of psychology in, 227–29
educational market: analogy to rent control, 168; as authoritarian, 170–73; as bureaucracy, 32–33; poor customer service in, 127; and students as number on a roster, 52. *See also* bureaucratic education
Einstein, Albert: and peer review, 126; persistence as cause of success, 243
Elder, Larry, *Double Standards*, 15
emergency rooms, and lack of excess capacity, 47
emotions: denial of by parents and coaches, 331; role in stating and respecting facts, 312–14; role of in judging advertising, 21
empowerment, in democratic schools, 155, 176
Enlightenment, The, philosophical errors of, 33
envy and cynicism of postmoderns, 35
epistemology: and argument from uncertainty, 301–4; as how-to discipline, 299–301
equality, as equal dignity, 26. *See also* dignity
Ericsson, Anders, on 10,000 hours of practice, 349
eugenics of early progressives, 110–12
Evita (musical): as Cinderella story, 366; heroine or dictator, 365–367
external control psychology: and authoritarian parenting, 264–65;

and dependence, 51; right to coerce others, 50–51; and theory of the big mouth, 224–26; and unilateral rejection of deadly habits, 221–24

facts, irrelevance of: in art, 365; and BS, 307–9; to identity activists, 93; and modern puritans, 278; and polylogism, 309–10; why, 311–15
faking, and lying and BS'ing, 45, 213–14
familial atmosphere of business, 52–53
federal law, Sovietization of, 68–70
federal prosecutors: and Javert, 69; as powerful and unaccountable, 87
feelings, primacy of in postmodernism, 144–45
fish metaphor, for removal of adult power and control over children, 154, 239–40
fixed vs. growth mindset, born that way vs. effort, 274–77
Flexner Report, and restriction of supply in medicine, 47
Foundation for Individual Rights in Education (FIRE), bipartisan defender of First Amendment, 143–46
Frankfurt, Harry: *On Bullshit*, 293–95, 307–9
Frankl, Victor, *Man's Search for Meaning*, 117–18
Freeman, Walter, ice pick lobotomist, 249, 251
free market in education: hole-in-the-wall experiments, 66–67; market (producers and customers) determines quality, 136; no grades or exams, 53–54; not one size fits all (Mao tunics), 161, 164; as rational alternative to force and fear, 173; teachers as peddlers of ideas, 159–61
free market in scholarly research, 125–6
free sample, and product trial, 27–28
free school movement, 176–78
free trade, unilateral: and internal control psychology, 221, 223–24

free will, as cognitive self-regulation, 316
friend, closeness of, as measured by distance from facts (reality), 315
Fuller, Robert: on rankism in *Somebodies and Nobodies*, 26–27, 181–82, 301; as social liberal, 26

Gagliardi, John, winningest coach ever, 349
Galbraith, John Kenneth, dependence effect, 22
Galilean personality, as politically incorrect scientist, 90–93
Galileo: independent judgment of, 206–7; and Inquisitional "correctness," 100, 125
gender, psychological basis of, 97
generalization, as inductive, 12
Gestapo-like tactics, of FBI, 62, 70, 114
Gibson Guitar, raided with Gestapo-like tactics, 62–63, 109
Ginott, Haim: *Between Parent and Child*, 202; "describe, don't evaluate," 201–3, 276
Glasser, William: *Choice Theory*, 49–51; deadly habits and connecting habits, 50–51; on independence, 240; and quality school, 183; schizophrenics "just lonely people," 246
Glazer, Myron Peretz, and Penina Migdal Glazer: social liberals, 78; *The Whistleblowers*, 77–81
Goertz, Donna Bryant, medication as the new spanking, 238
government: coercive institution, 62–65; killed the big bands and railroads, 74–77; not "our friend," 86–87
grade inflation, in 1894 and today, 156–57
Greek Dark Age, and recording of oral tradition, 43–44
Greenberg, Daniel, on independence and the free society, 240
Gretzky, Wayne, on lack of creativity in hockey today, 193–94
Groopman, Jerome: *How Doctors Think*, 48–49, 204–5

group projects: alleged simulation of reality, 186–87; and cooperative learning, 185–87

Hayek, F. A., on conservatives' use of coercion, 105
helicoptering: to prevent pain, 264; vs. dismissiveness, 277–80
Henninger, Daniel, on Americanized Maoism, 98, 99
Hicks, Stephen, *Explaining Postmodernism*, 34–36
Highet, Gilbert, on lecture and tutorial methods of teaching, 175
history, as applied science, 15
hitting, dogs and children, 229–32, 284
Hobbes, Thomas, and need for strong central government, 244, 304
Hofstadter, Richard, and social Darwinism, 113
Holmes, Sherlock, as applied scientist, 13
Holt, John: confidence killed by fifth grade, 208; and home schooling, 177; on praise, 202
honesty: and bribery, 45–46; and career in business, 44–46
Hong Kong, and general elections, 63
honor: and individualism, 270–71; as status and rank vs. self-esteem, 269–71. *See also* pseudo-honor
Hook, Sidney: *Out of Step*, 101–5; and Eastern vs. Western cultures, 312
Horrobin, David, on suppression of innovation, 124, 141, 142
hospitals: and branding, 97; and lack of excess capacity, 47
hostility, toward capitalism and advertising, 25
human nature, theories of, 41, 61, 104
hyperbole. *See* BS (bullshit)

Iago, as postmodernism's slow poison to modernity's Othello, 35
Ibsen, Henrik: independent judgment in *An Enemy of the People*, 206–7

ideas, power of, 47–49
identity activists, as enemies of Galilean personality, 92–93
identity, personal, determined by core evaluations, 317
imitation, and acceleration of product acceptance, 28
independent judgment (independence): can everyone practice it, 219–21; can it be taught, 221; meaning of, 206-8; objective in education, 228; statements of, 239–41
individual, as defined by the group, 34
inflation, centuries of, 42
influencers, besides advertisers, 20
injuries, overuse in youth sports: athletic trainers ignored by coaches, 356; breakdown exceeds build up, 355; excessive practices and games, 329, 334, 339
innovation in education, from outside establishment, 187–90
instrumentalism, Dewey's preferred name for his philosophy, 298
intelligence: ability to see and do before others, 319–20; and eugenics, 321; not inborn, 318–21; role of in independent judgment, 220; role of knowledge and interest in, 320–21
interest, role of in education, 163–66
internal control psychology: on choosing and controlling one's own behavior, 50; as foundation of independent judgment, 51
intersex people, and borderline problem in theory of universals, 94, 96
intrinsicism, essences and values external to consciousness, 43, 97, 296–98
introspection: required for good education, 212; skill to examine psychological premises, 317; valid method of science, 316
introversion: not same as shyness, 242; quiet persistence, minimal stimulation, 242–44
involuntary servitude, and Apple

Computer, 105–9. *See also* draft, military
IQ testing, as contrived, 321

Jackson, Phil, on anger and punishment in coaching sports, 347
Javert, "the law must be obeyed," 69, 281
Jobs, Steve, on independence, 239
Johnson, Thomas L., *The Real Academic Community and the Rational Alternative*, 170–73
judging others, 205
judgment, independent. *See* independent judgment
judgment, sound. *See* sound judgment
justice, social vs. individual, collectivist and individualist definitions, 96

Kafkaesque, description of blind peer review, 130
Kant, Immanuel: and altruism, 89; and duty ethics of chores, 287; and subjectivism, 43
Kentucky Fried Chicken, and alleged subliminal advertising, 20–21
Key, Wilson Bryan, and alleged subliminal embeds, 20, 24
Khan, Salmon: and flipped classroom, 198; *The One World Schoolhouse*, 197–99
Khrushchev, Nikita, 34, 314
Kimball, Roger, *Tenured Radicals* and crybullies, 149
Kohn, Alfie: on grade inflation, 156–57; *No Contest: The Case against Competition*, 21–23

ladder climbing, tactic of federal prosecutors, 69
law, non-objective, overly broad and vague, 68–70, 82–83, 144
League of Their Own, A: "no crying in baseball," 329–31; vs. crying on screen, *In the Line of Fire*, 330
learning vs. doing, separate actions, 178–80
lecture method of teaching, 174–75
Leonard, Thomas C., *Illiberal Reformers*, 110–13
liberalism, classical or market vs. social: and altruism, 38–39; similarities and differences, 37
libertarianism. *See* liberalism, classical or market
lifelong learning, and encouragement, guidance, motivation, 325–26
logic: applied to one's own psychology, 318; introspective science and art, 212, 316; as respect for facts, 314–15
Lukianoff, Greg, *Unlearning Liberty*, 143–46
lying: species of BS, 294; vs. dishonesty, 45; as way of life, 268

Magna Carta, and Bill of Rights, 43
"make trade, not war," 58
Maoism, Americanized, and its postmodern roots, 98–99
Marcuse, Herbert, virulent absolutism of and postmodernism, 146
marketing, and lack of attention to needs and wants of children in youth sports, 337
Martin, Brian, on students and the scholarly trade, 138–39
Masson, Jeffrey: on Freud's seduction theory, 258; *When Elephants Weep*, 256–58
McGovern Report, and low-fat diets, 303
McNamara, Joseph, father of community policing, 84–86
medical care before bureaucratization, 47–48
medical market: as bureaucracy, 32–33; and poor customer service, 47, 127
medical model of psychiatry, 245, 246, 250
medicine, socialized, as modeled on medieval guilds, 49
"men of hard science," 249–51, 258, 280
Mencken, H. L., and puritanism, 306
method of education: and development of the mind, 167–68; primary to content, 166–68
Milgram obedience experiments, 211
Milken, Michael, younger brother threatened with prison, 68

Miller, Alice, *For Your Own Good*, 259–60, 261
Mises, Ludwig von: on academic freedom, 143; on bureaucracy, 120–21, 281, 283; on courting favors of the powerful, 23; economic calculation in socialism, 88; not silenced by wars, 44; on theory and history, 15
Mises Institute, and giveaway of *Omnipotent Government*, 29
Miss Brimsley cartoon, who really failed, 139, 197
Monckton, Christopher, Viscount of Brenchley, and wall-to-wall Marxism, 91, 93
monopoly: and four-firm concentration ratio, 24; as government-granted privilege, 25, 168; and occupational licensing, 23, 25, 33, 47, 136, 244; and rent control, 168–69
Montessori schools: and early learning, 163; choice in education, 193; and grades, 183; independence the goal, 67
monument builders, as expecting gratitude and prestige, 60
moral treatment movement: destroyed by ridicule and condescension, 249; in psychiatry, 248–251
motivation, intrinsic vs. extrinsic, 22–23
Mozart, Wolfgang Amadeus, on response to copiers (music pirates), 30
Ms. Mentor (Emily Toth), on the literary perspective of academia, 135

Napolitano, Andrew, on the involuntary servitude of Apple Computer, 106–7
Neill, A. S.: on independence and the free society, 241; on spanking and adult rage, 234
Nelsen, Jane, *Positive Discipline* and family meeting, 210
New Left, opposed by Sidney Hook, 102
nutrition studies, and low-fat vs. low carbohydrate diets, 302–4

obedience to authority: defeats creativity, 194; premise of government schooling, 162; and stage mother syndrome, 332–34
Objectivism, on patents and copyrights, 30
objectivity, as adhering to facts, 308
observation, fundamental method of science, including psychology, 234–36
occupational licensing: monopoly of the many, 168; and restriction of supply, 25. *See also* monopoly
Ogilvy, David, on advertising messages, 201
Oliner, Samuel P., and Pearl M. Oliner,*The Altruistic P,ersonality*, 90
one size fits all: and class participation, 291; discourages creativity, 193; meaning of, 164
one-time learning, mistaken assumption of adults, 162–63
oral vs. written presentations, essentialization vs. detail, 174–75

Packer, Edith: and core evaluations, 318; and introspection, 212; on self-esteem and personal identity, 221; on subconscious motivation, 277
Palmer, Craig, as Galilean personality, 92
parents, on being child's friend, 264–66
Palyi, Melchior, on origin of socialized medicine, 49
patents and copyrights: in perpetuity, 129; and creativity, 31, 129; as intellectual property, 30, 128–30; as monopoly, 30, 129
Paulinus of Nola, as renouncing material life, 42
Peace Corps, and volunteer vacation movement, 59
peer review: in academic research, 123–26; blind review ended by *British Medical Journal*, 130; the

need for objectivity in, 130–32; and suppression of innovation, 124, 130
perception, subliminal, as self-contradiction, 20
Perry, Bruce, on trauma in childhood, 260–61
PhD cop. *See* McNamara, Joseph
PhD kings, and the poor and downtrodden, 40
philosophy, on instilling confidence in business career, 46
Piaget, Jean: and concrete operations, 208–9; on decentering, 131
piracy: market function of, 27–31, 128; and word-of-mouth communication, 28
pity, as contemptuous sorrow, 40
plagiarism: difficult to prove, 194–97; and ignorance vs. dishonesty, 138–40
play, unorganized, in sports: develops better perception and decision making, 334, 359
police: and drug war, 73, 79, 84; militarization of, 71–72, 83, 84, 86; and unarmed suspects, 85
political correctness: and demands vs. capitulation, 149–51; and group balkanization, 34; the new McCarthyism, 143–46
politics: as a bore, 36, 62–65, 113–17; not boring after 2016, 65, 117
polylogism, Marxist: epistemological relativism, 93, 99; and right to lie, 309–10
Popper, Karl, and falsificationism, 322
positivism, logical, and denigration of Freud, 322
postmodernism: on equating words to action, 144; as rejection of Enlightenment values, 34–36; shift from red to green, 35; and use of "narrative," 99
practice: and off-season rest, 351; 357; quantity vs. quality, 349–50; skill as improving with age, 349
praise: direct or excessive, 202-3; of quitters and failures, 262–63
premises: beliefs, values, and emotions, 235; need to examine, 234–36

price attack, how marketers respond, 30
price controls, cause of shortages, 48
principles, teaching, lay foundation for independence, 208–10
prisoners of war, and torture, 284
privacy vs. security, 107–9
privatization of educational and rental apartment markets, immediate increase in supply and variety, 170
privilege. *See* rankism
profit management: and loyalty to customers, 80–81; method of running a business, 31
progressives, early: excluded "inferior" groups, 111; as fascist, 110–13
protectionism, of patents in nineteenth century, 129
pseudo-honor: of neoconservatives, 271–74; and pseudo self-esteem of the elite, 40, 272–73; tribal concept, 271
psychiatry, modern: barbaric restraint, 244–48; chemical imbalance theory of, 252–55; and symptom-exacerbation experiments, 250
psycho-epistemology: and BS, 294–95, 308, 311; of fixed and growth mindsets, 274–75; mental habits that determine personality, character, behavior, 214–15, 316–17
psychology: as influencing perception, 41; internal vs. external control, 50–51; in judging ignorance vs. dishonesty, 139–40; primacy of, 227–29
public service, as promoting peace and prosperity, 57–59
puffery, as extravagant praise, 201
puritanism: and chores, 287; and helicoptering, 278
putsch mentality, after November 2016 election, 117

quality school, Glasser's coercion-free version, 183
quitters and failures: healthy to quit and fail, 262–63; name calling destroys resilience, 263

racism, as origin and motive of minimum wage laws, 99
Radack, Jesselyn, harassed for doing job as attorney, 80
railroads, freight, and price controls, 75–77
Rand, Ayn: on altruism, 88–90; and anti-concept, 20; "check your premises," 235; and communists' right to lie, 309; on Descartes and the Witch Doctor, 42–43; on distinction between esthetic judgment and taste, 132; honor as self-esteem, 269; on independence, 241; Mike Wallace 1959 interview of, 40n36; moral vs. practical, 59–61; prediction of new Dark Age, 42; role of emotion in beliefs of "sincere" altruists, 313–14; smallest minority on earth, 96; socialism dead as moral ideal, 33; trader principle as justice, 224
rank, as earned and natural, 26
rankism: as abuse of rank, vestige of aristocratic class, 26; and teacher-professor condescension, 25, 26, 180–82, 301
rationalization, in criminal personality, 314
Rauch, Jonathan: introverts little understood, 226; *Kindly Inquisitors*, 146–48; offendedness as start of learning, 147
reality, as known only through feeling, 34
Reardan, Linda, on Descartes and consciousness, 43
Reisman, George: on job creation, 57; capitalism as cure for racism, 99; on monopoly, 168
relativism, epistemological and moral: and authoritarianism, 93; and virulent absolutism today, 304–7
reason, effectiveness narrowed in nineteenth century, 34
Reed, John R., and minimal practice for baseball team, 349
Reed, Ken, and Walter Byers, on elimination of college athletic scholarships, 348

rent seeking: and one-upmanship in politics, 309; and special interest groups, 87; violates rights, 62, 114
Republicans, as paying lip service to free markets, 63
Ripken, Jr., Cal, on attributing success in professional baseball to high school soccer, 358–59
Robinson, Ken: on creativity as objective in education, 192–93; on real goal of college professors, 66
Rockwell, Lew, on American conservatism, 38
Rogers, Stuart, on movie theater hoax, 20
Rome, decline of, 42–44
Rosen, Andrew, *Change.edu*, 188
Rousseau, Jean-Jacques, on child as small adult, 161, 167
rules: and budget of bureaucracy, 32; as commands for obedience, 208–9; intent and motive absent in zero tolerance, 305; "rules are rules" as bureaucrats' refrain, 31–32, 142, 281; and stick motivation in youth sports, 328
rule by experts: in government education, 164; and occupational licensing, 25, 168

Sacks, Oliver, on faulty memory, 196
Samenow, Stanton, *Inside the Criminal Mind*, 267–69
Sayre's law, 133
scholarly research: and "playing the game," 128, 140; flaws of, 140–42
scholarships: not necessary for college education in most states, 343; obsession with in youth sports, 343–45; rarity of so-called full ride, 344
schools, non-establishment: for-profits, 188; Khan Academy, 189; parent funded in India and Nigeria, 189
scientific management, and free school movement, 176–77
Scroogenomics, on gift giving, 54–55
self-esteem: development of, 317; as objective in education, 227–29; pseudo, 40, 272–73; and upward mobility, 41

Index • 379

Semmelweis, Ignaz, death in insane asylum, 251
service learning, and coerced altruism, 39–41
service, national. *See* draft, military
servitude, involuntary. *See* draft, military
Seven Countries Study of nutrition, and selection bias in, 303
sheet music publishers vs. phonograph and player piano industries, 30
Silverglate, Harvey: on DOJ's "sick culture," 70; *Three Felonies a Day*, 68–70
situation. *See* disposition
socialism: of medical care, 47–49; as moral ideal for Sidney Hook, 105; as ultimate end of Jeffersonian democracy, 102
Socrates: and Athenian "correctness," 100, 125; independent judgment of, 206–7; as whistleblower, 77, 80
solipsism, as dead end of animal behaviorism, 257
sound judgment: accumulated knowledge in, 205; meaning of, 206; as objective in education, 167, 207
Sowell, Thomas, on micro-totalitarianism, 149
Snowden, Edward, and enemies who want death penalty, 77
spanking (smacking): anger as motivation for, 233; humiliation as consequence of, 232; severe version as tool of slave owners, 231; should it be a felony, 232–34
sports, life lessons from: coach abuse, 340; cost of travel and club, 348; independent thinking, 341; career beyond youth and professional, 342; overuse injuries and time off, 347
sports, multiple: better players and teammates, fewer injuries, 339, 355; vs. single-sport specialization, 357–60
spin: as fabrication, 294; original meaning, 308
stage mother syndrome: achievement by proxy, 329; in *Gypsy* (musical), 332; and obedience to authority, 333–34; and pressure-cooker atmosphere, 334–35; or tiger mom, 332–34
Stanford Prison Experiment, 210–12
statistical projection or inference: vs. scientific generalization, 322–24; where valid in science, 324
sterilization, as used by early progressives, 112, 247, 321
Stewart, Martha, press release taken as securities fraud, 70
stick motivation: and chores, 285–88; and class participation, 288–91; as extrinsic motivation, 327–29
Stoics, as teachers of Roman sons, 42
students: feeling important, 52; math skills and grade inflation, 155–157; as paying customers, 27; quality of today, 155–59
subconscious: conscious perceptions shaped by, 24; influence on conscious behavior, 212–13; role of in emotions, 21; and von Domarus principle, 215–17
Sudbury Valley and Summerhill Schools, 153–55, 162, 165, 183–85, 209, 239–40
Swartz, Aaron, as persecuted by DOJ, 70
SWAT teams: botched raids, 71, 73; and Gestapo-like raids, 62–63, 70, 71–74, 109; and killing of dogs, 72–74
Swiss cheese holes, filling gaps in learning, 197–99
Szasz, Thomas, on psychiatry as alchemy and astrology, 247

talkers: know what's right for others, 225; vs. quiet people, 224–26
tardive dyskinesia, effect of psychotropic drugs, 245, 254
Taubes, Gary, *Good Calories, Bad Calories* and *Why We Get Fat*, 302–4
teaching: before doing, as saving time, 179; requires patience, 326–27
technocracy, 176–177
television, and *Hamlet*, 157

tenure, golden handcuffs of, 126, 133
testing: contrived nature of, 191–92; open-book vs. memory, 190–92
tiger mom: coercing children to do the "right" things, 66, 332–34; conventionality of, 334. *See also* stage mother syndrome
trains, passenger, and featherbedding, 76–77
trigger warning, and campus censorship, 147–48
Tucker, Jeffrey, on banned products, 98
Twain, Mark: on copyright in perpetuity, 30; on plagiarism, 195–96
twin studies, 320–21

universals, theory of, as fundamental to science, 104, 258, 322–24
Valenti, Jack, on copyright in perpetuity, 30
value theories, as sciences of guidance, 299–301
Vicary, James, and the movie theater hoax, 19–20
Von Domarus, Eilhard, on the subconscious and fallacy of undistributed middle, 215–17
vote, the: as not essential to genuine liberalism, 64, 103–4; as restrained by individual rights, 104

waltz, the, as life in three-quarter time and effortless joy, 363–65
Washington, George, myths taught to children, 157
Watts, Anthony, and Bill McKibben's reliance on emotion, 312–13
Weber, Max, on bureaucracy, 283
Welch, Jack: as example of growth mindset, 276; and Suzy Welch, on hiring the most talented, 134
whistleblowers, in bureaucracy, 77–81
Whittaker, Robert: *Anatomy of an Epidemic*, 251–55; *Mad in America*, 248–51; smeared and cancelled, 250
whole child, as development of mental and emotional life, 167
Wichita Collegiate, teachers learned to innovate, 159
Williams, Walter: on academic fascism and denial of free speech, 150; *All It Takes Is Guts*, 14; on racist origins of minimum wage laws, 99
Wilson, Woodrow, re-segregated Washington, DC, 112–13
Woodbridge, F. J. E., influenced John Dewey, 295–96
Wooden, John: on competing only with self, 65, on competition, 22

Yochelson, Samuel, and Stanton Samenow: *The Criminal Personality*, 280; and the non-arrestable criminal, 280–83
youth sports: adult dominated, 66, 351; career beyond college, 342; fraud and exploitation in, 341; more important things in life than, 334–37; recreational vs. travel (or club), 335; winning the only thing, 66–67

Zimbardo, Philip: *The Lucifer Effect*, 210–13, on shyness, 226

Cover by 1106Design, www.1106Design.com

Interior design by Kirkpatrick Books

Main text: Warnock Pro

Headings: Myriad Pro

www.ingramcontent.com/pod-product-compliance
Lightning Source LLC
Chambersburg PA
CBHW031404290426
44110CB00011B/249